THE BOOK OF LOVE

CYNTHIA MARKOVITCH

BALBOA.PRESS
A DIVISION OF HAY HOUSE

This book is a work of non-fiction. Unless otherwise noted, the author and the publisher make no explicit guarantees as to the accuracy of the information contained in this book and in some cases, names of people and places have been altered to protect their privacy.

Balboa Press books may be ordered through booksellers or by contacting:

Balboa Press
A Division of Hay House
1663 Liberty Drive
Bloomington, IN 47403
www.balboapress.com
844-682-1282

Because of the dynamic nature of the Internet, any web addresses or links contained in this book may have changed since publication and may no longer be valid. The views expressed in this work are solely those of the author and do not necessarily reflect the views of the publisher, and the publisher hereby disclaims any responsibility for them.

The author of this book does not dispense medical advice or prescribe the use of any technique as a form of treatment for physical, emotional, or medical problems without the advice of a physician, either directly or indirectly. The intent of the author is only to offer information of a general nature to help you in your quest for emotional and spiritual well-being. In the event you use any of the information in this book for yourself, which is your constitutional right, the author and the publisher assume no responsibility for your actions.

Print information available on the last page.

ISBN: 979-8-7652-2650-6 (sc)
ISBN: 979-8-7652-2652-0 (hc)
ISBN: 979-8-7652-2651-3 (e)

Library of Congress Control Number: 2022905489

Balboa Press rev. date: 04/22/2022

CHAPTER 1

NARROWLY ESCAPING CHILDHOOD

In August of 2016, my husband and I abruptly moved from Mt. Pleasant, Texas to Colorado Springs, Colorado. We're in walking distance to the Garden of the Gods. For the first three months I did nothing but hike and party. I thought cool! Was this how the rest of my life going to be? Hiking daily and partying at night. I began thinking something was going on for us to have moved here in such a whirlwind but didn't know what. Maybe God wanted to talk to me about something. Maybe I was in some kind of trouble with him, considering my past. I was having so much fun and felt like a teenager on a permanent vacation. Still, I was suspicious and wondered why I was here and when this vacation was going to end.

On December 28, 2016, something spoke to me and told me it was time to write The Book of Love. That must be why I was here! You see, I was told by a higher power, energy, entity, alien, or perhaps even god, over 30 years ago that I'd write this book. It was so long ago I thought it wasn't real and would never happen. On New Year's Eve my husband said, "I think now is when you're supposed to write that book you talked about a long time ago." I replied, "Wow! Something spoke to me and said the same thing the other day. What a strange coincidence!" I guess it was time.

I began to write but had no idea what to say. I'd never written a book before. Then something said, "Start with your first memory on Earth." I became confused and was like what? This book is about me? And why was I supposed to write it? Maybe because of my strange eventful childhood or the crazy vivid dreams I've had in the past? Perhaps it was because I was an exotic dancer named Venus the Goddess for many years, or the path in life I chose to take. Maybe I will know myself better or you will know me better.

It was the mid-sixties, and the young were revolting against the terrible war going on. They were called hippies and preached peace and love. They smoked pot, took acid, and loved rainbows. I was born in St. Louis Missouri and was named CYNTHIA which meant MOON GODDESS or THE BRINGER OR REFLECTOR OF LIGHT...**IT WAS THE DAWNING OF THE AGE OF AQUARIUS. THE TIME OF USHERING IN LOVE. THE AGE OF THE GREAT AWAKENING!**

I had two older brothers and many thought one of them was my twin because we looked so much alike. My first memory was sitting in my highchair eating Trix and watching Captain Kangaroo. Life was simple. My parents divorced when I was young because the families didn't get along with each other. My grandma was mad at my dad because he got my mom pregnant when she was a teenager and ruined her dance career. My dad's mom was mad at my mom because she accidentally burned their house down.

We moved to a large two-story house on Morganford in St. Louis. It had a big basement and backyard and looked like a giant white barn. My mom remarried, had another son, and divorced not long after.

I was around four and my grandma was over babysitting. She wasn't my real grandma. For some reason my mom was awarded by the state to live with her uncle and aunt at age two. But my mom knew who her real parents were. Anyway, my dad stopped by to give us presents for Christmas, but my grandma wouldn't let him in. When I found out it was my dad at the door, I started crying for him, but she told me to shut up. She wouldn't let me see him. She told him to leave the presents on the porch and go away. When he was leaving, I ran to the window yelling and crying for him, but he didn't hear me. I had tears rolling down my cheeks as I saw him get in his car and leave. That made me very mad at my grandma and I didn't like her anymore. I didn't see my father for a long time after that. My present was a two-story tin doll house with all the furniture and a family. I cherished it because it was all I had to remember him by.

Not long after we moved in something terrible happened to my mom. While two of my brothers and I were next door playing, a very bad man rang the doorbell at my house. My brother answered and the bad man put a gun to his head! He locked him in the closet, then tied my mother up and did terrible things. The neighbor got a good look at him when he left and was arrested but wasn't prosecuted because the neighbor was afraid to testify against him.

I had a very scary incident with a teenage babysitter down the street. As soon as my mom dropped me and my little brother off, she got a big butcher knife out and was threatening to kill us. My little brother was lying on the couch, and I was standing in between them trying to protect him. I was crying and begging her not to hurt us. Just then the next-door neighbor pulled up outside and I knew her. The babysitter told me to wipe my tears and wave to her as if nothing was going on. I did. Then she put the knife to my throat and told me if I told anyone she'd kill us. Then she put the knife away and tried to convince me she was just playing a game. As soon as I got home, I broke down in tears and told my mom. I didn't think she believed me because she didn't confront the babysitter, but never took us back there.

My older brothers had a friend who lived several blocks down the street, upstairs on top of a business. I went to his apartment to see if my brothers were there so I could play with them. My brothers weren't there but I was invited in to play. It was getting dark, so I told him I needed to go home. Instead, he tied me to a chair and his parents got out a gun and said they were moving to California and didn't have a little girl and always wanted one, so they were taking me with them. I saw their belongings packed in boxes and began to panic, crying and begging them to let me go but they wouldn't. I heard my brother outside calling me and they told me if I called back to him and he came upstairs, they'd shoot him. I was crying and very scared, but I screamed his name out real loud. They quickly untied me, and I ran down the steps as fast as I could, past my brother at the bottom and didn't stop until I got all the way home. I immediately told my mom what happened, but I didn't think she believed me about that neither. Before they moved to California, I saw the boy one more time. While walking to the corner store to get some candy he started running after me, so I ran into the store crying and told the cashier someone was trying to get me. She went outside but saw no one. I had her watch me run down the block until I was almost home. Because my mom didn't seem to believe me it caused me to have bad nightmares that she was a witch trying to burn me in a fireplace like Hansel and Gretel.

My mom remarried a Cadillac dealer and my grandma really liked him because he had money. My mom was warned he was a womanizer but married him anyways. He was good to us until they married, then he turned into a terrible monster. The police came to our house often. He'd beat my mom up and break all the glass in the house. Then he'd replace it all and beg for forgiveness. When the police came, he always left so my mom didn't have to get us kids out of bed and find a place to stay for the night. He beat my brothers with dog leashes, but never beat me. When we got in trouble, he'd put shaving cream in our mouths and made us keep it there until he told us to swallow it. That gagged me. I hated lime scented shaving cream and always hoped I got the cherry scented. One time my little brother was taking a bath upstairs and didn't notice the tub overflowing. The water leaked downstairs into my parent's closet and got everything wet. When my stepdad saw that, he beat him with the buckle of a belt. He didn't stop until my mom pulled him off. I was so scared and thought he was going to kill him. He was bruised from head to toe, and I felt so sorry for him.

Our stepdad bought us a basketball and me and my brothers went in the alley to play. We lived on a big hill and the basketball got away from us. It rolled down the hill and another hill then another and out of sight. We couldn't find it anywhere. My stepdad got mad and put shaving cream in our mouths and took all our money away. I had a plastic bunny bank that was a foot tall and almost full. I'd been saving money in it my whole life. He took all of it.

We had to stay in bed on the weekends until my parents woke up. I'd lie in bed staring at the ceiling and walls waiting for the housekeeper to get us. I always saw a headhunter with feathers on his head in the design on the wall and it scared me all the time.

Everyone in the family was a different religion. One grandma Catholic, my real grandma and mom Lutheran, and my stepdad Baptist. So, everyone went to different churches. I went to all of them depending on who I was with. The Catholics had the prettiest churches but the scariest music. I was always mesmerized by the beauty of the stained-glass windows.

My parents didn't go to church much, but on Sundays, they made the kids walk to the Lutheran Church ten blocks away. I think the reason they sent us was to get rid of us for a while. My favorite song at church was This Little Light of Mine and I enjoyed the cookies and Kool-Aid.

One day on the way home from church an old man let us pick berries in his backyard and have cookies and Kool-Aid. I went inside to help, and we took the treats out to my brothers. He brought me back in the house and locked the door. He started trying to touch me under my dress. Just then my brother knocked on the door, so he stopped. I ran outside and told my brothers we needed to leave right now. I didn't tell anyone what happened. Every Sunday my brothers wanted to stop there but I refused to go to his house again.

One time I stole a small angel food cake with pink icing from the corner store. I felt so bad I couldn't eat it. I took it back to the store crying and told the cashier what I did. She said it was alright but don't do that again. That still didn't ease my guilty conscience and I woke up from a nightmare, so I woke my mom up crying and told her what I did. She also told me it was alright but not to do it again or I'd have more nightmares.

I had a toy animal stuffed with rainbow colored plastic bread wrappers cut into ribbons. Me and my kitty cat were having a party in the backyard, and needed decorations, so I popped it open and put the colorful plastic ribbons all over the yard. I thought it looked very pretty. I was so proud of it that I got my mom and showed her. When she saw it, the look on her face was awful! She was shocked and angry. I had no idea I was doing anything wrong. I was just having fun, but she made me clean it up immediately.

Another time I wanted to play with my tea set in the front yard, but my mom said no and told me to play in my room. Instead, I threw the tea set, and all my toy dishes out of my second story bedroom window. Then I climbed out my window and on to the top of the front porch roof, then climbed down the rail of the porch to the ground. When my mom found out she was very mad and threw all my dishes away. I begged and pleaded and cried for her to get my toy dishes out of the trash, but she wouldn't.

One time I did a big no-no. I got an empty can and me and my little brother went door to door pretending to raise money for an organization. When we got home my mom asked where we got all the money, so I told her. She got mad and made us go back to everyone and tell them what we did and give all the money back. I was so embarrassed.

I had a girlfriend in kindergarten and her mom picked me up and took us to the park for picnics. I really enjoyed it. She moved away and it made me so angry and sad that I wiped her completely out of my memory. A year later she moved back and tried to tell me who she was, but I didn't remember her and wanted nothing to do with her. That made her sad, so she started crying. Twenty-five years later I remembered who she was and felt bad about the way I acted. The memory is a strange thing.

I was a tomboy growing up probably because I had three brothers. I didn't dream of getting married or being a princess but sometimes the neighborhood boys played a game called Capture the Queen. I was the queen, and my brothers were on my side. The boys from the neighborhood tried to steal me and keep me captive until I was rescued. It was a fun game and went on for hours. We also played King of the Mountain. One person got on top of the hill and tried to stop anyone from getting to the top. Whoever made it to the top became the new king and had to defend the hill.

I liked to jump on my bed but one time I fell off and hit my head on the steel frame and had to get stitches. Once my mom was spanking me and I wiggled free and busted my cheek on the wall and had to go to the hospital again. Now I have two big scars on my face. I also got hurt and have a scar on the front top of my head. I don't remember how I got it, but funny my scars look like I've had a lobotomy.

Me and my brothers were eating SpaghettiOs and saw a spider come down from the ceiling on a single string and land in my food. My brothers thought that was extremely funny and were laughing and I yelled for our mom. She came in and I told her a spider was in my bowl. She said, "No there's not! Just eat your food!" Then she stirred it all up. My brothers thought that was even funnier and laughed more. At my house if you didn't eat what was made then you didn't eat. That night I didn't eat. I wasn't going to eat a spider.

Before we lived in the house, a lady named Nellie died in the bathtub and was said to haunt the house. The upstairs toilet flushed with no one there and dishes fell off shelves in the kitchen. My oldest brother saw her one night when he was at the top of the stairs. He said she was at the bottom, glowing white, wearing a white nightgown, had no feet, and floated above the floor! That scared him so bad he ran into my mom's room crying uncontrollably and sat in her lap. That looked funny because he was around 12 years old. My little brother said he saw her in his upstairs bedroom window, and she was wearing curlers in her hair and had a scarf over the curlers and was glowing white. It terrified him also. I never saw Nellie and she never bothered me, so I wasn't afraid.

My mom whistled very loud without using her fingers and that's how she called us to come in from outside. You could hear it a few blocks away and when she whistled you better come home right away, or you'd be in trouble. One night she whistled but none of us came home. She couldn't find us, so she called the police. Here's the story. It was just getting dark, and my brothers and I were playing in the backyard. They told me to ask our mom if we could go in the alley to play. When I went inside, she was on the phone, and I asked her. She was saying yes to the person on the phone, but I thought she was saying yes to me. I told my brothers she said yes, so we went in the alley and somehow, I got lost. I didn't know which way to go to get home. I ended up in front of a house where two twin teenage boys lived. Their mom saw me and told me it was getting dark, and I needed to go home, but I was too afraid to tell her I was lost. She went back in her house and the two twin boys noticed something was wrong because I didn't go anywhere. One of them asked if I was lost and I told them yes. One told me to follow them into the backyard and they'd show me the way home. When we got there, they threw me on the ground and pulled my pants and underwear down. One held their hand over my mouth, so no one heard me screaming. I struggled to get free, but they were too strong. Just then we heard and saw police sirens in the alley, so they immediately let go and took off running into the front. I pulled my pants up and climbed over the chain fence just in time for the police to see me in the alley. They opened the back-car door, and my three brothers were sitting in there, so I got in and they drove us home. When my two oldest brothers got out, they got whipped right there on the street. I didn't get in trouble and didn't tell anyone what happened because I was way too afraid.

Another time my little brother and I were playing in the front yard and a car pulled up and two hippie guys got out and came towards us. I grabbed my brother by the hand and yelled, "RUN!" We ran in the house and yelled for our mom. I told her what happened, and we looked out the window just in time to see the men get back in their car and take off. I was very scared. I felt they were trying to kidnap one of us.

My little brother started acting up lighting fires between the houses outside. One afternoon he caught one of the bedrooms on fire and got scared and hid under the bed. It was a big fire, but my parents kept it under control until the fire department arrived and put it out. They found him under the bed unharmed. The whole room had to be remodeled. After that my mom took him to the fire station to show him what people looked like when they got badly burned but that didn't stop him. He also went to school every day and threw his lunch in the trash and told his teacher his mom sent him with none.

I became afraid to sleep at night because I thought I might die in a fire. I was very leery of people I knew and didn't know. I didn't trust anyone and wasn't really close to anyone. I always tried to be aware of my surroundings. When I walked down the street and a car passed by, I ducked behind a parked car until it passed. I was so afraid of being kidnapped! School was getting hard because all I wanted to do was sleep in class.

What I liked about being rich was having a maid to cook, clean, and wash my hair. I liked eating shrimp and steak and riding in a new Cadillac every week. Especially the convertibles. I liked sitting in the back and having the wind blow through my hair while listening to the songs SOME KIND OF WONDERFUL by GRAND FUNK, BLACK WATERS by

THE DOOBIES BROTHERS and YOU SEXY THING by HOT CHOCOLATE. ***I believe in miracles. Where you from? You sexy thing! Where did you come from angel? How did you know I'd be the one? Oh! It's ecstasy!***

Another song I liked was by PAPER LACE called THE NIGHT CHICAGO DIED. ***Daddy was a cop, on the east side of Chicago. Back in the U.S.A. In the heat of a summer night. In the land of the dollar bill. When the town of Chicago died, and they talk about it still. When a man named Al Capone, tried to make that town his own! And he called his gang to war with the forces of the law! And the sound of the battle rang through the streets of the old east side. Til the last of the hoodlum gang had surrendered up or died. And I asked someone who said, "Bout a hundred cops are dead!" And there was no sound at all but the clock upon the wall. (tick-tock tick-tock) Then the door burst open wide! And my daddy stepped inside! And he kissed my mamas face! And he washed her tears away!***

One night I woke to the sound of my stepdad yelling at my mom and loud glass breaking. He said he was going to burn the house down. My mom went to the back porch to get away from him and he went upstairs and pushed the air conditioning unit out the window hoping it landed on her, but he missed. After the yelling and glass breaking stopped, I crept downstairs to see what was going on. My mom was on the floor sobbing in a pile of glass. I asked if I could help clean the mess, but she told me to go back to bed before he came back and saw me up and I got in trouble. I went to my room and cried myself to sleep. I was so sad because I couldn't do anything to help her. I hated seeing my mom like that and I hated that man.

My stepdad liked to watch Star Trek and when it was on, he wanted everyone in the living room to watch. I didn't like it because the aliens were too scary. I liked the kid show Lost in Space. When Star Trek was on, I brought my Barbie, her beach van, and all the accessories into the living room and set it all up. I pretended Barbie and her friends were at the drive-in and played with them instead of watching TV. My favorite Lost in Space episode was Centauri 5 when aliens pretended to be humans. Whenever the music and party lights came on all the young people had to dance until it stopped.

I told my mom I wanted curly hair, but she replied, "You don't just get curly hair. You're born with it, but you can get a perm someday." When in church, I learned you could pray to God for things, so I prayed for my stepdad to go away forever and for curly hair. Then soon forgot all about it.

I became ill with tonsillitis and was scheduled to have them taken out the next day. I was very afraid to go to the hospital but when I woke, I was all better. My parents didn't believe me and took me to the hospital anyway. I was checked out and was fine. How did that happen? Was it the power of my mind? God? Just a coincidence or what? I never had problems with my tonsils again.

My stepdad took all of us to the drive-in on the weekends. We saw very scary movies like The Exorcist, The Texas Chainsaw Massacre, Rosemary's' Baby, Last House on the Left, The Devils Rain, House on the Haunted Hill, The Man With Two Heads, and Rabid. I saw all those movies before I was nine years old. I don't know why my parents took such young kids to see those movies. I became even more afraid and had terrible nightmares. After the movies were over, they played dirty porn on the screen. Sometimes I woke up and saw it and they told me to go back to sleep.

I couldn't watch the news because it was too scary. There was a man going around murdering young women and putting their bodies in 50-gallon drums and filling them with concrete. Another man was killing blonde ladies and that scared me because I was blonde. During Halloween a young girl was kidnapped about three miles away and was found chopped up in a sewer. That was way too scary for me.

I saw the movie Geronimo and it was very sad. I didn't like what white men did to the Indians. I was attracted to Indians. I liked the long black hair, dark eyes, muscles, and tan skin. There was a commercial that played on TV about littering. It had an Indian next to a river with a tear running down his cheek with a bunch of litter around him. Whenever it came on, I cried because it was sad how bad people treated earth.

When I was in second grade my older brothers and I walked 8 blocks to school. We began having problems with some older boys that went to a private Catholic school. We had to pass each other from opposite directions. We called them The Kneehouse Gang and they called us Goldilocks and the Three Bears. Every day they beat my brothers up with belts and broke our lunch boxes. My stepdad got tired of it, so he gave us dog chains to defend ourselves. When I went to school, I hung the dog chain in the coat room. The teacher noticed and told the principal, and he called my parents. My stepdad told him the situation, but they still said we couldn't bring dog chains to school. When nothing was done to stop the harassment, my stepdad took matters in his own hands. One morning he followed us to school without being seen. When the gang jumped out to attack us, my stepdad jumped out from behind a parked car and started beating them up. Some of them ran away but he got ahold of one and began punching and choking him. He picked the kid up off his feet, while holding him by the throat. He threatened to kill them if they didn't stop bothering us. It worked because they never messed with us again. That was the only good thing that man ever did for us.

I had a problem with a girl in my class. She was picking on me at lunch and wouldn't stop. She had big buck teeth, so I called her Bucky. She slapped me across my face and said she's going to meet me outside after school. By the end of the day all the kids heard we were going to fight. I really didn't want to but if she cornered me, I would. It was the end of the day and lots of kids were outside waiting to see us fight. I went outside and the kids formed a ring around us, and I couldn't go anywhere. Everyone wanted us to fight. Round one went good for me, and we broke up, but she wanted to fight more. Round two also went good for me and we broke up again. She still wanted to fight more but I didn't want to, so I ran away. She caught up with me in a stranger's front yard and we fought again. This time I got her in a position she couldn't move and beat the shit out of her. We broke up and I was trying to walk away but now her friend wanted to fight and I didn't know why. I walked on home. The next day at school I saw she was pretty bruised up and had black eyes and a big fat lip. She never messed with me again and neither did any of her friends.

The last time my mom and stepdad got into a fight he hurt her bad. He broke her collar bone and nose and bruised her all over. She had to stay in the hospital for a while. I cried myself to sleep every night she was gone. I really missed her and couldn't wait for her to come home. She finally had enough and told him she wanted a divorce.

At this point my stepdad was desperately trying to win my mom back. He bought her a cute puppy that costed $500, and my mom named her Foxy. Then he took all of us to Disney Land in Florida. When we got back my mom still wanted nothing to do with him and soon divorced him. I was so happy.

Life was hard on my mom after she divorced. She had to work two jobs just to try to make ends meet. Having milk was a luxury. I had to do lots of cooking, cleaning, grocery shopping, and laundry. The thing that scared me most was when I had to light the gas stove because it was so dangerous. Me and one of my brothers would carry the laundry six blocks to the laundromat when we had no washer or dryer. The extra work was worth not having that terrible man in our lives anymore.

My older brothers began acting out by smoking, stealing, and skipping school. One of them became violent towards our mom, so she called our real dad who lived in Texas with his new family and asked if he'd take him. He agreed and was coming in the summer to pick him up. I was so excited because I hadn't seen or talked to my dad for so long. I was nine years old now and still had the doll house he gave me. He came with his wife and their young son. They visited a few hours and went on their way to La Feria Texas with my brother.

It was my mom, me, and two brothers living in the big two-story house, and it was spooky to be alone. I was scared at night when my mom went to the bar down the street to waitress and left us home alone. I was afraid a stranger would break in and hurt us, or the house would burn down. During the day she worked at a hamburger joint, and also worked on getting her cosmetology degree. I quizzed her on her homework when she was home. I hardly ever saw her, and I had to get me and my brothers up for school in the mornings.

My mom gave me $10 and a list of groceries to get. On the way I lost the money, so I went back home and told her. She replied, "Go back and look for it and don't come home until you find it!" I went walking the same way I started but couldn't find it anywhere. I wondered if I'd be able to go home again or if my mom was just saying that. I started crying because I couldn't find it and didn't know what to do. Did she really want me not to come home if I didn't find it? Even if it got dark? And where would I go? Finally, I saw it laying in the gutter of the street and was very relieved. I did the shopping and went home.

My little brother was still acting up, starting fires, throwing his lunch in the trash, and skipping school. Our mom put him in a boy's home that was run by the state. They wanted her to sign her rights over to them, but she refused. The state found a foster home to put him in and his foster parents wanted to adopt him, but she also refused that. She then sent my other brother to our dads.

Now it was just me and my mom in the big spooky house and I was in fourth grade. When she left at night to work or on a date, I was very afraid to be alone without a parent. I couldn't sleep at night because I was still afraid a bad man would break in and hurt me, or I'd die in a fire when I slept. I stayed up at night the best I could, watching TV until it went off air. School was hard because I was so tired all the time and I started falling behind in class. All I did was look out the window and daydream about the cutest boy in class named Steven. Sometimes I fell asleep. On my report card my teacher wrote a note that said, "All Cindy does all day is daydream out the window." So true.

My mom was very beautiful. Lots of men dated her and wanted to marry her but she wasn't ready and turned them all down. She got her cosmetology license but eventually took a job in a factory due to transportation problems. She met a nice man at work but wanted nothing to do with him because he was in the middle of a divorce. He was very persistent and followed her around all the time and gave her rides back and forth from work. They finally started dating and he soon moved in. He was very nice to us.

I loved roller skating on the weekends and was very good at it. The rink was eight blocks away and the only way I could afford to go was to win the skating contest and get free passes. I won all the time against the teenage girls, so that made them mad. At the end of the night, they'd wait outside to beat me up. I'd leave early or run out the door past them as fast as I could and didn't stop until I got home. I enjoyed watching women's roller derby every Sunday. When I grew up, I wanted to be a Roller Derby Queen.

My real grandma and her husband lived several miles away and had parties all the time. I loved going there! I had two aunts and one worked in the bars. When I stayed the night, I watched her put on makeup before work. She was so pretty. I wanted to grow up to be just like her. The other had long black hair and looked like an Indian. Her husband had very long hair and was very good looking, but he was a womanizer and beat my aunt all the time. She eventually divorced him. My grandpa was also a womanizer. At a party my grandparents got into an argument, and he slapped her in the face so hard I thought her head was going to come off. Everyone saw it and froze in shock. No one knew what to do. My grandma ran to her bedroom. They split up and he came to stay with us until he figured out what to do. I was very mean to him after what he did to my real grandma. I called him names and cussed him out when my mom wasn't around. We didn't get along and I couldn't wait for him to move out. My grandma divorced him.

Around this time my hair started going crazy. It got wavy and I didn't like it and ironed it straight. I just wanted straight hair! The kids at school teased me about my hair and called me crash helmet. I hated my hair so much.

My mother use to read Tarot cards. Years before, when my mom and dad were married several of our relatives were having a get together. Someone started reading cards and my uncle got the card of death. Everyone laughed and thought nothing of it. That night on the way home he died in a very bad car accident. His head was totally severed from his body in the wreck.

My mom hadn't used the cards in years, but out of the blue, she wanted to read my future. She set the cards up and told me she saw a long trip, far away, in my near future. That made me very excited! Soon after that my mom said my dad was coming to pick me and my little brother up to spend the summer with him. I was very excited about it and couldn't wait to go but didn't trust my mom would come pick me up when summer was over and made her promise to. She promised so I agreed to go. My dad showed up with his family and my two older brothers. We piled in a camper shell on the back of his truck and left for La Feria.

We arrived at my dad's house way out in the country on Rabb Road. It was a dirt road and we only had two neighbors. One lived a quarter mile away and the other a mile away. We were surrounded by grapefruits, lemons, green peppers, and cotton plants. I liked going to the field and picking food and eating it, but we really weren't allowed. The closest neighbor had three teenage daughters older than me. Me and the youngest girl became friends. She had very strict parents.

Her parents had a big hog in a pen outside. He was very mean and didn't like people. If you got in his pen, he chased you and tried to bite you. He smelled very bad. Nevertheless, we'd jump on his back and ride him like a bull. If he bucked you off, you'd better get out of his pen quickly. It was so much fun. I really liked going to her house and riding the hog. One day I went over, and everyone was standing around a fifty-gallon drum with a fire under it. I asked what they were doing. They said they were cooking the hog. I got a confused look on my face and then I got sad. I didn't know he was raised to be eaten. I went home and cried but didn't let anyone know I was upset.

We had a chicken that sat on a giant pile of eggs that never hatched because we didn't have a rooster. I asked my girlfriend to give me a fertilized egg from her chickens because I wanted it to hatch the day my mom was to pick me up. She didn't want to give me one because she was afraid her dad would notice it missing. I said, "Look at all these chickens! He won't notice one egg missing." She assured me he would but gave me one anyways and I put it under our chicken. The next day her dad came over and told my dad he wanted it back. Her dad was quite angry. My dad told him, "No, just let her keep the egg." I think my dad paid him for the egg so I could keep it.

My brothers and I went swimming in the canals and they scared me by saying there were poisonous fish and snakes in them. They'd tease me and yell they saw some and I'd frantically try to get out. The canal walls were slanted and slimy and very hard to get out of. They also liked pulling the tails off lizards and putting them down my shirt to watch me freak out.

It was time for my mom to pick me and my little brother up and I was so homesick and missed my familiar surroundings. I was packed and ready to go. The day she was to pick us up, I went out and checked the egg. It was hatching! I was so excited! I couldn't wait to show her the baby chick. The mama hen was also very excited that her egg was hatching. She was very possessive of her new chick, and it was hard to get near it. My mom arrived and I showed her the baby chick I got to hatch, and she thought it was cool. Then my mom dropped a big bombshell on me. She said she wasn't taking me home with her. She was only taking my little brother. That crushed me! I was devastated by the news and began bawling my eyes out. She promised me! She said I needed to stay here to take care of the baby chick. What a load of crap. I just wanted to go home. I felt as if my mother just abandoned me, and my heart hurt so bad. Now I didn't trust anyone, and my mother was just a big liar to me. I couldn't stop crying so I went to my room and waited for her to leave. When it was time for her to go, I was so mad and sad that I didn't even want to come out to say bye. But they made me. She left and took my little brother.

My dad made us call our stepmom mom, and I didn't like it. I didn't think you should be forced to call someone mom if they weren't. The reason was they didn't want their children calling her by her first name. I did it so I wouldn't get in trouble. We also weren't allowed to use the word man in this manner: Hey man what's going on? or How's it going man? If we did, we got slapped upside the head.

School started and I was in fifth grade. The population where I lived was 99 percent Hispanic. I felt so out of place and couldn't speak the language. I felt like a foreigner in another country and was constantly teased by classmates because I was white with long blonde hair. I was smarter than most of the kids in my class and became a straight A student. Getting good grades was very easy now.

One day my dad wanted me to stay home and babysit my 7-month-old sister. I told him I didn't want to, I wanted to play with my friend down the road. He didn't like my answer, so he slapped me so hard upside my head that I flew over the couch and landed behind it on the floor. That shocked me! I learned quickly if my parents asked me to do something I did it with no back talk.

My dad was in the Vietnam war and acted like a military man when disciplining us. Sometimes he'd say jump and if you didn't reply how high or jump, he gave you a smack upside your head. If he said frog, then you had to jump, or you got smacked. I think it was like a game to him, but I didn't like it. Sometimes he pinched my underarm on the sensitive area and it hurt really bad and left bruises. It made me cry. For some reason he thought it was funny. Sometimes he'd say I had a big butt and made derogatory racist statements to me. I just ignored him.

My dad sold the house in La Feria because he wanted to build one. He bought a tiny travel trailer for me and my two brothers to live in while he and his new family stayed in a motel. It was wintertime and cold in the trailer. Thanksgiving came and me and my brothers had turkey pot pies. I don't know what my dad and his new family did because we weren't allowed in the motel room. It kept raining and my dad couldn't build the new house until it stopped.

My brothers sometimes went to the woods and caught rabbits and cooked them over a fire. I wanted nothing to do with that. The thought of eating a cute little bunny rabbit sickened me.

Christmas morning came and me and my brothers got nothing. Our parents had a small Christmas tree in the motel room with presents for our little brother and sister. The managers of the motel had a daughter that was my age, and we were good friends. I went to her house, and she showed me all the presents she got and asked what I got. I told her I didn't get anything. Her parents felt bad and put $5 in an envelope and gave it to me. I spent the day at her house playing with her toys and having dinner. I felt closer to her family than I did my own.

My dad couldn't wait any longer for the rain to stop because he was running out of money and couldn't keep paying to stay in a motel. He bought a big house in Santa Rosa, Texas. It used to be a doctor's office and was very spooky knowing surely some people died there.

I changed schools and was still smarter than most kids in my class. When my brothers got bad grades, my dad spanked them with a belt. I didn't want that to happen to me, so I made sure I did my schoolwork and got good grades. My dad paid money for good grades. I loved report card day because that meant payday.

My brothers were swinging me on a tree swing, and I was yelling for them to stop because they were swinging me too high. I was very scared yelling, "The rope is going to break! Stop! Stop!" They thought it was funny and swung me higher. Suddenly, on a backswing, the rope broke. I hit the tree with my back and rippled down the two by fours nailed into it like a ladder. I'm sure it looked funny like in the cartoons. I hit the ground and had the wind knocked out of me. My brothers thought it was hilarious, but I didn't! It took a few minutes to recover from the daze, and I had bruises on the back of my body in the shape of a ladder.

I was babysitting my little sister and took her to my friend's house. She was at the potty-training stage, so I kept asking her if she had to pee. She kept saying no, then peed in her pants. I really didn't know how to discipline her, so I gave her a couple swats on her butt, and she cried. I left no mark or really hurt her. My girlfriend's mom called my parents and told them. My parents were furious! That's the way I was being raised and I didn't know any other way to discipline her. When I got home, I got slapped upside my head and chewed out. I thought that was wrong and unfair. My dad spanked us but not his new kids. Even when my little brother was being a spoiled monster. He didn't treat us like he treated his new family.

My dad put locks on all the food cabinets and the refrigerator doors so we couldn't get in them. When me and my older brothers weren't around, they'd give my little brother and sister sweets. Me and my brothers were only fed at mealtimes. I hated when my stepmom made liver and onions or butter beans! I'd put the beans on a spoon and pass them under the table to her and she ate them for me. If she didn't, I swallowed them whole. I really liked her tacos and burgers. Me and my brothers got free breakfast at school in the mornings, so I liked to go to school to eat. All the lunch ladies were very nice to me.

At school they put together a book of poems that kids wrote so I wrote this for it:

The Mill

If I were a mill on top of a hill, I'd wheal and squeal so loud that the people wouldn't be proud. I'd be so happy and gay, because the wind would turn me all day, and when night comes, I'd rest, so the next day, I could do my very best.

One of my older brothers was a know it all. He had to always be right and have the last word on everything. We got in an argument one time over how to spell the word ad like in a newspaper ad. He insisted it was spelled add. I told him add is when you add numbers. He still insisted I was wrong, so I got a newspaper and showed him the word ad over and over in it. He said they must have spelled it wrong. I just laughed and knew not to argue with him anymore.

My dad on the other hand was not as easy going with him. One day he had enough of his attitude and lost his patience. My brother wouldn't shut up after my dad told him to. He just wanted to keep arguing. My dad took him in the family room, tied his hands together, and put a gag in his mouth. Stood him on a chair and strung his hands above his head and tied him to a wooden ceiling beam and made him stand on the chair for a while. That terrified me and I felt extremely bad for my brother. I don't think my dad understood the physical abuse me and my brothers went through with my stepdad. That was probably why they were acting out. I was afraid to get in trouble and did my best to follow the rules.

My little sister got sick with something that made blisters in her mouth. They took her to the doctor and got medicine. Then I came down with it and we had it at the same time. My dad made me gargle with warm saltwater. I was screaming and crying it hurt too much and my nose started bleeding and he just walked away. The medicine she got wasn't working so they got her new medicine and gave me her old medicine. Why would they think it was going to work for me if it didn't work for her? She quickly got better, and they gave me the medicine that was left. I too quickly got better. I felt like a second-class citizen in this family.

When my parents didn't want me and my older brothers around, they dropped us off under a bridge way out in the country to spend the weekend. It was ok sometimes, but I didn't like to spend the whole weekend there. One night was enough for me. At night when we slept under the bridge, I was afraid of snakes, wild animals, and the thought of a bad stranger showing up and hurting us. If we had an emergency there was no way to get help. I couldn't wait to get back home, take a nice warm bubble bath, and get in a soft bed again.

I liked it when it was time to go fishing to stock the freezer. My dad was in the coast guard reserves and at night we went to the base on the gulf shore and fished for hours. You never knew what you were going to catch. It was nonstop fast fishing. I didn't like to catch ribbon fish. They weren't edible and had very sharp teeth and were hard to get off the hook. My dad killed them, chopped them up, and threw them in the water for chum. When we got home and it was time to kill, skin, and fillet them, I wanted no part of it. That was too gross for me, and I didn't like to eat fish.

I just turned twelve and started my period but didn't feel close enough to anyone to tell them something so personal. I had to tell someone. I took my stepmom aside and told her, but she didn't believe me. She said I was too young. I was confused at what to do. I insisted that I did. She took me in the bathroom, and I showed her and then she believed me. At the dinner table my dad started teasing me in front of everyone in a roundabout way and made stupid remarks about it. I was so embarrassed in front of everyone. Sometimes the people in my family had no empathy for others. I felt like a live-in babysitter and a maid.

Early one morning I did something very strange. It was just getting dawn when I got out of bed and walked in my sleep to the next-door neighbor's backyard. I stood there staring at the sky. My dad happened to look out the window and saw me standing out there in my nightgown. He came outside where I was and asked me what I was doing. I told him the neighbor took my bra and I was getting it back. He realized I was sleepwalking and walked me back to my room and I got in bed. When I woke that morning, my dad asked if I remembered anything and I replied, "Yes I remember it." I didn't tell him what I remembered nor what I was staring at in the sky. I was standing at the edge of a giant cliff overlooking the ocean. I could feel the wind blowing through my hair and smell the ocean breeze. I could hear and see the waves crashing the shoreline below. The sun was in the sky in front of me and it was very big and bright and beautiful. It was shining red, yellow, and orange, and was so spectacular and mesmerizing. Everything felt serene and I didn't want to stop staring at it. That was when my dad came out and got me.

I met many of my dad's relatives. My grandma, grandpa, aunt, uncles, and cousins. My grandpa was very tall, very nice, and had a long white ponytail. My grandma on the other hand was a whole different story. She was very small and quite mean. When you were at her house and it was time to eat, when she called if you didn't show up in five minutes, she threw your plate of food in the trash, and you didn't get to eat. I didn't like going to my grandparents because they had stinky goats. They also made my brothers and me practice square dancing together. I hated it. My great grandma who I never met was a full blooded Cherokee Indian named Elsie Bear.

My dad's sister was even stricter than my grandma. After her husband died in the car wreck I talked about earlier, she remarried. He also died and she remarried again. He died too and she was now on her fourth marriage. She reminded me of the wicked witch of the west. I was sleeping over one time and she was at work. I wanted something sweet to eat but all they had was green Jell-O. About 15 boxes. I didn't like the flavor of lime Jell-O but wanted something sweet. I told my cousins, "Let's eat a box of Jell-O." They replied, "NO! Our mom will find out and we'll get in lots of trouble!" I didn't believe them and replied, "Look at all of the green Jell-O! She'll never notice if we eat one." So, we ate a box. As soon as my aunt got home, she flew through the door very fast like a witch on a broomstick and went to the cabinet. She opened it up and yelled, "WHO ATE MY GREEN JELL-O!" We told her we all did. I was really scared of her. All my cousins went to my aunt's bedroom and had to pull their pants down to their ankles and got spanked with a belt by their stepdad. These were teenage girls. I felt her husband was a pervert. Later in life he was robbed and murdered at the beach while sitting in his truck. But they didn't spank me because I wasn't their child. I apologized to my cousins.

One of my older cousins came over and we rode our bikes to the school yard. No one else was there but me and her, then five teenage Hispanic boys showed up, so we decided to leave right away. Before we could go, the boys grabbed me off my bike, threw me on the ground, and started trying to tear my clothes off! My cousin took off and left me there. I was fighting, punching, scratching, kicking, and screaming, trying to get them to stop! Then as quickly as it started, they stopped and took off running. I had no idea what made them stop and run away. I got up and was disheveled and got my clothes straightened out. I got on my bike and took off as fast as I could for home. When I got there, I found my cousin hadn't told anyone what was happening to me. She was just sitting on the couch. That kind of made me mad at her. So, oh well, that was over, and I never told my parents about it. It was very embarrassing to go to school every day and face the boys who attacked me.

My dad was a meat inspector and bought a slaughterhouse. It was way out in the country and looked like it was in the movie The Texas Chainsaw Massacre. It was very scary, and I hated going there. It smelled bad all the time and there were flies everywhere. Dead skinned carcasses hung from meat hooks with blood and guts all over the floors. One room was a salt room for hanging and drying hides. It was an awful place to go, and I hated when my parents took me there. It was disgusting. I was happier staying at home babysitting my younger siblings and was sometimes paid a dollar an hour.

My dad went to ranches and picked up their dead animals and brought them to the slaughterhouse to be butchered for zoo meat or dogfood. The hides were sold to personal buyers. The ranchers were happy because they didn't have to deal with their dead animals anymore. He soon had contracts with many ranchers, so business was doing great.

My dad made my brothers work at the slaughterhouse at night and go to school during the day. I'm sure that affected their grades. They had it so much worse than I did, and I felt very sorry for them. One day I was at school and a teacher asked me to ask my brothers if they could shower better. I explained to her they worked in a slaughterhouse at night and the smell of dead animals was very hard to get off you. The teacher said no more about it. They got paid to work but they probably would've rather just had a normal childhood instead of the money.

The ranchers saw how much money my dad made from their dead animals, and they decided to break their contracts and butcher their own dead animals. My dad got a lawyer and was suing the ranchers for a million dollars. The case was going well, but one day the lawyer didn't tell my dad they had a court date, and no one showed. Not even the lawyer. So, the case was dropped. I think the lawyer got paid off by the ranchers to get rid of the lawsuit.

My dad decided to tear down the slaughterhouse and sell the land. That made me very happy. He used his old pickup truck and some big chains. He attached the chains to the truck and the building to pull the concrete structure down. Me and my brothers were sitting on the tailgate to get a good view. My dad was in the truck and was just getting ready to pull forward when suddenly, he stopped, got out, and told us to get off the tailgate because the building might land on us. We all got off and my dad went ahead and pulled the building down and the wall landed on the tailgate and ripped it right off. If we had stayed on it, we would have gotten our legs crushed or worse! We were so lucky my dad noticed the danger before he pulled the building down or it could have been a giant tragedy. That was the end of the horrible slaughterhouse.

I made a few friends at school but most of the kids were mean to me because I was white. There was a girl who always picked on me at school and I got tired of it and one day she fell asleep at her desk, so I tied her shoestrings in knots to the legs of her desk. When the bell rang, she jumped up and fell flat on her face. I laughed at her and walked away. I don't know how she got out of it. She wanted to fight after school, so she followed me to the vacant field in front of my house. We had a good fight, but I whooped her ass. She decided to be my friend after that.

I wanted to be a cheerleader and went through tryouts and was picked. I was so excited! I went home and told my parents I needed some money for supplies and a uniform, but they said they couldn't afford it and I was really bummed out about it.

I played on a softball and basketball team at school. The girls on the basketball team were mean to me and always tried to trip me during practice even if I was on their team. I was like what the hell are you tripping me for? I'm on your team! They thought it was funny to see me fall but it really annoyed me.

My nickname was Cindy and when I walked by the Hispanic girls playing jump rope, they'd start singing this song to tease me. Cindy-rella dressed in yella went upstairs to kiss a fella. Made a mistake and kissed a snake! How many kisses did it take? 1 2 3 4 5 6 7 and so on. I thought that was weird and creepy.

It was time for yearbooks and class pictures, but we couldn't afford a yearbook. The lunch ladies liked me so much they all chipped in and bought me one. They said they wanted me to remember them and the time I spent at their school. I thought that was so sweet and thanked them. When we took the class picture, I was the only white girl, and was front and center holding the class sign.

Girls wanted to write in my yearbook even if they weren't really my friends. I didn't care so I let them. I paid no attention to what they wrote at the time. Looking back on it I never noticed how many girls wrote, "I hope you find the man of your dreams!" I guess it must have had something to do with the Cindy-rella song they always sang to me.

My favorite show to watch was Dr Shrinker. He was a madman with an evil mind who shrunk people. He was an evil scientist.

Two blocks away was a Baptist Church and the preacher had a granddaughter, and we became friends. I went to church with her on Sundays to get away from my family. I really liked going there to play because they had a game room with a foosball table and other games. Her family convinced me to accept Jesus and wanted me to get baptized by water in front of the congregation. I was supposed to do it that weekend but out of the blue my mom called and wanted me to come home. I was so excited! I just wanted to go home to my old house and see my old friends and go skating every weekend again. I packed my belongings and immediately flew home.

My mom and her boyfriend picked me up and told me they had a big surprise for me when we got home. That made me very excited, and I couldn't wait. I couldn't imagine what it could be.

We pulled into a trailer park in the country and my mom yelled, "Surprise, we're home." I was confused. This wasn't my home. My mom sold the house and bought a 2-bedroom trailer. That wasn't the pleasant surprise I was hoping for. I wanted to go back to the house I was familiar with. We went inside and it was nice enough. I looked for my belongings I had before I went to my dad's. My dolls, roller skates and so forth. But they weren't there. I asked my mom where my stuff was, and she said she didn't think I wanted it anymore, so she got rid of it all. I was bummed out about everything. Life was just one big disappointment after another. We lived in House Springs Missouri, and I didn't know anyone. I wasn't very good at making friends and usually felt like an outcast or a misfit.

I was listening to the radio trying to win tickets to Six Flags and was the right caller and won. A week later I was listening again to win tickets to Journey. I was the right caller and won again! I was so excited I was going to see Journey. They asked me if I won anything in the last month from their station and I told them I did thinking I might get another prize for winning twice. Then they told me I couldn't win twice in one month and wouldn't be getting the Journey tickets. I tried to trade the tickets, but they wouldn't. I was so bummed out.

My brother came to visit from the boy's home, and I took him to a place called Pismo Beach to swim. It looked like a beach but was really a river. It had a giant waterfall just past the place we swam. It rained a lot, so the river had a very strong current. I told him to stay close to the bank, so the current didn't sweep him over the waterfall. We were swimming next to each other, but he didn't listen to me, and the current grabbed him and started taking him away. He was yelling for help, so I grabbed him and threw him up in the air out of the current. Then the current swept me away and I was stuck at the top of the waterfall. I couldn't move or I'd go over the falls. It was very slippery from the slimy moss. If I went over the falls, the rocks would really hurt me. A bunch of guys made a chain and rescued me. I was embarrassed and upset with my little brother.

Whenever my little brother visited, I loved to put on concerts for him. I put party lights up, got a fake mic, and set my few stuffed animals up like they were the audience. My brother was the only real live person. My favorite was acting and singing the entire album Bat Out of Hell by Meatloaf.

School started and I was in 7th grade. It went ok and I adjusted well to everything. My aunt, uncle, and cousin moved in a few trailers down from us. I wasn't happy about it because my aunt was very strict and a nosey tattle tale. I started smoking cigarettes and just knew she was going to catch me and tell.

My best friend was several years older than me. Her hair was very curly, and we both blow dried our hair straight and I had the Farrah Faucet look. I loved going to her house to swim, play Spades, ping pong, and spend the night. We liked going to the five and dime store and playing a game. We'd steal things from the store and add it all up. I guess my conscience took some time off. Whoever had the highest amount was the winner. One time we were doing it and she got caught. They wanted to search her purse, but she refused. We ran out the store, got in her car, and took off. We never did that again.

There were two girls at school that loved to pick on me. They'd steal my books and notebooks and put their names on them. They were just terribly mean to me and always called me names and hit me for no reason. They'd throw things at me in class and make spit balls and spit them at me. I got tired of it so one day I got a big thorn that was about three inches long and very sharp. I saw them walking to class and ran up behind them and poked one of them really hard in their ass with the thorn. She jumped in the air like she was a cartoon character! It was so funny! I started laughing at them and told them they better leave me alone or something worse might happen. They never bothered me again.

My mom and her boyfriend married in a small Baptist church after he divorced his first wife and now, I had two older red headed stepsisters. Sounds like a Cinderella tale getting ready to start.

One of his daughters was a couple years older than me and moved in with us. I was excited to have a new friend and sister and was willing to share my room.

My oldest stepsister who was very nice came to visit and brought her boyfriend and they liked to smoke pot, but I'd never tried it. Her boyfriend brought some called Hawaiian. When it got dark, we all got in the car to go get high. After we smoked a joint, I was high, and felt good. But somehow her boyfriend was driving the wrong way down a one-way service road and all the cars were beeping their horns, flashing their lights, and pulling over so they didn't hit us! He realized it and quickly turned the car around. Wow! We almost had a terrible car wreck!

The skating rink in town had an all-night skate-a-thon and me and my stepsister were supposed to go but instead we went to these older guys house and spent the night drinking, smoking pot, making out, and listening to music. We hadn't noticed the big snowstorm outside that sent over a foot of snow. We couldn't make it back to the roller rink before our parents were to pick us up. When we finally got back to the skating rink our parents were already there waiting. We knew we were in lots of trouble. We both got grounded and my mom cut the cords off my stereo and TV in our bedroom.

It bothered me when my stepsister's girlfriend came over and sat in my stepdad's lap and flirted with him in front of my mom. She was a full-grown woman with giant boobs and kissed and hugged on him. I didn't know why my mom put up with that. I knew my next-door neighbor was cheating on his wife with her. That's probably why I didn't like her sitting in my new stepdad's lap. My stepdad liked it. He thought she was a hot 17-year-old. If it was me, I'd have kicked that hussy out and told her to never come back.

My mom and stepsister fought all the time and life was miserable. She blamed my mom for her parents' divorce. They had a giant fight, and it became physical. After throwing punches my mom grabbed her by her hair and dragged her across the floor towards the front door. I tried to get them apart but couldn't. My mom threw her out the door and told her she couldn't live here anymore. My stepsister told our friends that I helped my mom beat her up but that wasn't true. All our friends were mad at me because they believed her. No one was my friend anymore.

Sometimes my best friend picked us up for school and we rode around getting stoned. On this morning it was very cold and snowed a lot. We were getting ready to leave and she said she wasn't taking me to school anymore. Only my stepsister. They told me to ride the bus. That confused me. Then I understood. She didn't want to be my friend anymore because of the lie my stepsister told.

My stepsister moved out very soon after the fight and all my friends were my friends again and all was well except for one thing. My ankles were swelling and bothering me again. All my life my ankles felt weak and wobbly and sprained easy. My mom took me to the doctors, and he said I had children's rheumatoid arthritis and there was nothing he could do. I got a permanent pass to get out of P.E. and was happy about it. I paid no mind to what the doctor said and went on with my life.

A girl in my class told me a couple boys next door were going to watch some stag films in their garage and wanted to know if I wanted to go. I had no idea what a stag film was but told her I'd go. I snuck out late at night and we went into the garage with the two boys, and they put the film on. To my shock it was a sex video! I was so embarrassed I couldn't even watch it or look at anyone. All I could do was giggle. After a few minutes I told them I had to go.

One afternoon me and the same girl were walking on a dirt road out in the country. We weren't expecting to see anyone.

Two young boys approached, and I recognized them from school. We only knew each other in passing. They were brothers and had very beautiful long curly bright white hair. The oldest one I thought was cute asked if I wanted to buy a joint for two dollars. I replied, "That's an awfully small joint for two dollars." He said, "Trust me. You'll get really high. It's angel dust." I had no idea what angel dust was and thought it was just the name of the weed. Like Hawaiian or Sinsemilla. We both smoked it and got so fucking high. I felt like I was in a big foggy cloud. My feet felt like they had concrete stuck to them and I had a hard time picking them up to walk. I was laughing so hard and I'm sure I looked funny trying to walk. I'd never been that high before. I guess they called it angel dust because it made you feel like you were in the clouds. I couldn't wait to go to school to see the boys, but I never saw them again.

I was babysitting for a lady who lived far out in the country, and it was spooky at her house at night. I made sure all the windows and doors were locked. The next morning, she came home and went to bed. I was sleeping on the couch and woke to see a man standing in the living room looking at the stereo. I said, "I'm thirsty. I need a drink of water." He got me a glass of water and I drank some and gave it back to him. He said, "Now you can go back to sleep." When he left, I was woken again by the noise of the screen door slamming and I went back to sleep. When we both woke up, I told her, "I think your husband was here." Then told her what happened. She was confused and alarmed and replied, "I'm divorced! My husband's not around here!" She called the police and reported it. The police searched the neighborhood and found a guy fitting the description I gave, going around on his bike stealing from houses and was arrested for having stolen property. That was quite scary. If he was a really bad man, he could've really hurt us.

Most of my girlfriends were older than me and we talked about sex a lot. I was still a virgin and my girlfriend said I should keep some contraceptives in case the time came I wanted to have sex. She gave me some foam and condoms, so I put them under my bathroom sink and thought no more about it. Me and my mom never talked about sex or girl things. She was going through my bathroom and found the condoms and totally freaked out. She kept yelling at me over and over, "What's this! What the hell is this! You wait until your grandma gets here and sees this!" She was so mad she wouldn't stop yelling at me. I told her I wasn't having sex and only had those in case I did. I wanted to be responsible and not get pregnant. My mom put the contraceptives on the living room coffee table for all to see. When my grandma arrived my mom said, "Tell your grandma what this stuff is! Go ahead and tell her!" When I did, she didn't say anything negative about it. She had no response. I think she was on my side because my mom got pregnant when she was 15 and I was trying to be more responsible. After my grandma left my mom threw all the contraceptives away.

Sometimes I snuck out at night and went a couple trailers down to party with older guys. My aunt who lived a few trailers down saw me come home as the sun was coming up and later told my parents. They came in my room where I was trying to sleep my terrible hangover off and made me clean it. I did it in agony. My hair felt like it was standing on its ends. That didn't make me a bad person or a sinner. Teenagers will be teenagers.

There was an older man that was good looking with long brown curls, dark brown eyes, and drove the ice cream truck in the neighborhood. He sold pot out of it, and we became friends. I rode around with him, ate ice cream, and got stoned. One day he asked if I wanted to drive the ice cream truck on the back roads. I drove very slowly because I was afraid, so he put his foot on mine and floored the gas. We were side swiping trees and trying not to wreck! He was laughing like a crazy madman the whole time. When he stopped flooring the gas we came to a stop, and I had a very puzzled and scared look on my face because I didn't know why he did that. Both side mirrors were knocked off and the sides were all dented. I looked at him with big eyes and said, "Sorry!" He started laughing and replied, "That's ok, insurance will pay for it."

One time we went to his house, and I found out he was married but I never met his wife. He was growing a lot of pot plants indoors and showed me them. I'd never seen that much pot before and was amazed. I wanted to pick some buds, but he said, "Nope, they're not ready yet." We got stoned and he took me home.

The ice cream man never came on to me, but one day he asked me to marry him. I just started laughing and replied, "No, you're already married." He replied back, "I'm a minister and have a license to marry people and I can marry more than one woman. I can marry us right now if you want." I just laughed more and declined his silly offer.

There was a college guy in the trailer park visiting his older brother. He had long dark curls and deep dark brown eyes with a cute smile and tan skin. He looked like an Arabian. I was very attracted to him! He'd pick me up and we rode around getting stoned. He was such a gentleman and never tried to kiss me until late one night he asked if I wanted to go skinny dipping. He said he knew a swimming pool out in the country where no one would notice us. We went there and climbed a tall chain link fence and stripped down to our underwear and got in the water. We were cuddling and was just getting ready to kiss when we heard a man yell from the distance, "You have 5 minutes to get out of the pool and leave before I call the police and come over there with a shotgun!" Then we heard the clicking noise of the shotgun, so we hurried out of the pool, got dressed, climbed back over the tall fence, and got in his car and took off! I was scared at first, but afterwards, we both laughed. We rode around a little, got stoned, and then he took me home. We were both too shy to come onto each other and never ended up kissing. On another occasion I was skinny dipping with some friends at night and got busted by the police. It was embarrassing coming out of the water in my underwear with bright lights on me.

For some reason I was unhappy and wanted something different and was going to run away and stay with some friends of a friend. They were to pick me up in the morning after my parents left for work. I skipped school, packed my belongings, and waited. Just then I heard a car pull up, so I looked out the window. It was my parents! I threw the bag in the closet and hid under clothes, hoping they wouldn't find me. My mom was yelling all through the house for me, but I wouldn't come out. I was way too afraid. She slid the closet door open and saw me at the bottom and dragged me out and punched me in the face! The school had called my mom at work and told her I didn't show up, so my parents immediately came home to find out what was going on. My mom yelled, "What are you doing? Running away?" I replied, "Yes!" She said, "Good! I'm glad to see you're packed! Grab your bag! You're going to your dads right now!" They took me immediately to my real dads a couple hours away and dropped me off in Mexico, Missouri. He lived above a dance studio. When you first walked in there were two bunk beds. I had the top bunk and my little brother slept on the bottom. There was absolutely no privacy because my bedroom was really the living room. My two older brothers shared a room and my parents and little sister shared one. I really hated it there.

At school there was a boy in class who sat next to me and was always mean to me. He'd say I was ugly, I stunk, and picked on me every day. I hated going to that class knowing he was going to be there. I guess he wasn't happy with his life, so he took a shotgun and committed suicide. I felt bad for him and went to his funeral. It felt strange going to class sitting next to his empty desk after he died.

I called my mom long distance without permission and when my dad got the phone bill, he was extremely mad and slapped me upside the head. Then he put a lock on the phone so I couldn't use it any more without permission.

I started cleaning houses and babysitting so I'd have some money. That was how I paid for things I wanted and clothes to wear because my parents rarely bought me anything.

I had an older step cousin who was very crazy. He came over one night when my parents were gone and asked if I wanted to go cruising. He was driving a beautiful white Cadillac. It was so nice. We went to the country, and he said, "Ok, let's have some real fun!" I didn't know what he meant and was kind of scared. I wasn't sure what he was talking about. He put his foot on the gas and floored it. He was knocking down stop signs, street signs, and driving in and out of fields. I got scared and was yelling for him to stop. He thought it was funny and kept doing it and laughing like a crazy person. When he was done, the beautiful Cadillac was beat all to hell. He took me back home and dropped me off. I didn't tell my parents about it but decided to stay away from him.

He came over again when my parents were gone. I answered the door and he said he wanted me to help him break into a house and needed someone small to climb in the window and unlock the door. I told him, "No! I don't want to get into trouble!" He pulled me outside on the two-story balcony, picked me up by my ankles, and held me over the ground and said he was going to drop me if I didn't do what he wanted. I still said no. He let go of one ankle and was holding me by the other one above the ground and said he was going to let go if I didn't help him. The drop was over 30 feet. I was so scared I agreed. We went to a trailer, and I crawled through a small window and unlocked the door. He got four expensive tires with fancy rims then took me back home. I was so afraid of getting in trouble that I didn't tell my parents and never answered the door for him again. He ironically died at a very young age from a heart attack.

I was depressed and hated the world. I had a girlfriend that was unhappy too and suggested we take a bunch of her mom's pills and end it all. I agreed. That night we got several bottles of pills and split them all. I went home and got in bed to go to sleep and never wake up. About an hour later there was a knock at the door. It was the police! They told my parents my girlfriend was in the hospital overdosing and was having her stomach pumped and they wanted to talk to me. They said, "You're not in any trouble. We just need to know the truth. How many pills did you take?" I replied, "We split all the pills." They started asking me questions like, "How old are you? What's your full name? What year is it? What town are you in?" I was buzzed but wasn't sick or incoherent, so the police left. I went back to sleep. The next morning, I was still buzzed and didn't go to school. When I saw my girlfriend, we talked about how stupid we were and said we'd never do that again. Me and my parents never discussed the incident.

I had a step cousin my age that got pregnant, so my parents put me on the pill, but I was still a virgin. I started dating and having sex with a man about nine years older than me and he was pretty good at it. He didn't just think of his own pleasure but also mine. We dated for a while and my parents knew but said nothing. Sometimes on the weekend I spent the night at his house but told my parents I was at my girlfriends. One night I was with him, and my parents saw my girlfriend and asked where I was. She told them she didn't know. Now I was busted. When I got home the next day my parents told me they knew I was at my boyfriends. They didn't say any more about it and I didn't get in trouble. They probably thought if they didn't make a big deal about it, we'd stop seeing each other.

When I did things that disappointed my dad he'd sigh and say, "Sin, sin, sin, what are we going to do with you?" And when I was bossy, he'd say, "Who died and made you the queen bee?" I just ignored him.

My family moved to a two-bedroom house in the same town. My oldest brother went into a work program to learn how to be a welder and the other moved back with our real mom.

It was the end of ninth grade and my cute algebra teacher was handing final grades out to everyone. As he did, he made a comment to the class about each student. Then it was my turn. I really did bad in algebra and didn't think I was going to pass. He handed me my report card and said, "The only reason I passed you is because you have a really nice smile." Then he smiled at me. I was happy I passed but embarrassed that he said that in front of the whole class.

A girlfriend asked if I wanted a tattoo, and I did. She tattooed my boyfriend's initials on my shoulder. I thought she was going to do small single line initials but instead she did big black block letters. OMG! My parents were going to see it, and I'd be in so much trouble! I was freaking out! All I could do was try to hide it. A few weeks went by, and my dad saw the tattoo but didn't get mad and I was amazed he said nothing about it.

I decided not to see my boyfriend anymore because he wanted me and his friend to have sex together and that made me very mad, so I stormed out and had no plans of seeing him again. The next time I saw him around town he told me his friend (that he tried to get me to have a threesome with) was just killed in a terrible car accident with a train. He was supposed to be with them that night but decided not to go. He was very lucky he didn't. Steve was dating someone else named Cindy and we never saw each other again.

My real mom was calling my dad and telling him about Jesus and the new church she went to. It was a non-denomination, new wave, holy rolling, charismatic church. Whenever he was done talking to her, he'd say my mom was a Jesus freak and tease me about it. I didn't like that.

A step aunt had me come over to babysit her four young daughters when needed. One day she told me she was very tired all the time. I told her to try over-the-counter caffeine pills like I took once in a while. I didn't think I was doing anything wrong. After all it was just like having a cup of coffee and my parents let me drink coffee. She told my parents and my dad confronted me. I told him they were just over-the-counter caffeine pills, but that infuriated him. He slapped me upside the head, and yelled, "Do you want me to call your mom and tell her?" I replied, "I don't care! I don't think I did anything wrong!" He said nothing more about it but was really mad.

My parents and siblings went to Texas for vacation, and I stayed with some friends of theirs. They had two young sons and a very nice two-story house. I stayed in their guest room and the bed was so comfortable. I loved coming home from school and being able to nap and have someone else cook dinner. I felt like I was a real part of their family. I didn't want to go home when my parents came back.

I was dating a 20-year-old with long brown hair down to his waist and he was hot and sexy. He was separated from his wife. After a couple weeks of dating, we had sex. Bummer! He wasn't very good at it, and I didn't get much pleasure out of it. A few days later he went back to his wife, and I was ok with it. A couple weeks later his wife wanted to have a word with me in the alley. We went into the alley, and she swung on me and hit me right on my cheek. I attacked her back and got her on the ground in a position she couldn't move and proceeded to pound her face. I stopped and asked if she had enough or wanted more. She said she was done so I let her go and she got up. Then she attacked me again and we were going at it until we were both too tired to fight and I left. I beat her up pretty good but all I had was a big bruise on my cheek from her first punch. When I got home my dad asked how I got the bruise, so I told him. We lived in such a small town that it already got back to him. My dad said that should teach me not to mess with a married man. I ignored him and walked away.

I didn't like living at my dad's because I didn't feel like part of their family and was never invited to go anywhere with them. All I did was babysit and clean the house. Me and my dad got into a big argument, so I went to the courthouse and told them I wanted to be removed from my family and go into foster care. They called my dad to come, and they all convinced me to forget about it and go back home. I finally agreed. We didn't talk about anything when we got home.

My parents were moving back to Texas and asked if I wanted to go with them or move in with their friends I stayed with before. I was so excited to move in with their friends. I really liked it there at first. I napped after school, did my homework, and had a mom to cook dinner. I felt like a real part of their family. Not long after I moved in things changed. They bought an ice cream shop in town, and I had to babysit every day after school, make dinner, and clean the house. I also had to work in the ice cream shop sometimes and do all the dishes for the shop. This was ruining my nap time, school homework, and my social life. I felt like a slave again and wasn't happy. They said they'd pay me $3 an hour for working at the shop but when payday came, they only paid me $1 an hour. I was upset about it and didn't want to work there anymore, but I was forced to. They also took me off the pill and told me I couldn't have sex anymore. What a bad idea because I wasn't going to stop having sex!

I tried to get a part time job after school to get away from the house but was only 15. All the places I applied told me I was too young and to come back when I was 16. I was bummed out about it and had to figure another way to spend time out of the house. I became a volunteer candy striper at the hospital and hoped I was going to be with newborns, but I worked in the elderly ward. I had to feed old people who couldn't feed themselves and it was hard to get pureed peas in a person's mouth who barely woke up. I didn't care for that job, but it was better than being at home.

I didn't want to live with my foster parents anymore, so I moved next door to a girlfriend's house, then I quit school with two weeks left to go. She was 18 and lived with her dad. I went to get my belongings from my foster parents and what money

I saved. When they found out I was moving they took all my money and only let me have my clothes.

I called my real mom to come pick me up and she was very happy about it but couldn't get me until she had time off work. She started sending me $10 a week and told me to keep in touch with her until she could come get me.

I went to visit some friends in town, but they weren't home. Their father was and he said, "I'm going to pick them up. Do you want to go with me? I'll let you practice driving." I knew him and thought I could trust him. He said he had to make a stop first. We went to the country and came to a locked chain link fence. He unlocked it and drove in. Then we went into the building where there were lots of bunk beds everywhere. It was some kind of camp. I was sitting on the bed waiting for him to finish what he had to do when suddenly, he began attacking me trying to pull my pants off! We struggled with each other for what seemed like a long time, then he finally stopped. I got myself together and ran to the truck. He promised if I got in, he wouldn't bother me again and would drive me back to town and drop me off where I wanted. I was scared but had no other way back to town and had no idea where I was. He kept his word and dropped me off in town. I walked back to my girlfriend's house where I was staying. I never reported it but should've.

I was at my girlfriend's house alone with her dad and he pulled his dick out and said, "I'll give you ten dollars to play with it." I yelled, "Hell no! Get the fuck away from me!" He went to work and when my girlfriend came home, I told her what happened, but she didn't believe me. We got in a big fight, and I told her, "Your dads a pervert!" I went down the street to another girlfriend's house and told her mom what was going on. She said I could stay there until my mom came to get me, but I had to pay her $10 a week. I agreed and moved in.

I called my favorite step aunt and told her what was going on and she had a brother-in-law who lived in town and said I could stay with him for free until my mom came. I moved in and cooked and cleaned house sometimes.

One night I had bad cramps and was 2 weeks late on my period and thought I must be pregnant. I was having a miscarriage but wasn't close enough to anyone to tell. After a couple hours a small jelly-like ball, the size of a quarter, came out and it was over. My cramps were gone, and I started my period. I didn't tell anyone, not even the guy I got pregnant by.

A month went by, but my mom still couldn't pick me up. I started dating a guy that was 20. I told him I was moving soon, and he said that was ok and still wanted to see me. He gave me a diamond promise ring and said he'd visit me on the weekends.

My mom realized she wouldn't be able to pick me up, so she sent a bus ticket. My step uncle took me to the bus station and dropped me off. A cute guy sitting next to me on the bus asked if I wanted to get high and loaded a small pipe and told me to go in the bathroom to smoke it. So, I did. Man! That was some good weed! I was so high. When I met my parents, my eyes were bloodshot, and I was paranoid they'd be able to tell I was stoned.

I wasn't the best or the worst child in the world, but I was a good person at heart. I didn't have the best or worst childhood and didn't have the best or worst parents. It was all just ok. There were many children in the world who had it a lot worse than me. I got lucky to escape many close calls.

CHAPTER 2

THE CHURCH CULT

My parents picked me up at the bus station and I was really stoned. My mom kept telling me about the new church they were going to. It was a non-denominational charismatic, new wave, holy rolling church. She asked me to go with her, but I declined. She went on and on about it and started harshing my buzz.

We got home and my older brothers were there but the youngest was still in the boy's home. I slept on the couch in the living room because my brothers had my old bedroom.

Every time my parents went to church my mom begged me to go but I always declined. When she got home, she'd tell me how wonderful the church was and about the Holy Spirit. She said it was like having a private line to talk to God and came with gifts like speaking in tongues, prophecy, and healing. That excited me at first but then decided I didn't want anything to do with it. My mom hadn't been able to receive the Holy Spirit with evidence of speaking in tongues. She said God told her she couldn't receive it until I did, and she desperately wanted it. She tried to receive it before but still couldn't speak in tongues. She kept begging me to go with her.

I finally relented and said I'd go one time. It was a small church with about 50 people. It was very plain and had fold up chairs. When the preacher took stage, my eyes almost popped out of my head! He was so fucking hot! Six foot six, broad shoulders, muscular, jet-black hair, dark eyes, and mustache with a beautiful smile. Oh shit! That couldn't be good. But he was married. Bummer. I was way too young for him anyways. The service was boring, but I liked the singing. At the end of the service, the preacher asked if anyone wanted to come to the front for a healing or to receive the Holy Spirit. I watched what he was doing on stage. He laid his hands on them and spoke in tongues and said, in Jesus' name receive your healing or the gift of the Holy Spirit. Some people passed out and fell to the floor. I thought they were just weak, or it was fake. Afterwards my mom asked me what I thought and wanted to know if I was going again. I told her it was ok. I'd go. That made her happy. She had no idea I was only going to see the hot preacher.

The church used scare tactics and preached about it being the end of time and if you didn't accept Jesus as your Lord and Savior you'd be cast into the eternal fires of hell. It was starting to scare me! They said we were in Revelation time.

After going for a while, I wanted to see what it was really about. At the end of the service the preacher called people to the front like he always did. I went up there and about 10 other people did also. I was standing there, and the preacher laid his hand on my forehead and said, "Receive the gift of the Holy Spirit in Jesus name!" Then he went on to the next person and did the same. I was confused. Nothing happened. Other people he laid hands on started speaking in tongues and going into the spirit and falling to the ground. Now I thought this was a bunch of fake bullshit. I turned around and looked at my mom with a puzzled look on my face. I didn't feel anything. A little old lady with long white hair was sitting in the congregation and saw I was confused. She asked me if I received the Holy Spirit and I told her I wasn't sure. She took me into a little room with two chairs that faced each other. She asked God to let me receive the Holy Spirit in Jesus name, then touched me lightly on my forehead with one finger. When she did, it felt like a cork popped out of my throat and I began speaking in tongues. I felt like something inside of me had been released like I was a bottle holding something inside. I started crying because it felt so good when it was released. It felt like what was bottled up inside me was now also surrounding me. It felt like I released my Holy Spirit, not received it. When I came out my mom could tell I had The Holy Spirit because my face was glowing red. On the way home she asked if I received it with the evidence of speaking in tongues and I told her I did. She was so happy for me, but still couldn't do it herself. She wanted me to speak in the spirit, but it was embarrassing. I did it anyways to prove it. She wanted me to help her receive the gifts of the Holy Spirit with the evidence of speaking in tongues. We got home and I laid my hands on her forehead and said the words, "Dear God please let my mom receive the gifts of the Holy Spirit with the evidence of speaking in tongues." Nothing happened. She said her tongue was moving funny in her mouth and she had no control over it. I replied, "You have it! Now let it out of your mouth." She started speaking in tongues and was overjoyed.

We didn't get along with the managers of the trailer park because their son pulled my bikini bottom down at the swimming pool, so I beat him up. They confronted my parents about it but said nothing more when they found out what he did.

My brothers came home one day with a friend from their past and were excited to tell my mom. He said he lived on Morganford. I thought hmmm could this be the boy who tied me up and his parents threatened to kidnap me? I asked him, "Did you live on the second story above a business on Morganford?" He replied, "Yes." I asked, "Did you move to California after that?" He replied, "Yes." Now I knew it was him! I took my mom aside and told her they were the ones who tried to kidnap me when I was very young, and I didn't want him or his parents around me. My mom blew me off and replied, "Well you have Jesus in your heart now and you should forgive him and just forget about it." Whenever he came over, I went to my parent's room and stayed there until he left because he creeped me out. What a wild coincidence to come across them again.

My brothers had another friend who was a shady character. He was a pothead, a thief, and was always in trouble with the law. He came over one afternoon when my parents were at work. I was napping in their bedroom and was awoken by him trying to touch me. I freaked out and started yelling for him to get the fuck out. He got scared and left the room. I told my brothers what he did and told them to make him leave. They wouldn't so that made me very mad. I called a policeman who lived a few trailers away and told him what happened, and he knew who I was talking about and came right over. He kicked the guy out and told him if he ever came back again, he'd arrest him. My brothers got mad at me, but I didn't care. My parents didn't like the guy and were happy he didn't come over anymore.

The church was having water baptizing and me and my parents went. It was at a person's house in their swimming pool. They had a big party and we got baptized, but it was nothing spectacular. Just dunked under water and the preacher asked God to baptize us in the name of Jesus just like you see at any normal church.

Soon after that, the church was having a thing called a bible advance. It was the same as a bible retreat in other churches. This one was kind of different though. They only wanted all the women to attend and dress in white to marry Jesus. I thought that was kind of strange. We went far out in the country to a beautiful place. I had lots of fun before the ceremony. There was horseback riding, hiking, and breakfast every morning outside, then it was time for the ceremony. Only women were invited, and we were all dressed in white. I was the youngest. I began to not feel right about what was going on. I was having second thoughts about it. I guess you could say I was getting cold feet! The lady performing the ceremony said we'd all be hand maidens to God. I was confused and didn't even know what that meant.

The lady on stage performing the ceremony called me and several other ladies to come to the front so she could lay hands on us. I was standing up there looking around thinking this was just crazy. She laid hands on the lady next to me and the lady started shaking, did a flip in the air, and landed on her back, and then went into the spirit speaking in tongues. That scared the shit out of me, so I didn't want her to lay her hands on me, but I didn't know how to get out of it! The lady on stage saw how frightened I was and said, "Don't worry, she'll be alright. She was just touched by God." On my turn, the lady laid her hands on me and said something I don't remember. It felt like I was being shocked by electricity and I fell down crying! I thought she must have had some sort of a shocking devise on her, while she stayed grounded. When she touched people, she didn't get shocked herself. She assured me I'd be ok, and that God had just touched me. I didn't think that was God. I felt like I was shocked with a cattle prod but said nothing about it to my parents. I wasn't stupid. I knew what it felt like to be shocked by electricity. I thought that was all very weird and thought about not going to church anymore.

Soon after that the church had a seminar at a big fancy hotel called The Grand. The topic was Revelation. I didn't know much about it and went with my parents. It was about the end of times and Jesus and The Devil were coming to earth to have a big war. The final battle. So scary! They said there'd be a new money system. No one would be able to buy or sell anything unless they had the mark of the beast and there'd be a one world market. They said God's children would be marked with a seal and would be protected from all of this and if you weren't saved by Jesus and didn't believe in him, you'd spend eternity in a fiery pit called Hell. Hearing that really frightened me, so I decided I better not leave the church and stayed out of fear at the threat of the wrath of God and spending eternity in Hell. I wanted to believe in Jesus, but they said he is my God and I felt something very fishy about the contradiction God the father and God the son Now I was supposed to walk in blind faith. That didn't sound like something my God would want me to do if my eternal salvation was on the line, but I went along with it. I told God I didn't want Jesus to come back right now. I wanted to live a normal life, get married, and have children. I didn't want to deal with religion,

God, Jesus, Lucifer, Satan, the Devil, or the Holy Spirit. Then something spoke to me softly and said, "I want you to name your first-born son Michael after the archangel in Revelation." I didn't know who said that, but I agreed and went on with my life. I just assumed it was God.

My mom was having a strange problem. She'd wake up in the middle of the night and felt like she was being strangled or choked. It happened every night, so she went to the doctor, but he couldn't find anything wrong and told her she had surgeryitis and just wanted to be operated on. She went through the choking feeling every night and couldn't breathe and went to another doctor. He told her the same thing as the first doctor. She was upset and didn't know what to do. She decided to see one more doctor and he examined her and sent her immediately to the hospital to x-ray her throat because he felt a tumor in it. She had a tumor on the outside of her windpipe that grew roots and wrapped around the windpipe choking her. He did immediate surgery, and she had no more problems breathing. Doctors are only practitioners. We are what they practice on.

After that my mom had bad pain in her abdomen. X-rays showed she had a tumor the size of a grapefruit under her rib cage. She was admitted in the hospital and scheduled for surgery the next day. That night a lady who my mom had never met, came to her hospital room and said, "God spoke to me and told me to lay my hands on you and pray for a healing." Even though my mom didn't know her, she agreed. The young lady didn't touch my mom but held her hand over her stomach and prayed. My mom said she got a very warm sensation where the tumor was. After that the young lady left. The next day, she told her doctor what happened and demanded a new x-ray before surgery. The doctor thought it was a waste of time but did it to prove the tumor was still there. But to the doctor's amazement the tumor was miraculously gone. The doctors were baffled.

Several weeks after that it was early in the morning, and I was sleeping on the couch. I heard my mom screaming and it woke me, so I ran to her room in a panic to see what was wrong. I threw the door open and yelled, "What's wrong?!" Then I closed the door real fast because I realized my parents were having sex and I was so embarrassed.

My oldest brother fixed my stereo wire after our mom cut the cord, but he wouldn't let me use it. All he played was rock and roll from scary bands like Ozzy Osbourne and Black Sabbath. He played it as loud as it would go when my parents were gone. The managers of the trailer park told my parents if that didn't stop, we'd get evicted because the neighbors complained about it. He didn't stop playing loud music, so we got an eviction notice.

We were sitting around the house one day and my mom yelled, "Oh! I just got a message from God!" He said, "I'm going to send you an addition to your family. I'm going to send you another animal." I thought my mom was off her rocker and had gone cuckoo. One of my oldest brothers was away and when he came home, he had a tiny black kitten. He found her on the side of the road and tucked her in his coat and rode with her over 100 miles on his motorcycle. We all felt it was a kitten for me, but I thought was this really a gift from God and why would he be sending me gifts? I looked her over and thought she had a piece of white fuzz on her. When I tried to pull it off, she went flying in the air. She had one white spot on the tip of her tail and the rest of her was all black. She looked like she'd been a white cat that was held by the tip of her tail and dipped in an ink well. So, I named her Inky. She was about 4 weeks old and had to be taught how to drink and eat from a bowl. She was so cute. I loved her so much. Was that just a coincidence or really a gift from God?

My mom still had her little dog Foxy from her ex-husband. A little schnauzer showed up on our porch and we didn't know why. He wouldn't go home. When Foxy came out, he got very excited to see her. We didn't understand it because she was fixed. He stayed out there for two days and on the 3rd day my mom finally let him in. He was in love with Foxy. It was so cute watching them together. He was such a gentleman and always let her eat first, go out the door first, and followed her everywhere to protect her. I didn't know two dogs could really fall in love like that. His owners lived down the street and when they saw their dog in our yard they came over and took him home. A couple hours later he was back at our house wanting to be with Foxy. We let him in again and the dogs were very happy together. His owner came over and got him again. They put him outside on a leather leash, but he chewed through it and was back at our house in no time. His owners blamed us because they couldn't keep their dog at home. We explained to them their dog was in love with ours, but they didn't care. They just wanted their dog, and we always gave him back. They were truly in love.

My parents said they felt God was calling them to the main church in Texas where our pastor trained before he started his own ministry. The church was in Farmers Branch. My parents weren't sure if they were truly being called there by God, so they asked the pastor, "How do we know if this is from God?" He replied, "If God meets you there then you know it's from God."

We sold everything we owned except for some clothes and a few small items. My mom made me throw all the rock and roll music away. She said, "Rock and Roll is Devil music and I want you to break them into pieces and throw them away and don't listen to it anymore!" I reluctantly did what she said. They sold the trailer and got my little brother out of the boy's home, and I quit school. We'd soon be moving to Texas.

My boyfriend called and said he was dating someone else, and we knew each other, and he wanted his ring back. I told him, "That's great! I'm getting ready to move and I didn't know how to tell you or what to do with the ring?" He said they'd be up this weekend to get it. I was more excited to see my old girlfriend than him! Ironically, in my phonebook under the letter B were only two listings and it was theirs. What were the odds they'd meet and date each other? They arrived and my girlfriend wouldn't talk to me or even get out of the car. I didn't understand because we were such good friends before. I told her I had no hard feelings, and still wanted to be friends and invited them to stay for a bit. I guess it was too weird for her, so my ex-boyfriend got his ring and they immediately left. That wasn't how I thought it was going to go. They drove over two hours to get here and stayed 5 minutes. I was hoping we could all still be friends. But I guess not.

I still didn't like my hair and blow-dried it every day to get the waves out and was still sporting the Farah Faucet look. My hair color was a pretty strawberry blonde, but I didn't even think about when I asked God for curly hair a long time ago.

One night I woke from a very scary dream: I went to this old spooky house and knocked on the door and a real old lady answered. She had twin girls. One on each side of her. The old lady invited me in. It was very creepy like a haunted house. The old lady took me to a closet, opened it up, got a big broken cross out of the bottom and showed it to me, then put it back in the closet. I was confused and had no idea why she did that. Then she said, "There is a secret passageway out of the house." But said no more about it. She took me to the garage, and I saw wood steps nailed to the wall that went up to an attic. She looked up at the attic and yelled, "Don't go in the attic! There's Demons in the Attic!" Then the twin girls were trying to get me to go into the attic, but I got really scared and ran out of the house as fast as I could. I immediately woke from my dream in a sweat and was confused and scared. I went back to sleep and when I woke that day, I told my parents about it, but they thought nothing of it

The next night I had another dream, but this one was fun. An angel with real big, beautiful, rainbow wings came to my trailer while I was sleeping and woke me. The angel said come outside and follow. The angel was so beautiful and mesmerizing that I followed the angel out the door and I saw her flying in the sky, so I followed out of the trailer park and down the highway. We came to the gas station on the highway that I recognized and then I woke up! I wondered what it was all about.

The next night I had another dream and this one was scary. I dreamt there were a bunch of demons all over the outside of our trailer trying to get in but couldn't. Then I was in the middle of a place that looked like Stonehenge. Dinosaurs and demons were trying to get in, but the circle of Stonehenge protected me somehow. Then I woke up thinking what a very strange dream. Sometimes I was afraid dinosaurs would get me, but that wasn't possible considering they were extinct. I went back to sleep and had another strange dream! I was on top of the moon and spirits came to me and I'd direct them which way they were supposed to go to get to their destination. Then I woke up laughing because if that dream was true, I'm sure I sent many the wrong way because I was really a dizzy blonde with no sense of direction. I could get lost just going around the block.

We packed our belongings in a small U-Haul that was pulled behind the car. We wanted to take the dog that was in love with Foxy, but they wanted two hundred dollars for him. We were on a tight budget and couldn't afford it. I told my mom to take him anyways because we shouldn't break up true love. I begged her, "Please, please take him with us! Don't separate them! They are really in love with each other!" She said, "No, it wouldn't be right." I went away and cried because it made me sad. That was the end of their love story. They never saw each other again.

It was Oct 30th, 1982. We left but told no one. I remember the year because the St. Louis Cardinals won the world series. It was me, my mom and stepdad, one of my older brothers and my youngest brother. We also had three cats and two dogs. We set out for Texas and had no plans on what to do when we got there. We didn't know anyone there or what to expect when we arrived.

It was late Halloween night when we arrived. We had nowhere to go and weren't sure what to do because we knew no one in Texas. My parents drove to Farmers Branch to see the church we'd be attending. When we pulled in there were several cars on the lot with several people standing around. My parents told them we just came from House Springs Missouri and had been going to a branch of their church but came here to go to theirs. My parents asked them what they were doing so late in the parking lot, and someone replied they just gotten back from a bible advance, and someone locked their keys in their car. They were all waiting for someone to return with an extra set. They said they knew God had a reason for this but wasn't sure what it was. Amazingly one of the ladies was from the exact little town we were from and had moved to Texas a year earlier. Wow what a coincidence! They figured we must be on a mission from God and called us The Mission Family. I thought that was all very strange. What mission were we on? When the lady from House Springs found out we had no place to go, she gave us the keys to her apartment and said we could stay there, and she'd stay with a friend until we figured out what to do. That was so nice of her. Was that what the pastor meant by, if it was from God, he'd meet you there? Or was it just a coincidence?

We were sitting in her living room one night when the front door opened, and a strange black man was standing there! Our dog Kiki immediately jumped up on him, knocked him to the ground, got on top of him, and started growling like she was going to bite his face off! He froze. My dad called Kiki off and the guy jumped up and said, "Sorry I thought this was my apartment!" Then he took off running away as fast as he could. It all happened so fast, then was over. Kiki was a very good guard dog.

The new church was way bigger and fancier, and the preacher looked like a vampire. He seemed scary to me. They had comfortable chairs like in a movie theater. Not cheap fold up ones. There were over a thousand people that attended. Everyone was very nice and accepted us into the congregation. This church was the same as the one we came from. Non- Denominational,

Charismatic Holy Rollers. After service was over, we got together with a bunch of people from the congregation and went out for coffee and food. It was lots of fun. I was bummed out when my parents couldn't afford to go with everyone because that was my favorite part.

My parents found a nice house in a good neighborhood in Garland. Me and my little brother went to enroll in school, but they said we missed too many days and had to wait until next year. I got a job at Mr. Gatti's Pizza and all my money went towards helping my family pay bills.

Rent was very expensive, and we had problems paying it. My parents took on two borders they knew from roofing work. They were strange. One was very tall and reminded me of Lurch from the Adams Family and the other had one blue eye with white eyelashes and one brown eye with black eyelashes. I thought they were both very creepy! I did the grocery shopping and cooking for everyone because my mom was a terrible cook. I needed to feed seven grown people every night, so I cooked fried chicken and beef stew a lot because it was cheap.

We still couldn't keep up with rent so one of the borders said he knew a little old lady in Oak Cliff who rented rooms and would ask if she'd board all of us. She agreed. She lived off Kiest and Garapan on Llewellyn Street. When we got to the front porch, I got a bad feeling about the house. I told my parents, "Wait! This is the house in my dreams! I don't want to stay here!" My mom replied, "You have Jesus on your side now. He'll protect you." I still didn't want to go in. They knocked on the door and a little old lady who could barely see opened it and a strange gray matter, apparently invisible to everyone else, came out and tried to engulf me. I started crying and freaking out! I didn't want to go in. I was terrified of the grey matter I saw in the shape of a spirit. My parents calmed me down and convinced me I'd be ok because Jesus was with me, so I went in. The house looked like it belonged in an old horror film. Cobwebs everywhere. Spiders, cockroaches, water bugs, and fleas, infested the house. Everything had thick dust on it. Mice and rats ran around freely. She had no back door, only a screen door, and all the doors inside were missing their doorknobs. I thought that was very strange. It was quite spooky. I told my parents I could prove to them this was the house in my dream. I went straight to a bedroom, opened the closet door, dug a little in the bottom of it, then pulled out a big broken cross. I became terrified! Could this all be real? I showed the big ceramic broken cross to my parents and told them this was in my dream that I told them about right before we moved here! They didn't think anything of it, but that disturbed me, I didn't think they believed me. After I found the cross, I tried to figure out if all of this was real. I went into the garage to see if it had wooden steps nailed to the wall leading to the attic, and it did. Then I told my parents, "In my dream there were demons in the attic and a secret passageway out. This is the house in my dream!" I didn't want to stay there. But what was I going to do? I really didn't have much choice.

The little old ladies name was Vera. She had one male border already. We were all trying to figure out where everyone was going to sleep. I ended up in the master bedroom with the king-sized waterbed.

We cleaned everything up and got rid of the infestations. We put a new backdoor on and doorknobs on all the doors. I started talking to Vera about her life and she told me she had twin daughters that died very young. Her son and her husband died in separate car crashes and her granddaughter was deaf. She had one remaining daughter. I thought wow! That was all so tragic.

There was something else very strange at her house. It had a phone in the middle of it, but you couldn't make calls out. You could only receive calls. That puzzled me. You had to call the operator to place a call, and she'd tell me to deposit a quarter, but there was nowhere to put money. I'd tell her I did put money in, then she'd connect me to the number. What the hell was going on with the phone? It must have somehow been connected to a payphone.

Our indoor cats were getting out of the house, and we didn't know how. I told my mom in my dream there was a secret passageway out. I decided to look for it, so I went into my bedroom and looked in the bottom of the closet and found a little tiny door with a little tiny knob. I pulled on the knob and opened the door. It went to the outside and had a spring that made it close back up. That was how the cats were getting out. Yes! That must have been the secret passageway out I was told about in my dream. But why did I have those dreams? Was it all just coincidence?

I had a couple guys trying to court me. One came over all the time and was nineteen, blonde haired, and blue eyed, but I wasn't interested because I liked guys who looked totally different than me. He just wasn't what I was looking for. The other was 20 and brought me flowers, stuffed animals, and exotic plants all the time. I wasn't interested in him either. He wasn't bad looking and did have black hair and dark eyes but didn't have that unique look I was looking for.

We were sleeping one night when my mom woke to the smell of smoke. She went into the family room where my brothers were and saw three separate fires in different locations. She started yelling, "Fire! Fire! Fire!" We all woke up and came running out of our rooms. I picked the phone up to call the fire department. I told the operator my address and said our house was on fire and we needed the fire department. She replied, "Mam, are you at a pay phone?" I sternly replied, "No, I'm in the middle of the house and it's on fire!" She replied, "No, you're at a pay phone." I told her, "No! I'm not! Just call the fire department and send them here!" She finally agreed and we hung up. My parents put the fires out and the fire department showed up and saw the fires were out, then wrote a report and left. So, someone in the house lit three different fires in three different locations and wrote on the kitchen mirror in big black bold marker SATAN IS KING. I had my suspicions about who did it. But said nothing. My parents said nothing more about it.

Our church was very far away from where we lived and sometimes, we didn't have gas money to get there. My parents got a podium and turned it into an alter to have church at the house. My stepdad was always the preacher and at the end we prayed. I'd go into the spirit and speak in tongues like at the church. When you did, someone was supposed to interpret the message. When it was over, I'd ask what the message was and was always told, there was no message. I got tired of hearing that, so I quit going to service in the house. If there was a message from God, no one gave it to me.

Not long after the first fire there was another fire in the house while we slept. I had to do the same thing I did before with the operator and convince her I wasn't at a pay phone. I was in fact in the middle of the house. She finally agreed to get ahold of the fire department. We had the fire out again before they arrived. They made another report and left. I was afraid to go to sleep at night because I might burn in a fire. Sleeping on the waterbed made me feel a little safer from the fires for some reason.

I got a new job as a phone salesperson selling subscriptions of the Dallas Morning News. On my second day they gave me a list of names to call from the phone book and I had a sheet in front of me with the pitch I was to use to get people to subscribe. A couple of hours later I had the name John. I called the number and a guy named Steve answered. I gave him my pitch and he replied, "Hold on I'm not the one who makes those decisions here." He handed the phone to his roommate John, and I gave him my pitch. He asked me, "How old are you? I told him, "17." He asked, "How tall are you?" I replied, "Five foot." Then he asked, "What color hair and eyes do you have?" I replied, "Blonde hair and blue eyes." Then he asked, "How much do you weigh?" I told him, "100 pounds." I guess he liked all my answers because he said, "I'll make a deal with you. If you go out on a date with me, I'll subscribe to the newspaper." I agreed and kept his number and said I'd call him later and he subscribed.

The next day I went to work my boss took me in the office and said, "I heard your conversation with that guy yesterday. This is not a dating service and I'm going to have to let you go." Bummer. I got fired over a man I never met.

I got a job waitressing at Kips restaurant. My parents went there often, and we knew the managers. I never waitressed before but learned very fast and made good money. I still gave all my money to my parents to help pay the bills.

I decided to go ahead and call John. I told the operator the pay phone stole my money and asked her to connect me, and she did. We set a date for him to pick me up that weekend. I had no idea what to expect. If I didn't like anything about him, I'd tell him I didn't want to go out with him. This was weird. I'd never been on a blind date before. I didn't really have any clothes to wear except for a few church dresses. I was very poor, and all my money went to my family. I felt like Cinderella whose fairy godmother fell asleep on the job.

Before John arrived, the border that looked like Lurch said, "I have to check him out first to make sure he's ok. If I don't like him, I'm going to tell him to leave." John came all the way from Dallas to Oak Cliff to pick me up and when he knocked on the door, Lurch opened it. I'm sure John was a little shocked to see a six foot plus scary man staring down at him. I pushed the border aside to see. When I saw him, I was like OMG! What is my heart doing? My heart had never acted like that before. It was pounding so fast I thought it was going to burst out of my chest. He was the most attractive man I 'd ever met in my life. When he saw me, he got a big smile on his face, and we were both happy to meet each other. To me and my parent's amazement he looked just like our old pastor from Missouri that I had the hots for. The only difference was John was miniature size. Just the right size for me! He was about 5ft 5 with jet black hair, beautiful green eyes, and a mustache with a devilish smirk. He had a very nice-looking body and his cologne smelled enticingly alluring. He was very charming. I fell in love with him the moment I met him.

He took me to a nice little romantic Chinese restaurant and ordered us each a glass of wine. He asked me if I liked snow peas and I told him I'd never tried them. I said I didn't like any kind of peas. He told me he'd order them for me because he thought I'd like them. To my surprise I did like snow peas. He tried to show me how to use chop sticks, but I wasn't very good at it. He told me he was from Turkey, but I had no idea where that was. When the date was over, he took me home and gave me a little kiss and I gave him my phone number in case he wanted to go out again. I didn't think he'd call me because he was so sophisticated, and I was so much younger than him and smoked cigarettes. I was sure he didn't like that because he didn't smoke, but he didn't say anything about it. I would have quit smoking for him if he had asked me to. That's how much I adored him. I just left it at that, expecting to never hear from him again.

To my happy surprise he called a week later and wanted to go out again. He said, "Put on the sexiest clothes you have, and I'll come pick you up." I agreed but didn't have anything sexy to wear. Just another church dress. He picked me up and I thought we were going to go out. Instead, he took me to his apartment on Dallas Parkway where he lived on the second floor. He said he was going to make dinner for me and made a couple screw drivers for us, and we drank while he made spaghetti. Afterwards, we sat on the couch, and he put Pink Floyd on. I had no idea who they were. I wasn't allowed to listen to rock and roll. The song I remember was TIME. ***Ticking away the moments that make up a dull day. Fritter and waste the hours in an offhand way. Kicking around on a piece of ground in your hometown. Waiting for someone or something to show you the way.*** I told John, "That's Devil music and I'm not allowed to listen to it." He laughingly replied, "Pink Floyd is not Devil music!"

I used the restroom and when I came out John was standing right in front of me and had me pinned up against the wall, but not in a bad way. He was being very sexy and looking into my eyes. I asked him what the door next to me was and he replied, "That's my bedroom." I asked if I could see it and he said with a cute smirk on his face, "Only if you're going to have sex with me." Then there was what seemed to be a long awkward pause because I was thinking it over. I looked him deep in his gorgeous green eyes and said, "OK." We went in his room, got on his big bed, took our clothes off, and started having sex. Then it was over. It was all about him. He rolled over and went to sleep. He didn't even cuddle or hold me. He woke around three in the morning and drove me home and dropped me off. Now that he got what he really wanted from me I didn't expect he'd call again.

To my surprise he called a couple weeks later and said, "Put on a sexy skirt with no underwear and I'll be by to pick you up soon." I knew he just wanted sex again and I was game because he was the sexiest man I'd ever met. I really didn't have any sexy clothes. He came and picked me up and we drove about a mile away and he parked his little white car on the street. He was in the driver's seat, and I got on top. That was pretty ballsy of us considering it was broad daylight. He took me back home and dropped me off. I expected soon he'd find someone else to have sex with and would never see me again and I was going to leave it at that.

One morning we woke to the smell of smoke again but couldn't figure out where it was coming from. We looked all over and couldn't find the fire. Then I looked up and there was a giant black circle forming on the ceiling. The fire was in the attic! Here we went again with the phone. But this time there was no dial tone. I tried to get a dial tone to call the operator to get the firemen again, but no dial tone. I ran across the street to the neighbors and used their phone to call the fire department. They came and put the fire out in the attic and made another report. I was pretty sure I knew who was doing it but needed proof before

I told anyone. I didn't know how to get the proof and every night I was afraid I'd burn to death in a fire when I went to sleep.

Vera was away at her daughter's house in Waco when the last fire happened, and the phone line was burned. She got in a big fight with her daughter because she wouldn't let her have a twinkie. She ate twinkies all the time after we moved in because we laid hands on her and asked God to heal her. After that she ate what she wanted and never had any problems. When Vera told her daughter that, she didn't believe her and still didn't let her have a twinkie. It made Vera very mad so she tried to call us so we could pick her up. When she couldn't get ahold of us, she decided to walk all the way home. She got out on the highway and was walking when the police saw her and tried to get her in the car, but she refused. They wanted to arrest her for vagrancy, but she had more than five dollars on her. They had to let her go. She couldn't see very well and accidentally stepped out in front of a semi-truck and was killed instantly! ***Vera! Oh Vera! Where have you gone!*** At her funeral it was a closed casket because her body was so mangled. That was very sad and soon we had to move because her daughter wanted possession of the house. I kept Vera's sewing box to remind me of her.

Now the police wanted some people in the house to take polygraphs to find out who was setting the fires. The boarder that was there before us moved out before the last fire because he didn't like what was going on. I couldn't blame him. I would have moved too if I could. I didn't have to take a polygraph test, but my brothers and the other two boarders did. It came back saying my youngest brother didn't pass. I knew it was him and now maybe my parents would know it was him. Instead, he convinced them it wasn't him, and the polygraph was wrong. Now I really had to find out who was starting all the fires and needed proof. I turned to God and my Holy Spirit and asked them to help. I didn't like the place I was living in and was looking for a place to move without my family.

We didn't have a TV and I was bored so I turned the radio on one day to listen to rock and roll music. When I did, it scared me, so I turned it off! The song playing was BURNING DOWN THE HOUSE by THE TALKING HEADS. ***Burning down the house! My house! Here's your ticket. pack your bags. Time for jumpim overboard. Transportation is near. Maybe you know where you are. Fighting fire with fire! Gonna burst into flames!*** It scared me because someone was trying to burn down the house I lived in, and it was kind of a freaky coincidence that the music just said what was going on in my life. That was strange.

Now John couldn't call me anymore even if he wanted to because the phone line was burned.

About a week after Vera's death, I felt a higher power was talking to me. Some kind of an entity, energy, or maybe even God. It was getting dark out when something said, "Go to the gas station and call John and get his address and write him a letter." I thought that was very strange but went ahead and called him. I told him God told me to get his address and send him a letter. He laughed at me and didn't want to give it to me. I begged him and told him I was serious! He finally gave in. I went home to write the letter but didn't know what I was supposed to write. Pretty sure it started like this: Dear John. Hahaha! I don't remember what I wrote because it was so long ago. But it probably had something to do with all the fires at my house. I put the letter in an envelope, put a stamp on it, and just sat on the couch waiting. Then it spoke to me again and said, "NOW! PUT THE LETTER IN THE MAILBOX ON THE PORCH! DO IT NOW!" I was like, "Ok! Ok! Whatever you are, you don't have to be so pushy." I had no idea what the urgency was and thought it must be God talking to me. I went to the front porch to put the letter in the mailbox when I saw someone climbing in the bathroom window, so I yelled, "Hey! What the fuck are you doing and who are you?" By then the person already climbed through the window. Then I realized it was my little brother. I asked him, "What are you doing?" He replied, "The glass broke out of the window, so I was fixing it." I didn't believe what he told me and thought something was fishy about his story, but I wasn't sure what it was. I went back inside, and he was in the shower. Suddenly, the back of the house was on fire! Now I knew it was my little brother. He pretended to be in the shower and climbed out the bathroom window, went to the backyard, got a big bag of trash, shoved it up under the back of the house, and lit it on fire. So here I went again. I had to run across the street to a neighbor's and call the fire department. They came and put the fire out. Now I knew for sure it was him lighting the fires. I began looking for my first opportunity to move and get away from this family and house because no one was doing anything to stop him from lighting more fires.

My oldest brother stayed in Missouri when we moved to Texas. He wanted to come live with us and when he got to Oak Cliff, he only had our address, so he stopped at the fire department and asked to keep his belongings there until he found where we lived. He showed the fireman the address and they responded, "Yes, we know that address very well. There have been several fires there in the last month." They told him how to get to the house and he showed up with no problems. Coincidence?

I was thinking how I was going to get out of here. My boss at work was pretty good looking and I could tell he was fond of me, but he was much older than me. I went to work and told him what was going on at my house and asked if I could stay with him. He immediately jumped at the opportunity, so I moved in with him right away at his apartment in Carrollton. We soon became lovers. But he was terrible at sex. He was very good looking but very bad at sex. He had me quit my job and we played house for a little while.

I still wanted to see John, so I took a cab to his apartment, but he wasn't home. His roommate Steve was there so I hung out a little to see if John showed up. Steve told me John was gay and I shouldn't bother him anymore. I knew that wasn't true. I think

Steve was trying to be nice and spare my feelings because John most likely didn't want to see me anymore and I couldn't blame him with all the crazy shit going on in my life.

On the cab ride home, the driver told me to sit up front with him. About 15 minutes into the ride, he pulled the car over and parked. I wondered why he did that. Then he pulled his big hard dick out and said, "Do you want some?" I told him, "Fuck No! Put your dick back in your pants and take me home!" I didn't have any more problems with him after that, but it was very hard to trust people anymore.

The guy I lived with wanted to move to a ritzy new apartment in Arlington that didn't allow pets. He wanted me to give Inky away, but I couldn't do that. I hadn't told him how I got her or anything about my past. Only about the fires. I was relieved I could sleep at night without the fear of burning, but I wouldn't give Inky up. I called my mom and told her what was going on. My family had moved to Farmers Branch. I asked if there were any fires there and she said no. I asked if I could move back in, and she said yes. While my boyfriend was at work, I wrote a letter telling him I was moving out because I didn't want to get rid of Inky. I packed and my mom came and got me. I lived with her, my stepdad, three brothers, and five animals in a two-bedroom apartment. It was extremely cramped, and I had to sleep on the couch. Absolutely no privacy again.

A couple days later my ex-boyfriend showed up and begged me to come back, but I told him I wasn't interested. He said he was sorry, and I could keep Inky if I just came back but I still said no. If he had been good in bed, I'd have gone back with him. But I couldn't tell him that. He came over a couple more times begging me to come back, but the answer was still no. He finally gave up and quit coming over. I was over with that relationship for sure.

I got a job waitressing at Kips on Beltline. I took a cab to work because it was so far away. One day my feet swelled up like two balloons and I couldn't walk. My mom took me to the doctors, and again was told I had severe rheumatoid arthritis and there was nothing he could do but try to get the swelling down and gave me crutches to walk with. The doctor said it was so bad I probably wouldn't walk by the time I was 19. I paid no attention to him and eventually the swelling went down, and I was ok.

Me and Inky were so close she followed me around like a dog. One afternoon we were outside when a neighbor came out with his German shepherd. His dog was getting too close to me and Inky didn't like it. She ran after his dog and chased him around the complex. The man got very mad, and yelled, "You need to keep your cat on a leash!" I found it hard to stop laughing because I'd never seen a tiny cat chase a big dog around.

I quit Kips and got a better job across the highway at Cocos. I didn't like that I had to cross a big highway, so I still took a cab. We didn't have a phone and my cute neighbor upstairs let me use his to call cabs. We began having sex and he was pretty good.

One Friday he gave me a couple of Quaaludes and told me not to take both at the same time. Then asked if I wanted to go to a dance club with him that night and I did because I had a fake ID my girlfriend gave me. He said he'd come over that night to pick me up. I took a Quaalude and started getting ready. A half an hour later I didn't feel anything, so I took the other one. What a big mistake! I was in the bathroom brushing my hair when suddenly I was frozen holding the brush in the air. I couldn't move. I was totally out of it. My mom came in and saw me standing in a daze. She helped me to the couch, and I passed out until the next day. When I woke up my mom asked what was wrong so I told her I must have been having a flashback from something I took a long time ago. She believed me and said nothing more about it. I was bummed because I missed my date. When I saw him, I told him I was sorry for missing the date because I took both Quaaludes. He just laughed and said it was ok and we could go out next weekend.

Next weekend came, and he reminded me we were supposed to go out. This time he didn't give me any Quaaludes. I got all dressed up and we went to the Ritz dance bar. We went in and he went to use the restroom and said he'd meet me at the bar. He gave me $20 and told me to get what I wanted. I ordered a drink and while I was waiting for him a guy came up next to me and asked if I'd like to dance. I replied, "No thanks. I don't dance." Then he leaned into my ear and whispered, "You're going to regret that later. No one says no to me." Then he walked away. I had no idea what he meant but it sounded threatening. I paid for the drink, picked it up, took a little sip and turned around to see if my date was anywhere, then I passed out on the floor. When I came to, there was a crowd surrounding me. Just then I saw my date and he helped me up, got me to a table, and got me another drink because mine spilled on the floor. He asked me what happened, and I replied, "I don't know." I told him what the guy said to me, and we didn't know what to think about it. It was very strange. I looked around for the guy to point him out but didn't see him anywhere. I wondered if he slipped something in my drink when he whispered in my ear. I was fine the rest of the night and had a good time and we had sex afterwards and it was very satisfying.

I had an older girlfriend who lived in the apartment complex, and I went to her place, and she said her phone started working for no apparent reason. She said it wasn't supposed to work but oddly it just started working. She asked if there was anyone I wanted to call, but I didn't know anyone's number but John's. I called him to see how he was doing. He answered and I told him about the weird connection with the phone. We talked a few minutes and I asked if I could come see him, but he said, "No, put your girlfriend on so I can talk to her." I was bummed out he didn't even want to see me as a friend. I couldn't understand why not. He invited my girlfriend over and told her not to bring me. I was truly crushed. That really hurt my feelings. I'd never loved anyone like that before and didn't like the way he treated me. She left and went to see him. I went to the liquor store to get a bottle of whiskey to drown my sorrows. I was at the playground sitting on a swing drinking my booze, having my own personal pity party when I heard a voice softly say, "Don't be so sad. Someday you will grow up to be a queen." I looked around puzzled and wondered who the hell said that. Was that in my imagination? And the queen of what? I thought I must be losing my mind. I began laughing because I thought I was hearing things. When my girlfriend got back from John's place, she was very pissed off at him. She wouldn't tell me what happened, but said, "John is a jerk! Don't waste your time on him!" But I was so in love with him, and I didn't know how to get rid of these feelings. We didn't say any more about him. Not much later in life, I slept with a few of his friends in his bed when he wasn't home to get over him, and his roommate called him and told him while I was doing it. I left a bloody mess for him to clean up.

I went to church with my parents again and they were now security guards there. I started having strange dreams again. I dreamt the church had three balconies and I saw people sitting in them singing. When I woke, I told my mom and the next time we went to church they had put balconies in. That made me stop and think about my dream and how very strange that I dreamt it before it happened. Was that just a coincidence and if not, where was I getting this information from?

A few days later I had another dream that really frightened me. I dreamt God came over and was in a little green car. He said, "Get in I want to show you something." I got in and he was driving down the highway. Suddenly, I saw dismembered bodies all along the sides of the highway. It was a frightening sight to see body parts scattered everywhere. I got scared and asked God, "Where are we going?" He replied, "I'm taking you to the church to show you something." As we were taking the exit ramp to get to the church, God stopped and said, "Look down there." I saw a big ball of worms all entwined together squirming around in a pit. I was confused at what I saw and asked, "What is that?"

He replied, "Those are the people in the church. They appear to be alive but are really dead." I became confused again. He said, "Don't just look at the church from the inside out, but also from the outside in." Then he took me into the church and there were two giant movie screens. One on each side of the stage. He said, "Look at the screens." When I did, I saw a bunch of germs on them. Then God said, "The church is sick with a disease. I want you to leave the church and lead my people out. Do it now or they will turn to stone." In my dream I immediately got up and started telling everyone to leave the church because it was bad, but no one listened to me. I was in a panic! They all just ignored me and kept doing what they were doing. I got upset because I couldn't get anyone to leave the church. I asked God, "Why are they not listening to me?" He replied, "Because maybe they are not my people." Then I woke frightened and confused. I didn't want to go to the church anymore. I wondered, why God was picking on me. Why me? I'm not a leader. And where was I supposed to lead God's people to? I thought the church was where God and his people were. That morning I told my mom about the dream and told her I didn't want to go to her church anymore. She replied, "That's not God speaking to you in your dreams! That's the Devil! You should test the spirits before you get in their car and go for a ride!" She was quite angry at me and didn't like the dream I told her about.

To my shocking surprise the very next time we went to church there were two giant movie screens on each side of the stage just like in my dream and I pointed it out to my parents. I felt weird about it and started to get scared. Was that just a coincidence or was a higher power really talking to me in my dreams? The pastor explained they were going worldwide with their sermon via satellite and that's what the screens were for. We could see other people at other churches waiting to hear the pastor's sermon. I got kind of scared because this was very similar to my dream. Then during the service, a man sitting a few seats away from me, jumped up out of his chair and started yelling, "This is not God's church! This is a bad church! This church is sick with a disease! They are false prophets! You need to leave this church!" Now I was really scared. I didn't know what to do. The man kept saying it very loud until he was escorted out by security guards. That was so close to my dream! After service was over, I told my mom I wasn't going to go to that church anymore. She wasn't happy about it but what could she do? Now none of her children went to church with her. I just waited to see where God wanted me to go now that I didn't have a church anymore. I was very confused.

A few days later I had another strange dream. I was standing in a long line to get the mark of the beast, but there was another line you could get in if you didn't want the mark. The other line gave you little white pills to take instead of eating food. You had to choose which line you wanted to be in. I chose the one with the pills. I kept telling everyone that was in line to get the mark, to get out of that line and in the line that I was in. The people in the line to get the mark of the beast wanted the mark because without it you couldn't buy or sell anything, not even food. The people in line to get the mark wouldn't listen to me so I began crying. It was my turn in line and I got my pills for the week. I kept telling everyone to get out of the line that gives you the mark. But they still wouldn't listen. I started crying even more and didn't realize I ate all my pills. That made me cry even more! I had no pills left for the rest of the week and didn't know what I was going to do. Then I woke up feeling very puzzled because I didn't understand the dream. I told my mom, but she thought nothing of it.

Some time went by, so I called John to find out why my girlfriend was so upset with him. He told me, "If she lost some weight and didn't smoke, she'd be much prettier." Man, I thought that was mean. John wanted me to go to a seminar in Dallas and I agreed because I thought he'd be there. I went to his house to get the address and his roommate gave me the paper that read, Seven Seals and had the address on it. I became intrigued because I read something in the Bible about the Seven Seals. When I got there, I realized it was a restaurant called Seven Seas. It was misspelled on the paper. I went to the suite and there was no one else but me and the guy doing the seminar. He said they were an organization called The American Free Enterprise. T.A.F.E. for short. Their emblem was an American Bald Eagle with its wings strapped down as if to stop it from flying. He told me they were connected to the biggest computer in Brussels Belgium and had a giant book of everything you'd ever want to buy or sell. Then he showed me a big thick book full of all different kinds of products to buy. He said, "We have these white pills you can buy from the company. They are supposed to make you feel good like the Christians feel when they are high on Christ." When he mentioned the pills, I immediately had a flash back to the dream I had days earlier. I thought it was a strange, twisted coincidence how this resembled my dream. He gave me a few papers to look over and asked if I wanted to join for a small fee. I asked him more about the computer in Brussels Belgium, but he didn't want to talk about that. I told him, "I'll take these papers home and look them over and decide later." Just then I saw fire in his eyes, and he got very mad and yelled, "No! You can't take these papers with you! Give them back to me!" So, I did. I left with only the paper I came with and wondered what the hell that was all about! Must have been some kind of a pyramid scheme like Amway.

I lost my job at Coco's because I kept getting runs in my stocking. My boss said if it happened one more time, he'd fire me. It was Sunday morning, and I was getting ready for work. I put my brand-new pair of pantyhose on and got a big run in them. I couldn't go to the store to get new ones because back then there was a weird law called the Blue Law. That meant you couldn't buy certain items on Sundays and pantyhose was one of them. There was nothing I could do about it but go to work with the run in my stockings. I got there and the manager saw it and said, "I told you if you came to work that way again, I'd fire you. Your fired!" I explained to him I couldn't buy stockings on Sunday, but he replied, "That's not my problem." Now I had to find a new job right away. I got a job as a waitress at JoJo's on Beltline in Dallas, but it was much further away from home, so I still took a cab.

Our mom was furious that all her kids were acting up and wouldn't go to church with here anymore, so she told all of us to move out. One of my older brothers found a two-bedroom apartment on Alpha and Montfort in Dallas. We got the place together but only he could sign the lease because I was only 17. It was two stories with the bedrooms on top and was very nice. It had a big bathroom upstairs and a small one downstairs. There was a fireplace in the living room and a big swimming pool in the back. It was cozy. I liked it a lot and things were going well for me. I rented an entire house of furniture and bought a lot of tropical plants. The apartment looked beautiful. I was happy in my life.

My brother came home one day with a little green 1966 Dodge Dart. I was amazed! It looked just like the one in my dream where God came and picked me up and we went to the church and saw all the scary body parts on the way.

I needed a driver's license but didn't know anyone to take me and I didn't want to bother my parents, so I went by myself. I didn't study but passed the written exam. When it came to the driving, part I was very nervous! I was told I didn't pass because I didn't come to a complete stop at the stop signs and couldn't parallel park. Bummer. Well, I still had to get in the car and drive home by myself and I hoped they didn't notice and give me a ticket. I took the test again a month later and passed with no problem.

My oldest brother and younger brother had nowhere to go so we let them stay with us, but they didn't have jobs. My brother who everyone thought was my twin when we were young had a good job at a tire shop. It was only a mile away, but he always had problems getting to work on time.

I bought a big console TV, and my brother had a friend come over and hook the cable up illegally. There was a station called MTV. It was a music video channel that played rock and roll. The first song I saw was THE THRILLER by MICHAEL JACKSON and it scared the hell out of me because it was about demons, and I had just left the church and denounced the mainstream religion that was taught in America. Some of it went like this. ***It's close to midnight, something evil's lurking in the dark. Under the moonlight you see a sight that almost stops your heart! You try to scream! But terror takes the sound before you make it! You start to freeze! As horror looks you right between your eyes! You're paralyzed! Cause this is thriller! Thriller night! And no one's gonna save you from the beast about to strike! You're fighting for your life inside a thriller, killer! You hear the door slam and realize there's nowhere left to run! You close your eyes and hope that this is just imagination! Girl but all the while you hear a creature creeping up behind you! You're out of time!*** Then Vincent Price said in a very scary voice, **DARKNESS FALLS ACROSS THE LAND. THE MIDNIGHT HOUR IS CLOSE AT HAND. CREATURES CRAWL IN SEARCH OF BLOOD, TO TERRORIZE Y'ALLS' NEIGHBORHOOD. AND WHOSOEVER SHALL BE FOUND, WITHOUT THE SOUL FOR GETTING DOWN, MUST STAND AND FACE THE HOUNDS OF HELL, AND ROT INSIDE A CORPSES' SHELL!** Then more singing. ***Night creatures call and the dead start to walk in their masquerade! There's no escaping the jaws of the alien this time! They're open wide! This is the end of your life! They're out to get you! There's demons closing in on every side! They will possess you! Unless you change that number on the dial!*** Then Vincent Price talked again in his creepy voice. **THE FOULEST STENCH IS IN THE AIR! THE FUNK OF FORTY THOUSAND YEARS! AND GRISLY GHOULS**

FROM EVERY TOMB ARE CLOSING IN TO SEAL YOUR DOOM! ALTHOUGH YOU FIGHT TO STAY ALIVE, YOUR BODY STARTS TO SHIVER! FOR NO MERE MORTAL CAN RESIST THE EVIL OF THE THRILLER! HAHAHAHA! That really frightened me, and I didn't want to hear any more music like that! But I listened to this song called SAFETY DANCE by MEN WITHOUT HATS! ***It's safety dance. We can dance if we want to! We can leave your friends behind! Cause your friends don't dance, and if they don't dance, well, they ain't no friends of mine! We can go where we want to. A place where they will never find. And we can act like we come from out of this world and leave the real one far behind. We can go where we want to. The night is young and so am I. We can dress real neat from our hats to our feet and surprise with the victory cry! We can act if we want to. If we don't nobody will. And you can act real rude and totally removed and I can act like an imbecile! We can dance! We can dance! Everything's totally out of control! We can dance! We can dance! Everybody look at your hands!*** That song also scared me because it reminded me of getting the mark of the beast on your hand, so I decided not to watch MTV anymore. I began thinking about maybe going back to church again.

On my way home from work the car started sputtering so I pulled into the gas station next to my apartment. I didn't know what was wrong and my brother was at work. I didn't know what to do. The only person I knew was John. He lived close so I called him and told him my car was broken down on Alpha and Montfort. I asked if he could come look at it and tell me what's wrong. To my amazement he came right over. He looked at the car and said, "Well Cindy, you have to put gas in the car." He seemed quite perturbed at me because I didn't know cars needed gas. He showed me how to get gas and afterwards I invited him to see my apartment next door, but he declined. I really couldn't blame him after what I'd done, but it was very nice of him to come and help me.

My brothers introduced me to a friend who lived across the street. We liked each other and started dating. Several weeks into our relationship I went to his apartment early one morning and just before I wrang the doorbell, I saw him through the window lying in bed with another woman. I decided not to disturb them. The next time he came over I gave him the cold shoulder and told him I didn't want to see him anymore. He was confused and wanted to know why. I didn't give him a reason, and just told him I wasn't interested in him. He tried to get back with me for a couple weeks, but finally stopped coming over.

I met a guy at the pool hall across the street and he asked me out on a date. He also lived across the street. We went out and had a nice dinner and afterwards he invited me over to have a drink. After a couple drinks, it was getting late, and I had to work in the morning, so I told him it was time for me to go. I went to walk to the door, and he stood in front of it and got a very strange look in his eyes. It was kind of scary. Then he grabbed me by my arms very tight, and we were looking each other in the eyes, and I said with a very stern voice, "Look! You don't want to do this!" I gave him the look like we were getting ready to rumble and not in a good way. I could tell he wanted to force me to have sex with him. He could tell he was going to be in for a big fight. Then he let my arms go and I left and never went out with him again. What a jerk. If he'd have had just a little patience, I'm sure we would have eventually knocked boots.

Not long after that I became friends with a guy who lived in the same apartment complex. He invited me over for dinner and drinks, but I wasn't sure I should go after what happened before. He seemed like a nice guy. I decide to go ahead and have dinner with him. I was at his apartment, and we had a couple of drinks, and he hadn't started dinner yet. I began to wonder if he was going to make dinner. I told him, "I need to use the restroom." I went in and locked the door behind me. I peed and while I was pulling my pants up, he somehow unlocked door and attacked me! He was trying to pull my pants off and we struggled for what seemed to be a long time but was probably only a few minutes. When he couldn't get my pants off, he gave up. I got my pants zipped and buttoned and took off running out of his apartment. If any of those guys had physically hurt me, I would have reported it to the police but luckily, they hadn't. Man! What was wrong with these guys? They needed to learn some self-control!

I needed some extra money and met an older man in his late 50's through a lady in my apartment complex. He needed a cleaning lady, so she gave me his number and I called. He lived down the street in a nice big house. We met and he told me he was married and needed someone to clean the house once a week for $100 while his wife was away on business. I agreed and came over the next day to clean. After I finished, he paid me and was pulling my arm trying to get me to sit on his lap. I refused and was getting mad telling him to stop it. He told me his wife was out of town and he'd give me $100 more if I had sex with him. I angrily told him, "Hell No!" I left immediately and never went back. Bummer. I thought this side job would help me get ahead on my bills. The next week I didn't go to his house to clean, so he came to my apartment and asked why I didn't show up. I told him I didn't like the way he acted. He replied, "I still want you to clean my house even though you won't have sex with me." I told him, "Hell No! Get the Fuck out of here!" He left and we never saw each other again.

I was at the swimming pool one hot afternoon with Inky. I was floating on a raft, and she was laying in the shade. A lady came by and picked her up and started walking away with her! I yelled, "Hey! Where are you going with my cat?" She replied, "Oh! I didn't know this was your cat. I thought it was a stray and was going to take it home with me." I told her, "No. She's not a stray! She's mine! She follows me like a dog." The lady left and I thought how lucky I was not to be napping or Inky would've been gone and I wouldn't have known what happened to her.

I called John late one night and he answered. I asked how he was, and he said OK, but he had just woken from a scary dream. He said, "I was out on a small boat in the ocean and was fishing. Suddenly, I caught something big on my line and it started dragging my boat all over the water and I had no control of the boat. Then the water got very choppy, and the waves got big and then I woke up and heard a giant explosion in my room and got a little scared and pulled my covers up by my eyes and looked around but saw nothing and then you called. Do you know what it might mean?" I laughed and replied, "No. But I want to know, did you reel the fish in? Or did it get away?" He replied, "I don't know because I woke up." I was interested in knowing what happened to what was on his line. I laughed again and said, "Have a good night, goodbye." And we hung up.

Out of the blue the Dallas Morning News started being delivered to my apartment and I had no idea why. It was strange because I never subscribed to it and didn't really want it. They just piled up on the floor and I never read them. Then one day something spoke to me and told me to pick up the last paper and read it. I came across an article about the church I had attended in Farmers Branch. The article said someone had dug up a corpse from a graveyard and scattered the body parts around the outside of the church and put the head of the body in the women's restroom! When I read that my eyes must have gotten as big a saucers, because it was so close to the dream I had. I was quite shocked and scared. Was that just a coincidence? What was causing my crazy dreams and why me? It couldn't be normal. Was everyone going through the same kind of things I was? I showed the article to my parents and told them it was very close to the dream I had earlier. They just brushed me off and my mom felt I was talking to the Devil again. I told my mom, "I am totally done with that church. I am never going back. This article gives me the confirmation I was looking for that I was right in leaving." She wasn't happy about it but there was nothing she could do.

I was now a grown up and made my own decisions about my religious views.

My parents were still security guards for the church and saw things going on that they disagreed with. They saw the church wasted money on things like $500 doorknobs, $5000 Persian rugs, and very expensive cars while the church always begged for more money saying God would bless you if you gave the church money. Money! Money! Money! That's all the church cared about. They wanted your money for their own personal use. My parents didn't like that and finally quit going. My mom said the Holy Spirit spoke to her and gave her a message for the church. When she told me that I thought yeah right! All those times I went into the spirit and asked for the message but there never was one. Now suddenly, my mom had a message. I read it and wrote my own poem mixed with hers and put it away and thought no more of it.

My parents set up a meeting with the pastor who looked like a vampire, so they could give him the letter and I just had to go. To me, that was the equivalent of looking the devil in his face and knowing who he really was. We got there and my mom told him, "I have a message from the Holy Spirit for you." He read it and all he did was smile big and say, OK. We left and none of us ever went back. Later the pastor got in lots of trouble for misuse of money and his wife left him for having affairs.

Now I had no religion or church and just had God, Jesus, and The Holy Spirit with me. I felt lost at times and other times I felt I was found. I was very unsure about what I was doing in my life, denouncing the mainstream religion and what I was supposed to do with the rest of my life. I just went on being a teenager.

One of my brothers introduced me to these two guys, John and Kevin, and one sold pot. John had good weed and I liked to buy quantity at a good price. After I came over and bought weed a few times John got the hots for me and wanted to have sex. So, we went in his bedroom. He was pretty good. But it was over too fast for me. Now whenever I went over to get pot, he always wanted to have sex and would take my hand and say, "Come on let's go in my bedroom and have some fun." I always did but figured he must have a girlfriend because we only had casual sex.

I liked Kevin, but he was shy around me. He was always in his room working on this drawing called The Other Side. It started as a doodle and ended up being a two-year project. After me and John were done fucking, I'd go into Kevin's room and sit and watch him draw because he was very good at it. The drawings he did were very trippy. I figured he must have been doing some acid or mushrooms or something to come up with that stuff. I grew very fond of Kevin, and really didn't care about John because we weren't going anywhere with our relationship. I wanted to get with Kevin but didn't know how since I was already fucking his roommate.

One day I went to their apartment, and John wasn't there, but Kevin was. He invited me in, and we went into his bedroom so he could draw, and I could watch. Then I asked him if he wanted to have sex and he replied, "Yes!" We got naked and got into his bed and I was on top fucking him when suddenly, he started laughing and couldn't stop! Then I started laughing and couldn't stop! I figured he must have taken something. I tried to get him to straighten up so we could keep having sex, but he couldn't stop laughing. I got frustrated and I finally said, "Ok! I give up! This isn't working." We just laughed more and never tried again because he didn't ask me to. I think he was too shy to come on to me. He was such a sweet guy.

Kevin finished drawing The Other Side and showed me. Wow! I thought it was an incredible picture. It had four dead rock stars in it. James Morrison, Janis Joplin, Jimmy Hendrix and Brian Jones. Of course, I knew nothing about them but was totally infatuated with the picture. I asked Kevin, "So what does the picture mean?" He laughingly replied, "It's the meaning of life from beginning to end." That confused me but made me intrigued so I asked for a copy, and he happily gave me one. To me it seemed like a map to somewhere with a message in it and I'd stare into the picture trying to understand it. I went next door to the printing shop and asked the owner who was fond of me if he'd blow the picture up and he did. He made three copies. One in black and white on vellum and the other two were brown on clear plastic. I left one on John's doorstep at The Parkway, but he said he never received it.

My oldest brother and younger brother were doing some bad drugs. I think it was called crystal meth. It was some kind of speed. I snorted it and it burned my nose, but the high felt good. When I came down from it, I hated it. I couldn't eat, and my stomach hurt extremely bad. My oldest brother had the idea to sell it and make money. There was a guy he bought $100 worth from, and they'd shoot up half and sell the other half for $100. I explained to my brother he wasn't making any money. I told him he was only making his money back to buy more and keep him and his friend shooting dope for free. He didn't understand that. I told him he needed to quit doing that and get a real job so he could help pay bills. He didn't want to, so I had no choice but to kick him out. It was winter and I felt bad when I saw him standing on the street corner in the cold. The most I could do was give him a blanket and occasionally some food. Tough love was very hard. Whenever he came over to visit and get warm, he'd go into my bathroom for a while, and I soon caught on he was shooting up. I told him he couldn't use my bathroom anymore. Then when he came over, he started unlocking my windows so he could sneak in when I wasn't home. When I caught on to that I nailed the windows shut. When he came over after that he pulled the nails out without me seeing and I soon caught on to that too. After he'd leave, I'd go around to the windows and put the nails back in. Finally, I had to tell him he couldn't come over anymore.

My youngest brother worked at Taco Bell and was to get a small check in a couple days and was supposed to give it to me to buy groceries after I spent all my money on rent. Instead, he gave it to a drug dealer who convinced him he'd triple his money in a few days. When I heard that, I got very angry and told him he needed to find a new place to stay, and he immediately moved in with some friends. I had to eat Rice-a-Roni for the next couple days until I went to work. I was lucky I worked at a restaurant and could eat at least once a day.

I wanted the tattoo on my back covered up. My brother knew a guy who did home tattoos, and he came over and I told him what I wanted. He said he'd have to make the clouds dark, so they'd cover the initials. I didn't like the feeling being pricked by an electric pin over and over but suffered through it. It was a big tattoo on my shoulder, and it came out very nice. I was happy with it. It was a rainbow with dark clouds.

My brother was working at the tire shop and was breaking down wooden pallets to bring them home for firewood. While doing it, a nail went up through his shoe and into his foot and he had to go to the hospital. He got antibiotics and pain pills. While I was at work, he was home on pain pills and a few of his friends showed up to party. He passed out with his friends still there and I had money that I saved for rent on the fireplace mantle. When I got home, my brother was the only one there and was sleeping. He woke up and told me he had friends over but fell asleep and they left. I immediately got alarmed and checked to see if our rent money was still on the mantle. But it was all gone! I got so mad at him for falling asleep with people over and now I didn't know how I was going to pay rent at the end of the month. I got upset and started crying and went to my room. I had no idea how I was going to get all the rent money.

My brother went back to work several days later and was fired. Now I was really freaking out because I had no idea how I was going to pay rent! He immediately got a job at the print shop next door and all he had to do was step out of our apartment, take a few steps, and he was at work. As soon as he started working there the car broke down and his boss gave me rides to work and back for a couple days until it was fixed. He lived in the same apartment complex as us and was very nice to me and never made a pass at me even though I knew he liked me.

Rent was due soon and I knew I wasn't going to have the money on time. I didn't know what to do! Something spoke to me and said, "Get the last newspaper that came and go through the Help Wanted ads." I replied, "I already have a job. I don't need another one." Then it replied, "Just do what I said!" So, I was like, "OK! OK! Don't be so pushy!" I was going through the Help Wanted ads and the voice said, "Stop right there!" It was an ad placed by a topless bar called Dejavu. It read, Topless Dancers Wanted. No experience necessary. $200 a week plus tips. Must be 19+. I replied, "No way! That's like going into the darkness. I don't want to go there. I'm almost flat chested and weigh 100 pounds. I'm a stick figure. I don't even know how to dance or be sexy! And I'm only 18!" I said to the voice that spoke to me, "No! I don't want to go there!" The voice replied, "Just do it and I will meet you there!" So, I replied, "God is that you? If it's really you I'm going to tell everyone that you want to meet me in a titty bar and you're going to be in lots of trouble. I don't think your followers are going to like that. You in a titty bar while they're at church worshipping you on Sundays!" Then I started laughing! This couldn't be real and if it was who would I tell? I must have been losing my mind. But decided to go ahead and go to Dejavu on my 19th birthday.

The guy next door had some mushrooms for sale. I'd never done mushrooms and invited a few friends over to play cards and do some. I boiled them and made tea. We drank the tea and ate the mushrooms. We were all sitting around the table playing when suddenly everyone turned into giant playing cards. I started laughing my ass off. They looked so funny as giant cards. I felt like Alice in Wonderland. The furniture was moving around and looked like it was breathing. The next thing I knew the doorbell rang and I was immediately back to normal. The trip was over.

It didn't last very long, about half an hour. I wanted to get back into it but couldn't. The two guys I got the mushrooms from were weird. They had absolutely no furniture, TV, radio, etc. in their apartment. They had giant maps all over the walls and threw darts at the maps and then said strange stuff about wars where the darts landed on the maps. That was freaky. They acted like they were some strange spirits talking through the guys. All the floors in the apartment were covered in an inch or more of pennies. I'd never seen anything like it before. They said it was from having penny wars. They were strange. I never saw them again after that.

CHAPTER 3

DEJAVU

On my birthday I drove the little green car to Dejavu and had no idea what to expect. I`d only been to regular bars a couple times. When I went in, I saw they had waitresses, and told the manager I wanted to apply for that position. He said they didn't need waitresses, they needed dancers. I told him I didn`t know how to dance and he replied, "That`s ok, you're pretty enough you don`t need to know how." He offered me a drink and told me to watch everything going on in the bar. I wasn't sure I could take my clothes off in public, but the other ladies seemed to be having fun, and money was flowing. The manager asked if I was ready to try. I had no idea I'd be auditioning and didn`t bring any dance clothes, only my heels. He got me some dance clothes, and told a lady named Venita, who was about 10 years older than me, to show me the ropes. The first thing she said was, "Do not follow in my footsteps!" Venita told me she was a married man's mistress. She took me to the dressing room where I changed then showed me how to get on center stage and the two side stages. You danced two songs on each stage. The bar reminded me of a strange temple for some weird reason. Everything focused to the main stage like it was a church. Then she took me to the DJ booth and told me to pick two songs for centerstage. I told them I didn`t know much about music and to play rock and roll. The DJ asked me what my dancer name was but I didn`t know what he meant. He said I needed to pick a dancer name that was not my real name. I didn`t know what name to use so I said Champagne. Ironically the music playing at the same time was LYNYRD SKYNYRD. ***What`s your name little girl? What`s your name? I'll find my limo driver take us to the show. I'll find a little queen***

and I know I can treat her right. What`s your name little girl? What`s your name? Shootin you straight little girl won`t you do the same? Won`t you come upstairs and have a drink of champagne! The next song was by THE ZOMBIES called TIME OF THE SEASON ***It's the time of the season, when love runs high. Let me try with pleasured hands to take you in the sun to promised lands. To show you everyone. What's your name? Who's your daddy? Is he rich like me? Has he taken any time to show you what you need to live?*** They called my name and the doors opened and I took centerstage. I was so nervous, and the lights were blinding. The strobe light was killing my eyes. All I could do was look at the audience and try not to look at the lights. The first song was over, and the doors opened, and I got off stage and took all my clothes off except for my G-string and heels and got back on center stage. All the flashing lights were so hard to deal with and I felt awkward being naked in front of the crowd, but I fake danced the best I could. There was a place on center stage if you touched a certain light, it shocked you! I made sure I stayed away from it. Since it was my first time on stage and my birthday, I was tipped very well! Later when I went on stage, they got me a cake and played, ***You say it's your birthday! Well, it's my birthday too yeah! Happy birthday to you!*** I made a lot of money on that set and stayed the rest of the day. I thought wow this was great. Now I can pay my rent on time. They asked if I was going to come back tomorrow, and I said yes. After all the place was like a candy store full of men, money, booze, and drugs. I had so much fun!

I went home that night and thought about what music to play and what name to use. I looked around and saw my mother's old tiara from when she was a young ballet dancer and decided to use it and call myself Princess Lusty. After all this was just an acting job and I could express myself through the music. When I was on stage the music was so loud that no one could hear me sing. I played songs like, I'M JUST A SINGER IN A ROCK-N-ROLL BAND/MOODY BLUES, and DREAM ON/AEROSMITH,

Half my life is written pages. You know it's true. All these feelings come back to you. Sing with me. Sing for the years. Sing for the laughter. Sing for the tears. Sing with me just for today. Maybe tomorrow the good Lord will take you away! I felt like I was in a movie theater or strange temple and was an actress. Dancers at Dejavu dressed in costumes, sexy dresses, or sexy lingerie.

The next day I went to work the music was saying ***Fame! Fame! Fame! What's your name! What's your name! What's your name!*** I put my tiara on and told the DJ I was Princess Lusty. The first song I picked was ALL YOU ZOMBIES by THE HOOTERS. ***Holy Moses met the Pharaoh, yeah he tried to set him straight. Looked him in the eye! Let my people go! Holy Moses on the mountain. High above the golden calf. Went to get the ten commandments. Yeah he`s just gonna breakem in half! All you zombies hide your faces. All you people in the street. All you sittin in high places, It`s all gonna fall on you! No one ever spoke to Noah. They just laughed at him instead. Working on his ark. Working all by himself! Only Noah saw it comin. Forty days and forty nights. Took his sons and daughters with him. Yeah, they were his real lights! Holy father what`s the matter? Where have all your children gone? Sitting in the dark. Living all by themselves! You don`t have to hide anymore! All you zombies show your faces!***

My next song was Time Keeps on Slippin Into the Future by Steve Miller. ***Time keeps on slippin into the future. I want to fly like an eagle let my spirit carry me. Til I`m free, oh Lord, through the revolution. Feed the babies, who don`t have enough to eat. Shoe the children, with no shoes on their feet. House the people living in the street. Oh, there`s a solution!***

The next time I danced I played MAGIC POWER by TRIUMPH. ***Somethings at the edge of your mind. Something you`ve been hoping to find. Not sure what it is. There you hear the music, and it all comes crystal clear. Music does the talkin says the things you want to hear. I`m young! I`m wild and I`m free! I`ve got the magic power of the music in me! Brings her closer to her***

dreams. A little magic power makes it better than it seems! She gets the magic power of the music in me. If you`re thinking it over, but you just can`t solve it out. Do you want someone to tell you what they think it`s all about? Are you reachin for the top? Well, the music keeps you going now and it`s never gonna stop! The world is full of compromise and infinite red tape! But the music's got the magic! It`s your one chance for escape! Turn me on and turn me up! It`s your turn to dream! I`m young! I`m wild and I`m free! I`ve got the magic power of the music in me!

The bar must have recently opened because they didn't have very many dancers. Sometimes I had to go back on stage as soon as I got off. That was very tiring. The five-inch heels were killing my feet, being on my tippy toes.

Barely detectable by me, a strange subliminal dialogue began with the music, and it went like this: WHO ARE YOU by THE WHO: ***Who are you? Who? Who? Tell me who the fuck are you? I really want to know! I know there's a place you walked where love falls from trees!***

I responded with PAT BENATAR. ***We are strong! Searching our hearts for so long. Both of us knowing love is a battlefield./Isn`t love primitive? A wild gift you want to give. Break out of captivity and follow me stereo child. Love is the kill and your hearts still wild. I am the warrior! Who`s the hunter? Who`s the game? I feel the beat call your name. I hold you close in victory. I don't want to tame your animal style. You won`t be caged in the call of the wild. Yes, I am the warrior! Victory is mine!***

THE BAR MUSIC: *VICTIM OF LOVE/ THE EAGLES.* ***What kind of love have you got? You should be home but you're not! A room full of noise and dangerous boys, still make you thirsty and hot. There`s just one thing I don't understand. You got your stories to tell. Victim of love it`s such an easy part and you know how to play it so well. Some people never come clean. I think you know what I mean. You`re walking the wire. Pain and desire. Looking for love in between. Tell me your secrets. I`ll tell you mine.***

This ain't no time to be cool. Victim of love. I see a broken heart. What kind of love have you got?/One of these nights! One of these crazy lonely nights! Were gonna find out pretty mama, what turns on your light. The full moon is calling. You got your demons. You got your desires. Well, I got a few of my own! Someone to be kind to in between the dark and the light. One of these dreams. One of these lost and lonely dreams. We're gonna find one that really screams! I've been searching for the daughter of the Devil himself. I've been searching for an angel in white. I've been waiting for a woman who's a little of both and I can feel her but she's nowhere in sight! Coming right behind you! Swear I'm gonna find you in between the dark and the light! SEPARATE WAYS /JOURNEY. ***Survive the tide love divides. Someday love will find you and break those chains that bind you! One night will remind you how we touched and went our separate ways. If you must go, I wish you well love. You'll never walk alone my love. Take care my love! True love won't desert you. You know I still love you!*** SPACE COWBOY/ STEVE MILLER. ***Some people call me the space cowboy. Some call me the gangster of Love. People talkin about me say I'm doin you wrong. You're the cutest thing I ever did see. Really love your peaches want to shake your tree.***

I played GLORIA GAYNOR. ***At first, I was afraid! I was petrified! And so your back! From outer space! I just walked in to find you hear with that sad look upon your face! I should have changed that stupid lock! I should have made you leave your key! If I'd a known for just one second you'd be back to bother me! Weren't you the one who tried to break me? Did you think I'd crumble? Did you think I'd lay down and die? I'm not that chained up little person still in love with you. So, you felt like dropping in and just expect me to be free? I WILL SURVIVE!*** TUSK/ FLEETWOOD MAC ***Why don't you tell me what's going on? Why don't you tell me who's on the phone? Why don't you ask him who's the latest on his throne? I can still hear you saying you would never break the chain***!

BAR MUSIC WENT: COLD AS ICE/ FOREIGNER. ***You're as cold as ice! You're willing to sacrifice our love! Someday you`ll pay the price I know!*** ROCK YOU LIKE A HURRICANE/ SCORPIONS ***So what is wrong with another sin? The bitch is hungry and wants to tell. So give her inches and feed her well. I`ve got to leave it`s time for the show. Lust is in cages til storm breaks loose! The wolf is hungry he wants his show. He`s licking his lips. He's ready to win. On the hunt tonight for love at first sting!*** AMERICAN GIRL/TOM PETTY ***She was an American girl raised on promises. She couldn't help thinkin that there was more to life somewhere else. Afterall it was a great big world with lots of places to run to. And if she had to die tryin she had one little promise she was going to keep.*** VOICES/RUSS BALLARD ***If you could see my mind. If you really look deep. Then maybe you'll find that somewhere there will be a place hidden behind my comedian face. You will find somewhere there's a house. Inside that house is a room. Locked in the room in the corner you see, a voice is waiting for me to set it free. I got the key. Voices! I hear voices! I locked it away in my imagination but I'm the one who's got the combination. Some people didn't like what the voice did say so I took the voice and locked it away. I got the key. Don't look back! Look straight ahead! Yesterday's gone! Don't turn away you can take it on!***

Ok, so the music was all too crazy for me, and I wasn't really paying attention to it. I just wanted to have fun, so this was the kind of music I played. HOLD THE LINE/TOTO ***Hold the line! Love isn't always on time!*** GIRLS JUST WANNA HAVE FUN/CYNDI LAUPER ***The phone rings in the middle of the night! My father yells whatcha gonna do with your life?! Oh, daddy girls just want to have fun. Some boys take a beautiful girl and hide her away from the rest of the world! I wanna be the one to walk in the sun!*** ALL SHE WANTS TO DO IS DANCE/DON HENLEY ***They`re picking up the prisoners and putting them in a pen, and all she wants to do is dance! Rebels been rebels since I***

don`t know when! All she wants to do is dance, dance! Can`t feel the heat comin off the street! She wants to party! She wants to get down! DANCING DAYS/LEDZEPPELIN ***Dancing days are here again. I`ve got my flower. I`ve got my power. I`ve got a woman who knows. You`ll be my only. My one and only! Is that the way it should start? Crazy ways are evident by the way you wear your clothes. Sipin booze is precedent as the evening starts to glow.*** DANCING WITH MYSELF/BILLY IDOL ***When there`s no one else in sight in a crowded lonely night, I wait so long for my love vibration and I`m dancing with myself. So let`s sink another drink, cause it'll give me time to think. If I had the chance I`d ask the world to dance! Well, I looked all over the world at every type of girl, but your empty eyes seem to pass me by and I`m dancing with myself.*** DANCING IN THE STREET/DAVID BOWIE ***Calling out around the world, are you ready for a brand-new beat? The time is right for dancing in the street! All we need is the music. The sweet, sweet music. There will be music everywhere! It doesn`t matter what you wear just as long as you are there! It`s just an invitation across the nation. A chance for us to meet. They`ll be laughing, singing, music swinging, and dancing in the street! Just as long as you are there!*** DANCE THE NIGHT AWAY/ VAN HALEN ***Have you seen her? So fine and pretty. Fooled me with her style and ease. And I felt her from across the room! Yes, it's love in the third degree! Come on and take a chance. You're old enough to dance. Dance the night away! A live wire. Barely a beginner. But just watch that lady go! She's on fire! Cause dancin gets her higher than anything that she knows! Dance the night away!*** LET'S DANCE/DAVID BOWIE ***Put on your red shoes and dance the blues to the song they`re playing on the radio. Let's dance, while color lights up your face! Sway through the crowd to an empty space. If you say run. I will run with you. If you say hide. I`ll hide. Let`s dance for fear your grace should fall. You could look into my eyes under the moonlight. The serious moonlight! Let`s dance!*** AND WE DANCED/HOOTERS ***And we danced, and***

we danced, swept away for a moment by chance. And we danced. And danced. And danced.

The bar played ROCK AND ROLL ALL NIGHT by KISS. ***You show us everything you got! You keep on dancin and the room gets hot! You drive us wild, we`ll drive you crazy! The party`s just about to let you in!*** HEAVENS ON FIRE/ ***I look at you and my blood boils hot! I feel my temperature rise! I want it all! Give me what you got! There`s hunger in your eyes! I`m getting closer baby hear me breathe! You know the way to give me what I need! Feel my heat! Takin you higher! Burn with me! Heaven`s on fire! Angel fly! Heaven`s on fire! You`re comin closer I can hear you breathe! You drive me crazy when you start to tease! You could bring the Devil to his knees***! GIRLS GOT RHYTHM/AC/DC ***I've been around the world! I've seen a million girls! Ain't none of them got what my lady she's got! She's stealing the spotlight! Knocks me off my feet! Enough to stop a freight train or start the third world war! You know she moves like sin and when she lets me in, it's like liquid love!*** ROCK CANDY/MONTROSE ***When you need a friend through thick and thin. Don't look to those above you. When your down and out, ain`t no doubt, nobody wants you! When you`re 19 and reachin for your dreams. Don`t let no one reach it for you! Stretch your arms and take a chance. If it can be done, you can do it!*** AIN'T TALKIN BOUT LOVE/VAN HALEN ***You may have all you want but I got something you need. Ain`t talkin bout love! I`ve been to the edge and I stood and looked down. You know I lost a lot of friends there baby! Ain`t got no time to mess around! If you want it, got to bleed for it***!

I just wanted to party and have fun and not pay attention to the music. I was having so much fun I forget I was called to Dejavu by some strange higher power that I thought was God.

I still felt like I was searching for something. Not sure what it was. Me? God? Jesus? The truth? A mate? Love? Maybe all the above. I worked the dayshift 10 to 7 because the night seemed like a wild out of control zoo.

Lots of men came in and asked me, "What`s a pretty young girl like you doing in a place like this?" I'd say, "I`m waiting to meet someone here." Men also asked me, "Does the carpet match the drapes?" I didn't know what they meant until a dancer told me. It seemed they wanted to know if my pussy hair matched my blonde hair on my head. And yes, it did.

When I was on stage, I liked to sing the songs I played. THE EDGE OF SEVENTEEN/STEVIE NICKS ***Just like the white winged dove sings a song sounds like she's singing. I went today! Maybe I will go again tomorrow! Well, the music there was hauntingly familiar! And I see what you're doing. With the words from a poet and the voice from a choir and a melody. Nothing else mattered! Then suddenly there was no one left standing in the hall! I went searching for an answer up the stairs and down the hall. Not to find an answer. Just to hear the call of a night bird singing, "Come with me." I hear you in the morning. And I hear you at nightfall. Sometimes to be near you is to be unable to hear you, my love.*** DREAMS ***Now here you go again you say you want your freedom. Well, who am I to keep you down? It's only right that you should play the way you feel it. But listen carefully to the sound of your loneliness. Players only love you when they're playing. Women they will come, and they will go. I see the crystal visions. I keep my visions to myself. It's only me who wants to wrap around your dreams and have you any dreams you'd like to sell? She rings a bell. Dreams unwind. Love's a state of mind. Will you ever win?*** SISTER OF THE MOON ***Intense silence as she walked in the room. Her black robes trailing. Sister of the moon. A black widow makes more sound than she. She was dark at the top of the stairs, and she called to me, and I followed as friends often do. The people they love her and still they are the most cruel. She asked me, "Be my sister? Sister of the moon?" Some call her sister of the moon. Some say illusions are her game. Does anybody know her name? So we make our choices when there is no choice and we listen to their voices ignoring our own voices.*** AFTER MIDNIGHT/

ERIC CLAPTON ***After midnight we're gonna find out what it is all about! We gonna give an exibition! We're gonna find out what it is all about!*** BOHEMIAN RHAPSODY/QUEEN ***Is this the real life? Or is this just fantasy? No escape from reality. Open your eyes. Look up to the skies and see!*** WE ARE THE CHAMPIONS/QUEEN ***I've paid my dues time after time. I've done my sentence but committed no crime! And bad mistakes I've made a few! I've had my share of sand kicked in my face! But I've come through! I've taken my bows and my curtain calls! It's been no bed of roses. No pleasure cruise. I consider it a challenge before the whole human race and I ain't gonna lose! We are the champions of the world!***

I was driving the car back and forth to work, but on my way home one night, it started smoking so I pulled over and left it. I had no idea cars needed oil and it was bone dry. I didn`t know anyone well enough to ask them to drive me to car lots until I found one and didn`t want to bother my parents who I had not told I was a dancer, so I got a cabby to drive me around for the day for $100. It took most of the day, but I got a cute little orange hatchback pinto.

One morning before work, I put my tiara on, sexy lingerie, and an overcoat. I went to see John hoping to have sex with him, but he wasn't interested and I couldn`t blame him after how I burned our bridge. He was the first person I told I became an exotic dancer named Princess Lusty. I did to him what Janis Joplin did to Leonard Cohen at The Chelsea Hotel. I left and went to work and never bothered him again.

As a dancer you had responsibilities even though it was a party all the time. I had to make sure I was on time for my shift all week, so I got my shift pay. One minute late blew the entire weeks' pay. Some dancers didn't care about the $200 a week for working six days on time. They showed up when they wanted. I had to make sure I didn't get too drunk or miss my call for stage. Definitely don't take too many drugs. Sometimes I missed my cue for center stage because I was busy table dancing and not used to being called Princess Lusty. I had to remember what dancer I danced after and try to be ready. Sometimes I went on center stage undressed if I missed my cue. It really didn't matter though. No one really cared. Becoming a dancer opened lots of doors. Some good. Some bad. All dancers had to decide which paths they wanted to take. For sure I didn`t want to get mixed up with the wrong crowd and get addicted to something or catch something. I'd been lucky enough so far to never have caught any kind of disease as promiscuous as I'd been in my past.

I had to learn the ropes fast, so I didn't get screwed over by anyone. Things I had to learn were: 1. Don't let your clothes out of your sight or they might get stolen by customers or dancers. Dancers stole them to sell in other bars and customers stole them for souvenirs and God only knows what else they did with them. 2. Don't lend your clothes to other dancers. They will ruin them and give them back to you in terrible condition. 3. Don't lose your money. 4. Always keep your eyes out for free money on the floors. Free money is fun easy money. 5. Don't let men scam you by tipping you fake money or paper. 6. Watch your drink at all times and take it with you wherever you go. 7. Don't get drunk and pass out or dancers might mess with you by painting your face, putting underwear over your head, or putting Cheetos in the crack of your butt.

I had to learn those lessons fast and sometimes the hard way. But I learned quick. One time I was table dancing and the man tipped me $100 in ones for a song. I looked like a Christmas tree made of money. I started dancing another song and when I turned my back, he plucked money off me and re-tipped me with it. He did it a few times and I caught on. I took all my money off and held it in my hand.

There were two dancers that were close friends who did things after hours with customers. They'd figure out if the guy had money, and if they did, the two dancers ganged up on him, got him drunk, and took all his money. They did things I wouldn't do. If they were messing with a customer like that, I didn't go around him because the customer expected me to do what they were doing. I just had to wait for my nice customers to show up. The ones that gave me easy money for doing nothing but dancing.

I had a problem with a dancer named Blue Eyes. She came to me and told me I couldn`t dance for her customers. Because once they met me, they wanted nothing more to do with her. I told her, "Fuck you bitch! I'll dance for whoever I want! You don`t own the customers!" She didn`t like my response and followed me in the restroom and cornered me. A couple of her friends followed her in to see what she was going to do. She started yelling at me, telling me I can`t dance for her customers and of course I told her off again. I refused to backdown and she swung on me and missed. I went off on her and started beating the crap out of her while her friends watched. Then I grabbed her long black hair and started banging her head into the porcelain sink while I was telling her, "I`m sorry you're making me do this to you!" You see I`m a very nice person and don`t like to fight, but when I`m cornered and have no choice, I can turn into a giant monster!" I was in such a rage I couldn`t stop and the other dancers pulled me off. When it was over, I told her, "Don`t ever fuck with me again! And I will dance for whoever wants me to dance for them!" I walked out and she composed herself, got her things together, and left for the day. A few days later she came back, and I took a look at her and said, "Hey Black Eyes! Do you want to fuck with me again?" She shook her head no, lowered it and walked away. I didn`t have any more problems from her and she soon quit.

A few days after that, an oriental lady that was about 40 started some shit with me. She had fake boobs and had a special trick. She could bend her middle finger and her nipple sucked in. I guess the doctor that did her boob job connected something. I was dancing on the side stage, and she was sitting at a table next to the stage with a man. I stepped down for a moment to dance a little and get my tip as we all did. When I went to get back on stage, she grabbed my hair and jerked it! That pissed me off and I knocked the man's drink on the floor, picked the table up over my head, chased her around the bar, and into the dressing room. Now these were real bar tables weighted on the bottom, so they didn`t tip easy. With me being only 5ft tall and 100 pounds that must have looked funny. The table wouldn`t fit through the dressing room door so I put it down and ran into the dressing room after her. She was terrified. I told her if she ever touched me again, she wouldn`t get off that easy next time. She replied with her eyes wide in fear, "Ok! ok!". I went back out to the bar and took the table back where the man was sitting and put it down and apologized for the drink and offered to buy him another one. He replied, "Are you kidding? That was exciting! I had no idea someone as small as you could be so strong. Sit and have a drink with me." I`m sure it infuriated the oriental girl. She never fucked with me again.

There was another dancer who was a muscular lesbian and after every guy she danced for she'd French kiss. I thought that was so gross, French kissing every guy in the bar. When I danced for a guy after she did, they expected a French kiss from me. I was like, Hell No! I wouldn't go around French kissing all the customers for money. Some dancers let customers touch them in private places and some touched guys in their privates. I wasn`t that free with myself. I was a clean dancer and wouldn't French kiss men or touch them with my hands or let them touch me. I was just a big tease, and it was lots of fun. Some dancers prostituted themselves after hours. Not me! That was the wrong road!

It was February 28, 1985, and I'd been dancing for a month. It was almost time to go home and was on a side stage dancing when a good looking 6ft2 man with long dark curly hair, dark brown eyes, and a beard, came over and tipped me. He looked to be in his mid-twenties. He said, "I think you're pretty cute and sexy." I took his tip and blushed and thanked him for the compliment. When I got off stage and scoped the bar looking for one last victim of the day to dance for, I spotted the man who tipped me sitting at the back bar by himself. He was very nice looking but seemed too hippie for me. I waited for the song to be over so I could approach him and dance. The song playing was by SIMPLE MINDS: ***Hey, hey, hey! Won`t you come see about me? I`ll be alone. Tell me your troubles and doubts. Giving me everything, inside and out. Loves strange. So real in the dark. Think of the tender things that we were working on. Slow change may pull us apart when the light gets into your heart. Don`t you forget about me. Will you stand above me? Look my way, never love me. Will you recognize me? Call my name or walk on by? I won`t harm you or touch your defenses. Going to take you apart. I`ll put us back together at heart. Don`t you forget about me. As you walk on by. Will you call my name? Or will you walk away? I say Lalalalalalalallalalala***

I approached the handsome man and started dancing for him to TINY DANCER by ELTON JOHN. ***Blue jean baby. Pretty eyed pirate smile. You`ll marry a music man. Ballerina. You must have seen her, dancing in the sand. And now she`s in me. Always with me. Tiny dancer in my hand. Jesus freaks, out in the streets, handing tickets out for God. Turning back, she just laughs. Looking on she sings the songs. Only you can hear me.*** The song ended and he asked if I'd like to have a drink with him and I replied, "Yes, but I`m getting off work soon." I sat down, and he said his name was Steve and asked what my name was. I confidently said, "My name is Princess Lusty." We were having our drinks and he said, "Hey, I`m looking for this girl named Cindy. We have a date to The Firm concert tonight and we`re supposed to meet here at 7. Do you know where she is?" I was taken back by what he said and was confused. I knew I was supposed to meet someone or something here and I looked around thinking someone was playing a joke on me. Did I know him from somewhere? Had I made a date and forgotten about it? Then it dawned on me, and I said, "Oh! You must mean my girlfriend Casey! Her real name is Cindy. She already left." Casey liked to lead men on and make dates to get their money then skip out. She was married and had 3 kids. Her favorite song was ROCKY MOUNTAIN WAY by JOE WALSH because it said, ***Bases were loaded and Casey's at bat, playin it play by play!*** Then I kind of chuckled. I could see he was bummed out about it. I had no idea what he saw in her. I didn't think she was pretty, and her tits were saggy. She also took way too many hard drugs. But her and Venita were my closest friends in the bar. Then Steve asked me if I'd like to go to the concert with him. I didn`t respond right away because I was thinking about it. Then I replied, "Ok, only if you drive my car, and we get some weed." He said he had plenty of weed. I asked if we could stop by my place so I could change, but he said we didn't have time, so I went to the dressing room to change. Steve thought I was around 26 and had been dancing for years because of the way I danced and carried myself with confidence. I felt our meeting was very strange.

Steve was highly disappointed when I came out dressed in dark blue corduroys, a blue KZEW t-shirt, tennis shoes and a rabbit fur vest. He thought I was going to dress like a hot goddess stripper, but instead I looked like a poor Cinderella. He thought I was dressed ugly. I had no idea I'd be going out that night.

While driving my car Steve said, "So Princess Lusty, what`s your real name? Or do you want me to call you Princess Lusty all night?" Inside I was giggling, and replied, "My name is Cindy." I was thinking how ironically funny it was. What a crazy coincidence that he was at Dejavu to meet a girl named Cindy. Was he who I was supposed to meet there? When we were in line to get in the concert the couple next to us shared some cocaine. Even after that, I hadn't eaten dinner yet and was starving. Steve bought me a bunch of food and was shocked at how much I ate. I had no idea who THE FIRM or JIMMY PAGE was. The only song I liked was RADIOACTIVE. ***Well, I`m not uptight. Not unattracted. Turn me on tonight. Cause I`m radioactive.***

Radioactive! There`s not a fight. And I`m not your captive. Turn me loose tonight. Cause I`m radioactive! I want to stay with you! I want to play with you! I want to lay with you! And I want you to know! Gotta! Gotta set a date! Don`t be distracted! Turn me on tonight! Cause I`m radioactive! I want you to know! Gotta! Gotta set a date! Don`t stand too close! You might catch it! Radio! Radio! Radioactive! I really wasn`t interested in Steve. I wouldn`t let him hold my hand, put his arm around me, or kiss me when he tried. I told him I just wanted to be friends. He seemed to take it ok. He bought both of us shirts so we had something to remember our date. I thought that was very sweet of him. When the concert was over, he drove to his apartment at The Clusters which was only a few blocks away from Dejavu. He asked me up, but I declined. He couldn`t find his shirt so we looked all over in my car but couldn`t find it. He thought I stole it so I could give it to one of the many boyfriends he thought I had. I didn`t steal his shirt and I didn`t have any boyfriends. Great! Now he thought I was a thief and he didn`t come back to Dejavu. I really couldn`t blame him. After all I told him I just wanted to be friends and refused his advances. I went on with my life as a dancer.

I was at work and spotted this cute guy that looked just like the John that I really liked. Wow! Five ft. six, jet black hair, dark eyebrows, and moustache. The only difference was, he had beautiful baby blue eyes. When our eyes met it was like a kaleidoscope effect just like when Davy Jones met a girl he liked on The Monkeys. I was so excited over him and he over me. His name was Myles. He asked me out and of course I said yes. He came to Dejavu everyday to see me and came over to my apartment after work. After a week I started being confused. We hadn`t had actual sex yet. All he did was please me orally and go no further. Something wasn't quite right, but I wasn't sure what it was. One night at his friend's house I found out he liked to shoot coke. He asked if I wanted to and I said, "No thanks. I'll just snort a line." A couple days went by, and I was on centerstage when a lady came in, walked up to the stage and started tipping me a lot of money. She said, "I`m not here to cause any problems. I just wanted to tell you I`m Myles` wife and I wanted to see what caught his eye. He`s right. You are cute." She tipped me more money and walked out. It was a very awkward and an embarrassing situation and I couldn`t wait for Myles to come in so I could give him a piece of my mind. I was so pissed off! When he came in to see me as he did every day, I told him, "I had a visitor today." He replied, "Oh yeah, who?" I told him, "Your wife!" Then he got this uh-oh look on his face and asked what she said, so I told him. He replied, "She doesn`t mind if we see each other because we both see other people. We have an open relationship." I told him I never wanted to see him again and don`t ever come to Dejavu to see me.

There was a new legal drug going around the bars called Ecstasy and the dancers liked it. It was supposed to enhance sex and cost $25 a pill. You could tell what dancers were on it because they wore sunglasses in the bar because they didn't want people to look in their eyes. The music went like this: I WANT A NEW DRUG/HUEY LEWIS AND THE NEWS ***I wanna new drug! One that does what it should! One that won`t make me feel too bad or make me feel too good! One that won`t make me nervous wondering what to do! One that makes me feel like I feel when I`m with you!*** SUNGLASSES AT NIGHT/COREY HART ***I wear my sunglasses at night so I can see the love that`s right before my eyes!*** CHEAP SUNGLASSES/ZZ TOP ***Spied a little thing and I followed her all night! She had a west coast strut that was sweet as molasses! But what really knocked me out was the cheap sunglasses!*** THE FUTURE'S SO BRIGHT, I GOTTA WEAR SHADES/TIMBUK 3 ***Well I'm heavenly blessed and worldly wise. I'm a peeping-tom techie with x-ray eyes. Things are going great and they're only getting better. I'm doing alright, My futures so bright, I gotta wear shades.*** The dancers were having lots of fun on it, so I asked Venita to get me some. I took the whole thing, but don't think I was supposed to! The bar music went like this. WHITE RABBIT/JEFFERSON AIRPLANE ***One pill makes you larger and one pill makes you small. And if you go chasing rabbits and you know you're going to fall. Tellem all hookah-smoking caterpillar has given you the call. Go ask Alice! I think she`d know! When the men on the chessboard get up and tell you where to go. And you`ve just had some kind of mushroom and your mind is moving low. And the white knight is talking backwards, and the red queen is off with her head! Remember! What the dormouse said! Feed your head!***

I was feeling really funny and having a great time! I felt like an actress in someone else's play. The bar music was going LOW RIDER/WAR ***Take a little trip. Take a little trip. Take a little trip and see! Take a little trip with me!*** STEPPEN WOLFE/ MAGIC CARPET RIDE ***I like to dream. Yes! Right between the sound machine, on a cloud of sound I drift in the night. Goes far! Flies near! To the stars away from here! Well, you don`t know what we can find. Why don`t you come with me little girl, on a magic carpet ride? Well, you don`t know what we can see. Why don`t you tell your dreams to me? Fantasy can set you free. Close your eyes girl! Look inside girl! Let the sound take you away! Last night I held a lamp, someone took my lamp away! I looked all around. A lousy candle was all I found! Close your eyes girl! Look inside girl! Let the sound take you away!*** TWILIGHT ZONE/ GOLDEN EARING ***There`s a storm on the loose! Sirens in my head! Wrapped up in silence all circuits are dead! Cannot decode! My whole life spins into a frenzy! Maybe my connection is tired of taking chances. Help! Now I`m steppin into the twilight zone! This place is a madhouse! My beacon has been moved under moon and star! Where am I to go now that I`ve gone too far? So you will come to know when the bullet hits the bone! I`m falling down a spiral destination unknown! Double crossed messenger all alone! Can`t get no connection! Can`t get through! Where are you? When the hitman comes, he knows damn well he has been cheated! So***

you were gone, NO! When the bullet hit the bone! GIMME SHELTER/ROLLING STONES ***It's just a shot away! A storm is threatening my very life today! If I don't get some shelter, I'm gonna fade away! It's just a shot away! Love, sister!*** COME SAIL AWAY/STYX ***I`m sailing away. Set an open course for the virgin sea. Cause I`ve got to be free. Free to face the life that`s ahead of me. On board I`m the captain, So climb aboard! I look to the sea. Reflections in the waves spark my memory. We lived happily forever, so the story goes. A gathering of Angels appeared above my head! They sang to me this song of hope, and this is what they said, "Come sail away! Come sail away! Come sail away with me!" I thought that they were angels, but to my surprise! We climbed aboard their starships and headed for the skies!*** TWO TICKETS TO PARADISE/EDDIE MONEY ***I`m gonna take you on a trip so far from here! I`ve got two tickets in my pocket! Now baby we`re gonna disappear! We`ve waited so long! I`ve got two tickets to Paradise! Won`t you pack your bags we`ll leave tonight!*** FREE RIDE/EDGAR WINTER ***The mountain is high. The valley is low. And your confused on which way to go. So I`ve come here to lend you a hand and lead you into the promised land. Come on and sit by my side! Come on and take a free ride! It`s time to begin. You know all the answers must come from within.***

I started dating a male stripper named Paradise. We went to each other's bars to see each other. He invited me to his house for sex, but he was bad at it. I just wanted it to be over. It was the worst sex I'd ever had in my life. Later that night his roommate who was also a dancer came home and climbed into bed and tried to put the moves on me. I told him to get the fuck out! The next morning when we woke, I told Paradise I never wanted to see him again. I never went back to the male strip club, nor did he come to Dejavu and I never dated a stripper again.

It was three weeks into March and my brother lost his job next door at the printing shop for being late repeatedly. My oldest brother was still trying to get into my house when I wasn't home to shoot up and I had enough. I packed all my belongings and returned the rented furniture but didn`t know where I was going to go. I just knew I was going somewhere. Another week went by and I still didn`t know what I was going to do. Then something spoke to me and said, "Go to Steve's apartment, knock on the door, and offer him $50 dollars a week to sleep on his couch." I replied, "Are you fucking kidding me! You do know it`s April Fool's Day, right?! Is this some kind of April Fool's joke?!" We didn`t even really like each other and he thought I was a thief. Well, he was a gentleman, and did live very close to Dejavu. Na, that`s ok. I didn`t want to. Then the voice became stern and said, "Just do it!" I finally relented and gathered the courage to knock on his door. When he answered, he was quite surprised and happy to see me. I told him about my situation with my brothers, and what I was supposed to say. He replied, "Of course you can stay here." He followed me to my apartment, and we loaded up my boxes and I moved in. He had an old crappy couch, a 13-inch TV, and a microwave. In his bedroom was a little twin mattress on the floor. It was definitely a bachelor's pad. He didn`t even have a phone. I noticed two giant pictures on the wall. One was a warrior barbarian man with dark hair and a dark beard. He was holding a giant sword and was on a snow chariot being pulled by four white polar bears. It looked like he was coming from the north. It looked quite like Steve. The other was a hot chick in a bikini, with a giant snake wrapped around her. She had long blonde wavy hair and she too was riding on a chariot. Hers was pulled by a tiger, a cheetah, a lion, a jaguar, and a leopard. It was set in prehistoric times, and she looked like she was coming from the south. She strangely looked like me. That was kind of weird. It felt like this was some kind of set up. I just ignored it and went on.

After I moved in, I told Steve some of my past and how my life had been strange and that I didn`t understand what it all meant. He was a very good listener with no judgement. I really liked that. He enjoyed hearing the stories from my past. He was the first person I ever talked to about my life, and it felt good to finally tell someone about my crazy past.

When I went to work the music in the bar was REBEL YELL by BILLY IDOL. ***Last night a little angel came dancing to my door! She said, "Come on baby! I got a license for love! And if it expires! Pray help from above!" Because! In the midnight hour, with a rebel yell, she cried, "More! More! More!" She don`t like slavery! Won`t sit and beg! What set you free and brought you to me? What sets you free? I need you hear by me! He lives in his own heaven. I walked the ward with you! I`ve dried your tears of pain a million times. I`d sell my soul for you. For money to burn with you. I`d give you all! And have none, babe! Justa have you here by me! Oh yeah little angel!*** ANGEL/JIMMY HENDRICKS ***Angel came down from Heaven yesterday. She stayed with me just long enough to rescue me. And she told me a story about the sweet love between the moon and the deep blue sea. Then she spread her wings high over me. And my angel said unto me, "Today is the day for you to rise! Take my hand. Your gonna rise.*** " TOM PETTY/ REFUGEE ***You don't have to live like a refugee*** JUST WHAT I NEEDED/CARS ***I don`t mind you comin here and wasting all my time. Cause when you're standing oh so near, I kinda lose my mind! It`s not the perfume that you wear. It`s not the ribbons in your hair. I don`t mind you hanging out, and talkin in your sleep. It doesn't matter where you`ve been, as long as it was deep. I guess you're just what I needed! I needed someone to bleed!*** NO ONE LIKE YOU/SCORPIONS ***Girl It's been a long time that we've been apart. Much too long for a man who needs Love. I`ve missed you since I`ve been away. It wasn`t easy to leave you alone! It`s getting harder each time that I go! I can`t wait for the nights with you! I imagine the things we`ll do! I just want to be loved by you! There are really no words strong enough to describe all my longing for Love. I don`t want my feelings restrained***! HOT BLOODED/ FOREIGNER ***I`m hot blooded check it and see! Come on baby do you do more than dance? You don`t have to read my mind to*** *know what I have in mind! Honey you ought a know! Let me lay it on the line! I wanna know what you're doing after the show? Can we make a secret rendezvous? Just me and you? I'll show you lovin like you never knew! I'm a little bit high. You're a little bit shy! You're making me sing for your sweet sweet thing!* FEEL LIKE MAKIN LOVE/BAD COMPANY *When I think about you, I think about love. If I live without you, I live without love. And if I had the sun and moon and they were shinin I'd give you both night and day to satisfy Love. I feel like makin love to you!* SHE'S SO COLD/ROLLING STONES *I'm so hot for her and she's so cold! I'm the burning bush! I'm the burning fire! I'm the bleeding volcano! Yea, I tried re-wiring her! Tried re-firing her! I think her engine is permanently stalled! She's so cold like a tombstone! She's so cold! I dare not touch her! My hand just froze! But she's beautiful!* LET MY LOVE OPEN THE DOOR/ PETE TOWNSHEND *Let my love open the door to your heart! I have the only key to your heart! I can stop you from falling apart! Release yourself from misery! There's only one thing gonna set you free. And that's my love! Love can cure your problems. Let my love open the door to your heart!* ALRIGHT NOW/FREE *There she stood in the street! Smiling from her head to her feet! I said, "Hey! What's your name? Maybe we can see things the same!" I took her home to my place! Watching every move on her face! She said, "Look! What's your game baby? Are you trying to put me in shame?" I said, "Slow! Don't go so fast! Don't you think that love can last?" She said, "Love! Lord above! Now your tryin to trick me in love!"* WON'T GET FOOLED AGAIN/THE WHO *We'll be fighting in the streets. With our children at our feet. And the morals that they worship will be gone. The men who spurred us on, sit in judgement of all wrong. They decide and the shotgun sings the song. I'll tip my hat to the new constitution. Take a bow for the new revolution. Then I'll get on my knees and pray, WE DON'T GET FOOLED AGAIN! The change it had to come. We knew it all along. We were liberated from the fold that's all.*

Though I know the hypnotized never lie! Meet the new boss! Same as the old boss!

Steve told me he robbed a K-Mart in Ohio with a steak knife and the bag boy almost got his license plate number but was off by one. Steve found out because he knew someone who worked there. It was close to Christmas, and he threw all the checks in the bag into the river. Everyone who paid by check that day no longer owed the money. He paid his bookie then bought a frisbee of hash and partied. Wow! What a bad boy he was. I wasn't sure what to think of him. I hoped he wasn't a wanted man.

A disease called AIDS started and I became frightened that we could get it through mosquito bites, and we'd all have to wear plastic bubble suits for protection. I started to panic. Steve reassured me mosquitos couldn't transfer the blood virus from person to person. But I knew how quickly bugs adapted and changed. The disease broke down your immune system and you eventually died. It was passed by having sex or shooting up drugs with someone who already had it. It was spreading quickly among the gay community. There was no cure.

I got a strange feeling and told Steve I thought scientists were working on cloning people. Steve assured me we didn't have the technology to do that yet and I told him, "I don't know. I feel weird. For some strange reason I feel someone is trying at this moment." I was a little frightened and told him I was afraid someone will clone dinosaurs also. Steve told me dinosaurs would never live again because we won't have that technology in our lifetime. I think I was scared because when I was a little girl, I had nightmares of dinosaurs peeking in my windows and was afraid giant ones would crush me inside my house. That happened quite often, and I'd wake in a panic.

I showed Steve the picture of The Other Side and told him my friend drew it. He thought it was awesome. I told him I didn't know who the people were in the picture. He then gave me a crash course in 60s rock music. He told me who the four people were. Janice Joplin, James Morrison, Jimmy Hendricks, and Brian Jones. He played music from them, and I was infatuated with Morrison! I told Steve, "I want to go to a Morrison concert." He laughed and said, "He`s already dead." Bummer! Then he told me, "They're all dead." Wow! I had no idea. For some reason I stared at the picture thinking maybe there was a message in it, or I might see another picture in it like the 3D ones created many years later, but I never saw anything. Ironically, the four all died at the age of 27.

Steve's wasn't a hippy, but strangely he had the hot James Morrison look and I liked it a lot. He played everything he had from The Doors, Jimmy Hendrix, and Janice Joplin, but didn't have much from Brian Jones.

The Doors album I liked most was The American Prayer. It was a bunch of James Morrisons poetry made into songs. ***Is everybody in? Is everybody in?! The ceremony is about to begin. Wake up! You can't remember where it was! Had this dream stopped? Shake dreams from your hair my pretty child. My sweet one. Choose the day and choose the sign of your day. The day's divinity. First thing you see. A vast radiant beach on a cool jeweled moon. The music and voices are all around us. Choose they croon, the Ancient Ones, the time has come again. Choose now they croon beneath the moon beside an ancient lake. Enter again the sweet forest. Enter the hot dream. Come with us. Everything is broken up and dances. Indians scattered on dawn's highway bleeding. Ghosts crowd the young child's fragile eggshell mind. We have assembled inside this ancient theatre to propagate our lust for life. Oh great creator of being, grant us one more hour to perform our art and perfect our lives. We need great golden copulations. When the true kings' murderers are allowed to run free. A thousand magicians arise in the land. Thank you oh Lord for the white blind light. Gently they stir. Gently rise. The dead are new-born awakening. With ravaged limbs and wet souls. Gently they sigh in rapt funeral amazement. Who called these dead to dance? Was it the young*** *woman learning to play the Ghost Song on her baby grand? Was it the wilderness children? Was it the Ghost God himself? I called you up to anoint the Earth. I called you to announce sadness falling like burned skin. I called you to wish you well. To glory in self like a new monster. And now I call on you to pray. A military station in the desert. The Base. To come of age in a dry place. Holes and caves. Angels and sailors. Dreams watching each other narrowly. Jumped, humped, born to suffer. Made to undress in the wilderness. I will never treat you mean. Never start no kind of scene. I'll tell you every place and person that I've been. He maneuvered two girls into his hotel room. One a friend. The other, the young one, a new stranger. She's trying to rise. Peace on Earth. I'll always be true if you'll only show me Far Arden again! I have an ancient Indian crucifix around my neck. Lying on stained wretched sheets with a bleeding virgin. We could plan a murder or start a religion. I'll tell you this! No eternal reward will forgive us now for wasting the dawn! Back in those days everything was simpler and more confused. One summer night going to the pier I ran into two young girls. The blonde one was called Freedom. The dark one Enterprise. We talked and they told me this story. Now listen to this.... I'll tell you about Texas and the big beat. Soft driven slow and mad like some new language. Reaching your head with the cold sudden fury of a divine messenger. Let me tell you about heartache and the loss of God. Wandering, wandering, in hopeless night. Out here in the perimeter there are no stars. Out here we is stoned immaculate! The movie will begin in five minutes. The mindless voice announced. All those unseated will await the next show. We filed slowly, languidly into the hall. The auditorium was vast and silent as we seated and were darkened. The voice continued. The program for this evening is not new. You've seen this entertainment through and through. You've seen your birth your life and death. You might recall all the rest. Did you have a good world when you died? Enough to base a movie on. I'm getting out of here! Where are you going? To the other side of morning. Curses. Invocations.*

Weird bate-headed monsters. I keep expecting one of you to rise. We welcome you to our procession. All hail the American night! What was that? I don't know! But I tell you this man! I don't know what's going to happen. But I'm gonna have my kicks before the whole shithouse goes up in flames! Keep your eyes on the road your hands upon the wheel! We're going to the roadhouse! Gonna have a real good time! The back of the roadhouse they got some bungalows! They dance for the people who like to go down slow. You gotta thrill my soul! You got to beep-a-gunk-a-chuca-honk-konk-konk-kadanta-each-ya-puna-ney-cha-bap-lula-chao-pao-pati-cha-ni-saong-kong! Ashen lady! Give up your vows! Save our city! Right now! The futures uncertain and the end is always near! The world on fire. A big party last night. Back! Back! Going back in all directions! Thoughts in time and out of season. The hitchhiker stood at the side of the road. "Hi. How you doing? I just got back into town. I was out in the desert for a while." Riders on the storm. Into this house were born. Into this world we're thrown. Like a dog without a bone. An actor out on loan. Girl you gotta love your man. Take him by the hand. Make him understand. The world on you depends, our life will never end. There's a killer on the road. If you give this man a ride, sweet family will die. Do you know the warm progress under the stars? Do you know we exist? Have you forgotten the keys to the kingdom? Have you been born yet and are you alive? Let's reinvent the Gods. All the myths of the ages. Celebrate symbols from deep elder forests. Have you forgotten the lessons of the ancient war? We need great golden copulations! Do you know we are being led to slaughter? And that fat slow generals are getting obscene on young blood? Do you know we are ruled by TV? The moon is a dry blood beast. We live, we die, and death not ends it. Journey we more into the nightmare. Where are the feasts we were promised? Where is the wine? The new wine. Dying on the vine. We're perched headlong on the edge of boredom. We're reaching for death on the end of a candle. We're trying for something that's already found us. I seek to know you acquiring

soulful wisdom. You can open walls of mystery. Strip shows. How to acquire death in the morning show. TV death which the child absorbs. Death well mystery which makes me write. Forgive the poor old people who gave us entry. Taught us God in the child's prayer in the night. Ancient wise satyr sing. Stiffen and guide us lost cells. The knowledge of cancer. To speak to the heart and give the gift. Words, power, trance. I'm sick of doubt. Live in the light of certain south cruel bindings. The servants have the power. I'm sick of faces staring at me from the TV tower. I want roses in my garden. Royal babies. They are waiting to take us into the severed garden. Do you know how pale and wanton thrillful comes death in a strange hour? Death makes angels of us all and gives us wings where we had shoulders smooth as raven's claws. No more money. No more dress. This other kingdom seems by far the best. Until its other jaw reveals incest and loose obedience to a vegetable law. I will not go! I prefer a Feast of Friends to the Giant Family!

More favorite lyrics on his other albums. FIVE TO ONE ***Five to one baby! One in five! No one here gets out alive! The old get old and the young get stronger! May take a week and it may take longer! They got the guns, but we got the numbers! Gonna win yeah, we're taking over! Come on!*** LIGHT MY FIRE ***You know that it would be untrue. You know that I would be a liar. If I was to say to you. Girl we couldn't get much higher. The time to hesitate is through. No time to wallow in the mire. Try now we can only lose. And our love becomes a funeral pyre. Come on baby light my fire! Try to set the night on fire!*** LOVE HIDES ***Love hides in the strangest places. Love hides in familiar faces. Love comes when you least expect it. Love hides in narrow corners. Love comes to those who seek it. Love hides inside the rainbow. Love hides in molecular structure. Love is the answer.*** YOU'RE LOST LITTLE GIRL ***You're lost little girl. You're lost. Tell me who you are. I think that you know what to do. Impossible. Yes, but it's true. You're lost little girl.*** QUEEN OF THE HIGHWAY ***She was a princess. Queen of the highway. No one could save her. Save the blind tiger.***

WILD CHILD ***Wild child full of grace. Savior of the human race. Natural child. Terrible child. Not your mother's or your father's child. An ancient lunatic. With hunger at her heels. Freedom in her eyes. She dances on her knees, prince by her side, staring into the hollow idol's eyes.*** THE SPY ***I'm a spy in the House of Love. I know the dream that you're dreamin of. I know the word that you long to hear. I know your deepest secret fear! I know everything! Everything you do. Everywhere you go. Everyone you know. I'm a spy in the House of Love! I can see what you do. And I know.*** MOONLIGHT DRIVE ***Let's swim to the moon. Let's climb through the tide. Penetrate the evening that the city sleeps to hide. Let's swim out tonight, Love. It's our turn to try. Surrender to the waiting worlds that lap against our side. Nothing left open and no time to decide. We've stepped into a river on our moonlight drive. You reach your hand to hold me, but I can't be your guide. Falling through wet forests on our moonlight drive.*** TOUCH ME ***Come on and touch me girl. Can't you see that I am not afraid? What was that promise that you made? I'm going to love you, til the heavens stop the rains. I'm going to love you, til the stars fall from the sky for you and I.*** NOT TO TOUCH THE EARTH ***Not to touch the Earth. Not to see the sun. Nothing left to do but run, run, run. Let's run. House upon the hill. Moon is lying still. Come on baby run with me. The mansion is warm at the top of the hill. Rich are the rooms and the comforts there and you won't know a thing til you get inside. Come along were not going very far to the east to meet the Czar. Run with me. Let's run. Some outlaws lived by the side of a lake. The minister's daughters in love with a snake who lives in a well by the side of the road. Wake up girl! We're almost home! We should see the gates by morning. We should be inside by the evening.*** CRAWLING KING SNAKE ***Well I'm the crawling king snake and I rule my den. Don't mess around with my mate! Gonna use her for myself! You better give me what I want! Gonna crawl no more. Caught me crawlin round your door. Seein everything I want. I'm gonna crawl on your floor! Let's***

crawl! I have crawled awhile! Come on crawl! Get on out there on your hands and knees and crawl all over me! BEEN DOWN SO LONG ***Well I've been down so goddam long that it looks like up to me! I said Warden! Warden! Warden! Won't you break your lock and key! Why don't one you people come on and set me free***! CRYSTAL SHIP ***Before you slip into unconsciousness, I'd like to have another kiss. Another flashing chance at bliss. Enclose me in your gentle rain. The time you ran was too insane. We'll meet again. Tell me where your freedom lies. The streets are fields that never die. I'd rather fly. The crystal ship is being filled. A thousand girls. A thousand thrills. A million ways to spend your time. When we get back, I'll drop a line***. BREAK ON THROUGH ***You know the day destroys the night! Night divides the day! Tried to run! Tried to hide! Break on through to the other side! We chased our pleasures here! Dug our treasures there! But can't you still recall the time we tried. Break on through to the other side! I found an island in your arms! Country in your eyes! Arms that chain! Eyes that lie! Break on through to the other side! Made the scene! The gate is straight! Deep and wide! Break on through to the other side!*** WHEN THE MUSIC'S OVER ***When the music's over! Turn out the lights! For the music is your special friend! Dance on fire as it intends! Music is your only friend! Until the end. Cancel my subscription to the Resurrection! Send my credentials to the house of detention! I got some friends inside. The face in the mirror won't stop! The girl in the window won't drop! A feast of friends. "Alive!" she cried. Waiting for me, outside! Before I sink into the big sleep, I want to hear the scream, of the butterfly. We're gettin tired of hanging around. Waiting around with our heads to the ground. I hear a very gentle sound. Very near yet very far. Very soft yet very clear. Come today! What have they done to the Earth!? What have they done to our fair sister!? Ravaged and plundered and ripped her and bit her! Stuck her with knives in the side of the dawn and tied her with fences and dragged her down! I hear a very gentle sound, with your ear down to the ground. We want the world***

and we want it NOW! See the light babe! THIS IS THE END ***This is the end. Beautiful friend. My only friend the end. Of our elaborate plans. The end. I'll never look into your eyes again. Can you picture what will be? So limitless and free. Lost in a Roman wilderness of pain and all the children are insane. There's danger on the edge of town. Ride the Kings Highway. Ride the highway west baby. Ride the snake to the lake. The ancient lake. The snake he's long. Seven miles. He's old and his skin is cold. The west is the best. Get here and we'll do the rest! The blue bus is calling us. The killer awoke before dawn. He put his boots on. He took a face from the ancient gallery, and he walked on down the hall. Come on baby take a chance with us! Beautiful friend. It hurts to set you free, but you'll never follow me. The end of nights we tried to die. This is the end!***

My favorite song from JIMMY HENDRIX was All Along the Watchtower. ***There must be some kind of way out of this, said the joker to the thief. There's too much confusion. I can't get no relief! No reason to get excited, the thief he kindly spoke. There are many here among us who feel that life is but a joke. But you and I we've been through that, and this is not our fate. So let us stop talking falsely now. The hours getting late! All along the watchtower Princes kept the view. While all the women came and went. Barefoot servants too. Outside in the cold distance a wildcat did growl. Two riders were approaching. And the wind began to howl!***

I had a giant rainbow fiber optic light that turned in circles and changed colors. We set giant mirrors up to reflect the light in the entire living room while we listened to music. I had a great time.

Steve told me he took some acid called Stars when he was young and went to play racquet ball but was tripping too much. Him and his friends went to his house, listening to Bowie, Led Zeppelin, and The Doors. He told them to give him a pen and paper so he could write down the meaning of life. By the time someone got it for him, he had forgotten it. Every time he went to write it down, he forgot and not one word was ever written. When the song Break on Through by The Doors came on, he ran out his bedroom, down the hallway, and out the front door. He did a strange flip in the air and landed on his back. He thought he was breaking through something. His friends got him inside and calmed him down, but he was still tripping. That scared them, so everyone left but his best friend. Steve said when he peered out of his garage, he'd see lots of police coming around the corner with flashing lights, so he'd yell, "Love! Love! Love! Time! Time! Time!" and they'd go in reverse and disappear. That repeated itself for hours until he came down. In those moments, he truly believed that he was controlling the reversing of time.

A guy who knew me before I was a dancer came into Dejavu and recognized me. We had a drink and a couple dances, and he was looking for some coke. I told him I could get some because one of Steve's neighbors was a coke dealer. He came over, bought some, and asked if he could shoot up. Steve said it was ok, so he did. It knocked him out on the floor, and I got so scared I thought he died! We got him to wake up and he said, "Wow! That is some really pure coke!" When he left, I told Steve, "Never again! I do not want anyone to ever shoot up in my house again!" Me and Steve discussed shooting up and I didn`t want to and told Steve I didn`t want him to either, so we didn`t.

I had a regular customer at work who bought me a bottle of Dom Perignon and gave me $100 to rub my shoes in his crotch for about three minutes. He had a very strange foot fetish. When he was done, he gave me another $50 to buy my shoes and take them. I liked when he visited because he was fast easy money. One night, he came over to my apartment and Steve hid in the closet for security. The guy paid me $200 dollars to rub my shoes in his crotch fully clothed for less than half an hour then bought my shoes as usual. That was easy money, but it was too weird for me, and even weirder for Steve, so I didn't do it again.

The owner of Dejavu was very handsome with long black hair but was very scary like mafia. We didn`t associate with each other and I stayed away from him. The manager, his cousin David, on the other hand was always asking me to go out but I always refused. I didn't know why. He was nice-looking but there was just something about him I didn't like. Not sure what it was. One day before the bar opened, he came to the dressing room and told me he wanted to show me the work he did in the men's restroom. I thought that was strange and was quite leery of him. I decided it would be safe because other people were in the bar. I followed him slowly and cautiously into the restroom. He showed me the work he did. To my relief and surprise, he didn`t try anything. He was just proud of his new sink and tile work.

I began to find Steve attractive the more I saw him running around in his boxer shorts. But I didn`t know how to go about telling him I was interested in him. He left one day to fly to Ohio to visit family and I wrote a note telling him I wanted to have a real serious relationship with him. I put the letter in an envelope and laid it on the coffee table. He wasn`t supposed to be back for several days so I had time to think about it. I went to work and when I got home Steve had missed his flight and read my letter. Oh no! Oh shit! He told me he read it and said he was very sorry but he wasn`t ready for a serious relationship right now. Well, I guess I just had to accept that and move on. Steve went to Ohio the next day, and I found a cute guy and brought him over and had sex with him in Steve's bed. After he got back, I told him I had a guy over for the night and hoped he didn`t mind. He said it was ok and we went on living together as friends.

I was dancing on a side stage and a beautiful young dancer with long dark straight hair, dark brown eyes, and a gorgeous body, reached out and grabbed my boob! I was quite confused and asked her why she did that? She replied, "My husband is away in the military, and I'm not allowed to have sex with other men. Only women. I want to know if you want to have sex with me?"

I told her, "No way!" Yuck! I never had a woman come on to me before and it shocked me. I thought women were beautiful but didn't want to have sex with them. When I got home, I told Steve what happened. He half-jokingly suggested I bring her home to have fun. I also told him NO! After all, I still wanted a serious relationship with Steve.

On May 1st, I was napping and had the strangest dream. A spaceship came down and engulfed the apartment. Aliens were examining my brain and heart. I heard one of them say, "Her brain is ok, but something is blocking her heart." Another alien said, "Well what is it?" One replied, "It's Jesus." Then the other alien said, "Well get it out of there." Just then one of my eyes opened and started looking around in real life but I guess I was still in my dream but didn't know it. I saw three half-human, half-alien figures around me. Everything was white, and I was laying on a steel table. They started yelling at me and interrogating me asking if I was a spy. We telepathically talked, and I kept telling them I wasn't a spy. I could see I was in a spaceship that had a large window I saw out. I saw several other spaceships having a war in space. Then an alien took this long, skinny, silver devise and looked deep down into my eye, and said, "Nope, no spy in there." Then I immediately woke up and it felt so real that I was frightened! I started looking around and touching the furniture to make sure I was in my apartment!

This next month would be the strangest one I ever had in my entire life. This guy came into the bar one afternoon and he glowed like an angel. Light just seemed to beam from him. He had pure bright white curls and rosy red cheeks with a beautiful pearly white smile. With the way my life had been in the past I just tried to ignore him. When I walked by, he reached out and grabbed my arm and said very politely, "Will you have a drink with me?" So, we were sitting there with our drinks not saying anything to each other. Then he very calmly said, "God has a message for you." Then he smiled very big showing me his pearly whites. I was taken back by what he said and waited to hear what the message was, but he said nothing. I was confused. Why did he not tell me? I was so enthralled at what he would say that I couldn`t even hear the music. If he hadn`t looked like an angel from heaven I would have paid no attention to him. The bar music went like this: BLINDED BY THE LIGHT/MANFRED MAN ***Blinded by the light! Another runner in the night! She was blinded by the light! With a boulder on my shoulder feelin kinda older I tripped the merry-go-round. Little early pearly came by in his curly-wurly and asked me if I needed a ride!*** S.O.S./ POLICE ***I`ll send an S.O.S. to the world. I hope that someone gets my message in the bottle!*** VAN HALEN/DIVER DOWN/ SECRETS ***She ain`t waitin til she gets older. Her feet are making tracks in the winter snow. She`s got a rainbow that touches her shoulder. She`ll be headed where the thunder rolls. She comes like a secret wind. She`s as strong as the mountains and walks tall as a tree. She`s been there before. She`ll never give in! She`ll be gone tomorrow, like the silent breeze. You`re running blind. Question is, not does Love exist? But when she leaves, where she goes? I got a feeling she don`t know either. Wait like the wind. Watch where she goes.*** BECAUSE THE NIGHT/PATTI SMITH ***Take me now baby here as I am. Hold me close try to understand. Desire is hunger is the fire I breathe. Love is a banquet on which we feed. Come on now try to understand. The way I feel under your command. Take my hand as the sun descends. They can`t hurt you now! Have I doubt baby when I`m alone? Love is a ring on the telephone. Love is an angel disguised as Lust, here in our bed til the morning comes. With Love we sleep. With doubt the vicious circle turns. Without you I cannot live! I believe in love too real to feel. Because the night, belongs to lovers! Because the night, belongs to Lust! Because the night, belongs to Love!***

I was still waiting for the message, but he said nothing. He just kept smiling at me. I finally asked what the message was, but he wouldn't tell me. Alright, I was done with this nonsense and was a little annoyed that he said nothing! I finished my drink, and I didn't dance for him. I told him bye and walked away then he left. I thought maybe he was just crazy or trying to pull my chain. Later that day the same music played again. When I heard it say **Love has a rainbow that touches her shoulder** I was like, wow! That`s weird! I have a rainbow tatoo that touches my shoulder. I went and asked the DJ what song that was, and he said SECRETS by VAN HALEN off the DIVER DOWN album. Then I heard another song that said, **Love is an angel disguised as lust**, and I thought, oh shit! I'm using the name Princess Lusty. Could I possibly be Love? It all seemed very personal to me, and I started contemplating if maybe I was Love. When I got home that night, I told Steve about the incident and he replied, "Hmm sounds interesting."

Not long after that the bar got scary to me. Something strange was happening. The atmosphere in the bar got different and I didn`t like it but I wasn't sure what was going on. I could feel it coming in the air. The music was scary. It went like this. Black Sabbath/Black Sabbath ***What is this that stands before me! Figure in black that points at me! Turn around quick and start to run! Find out I'm the chosen one! Big black shape with eyes of fire! Telling people their desire! Satan's sitting there he's smiling! Watches those flames get higher and higher! Is it the end my friend?! Satan's coming round the bend! People running cause they're scared!*** RUNNIN WITH THE DEVIL/VAN HALEN ***I live my life like there`s no tomorrow and all I`ve got I had to steal! Runnin with the Devil! I got no love. No love you`d call real.*** N.I.B./OZZY OSBOURNE ***Some people say my love cannot be true. Please believe me, my love, and I will show you. I will give you those things you thought were unreal. The sun, the moon, the stars all bear my seal. Follow me now and you will not regret, leaving the life you led before we met. You are the first to have this love of mine, forever with me til the end of time. Your love for me has just got to be real. Now I have you under my power! Our love***

grows stronger now with every hour! Look into my eyes you`ll see who I am! My name is Lucifer! Please take my hand! SHOUT AT THE DEVIL/MOTLEY CRUE ***Shout at the Devil! He's the wolf screaming lonely in the night! He's a blood stain on the stage! He's the tear in your eye! Been tempted by his lie! He'll put your strength to the test and put the thrill back in death! Sure you've heard it all before! Be strong and laugh and shout at the devil!*** FLESH/BILLY IDOL FLESH! ***We want flesh! Flesh for fantasy! Face to face and, back to back, you see and feel my sex attack. We want flesh! Flesh for fantasy! It`s after midnight are you feelin alright? Turn on the light. Are you someone else tonight? Don`t ask questions there`s time for it all.*** HIGHWAY TO HELL/AC/DC ***Going down, party time, and my friends are gonna be there too! I`m on the highway to Hell! No stop signs! Speed limits! Nobody`s gonna slow me down! Like a wheel gonna spin it! Hey Satan! Paid my dues! I`m on my way to the promised land! Don`t stop me! I`m goin down all the way!*** PAINT IT BLACK/ROLLING STONES ***I see a red door and I want it painted black! No colors anymore I want them to turn black! I see a line of cars and they`ll all be painted black. With flowers and my Love both never to come back. I see people turn their heads and quickly look away. I look inside myself and see my heart is black. I see my red door. I must have it painted black! Maybe then I`ll fade away and not have to face the facts. It`s not easy facing up when your whole world is black. I could not foresee this thing happening to you. If I look hard enough into the settin sun, my Love will laugh with me before the morning comes. I want to see it black! Black as night! Black as coal! Paint it black! No colors anymore!*** I'VE SEEN ALL GOOD PEOPLE/ YES ***I've seen all good people turn their heads each day so satisfied I'm on my way! Make the White Queen run so fast she hasn't got time to make you a wife. Move me on any black square. Use me anytime you want. Don't surround yourself with yourself.*** PSYCHO KILLER/TALKING HEADS ***Can't seem to face up to the facts! I`m tense and nervous and I can't relax! I can't sleep cause my beds***

on fire! Don't touch me I'm a real live wire! Psycho killer! Better run, run, run! Run away! You start a conversation you can't even finish it! You're talking a lot but you're not saying anything. When I have nothing to say my lips are sealed. Say something once why say it again! You better run! Run! Run! Run away! RUN THROUGH THE JUNGLE/CCR ***I thought it was a nightmare! Lord it was so true! They told me don't go walkin slow. The Devil's on the loose! Better run through the jungle and don't look back! Two hundred million guns are loaded Satan cries, "Take aim!" Better run through the jungle! Over the mountain thunder magic spoke, "Let the people know my wisdom! Fill the land with smoke!"*** BURNING DOWN THE HOUSE/TALKING HEADS ***Watch out! You might get what you're after! Strange but not a stranger! I'm an ordinary guy burning down the house. Hold tight! Wait til the parties over! Hold tight! Were in for nasty weather! Here`s your ticket, pack your bag. Time for jumpin overboard. The transportation is here. Close enough but not so far, maybe you know where you are. Fighting fire with fire! Shakedown! Dreams walking in broad daylight! I'm Gonna come in first place! Gonna burst into flames! I don`t know what you're expecting staring into the TV set? I ain`t got nothing to say.*** DANCING IN THE DARK/BRUCE SPRINGSTEEN ***You can`t start a fire without a spark even if were just dancing in the dark. Messages keeps getting clearer. Radios on and I`m movin round this place. I check my look in the mirror. Want to change my clothes my hair my face! I ain`t gettin nowhere! There`s something happening somewhere. I just know it. You sit around getting older. There`s a joke here somewhere and it`s on me. I`ll shake the world off my shoulders. Stay on the streets of this town and they`ll be carving you up alright. I`m sick of sitting round here trying to write this book! I need a love reaction! You can`t start a fire sitting around crying over a broken heart or worrying about your little world falling apart.*** ROCK ON/DEF LEOPARD ***All right! I've got something to say! It`s better to burn out than to fade away! Gonna***

start a fire! Come on! Rise up gather round! Rock this place to the ground! Burn it up let's go for broke! Watch the night go up in smoke! No serenade! No fire brigade! Just a pyromaniac! What do you want?! Long live rock-n-roll! Ok let's go! Let`s strike a light! Gonna blow like dynamite! I don`t care if it takes all night gonna set this town alight! We got the power! We got the glory! Just say you need it and if you need it say yea! Were gonna burn this damn place down to the ground! Hahahaha! I'LL WAIT/VAN HALEN *You've got me captured. I'm under your spell. I have your picture, yes I know it well. Another page is turned. Are you for real? It`s so hard to tell, from just a magazine. You just smile and the picture sells. Look what that does to me. I`ll wait til your love comes down! I`m comin straight for your heart! No way you can stop me now! As fine as you are! I wrote a letter and told her these words. I never sent it she wouldn`t have heard. Her eyes don`t follow me. You can`t imagine what your image means. The pages come alive. Your magic greets everyone who reads. Are you for real? It`s so hard to tell. I`ll wait til your love comes down! I`m coming straight for your heart! No way you can stop me now!* IN THE AIR TONIGHT/PHIL COLLINS *I can feel it coming in the air tonight. Oh Lord. I`ve been waiting for this moment all my life! Well, if you told me you were drowning, I would not lend a hand. I`ve seen your face before my friend. I don`t know if you know who I am. I was there! I saw what you did! I saw it with my own two eyes! Wipe off that grin! I know where you`ve been! And it`s all been a pack of lies!* WAR PIGS/BLACK SABBATH *Generals gathered in their masses! Just like witches at black masses! Evil minds that plot destruction! Sorcerer of deaths construction! In the fields the bodies burning! As the war machine keeps turning! Death and hatred to mankind! Poisoning their brainwashed minds! Oh Lord yeah! Treating people just like pawns in chess! Wait til their judgement day comes! Now in darkness world stops turning! Ashes where the bodies burning! No more war pigs have the power! Hand of God has struck the hour! Day of judgement God is calling! On their knees the war* *pigs crawling! Begging mercies for their sins! Satan laughing spreads his wings!* FOR THOSE ABOUT TO ROCK/AC/DC *Stand up and be counted for what you are about to receive! We are the dealers! We`ll give you everything you need. For those about to rock we salute you! Heads will roll tonight! We`re just a guitar fire ready and aimed at you for a twenty-one-gun salute! For those about to rock! Fire!* HELLS BELLS *I'm a rolling thunder! A pouring rain! I'm comin on like a hurricane! My lightning flashes across the sky! You're only young but your gonna die! I won't take no prisoners! Won't spare no lives! Nobody's putting up a fight! I'm gonna take you to Hell! I'm gonna get you! Satan get you! See my white light flashing as I split the night! Cause if Gods on the left I'm stickin to the right! You got me ringing Hells Bells! Satan's comin to you! He's ringing them now! They're takin you down and dragging you around! He's gonna split the night!* FOR WHOM THE BELL TOLLS/METALLICA *For whom the bell tolls! Take a look to the sky, just before you die! It's the last time you will! For whom the bell tolls!* ROLLING STONES *Please allow me to introduce myself. I`m a man of wealth and taste. I`ve been around for a long long time. Stole many a man's soul to waste! I was there when Jesus Christ had his moment of doubt and pain. Made damn sure that Pilate washed his hands and sealed his fate. Pleased to meet you! Hope you guessed my name! But what`s puzzling you is the nature of my game? I stuck around when I saw it was a time for change. Killed the czar and his ministers. Anastasia screamed in vain! I rode a tank! Held a general's rank and the bodies stank! Pleased to meet you! Hope you guess my name! I watched with glee while your kings and queens fought for ten decades for the Gods they made! Let me please introduce myself! Hope you guessed my name! But what`s confusing you is the nature of my game? Just call me Lucifer, cause I`m in need of some restraint! So, if you meet me have some courtesy, Some sympathy, and some taste! Use all your well-learned politesse or I`ll lay your soul to waste! Tell me baby! What`s my name? Can you guess my name? I tell you one time!*

You`re to blame! Tell me sweetie! What`s my name? Come on little sister! What's my name!

So, I was at the pool table and just finished a game when a dancer named Yellow Rose was dancing on one of the new stages. It was a 10 foot long running stage and was only 18 inches wide. It was very dangerous and had a bar across the ceiling to hold on to. I didn`t know her well and she was always snooty to me. She had been telling everyone talent scouts were coming in to see her perform and she was going to become a famous dancer. I thought she was crazy because she really couldn`t dance and she had a pig face, but she had blonde hair almost like mine and the same height and body build as me. Her favorite song to play was THE DEVIL WENT DOWN TO GEORGIA by THE CHARLIE DANIELS BAND. ***The Devil went down to Georgia. He was looking for a soul to steal! He was in a bind cause he was way behind and willing to make a deal!*** I hated dancing to that song when we were both on stage because it was a very long country song, and I didn't care for country music.

Just then this song came on. THE REAPER/BLUE OYSTER CULT ***All our times have come. Here but now they`re gone. Seasons don`t fear the reaper. Nor do the wind, the sun, or the rain. We can be like they are. Come on baby. Don`t fear the reaper. Lalalalalalalala. Take my hand. We`ll be able to fly. Love of two is one. Here but now they`re gone. Then the door was open, and the wind appeared. The candles blew then disappeared. The curtains flew then he appeared saying don`t be afraid! And she had no fear, and she ran to him. Then they started to fly. They looked backward and said goodbye. She had become like they are.***

This is hard to believe but as the song was playing a strange dark mass of energy slowly entered the bar. It appeared as the grim reaper in his dark cloak and was three feet off the ground. He slowly floated past me to where the drinks were served and stayed there looking around holding his sickle. I was like, whoa, what the fuck is that! I backed up against the wall to become a wallflower. I was thinking, this couldn't be real. I looked around to see if anyone else saw it, but I guess not. I just watched to see what was going to happen. Then suddenly, a giant bright red Devil or Demon appeared on stage with Yellow Rose. He had horns on his head and was carrying chains. He put the chains around her neck and wrists. Then began beating her with a whip while holding the chains and it was all playing out on the stage. He just kept beating her over and over! It looked as if she was laughing sardonically. I was so freaking scared and confused. No one else saw what I was seeing! Then the Grim reaper slowly floated on out of the bar and the Devil disappeared as these songs played. ANOTHER ONE BITES THE DUST/ QUEEN ***Machine guns ready to go! Are you ready? Hey, are you ready for this!? Are you hanging on the edge of your seat? Out of the doorway the bullets rip to the sound of the beat! Another one bites the dust! I'm gonna get you too! Another on bites the dust!*** DON'T COME AROUND HERE NO MORE/TOM PETTY ***Don't come around here no more. Whatever you're looking for. Don't come around here no more. I've given up on waiting any longer. On this love getting stronger. You darken my door. Whatever you're looking for. Stop walking down my street. Who do you expect to meet? Whatever you're looking for! Don't come around here no more!***

I was confused and scared and wasn't even sure if it was all real. I didn`t know what to do. I needed to warn Yellow Rose! I went to the stage she was dancing on and told her, "Look. I know you don`t know me very well but whatever it is that you're into, you need to get out of it right now because it`s going to kill you!" She just laughed at me and went on dancing. I didn't know what more to do after that. She thought it was funny. I went on with my day as if nothing had happened. Sadly, she'd be dead within 24 hours. ***If that chick don't want to know then forget her!*** THE BOYS ARE BACK IN TOWN/THIN LIZZY.

The song playing now was by LED ZEPPELIN. ***Been dazed***

and confused for so long it's not true! Wanted a woman never bargained for you! Lots of people talk but few of them know! The soul of a woman was created below! Lord how they hypnotize! Here I come again! Try to love you baby but you push me away! Don't know where you're goin. Only know where you've been.

When I got home that night, I told Steve what I saw and told him I was scared. He just thought I was weird and didn't take me seriously. I cleaned my room and made everything perfect in case the Grim reaper was coming for me since I saw him. I know that sounds silly but if I was going to die, I wanted my bedroom to be immaculate. The whole ordeal had me shaking inside. It seemed to me Dejavu was a place where spirits and angels or deities came to meet each other for some strange reason.

The next day I went to work my girlfriends asked me, "Did you hear what happened to Yellow Rose!?" I replied, "NO! What happened?" as the fear in me grew. One replied, "Her boyfriend beat her to death last night!" I think I went into shock. Did I really see that? Could that have all really been real? What a wild coincidence! I kept myself composed, but when I got home, I told Steve what happened to Yellow Rose and broke down crying. If only I had done more. But I couldn`t tell anyone at work what I saw. They might have thought I was crazy. Me and Steve didn`t talk anymore about it but we both thought it was pretty weird.

I went to work again, and everything seemed normal but then the music started playing angel songs. SEND ME AN ANGEL by REAL LIFE. ***Do you believe in Heaven above? Do you believe in Love? Don`t tell a lie. Don`t be false or untrue. It all comes back to you. Open fire. Looking for Love calling Heaven above. Send me angel. Right now! But don`t give up. Don`t give up. Send me an angel right now! I`m here.***

Ok, so now I started looking around for the guy who was here before that looked like an angel. And there he was. I thought how funny it was and a strange coincidence for him to show up as the music played angel songs. I was curious as to what he may say. I went over to his table, and he bought me a drink. We didn`t say anything to each other. He just smiled and stared at me with his big beaming presence. He was very handsome and had cherub cheeks but seemed too old for me even though he had not one wrinkle. After some awkward silence he said, "God has a message for you." I replied, "Ok. What is it?" He said nothing more. Just silence. I was waiting for him to speak, but nothing. The music playing went like this. AMERICAN PIE/DON MCLEAN ***A long, long, time ago, I can still remember how that music used to make me smile. I knew if I had my chance, I could make those people dance, and maybe they`d be happy for a while. Did you write The Book of Love? And do you have faith in God above? If the bible tells you so? Do you believe in rock-n-roll? Can music save your mortal soul? And there we were, all in one place. A generation, lost in space. With no time left to start again. As I watched him on the stage, my hands were clenched in fists of rage! No angel born in hell, can break that Satan's spell! And as the flames climbed high into the night, to light the sacrificial rite. I saw Satan laughing with delight. The day, the music died.*** ROCK AND ROLL/LED ZEPPELIN ***It`s been a long time since I rock and rolled! It`s been a long time since The Book of Love! Let me get back baby where I come from!***

Suddenly, I heard a loud voice say, "YOU WILL WRITE THE BOOK OF LOVE!" I was like, what the fuck was that? Who the fuck said that? Did anyone else hear that loud voice? It didn`t come out of the angel's mouth and it wasn't in the music. I wondered, what was THE BOOK OF LOVE and what it had to do with me. Now the bar music playing was SISTER CHRISTIAN/NIGHT RANGER. ***Sister Christian oh the time has come. And you know that you're the only one to say, ok. Where, you going? What you looking for? You know those boys don`t want to play no more with you. What`s your price for flight? In finding mister right? Babe you know your growing up so fast. There`s so much in life, don`t you give it up until your time is due.***

But you're motoring. WHITE WEDDING/BILLY IDOL ***Hey little sister, what have you done? Hey little sister, who`s the only one? Hey little sister, who`s your superman? Hey little sister, who`s the one you want? Hey little sister. Shotgun! It`s a nice day for a white wedding! I`ve been away for so long. I let you go for so long. It`s a nice day for a white wedding! It's a nice day to start again!***

Ok I`d had enough of that nonsense and asked if he'd like a table dance and he replied, "Of course!" I danced and the song that played was VOICES by RAINBOW. ***I heard the sound of voices in the night. Spellbound, there was something calling. I looked around and no one is in sight. Pulled down. I just kept on falling. I`ve seen this place before. You were standing by my side. I`ve seen your face before. I know it`s a mystery. Do you remember me on the street of dreams? I knew you`d set me free. And here we are right back where we started. Maybe this fantasy is real. But it`s still a mystery! Do you remember me on the street of dreams? Running through my memory on the street of dreams You are on every face I see. Will we ever meet again? Do you know what it meant to be on the street of dreams? Never know just who you`ll see, do ya? On the street of dreams, you can be who you want to be. I can hear you calling me. I can feel you haunting me.***

The song was over, he tipped me, I put my clothes on and told him bye and he left. I didn't know what to think about that encounter and swept it under the rug and went on with my day.

Later that day I was dancing for another customer, and he said, "Look! You have the big dipper across your entire belly." I looked and sure enough there was a dipper in seven moles, and it spanned my entire belly. There were no other moles on my stomach except for 3 small ones that were positioned weird in the dipper. I thought, cool, but no big deal, and went on dancing and forgot about it.

When I got home that night Steve wasn't there. I turned the TV on, and a guy came on channel 13. He was called the star hustler and his name was Jack Horkheimer. It started like this:

Some people hustle pool. Some people hustle cars. But have you ever heard about the man who hustles stars? Jack Horkheimer the star hustler! Then he said, "Everyone knows about the big dipper and the little dipper, but very few know about the littlest dipper of them all." Ok so now he had my undivided attention! He said, "Pleiades is the smallest dipper with seven stars." Then he said something about it being made for The Goddess of Love and it had something to do with the seven sisters. Then something about Atlas. I looked down at the moles on my belly. All the moles were in the same position as the constellation Pleiades. Even the other three moles were in the same position on the TV as on my belly! Wow! My moles matched exactly! What a coincidence! Then he said, "If you have these marks somewhere on your body, then you are someone very special, and always remember to keep looking up!" Then I was like, what the fuck! Oh my God! I must be going crazy! The TV just talked to me! What was that all about? This was very weird! Am I tripping? This couldn`t be real! When Steve got home, I told him what happened but didn`t think he believed me. I showed him Pleiades on my belly, and he replied, "So. Ok you have a dipper on your belly. It's cool but no big deal." He thought I might be tripping, or made it all up and I told him, "Jack Horkheimer is real and he really said that!" I tried to find Jack again on the TV but couldn't. So, I couldn`t prove to Steve he was real. I also told Steve that a loud voice at work told me I would write The Book of Love someday. I was quite confused about why all this was happening to me, but I went on as if all was normal.

Steve was looking hot in his basketball shorts. I also noticed he had a cute white triangle in his beard and in a weird way him and my cat were a match. I wanted to have sex with him, but didn`t know how to approach him. I knew he didn`t want to have a serious relationship but I hadn`t dated anyone after the night he turned me down and I was wanting some sex. 6 foot 2, Great body, long dark curls, and dark brown eyes. Yummy! I`m hungry for sex. He was hot. I think I was falling for him. I told him about Ecstasy and said it was supposed to enhance sex and asked him if he wanted to try it with me. We took it in the evening, and he got his Pink Floyd (who I really didn`t know much about) albums out and I had the giant rainbow light illuminating the entire living room. When he put on the song WELCOME TO THE MACHINE I got really scared because the walls in the room started moving and I had to hold on to them so I wouldn't fall! It felt like I was in a spaceship that was taking off. Steve started laughing at me.

The music went like this: ***Welcome my son. Welcome to the machine. Where have you been? It's alright we know where you've been! You've been in the pipeline filling in time. Provided with toys and scouting for boys. What did you dream? It's alright we told you what to dream***!

When I got myself together, he was still laughing at me about how scared I got. I had no idea Ecstasy was hallucinogenic. I really thought it was just a drug that made you feel good. But I was ok, and thought it was funny too and the room was normal again. We got on the couch and started making out and were just getting ready to have sex when I started screaming as loud as I could, "No! No! I`m not ready! I`m not ready! Stop!" He stopped and calmed me down and said, "You`re ok. You're just tripping." Then he laughed at me again because he thought it was funny that I was so scared. I told him he turned into this big half human, half animal creature, with big horns and it really scared me! Kind of like the creature Pan. Then everything was normal again and we went on and had some trippy sex while listening to music.

Pink Floyd was mostly calm trippy music. Here's some lyrics. HEY YOU ***Hey you, don't help them to bury the light. Don't give in, without a fight! Hey you, would you help them to carry the stone? Open your heart. I'm comin home. Don't tell me there's no hope at all. Together we stand! Divided we fall!*** COMFORTABLY NUMB ***Hello. Hello. Hello. Is there anybody in there? Just nod***

if you can hear me. Is there anyone at home? Relax. I need some information first. Just the basic facts. Can you show me where it hurts? There is no pain you are receding. A distant ship smoke on the horizon. You are only coming through in waves. Your lips move but I can't hear what they're saying. When I was a child, my hands felt just like two balloons. Now I've got that feeling once again. I can't explain. You would not understand. This is not how I am. When I was a child, I caught a fleeting glimpse, out of the corner of my eye. I turned to look but it was gone. I cannot put my finger on it now. The child has grown. The dream is gone. BREATHE ***Breathe in the air. Don't be afraid to care. Choose your own ground. For long you live and high you fly but only if you ride the tide and balanced on the biggest wave.*** SHINE ON YOU CRAZY DIAMOND ***Remember when you were young. You shone like the son. Now there's a look in your eyes like black holes in the sky. Shine on you crazy diamond. You were caught in the crossfire. Come on you stranger! You legend! You martyr! And SHINE! You reached for the secret to soon. You cried for the moon. Threatened by shadows at night and exposed in the light. Come on you raver! You seer of visions! Come on you painter! You piper! You prisoner! And SHINE!*** SHEEP ***Hopelessly passing your time in the grassland away. Only dimly aware of a certain unease in the air. You better watch out! There may be dogs about! I've looked over Jordan and I have seen things are not what they seem. What do you get for pretending the dangers not real! Meek and obedient you follow the leader down well-trodden corridors into the valley of steel. What a surprise! The look of terminal shock in your eyes! Now things are really what they seem! This is no bad dream! The Lord makes me down to lie. With bright knives he releaseth my soul. Wave upon wave of demented avengers march cheerfully out of obscurity into the dream. Have you heard the news? The dogs are dead! You better stay home and do as you're told. Get out of the road if you want to grow old!*** ECLIPSE ***All that you touch, see, taste, feel, love, hate, distrust, save, give, and all you create and***

destroy. And all that is now. And all that is gone. And all that's to come. And everything under the sun is in tune. But the sun is eclipsed by the moon. BRAIN DAMAGE ***If the dam breaks open many years too soon. And if there is no room upon the hill. I'll see you on the dark side of the moon. You raise the blade. You make the change. You re-arrange me til I'm sane. You lock the door and throw away the key. And if the cloud bursts thunder in your ear. You shout and no one seems to hear. And if the band you're in starts playing different tunes. I'll see you on the dark side of the moon.*** WISH YOU WERE HERE ***So you think you can tell Heaven from Hell. Blue skies from pain. Can you tell a green field from a cold steel rail? A smile from a veil? Did they get you to trade your heroes for ghosts? Hot ashes for trees? Did you exchange a walk on part in the war for a lead role in a cage? We're just two lost souls swimming in a fishbowl year after year. Running over the same old ground. Wish you were here.*** *THERE'S NO WAY OUT* ***There's no way out of here. When you come in, you're in for good. There was a promise made. The part you played. The chance you took. There's no time to be lost. You'll pay the cost. So get it right. There are no answers here. When you look out you don't see in.***

I guess Steve thought I was into kinky sex and wanted to have fun again. He tied me to his bed and put the scary song on Tied to the Whipping Post. He got a big butcher knife and started scaring me with it. When he saw I wasn't having fun and was really scared he immediately let me go and apologized.

Not many days after that Steve asked if I wanted to go to the horse races in Shreveport Louisiana on Saturday and I told him yes.

It was the day before the races, and I was at work and the music was going like this: CRAZY TRAIN/OZZY OSBOURNE ***All aboard! Hahaha! Crazy! But that`s how it goes! Millions of people living as foes! Maybe it`s not too late to learn how to love and forget how to hate! I`m going off the rails on a crazy train! I`ve listened to preachers. I`ve listened to fools.***

One person conditioned to rule and control. The media sells it, and you live the role. You gotta listen to my words! Heirs of a cold war! That`s what we`ve become! Inheriting troubles! Crazy! I just cannot bear! I`m living with something that just isn`t fair! Who and what`s to blame? I`m going off the rails on a crazy train! CRAZY ON YOU/HEART ***If we still have time we might still get by. Every time I think about it, I want to cry! With bombs and the devil and the kids keep coming! But I tell myself that I was doin alright. There`s nothing left to do at night. But go crazy on you! Let me go crazy, crazy, on you! My love is the evening breeze touching your skin. The gentle sweet singing of leaves in the wind. And you don`t need to wonder. You're doing fine. My Love, the pleasures mine! Whatcha gonna do when everybody`s insane. So afraid of one who`s so afraid of you! I was a willow last night in a dream. Bent down over a clear running stream. Sang you a song that I heard up above, and you kept me alive with your sweet flowing love!*** SHOUT/TEARS FOR FEARS ***Shoot! Shoot! Shout! Shout! Let it all out. These are the things I can do without. Come on! I`m talking to you. In violent times you shouldn`t have to sell your soul! In black and white, they really, really, ought to know! Those one-track minds took you for a working boy. Kiss them goodbye. They gave you life. And in return you gave them hell! As cold as ice. I hope we live to tell the tale. And when you`ve taken down your guard. If I could change your mind I`d really like to break your heart.*** TOO LATE FOR LOVE/DEF LEOPARD ***Somewhere in the distance I hear the bells ring. And the lady cross the street she shuts out the night! There`s a cast of thousands waiting as she turns out the light! But it`s too late! Too late! Too late for Love! With a pocket full of innocence, the entrance is grand! And the Queen of the dream stands before them all! She stretches out her hand as the curtain starts to fall. But it`s too late! Too late for Love! Standing by the trap door aware of me and you. We're waiting for our cue. It`s too late for Love!*** LIFE DURING WAR TIME/TALKING

HEADS ***Heard of a van that is loaded with weapons packed up and ready to go. Heard of some gravesites out by the highway. A place where nobody knows. The sound of gunfire, off in the distance! I`m getting use to that now. Lived in a brownstone. Lived in the ghetto. I`ve lived all over this town! This ain`t no party! Transmit the message, to the receiver! Hope for an answer some day. I got three passports. A couple of visas. You don`t even know my real name! High on a hillside the trucks are loaded. Everything's ready to roll. This ain`t no party! This ain`t no disco! This ain't no foolin around! I ain`t got time for that now! You oughta know not to stand by the window! Somebody will see you up there! I got some groceries. Some peanut butter. Enough for a couple of days. But I ain`t got no speakers! Ain`t got no headphones! Ain`t got no records to play! Trouble in transit! Got through the roadblock. We blended in with the crowd. We got computers! We`re tapping phone lines! We know that that ain`t allowed! We dress like students. We dress like housewives or in a suit and a tie. I burned all my notebooks! What good are notebooks? They won`t help me survive!*** RUN LIKE HELL/ PINK FLOYD ***Run! Run! Run! You better make your face up in your favorite disguise! With your button-down lips and your roller blind eyes! The hammers batter down your door! Run! Run! Run! You better run all day and run all night and keep your feelings hidden deep inside!*** JUMP/VAN HALEN ***You got it tough! I`ve seen the toughest go around! You`ve got to roll with the punches and get to what`s real. Can`t you see me standing there I`ve got my back against the record machine? I ain`t the worst that you`ve seen! Can`t you see what I mean? You might as well jump! Go ahead and jump! Oh! Hey you! Who said that? Baby how you been? Might as well jump! Go ahead and jump!*** BREAK ON THROUGH/DOORS ***You know the day destroys the night! Night divides the day! Tried to run! Tried to hide! Break on through to the other side! We chased our pleasures here. Dug our treasures there. Break on through to the other side!***

The gate is straight! Deep and wide! Break on through to the other side!

It was about an hour before time to go home and Steve told me he wasn`t sure he'd be off work in time to pick me up.

The music started playing angel songs like ANGEL OF THE MORNING by JUICE NEWTON. ***There`ll be no strings to bind your hands. Not if my love can`t bind your heart. And there`s no need to take a stand. I see no need to take me home. I`m old enough to face the dawn. Just call me angel of the morning. And if we`re victims of the night I won`t be blinded by the light. Just call me angel of the morning.*** I was scoping the bar out for the man that looked like an angel, because I felt a presence and the music was talking about an angel, but didn`t see him anywhere. I turned to look behind me and there he was. Right behind me. His presence was almost blinding in a strange way. He didn`t have a table yet but asked me if I'd have a drink with him again and I said yes. He got a table, and we got our drinks, and he was as cute as ever. He said the same thing to me he said before, "God has a message for you." I replied, "Ok. What is it?" He said nothing and I was as confused as ever again. I sarcastically replied, "Well! I`m waiting!" He just smiled with his rosy red cheeks and pearly whites. I told him, "My friend might not be able to pick me up after work. Can you give me a ride home a few blocks away if he doesn`t show up?" He replied, "Yes. It would be my pleasure." I had my drink and danced for him and went on my way. It was time to go home and I didn`t see him in the bar. I went to the dressing room to get changed and Venita and Casey were there. Venita said, "I'm going to the races tomorrow." I told her, "I am too!" I asked her what she was going for and she replied, "Money!" She asked me why I was going. I replied, "Love!" Casey said, "I can`t go. I saw Jesus and now they're coming to take me away." Then Venita picked up a large eggshell that panty hose came in and cracked it against the wall and yelled to me, "You don`t get it do you?" Then her and Casey busted out laughing at me and I was confused by them. I told them, "Yeah! You all are just being fucking crazy! See you later." I went outside and the guy that looked like an angel was parked right in front of the door where I came out. I was standing next to his car, looking around for Steve but didn`t see him. Suddenly Steve pulled up behind the guy's car and that was crazy. They both drove the same car! Same color. Same model. Same year. I was looking at Steve and looking at the other guy and they looked the same. Only the other guy was much older. I thought how strange that was and told the guy, "My friend is right behind your car waiting for me." I thanked him for waiting and told him bye. Steve thought that was a strange coincidence, how they both had the exact same car. We laughed about it and said no more.

I went home that night and looked at the picture The Other Side, and in it was a lady with long blonde hair breaking out of a big eggshell. I wondered if somehow, I was going to break out of my shell in a weird way. Such strange thoughts.

Saturday came and me and Steve were driving to the races. Everything seemed normal but then I saw something hard to explain. Three spirits seemed to be jumping in and out of Steve. I saw God, Jesus, and Satan! I was quite confused and said to Steve, "Who are you?" He replied, "I will be anybody you want me to be." That was not the answer I was wanting, but then it stopped. That was very strange! Steve saw roses being sold on the road and bought me a dozen yellow ones. He didn`t know yellow roses were friendship roses and I was hoping for red ones. Then I got this overwhelming feeling that very soon Steve was going to ask me to marry him! We stopped for gas and the song playing was BEHIND BLUE EYES by THE WHO. ***If I swallow anything evil, put your finger down my throat. If I shiver, please give me a blanket. Keep me warm, let me wear your coat.***

I went in the gas station and suddenly felt like I was going to throw up. I didn`t know where to do it but when I turned around there was an empty 5-gallon bucket at the end of the isle for no apparent reason. I threw up in it and felt better. I went and told the cashier sorry I threw up in the bucket and she might want to get rid of it. Me and Steve left and went on our way. Everything seemed normal to me. When we got to the races, I started my period and bled through my cute blue jumpsuit and had to change into my pink one. We picked our horses and were at the fence waiting for the race. When the gun went off, the sky opened up and I could see into heaven! I felt like I was in the bottom of an ancient Roman colosseum and people in heaven were looking down at me and cheering. I took off running as fast as I could because I was very frightened. I felt like I was being looked at through a giant microscope in the sky. I ran all the way out of the races then stopped, turned around and looked up to see if the sky was still open. It wasn`t. All I saw now was a giant spirit in the sky. I yelled at it, "What do you want! Quit following me! Leave me alone!" The spirit said, "Take your clothes off." So, I did. All I had on was my red panties and a red bandana tied around my neck. Then it said, "Turn around." So I did. To my great surprise there was a huge fucking bull right in front of me with a nose ring, and a chain tying him to the ground! How long is that chain?! Ok, not long enough to reach me. So, I turned back around to the spirit in the sky and was very angry. I put my clothes back on and asked, "What the fuck was that all about?!" The spirit started laughing and said, "I just wanted to see if you were still listening to me." I replied, "Of course I am! You're a big spirit in the sky! But not anymore!" and I began to stomp away when the spirit yelled, "Wait! I need you to do something!" So, I was like, "What!" He said, "Follow me. I'll show you." I followed the spirit for a distance. It took me to a sewer pipe that went underground. There was a nasty puddle of water at the entrance with spiders and who knows what else in it. It was very yucky and gucky. The spirit said, "Take all your clothes off again." I did. "Now what?" "Step into the water." I hesitated. I didn't want to. When I did, my feet sank in the muck. I said, "Ok I did it! Am I done?" The spirit said, "Go down into the hole." But I was like, "No way!" Then the sky opened up again and I could see the people in Heaven cheering for me and the spirit was being a commentator. He said, "Will she do it? Will she do it for Love?" They were all cheering, so I did it. I took the plunge in the dirty nasty hole. It was horrible! The further in I went the smaller the hole got. I just kept praying to God and Jesus to get me out of this. The hole got so small that I barely fit through it and had to dig my nails into the ground and drag myself through. I began to get really scared at the thought this hole didn`t go anywhere and I'd be stuck there and die because there was no way to go backwards. After what seemed like forever, I finally saw a light up ahead and the hole started getting larger until I came to a little square concrete room about 3ft tall by 3ft wide with a big heavy grate on top. I looked up through the grate and saw people standing around outside. In a meek little voice, I cried out, "Please let me out." Then I heard a guy yell, "There`s a little girl down there!" They took the grate off and helped me out and I was covered in muck from head to toe. To my amazement I was standing next to a horse and a jockey and camera bulbs were flashing everywhere. The flash from the cameras were blinding me. It seemed I came out in the winner's circle! LOL! I was asked, "Who raped you?" I was confused by the question and replied, "Nobody raped me." A man took his shirt off and covered me and I was taken to a small medical station where I showered and was given a robe and a blanket and rested on a bed. I told them my friend was here and they needed to get him. They got Steve and brought him to me, and he had no idea what was going on. The police came and I told them I had taken some drugs previously but it had been more than a week ago. They decided I should go to the mental hospital. They told me the state would admit me and decide when I got out or I could admit myself and get out in three days. They put me in the back of a paddy wagon and Steve said he'd meet me at the hospital. I got there and everything was yellow! I was in a small room with a bed. Steve came in and for some reason I said to him, "Why did you lie to me?" That confused him and he had a tear rolling down his cheek. Then he turned around to walk away and never see me again and I said, "Wait! I`m sorry! I`m so fucked up and I don`t understand what`s happening!" He turned back around to me and hugged me, then we both cried. It was time for Steve to leave and we said goodbye. I admitted myself and was given a private room, a yellow gown, a bed with linens and a shower. Steve called his little brother when he got home and told him what happened. His main advice to Steve was RUN! He also called my mom and told my stepdad I was in the mental hospital, and he told Steve not to bother them again because it could cause my mom to have a nervous breakdown. Steve was sad for me because he felt I was such a nice, sweet, innocent, person and had no one to help me through this very tough time but didn't know what to do. The nurse took me to the common area where everyone else was. As soon as I walked in, this older lady with long white hair ran up to me and said, "Thank God you made it! God put me in here on purpose to give you a message and meet you when you got here!" I thought, was this craziness ever going to stop? She said, "God told me to tell you that there's a big war going on right now and you're safer here! He told me to tell you that everything is going to be ok and you're going to be ok!" I just wanted all this to stop! I didn`t respond to the lady and just looked at her like she was crazy. The nurse gave me a couple of pills and took me back to my room where I fell asleep. Shortly after that, the nurse came and woke me and told me it was time to see the doctors and took me to a small examining room. Two male doctors came in and asked me if I knew what I did? I replied, "Yes. I took Ecstasy a while ago and crawled down in a sewer." I told them nothing more. They asked me if I wanted to hurt myself or anyone else and I replied in confusion, "No! Why would I want to hurt myself or anyone else?" They didn`t answer. They listened to my heart and put these weird probes on my head with wires and were looking at a computer screen. When they were done, they said I was ok. As they were leaving, one of the doctors said, "Next time we come back to see you I expect you not to be on any hard drugs." I just said Ok but didn`t understand what they meant by next time. The nurse came in and took me to the common area again where everyone was. I saw this young girl about my age sitting at a big table alone but I didn`t know what happened to her. She was shaking profusely as if she'd seen something so terrifying that she was in shock. Or something terrible happened to her. I tried to comfort her but you couldn`t get close or she'd start screaming. I tried to talk to her but all she did was shake and sob. I asked her what happened, but she never answered. I felt so bad for her.

There was also a young teenage boy that puzzled me because he looked just like the boy that always picked on me in school who killed himself with a shotgun. I mean exactly like him! I felt like I was in the land of the living dead! He'd go up to this very big young guy and punch him in the face and run away laughing. The big guy was incapable of defending himself due to mental issues. He would just stand there. The third time the bully went to do this I stood in between them and yelled at him, "Stop it!" The bully didn`t like that so he got a cup of tomato juice and poured it over my head. That made me scream at the top of my lungs and go into shock! The nurses came running and thought I was injured because it looked like I had blood all over me! It was like a scene from Carey the scary movie. They asked me what happened, so I told them. I was shaking like crazy! The nurses took me to my room to shower and gave me more pills and told me to lay down and rest. I woke up not long after that and was confused about where I was. I got lost and went into another room across from mine and fell asleep. While sleeping, I had a dream I saw a giant alien war going on outside in the sky. Some aliens came in the hospital looking for me but didn`t find me because I was in the wrong room.

It was Sunday and I called my mom to wish her a Happy Mother's Day. I told her I was sorry but I didn`t believe in her religion and didn't think Jesus was my God and I had to find my own truth. Now I have denounced her religion. I told her I was a topless dancer at a bar called Dejavu named Princess Lusty. She asked why I didn`t tell her earlier. She said she was a dancer for two weeks and her name was Champagne Ice, and I should have used that name. She said she was covering for a friend on vacation, and it was such hard work that she never go-go danced again. Then she snottily said, "I think you were just supposed to be a waitress there! Not a dancer!" I told her I love her, and I had to go. How funny we both used Champagne as our first dancer names. What a coincidence! After I hung up, I suddenly felt free. Like I was not brainwashed by society to blindly believe what it had been forcing me to believe since birth. You could say I had lost my religion. I was starting fresh in my brain to search for the truth. I felt like I was born again. Later my mom told my real grandma that I was an exotic dancer and she replied, "That`s ok! It's an art form and takes a lot of talent to do that." I was happy my real grandma was so open minded about me being an exotic dancer.

I decided to spend the rest of my time here in my room and not go to the common area. The older lady that I saw when I first got there that talked crazy to me, quietly came to my room and said, "You know if you don`t do what they want they'll keep you in here as long as they want." I asked her, "What do they want?" She replied, "They want you to go into the common area and color in some coloring books and do some little projects to show you're ok." Shortly after I went to the common area and the same people were there. When I saw the bully, I looked him right in his eyes as I walked past him and thought, if he lays one hand on that guy again I`m going to turn into a big monster and go crazy on him, even though it might cause me to have to stay longer! He didn`t bother the guy again. At least not when I was around. I colored in coloring books and watched everyone around me. The scared girl that was crying and shaking was still in the same spot as before, doing the same thing. I was done coloring and made a little red heart shaped change purse. I did what they wanted and went back to my room to be alone.

It was Monday. Time to go home. Would Steve show up to pick me up? If not, I didn`t know anyone but my parents and didn`t want to call them for help. Steve showed up and I was so relieved because I didn`t know what I would've done if not. On the ride home we didn`t talk about anything that happened. I apologized to Steve and thought it must just have been from the Ecstasy we took weeks earlier and we never took anymore.

Steve told me he won a good amount of money at the races and felt that I was his lucky charm. He pulled out a little ring box, opened it and said, "If were still together a year from now I'll marry you." He gave me a promise ring with seven diamonds and put it on my finger. I was quite confused. Why didn`t he run from me? And what kind of a proposal was that? We had never even discussed marriage or said we loved each other yet. I'd never told a man that I loved him. I told him I'd marry him on three conditions. First, we had to name our first-born son Michael after the Archangel in Revelations because God told me to. He agreed because coincidently he had already picked that name for his first-born son. Then I told him, second, if Jesus comes back, I had to go with him because I married him in a strange ceremony at a church. He laughed and said, "It`s been a long time. Two thousand years since Jesus was here. I doubt he`s really coming back so, ok." I replied, "Well lots of people think he's coming back!" Steve replied, "Well that's just a chance I'll have to take." And the third was he couldn`t make me stop dancing. He agreed to all of it. Then I told Steve, "You know my life has been pretty crazy. If you know anything about what's going on you better tell me." He laughingly replied, "I don't know anything about what's going on in your life." After that I gave him a private dance to the songs Rebel Yell and White Wedding. Then we had some great sex. He was really good at it and always thought of my needs first.

Steve said, "I went to a titty bar and shook a whore tree and Love fell out. What were you doing up there? Hiding?"

I didn`t go back to work for a while. A month later I was taking a nap and Steve came home from work and saw me wrestling with something in my dreams and was afraid for me, so he shook me awake and asked, "What`s going on?!" I told him I was having a crazy dream that God, Jesus, and Satan, were all standing in front of me, and they said I had to choose one of them. I was wrestling with who to choose, so I told them, "I choose the one that has the most love for me." I was waiting for one of them to step forward when I was abruptly wakened by you!" Steve replied, "Somethings not right about that! Get yourself together! I`m taking you back to the hospital!" I told Steve, "I don`t understand why. It was just a strange dream." We were at the psychiatric ward in Dallas and of course everything was yellow, and they asked me what the problem was. I said I was having strange dreams and couldn`t sleep. It was late and Steve left. The nurse gave me a little cup with liquid in it and said it would help me sleep. I drank it and went into a tiny room with a small mattress on the floor to sleep. About an hour later I came out and went to the nurse's station and she was shocked to see me standing there. She asked, "Why are you up?" I replied, "I still can`t sleep." She gave me another dose, so I drank it and went back to the room to sleep. Suddenly, I felt very sick and dizzy. I needed to get to the restroom which was around the corner from my room. I stood up and all I could do was hold on to the wall and inch myself out of the room and into the hallway. I tried to yell for help, but I was too fucked up and no one was around to hear me. I inched my way to the bathroom by holding the wall. I tried to get in, but someone was in there. I tried to tell the person in the bathroom to hurry because I was going to throw up. There were no nurses around and if I didn`t get in the bathroom soon I'd make a big mess on the floor. I was still holding on to the wall best I could. Finally, the person came out and I made my way in and threw up. When

I was done, I inched myself, using the wall, back into my room where I immediately fell asleep until morning.

The next morning it was time to see the doctor. He asked me two questions. "Do you want to hurt yourself?" I answered, "No." He replied, "Do you want to hurt anyone?" I answered, "No!" He then said, "You're okay to go home today." The doctor gave me the number to a counselor and said if I ever needed help to call them. Steve came and got me and asked what they did. I told him, "All they did was drug me to get me to sleep." He replied, "Ok. I promise I'll never take you to the hospital again. If you have any problems or need to talk to someone about anything, talk to me. I'll be your shrink from now on. You don`t need to talk to anyone but me." I agreed and we went on with our lives.

I was going through the closet and found Steve's journal and read it. He only had three girlfriends before me and from what I read one of them liked to have kinky sex, one was a topless dancer, and another had three kids. I ripped the pages in the book and put it back in the closet. I didn't want him to write about me in it. He got it out one day and asked me what happened. I told him, "I didn`t like that book, but at least you can still read it if you want. I didn`t destroy it." He wasn't mad about it at all and threw his book of sexual escapades away.

I had read the story of how he lost his virginity. It was Spring Break, and he was 19 and in Atlantic City with his friends. He went to a bar by himself and saw a beautiful young hippie girl and thought to himself, I must meet her. He went and talked to her and discovered everything she said was a line from song lyrics. She talked in nothing but song lyrics! Steve was confused and intrigued at the same time. Most of what she said came from The Doors, Pink Floyd and Foreigner. Steve asked her if she wanted to party at his motel room and to his amazement she said yes! Steve took some Quaaludes before he went to the bar, then had several drinks. They got to his motel room, and he laid down on the bed and instantly passed out. When he woke, she was gone. He went looking for her and found her with his best friend after they just had sex on the beach. Steve asked to speak with her alone. She quoted some more music and the last thing she said to him was, "Don't look back" (Boston). Then she walked away. Steve was still looking for someone to lose his virginity to, but he was quite shy around women. He met a girl on the street and they both ended up at the motel room. She got on the bed and told Steve to pull the string that was between her legs. He was confused. He pulled the string anyway and a bloody tampon came out. He said, "What the fuck?" She said, "It's ok we can still do whatever you want." After a couple of minutes of sex, she was snoring. Not great for his ego, but Steve was finally happy he wasn't a virgin anymore.

Later that night Steve and his friend were walking on the Boardwalk and came to a fortune teller and decided to try it. Steve sat down for a reading and the lady started talking about virginity and blood. Steve was shocked, his eyes got big, and he started laughing hysterically. He was laughing so hard he could barely walk out the door! He was laughing and crying when he went outside and could hardly tell his friend what the fortune teller said.

I decided I needed to make some money but didn't want to go back dancing yet. I went to Dejavu to see if anyone needed a babysitter. I recognized the DJ Skip but none of the dancers. I asked him where Venita and Casey were, and he told me Venita died of AIDS and Casey never came back. I asked where David was, and he said he also died of AIDS. WOW! Ironically the music playing was ANOTHER ONE BITES THE DUST by QUEEN. ***And another one gone, and another one gone, and another one bites the dust! Hey, gonna get you too!*** I went to the dressing room and asked if anyone needed a babysitter and a dancer said she had a newborn and needed one. After babysitting for her I realized something wasn't right. Her baby was always brought to me dirty and didn`t have enough diapers or formula. After a few days she told me she couldn`t pay me for the night. I told her she could pay me the next day. But the next day she didn`t pay me again. After a week of not paying, I became suspicious. I made lots of money when I was a dancer. Why couldn`t she pay me? The next time she came over I told her this was the last day I'd babysit until she paid me. She didn`t bring any formula. Only a bottle of what I thought was juice but was grape Kool-Aid! I was pretty sure newborns weren't supposed to have Kool-Aid. I called her mom who was her emergency contact and told her what was going on. She told me her daughter was a drug addict and CPS was in the process of taking her baby away. She told me to call CPS and report what was going on so it would help her get her granddaughter faster. So, I did. I went to the store and got what the baby needed. When she came to pick her up, she still said she couldn't pay me. I told her I called her mom and CPS, and that I would not be babysitting for her anymore. I called her mom a week later to see what happened and she told me she had the baby now. I liked the baby, and Steve was very good with her. Someday I wanted one.

I felt it was time to go back to Dejavu but didn`t want to use the name Princess Lusty. I didn`t know what name to use. I went on a journey to find myself and did a recap of my life. I was a young girl in a non-denominational charismatic church and baptized by the Holy Spirit. I began having strange prophetic dreams and my parents were called by who they felt was God to go to the main branch where we were called The Mission Family. Then I was called out of the church by who I thought was God to a topless bar called Dejavu, where I called myself Princess Lusty and things got very strange. I felt my surroundings for some reason were trying to tell me I was the Goddess of Love, but I refused to believe it. I thought my life had been very strange and felt like I was a character from the Bible like Noah, Moses, or Jesus, in a weird way. I thought this was a ridiculous long shot, but as crazy as my life had been, maybe there was something in the Bible about The Goddess of Love. I felt that was impossible because no one had ever talked about The Goddess of Love in the Bible when I was in the churches. I looked in the book but didn't find anything about her. The only names I knew her by were Venus and Aphrodite, but no mention of them. Next, I went to the library and got some books on Astronomy and Mythology and looked up the constellation Pleiades and it had something to do with The Goddess of Love and the Seven Sisters. I really didn't understand it. I looked up all the other names for The Goddess of Love and came up with Ishtar, Ashtoreth, Asherah, Astarte, Isis, and Esther. I went back to the Bible and looked up those names and to my great surprise there was something about The Goddess of Love in the Old Testament in 1st Kings! It said something about her having temples here on Earth and people worshipped her. It angered God that she wouldn't follow him, and she had many that worshipped her. He burnt all her temples down and killed all the people who refused to worship him. I thought that was very mean of God to do. I looked no further in the Bible for any more about The Goddess of Love. Then I looked up what my real name Cynthia meant, and it said, the bringer of light or reflector of light and moon goddess. It was Greek. Then I looked up Steven's name and it was also Greek. It meant The King. I began to think this was all too strange. It seemed like God, or this higher power, was having lots of contact with me like he did with Noah, Moses and Jesus. I felt like the Goddess Love character in the Bible, but on a small scale. I was in a strange sex temple, and men gave me money, booze, dinner, flowers, stuffed animals, clothes, and jewelry. Surely, I couldn`t be The Goddess Love from the Old Testament! For some strange reason I felt like I had been here before and had done this in another life. I felt someone above must have been playing a joke on me or playing a weird game with me. I even thought it might be possible that I was an actress in a weird show that people in Heaven watched. So crazy! If I was her, what was I doing here and how did I get here? I became a little frightened because if I was The Goddess of Love, Satan would be looking for me to destroy me or sacrifice me! I started laughing because this was all too funny and couldn't possibly be real, could it? When I was on center stage, I felt like a preacher with my music. This couldn`t be good! I was confused about why I was being called back to Dejavu and what name to use. I wanted the right name. I decided on Venus the Goddess because that was the common name most people knew Love by and now, I'd wear a crown.

I went back to Dejavu, walked in and thought great, there goes the music again! DOORS ***Hello! I love you won`t you tell me your name! Hello! I love you let me jump in your game! She`s walking down the street! Blind to every eye she meets. Do you think you`ll be the guy to make the Queen of the Angels sigh? Hello! I love you won`t you tell me your name! She holds her head so high, like a statue in the sky. Do you hope to make her see you fool? Do you hope to pluck this dusty jewel? Hello!*** ZOMBIES ***It's the time of the season, when love runs high. And let me try with pleasured hands. To take you in the sun, to promised lands. To show you everyone. It's the time of the season for loving. What's your name? Who's your daddy? Is he rich like me? Has he taken any time to show you what you need to live? I really want to know.***

I told Skip my name was now Venus the Goddess and wore a crown instead of the tiara worn by Princess Lusty. It was now time to work on my show. I needed all the music about love and what related to my life, and I needed to learn how to really dance and put on a great show and not just prance around. The music I started with was SECRETS by VAN HALEN. It talked about a girl who was Love and she had a rainbow that touched her shoulder just like I did. Next was, LOVE AIN'T NO STRANGER/WHITESNAKE ***Who knows where the cold winds blow? I asked my friends, but nobody knows. Who am I to believe in Love? Lord have mercy! Love ain`t no stranger! I looked around and what did I see? Broken hearted people staring at me.***

All searching cause they still believe. Love ain`t no stranger! I ain`t no stranger! But when I read between the lines it`s all the same! Who am I to believe in Love?*** More music I did. PEOPLE ARE STRANGE/DOORS ***When you're strange, no one remembers your name. When you're strange, faces come out of the rain. When you`re strange. Streets are uneven when you're down. KILLER QUEEN/QUEEN ***At any time an invitation you can`t decline. Caviar and cigarettes. Well versed in etiquette. Extraordinarily nice. She`s a killer! Qu-e-e-e-n! Gunpowder gelatin dynamite with a laser beam! Guaranteed to blow your mind! Anytime! Recommended at the price! Wanna try? To avoid complications, she never kept the same address. In conversation she spoke just like a baroness. Fastidious and precise. She`s a killer! Qu-e-e-e-n! Dynamite with a laser beam! Guaranteed to blow your mind! Anytime! Drop of a hat she is willing. As playful as a pussy cat then momentarily out of action. Temporarily out of gas to absolutely drive you wild! Wanna try?*** YOU GIVE LOVE A BAD NAME/ BON JOVI ***Shot through the heart and you're to blame! You give love a bad name! An angel's smile is what you sell! You promised me Heaven but put me through Hell! Chains of Love got ahold of me! This is a prison you can't break free! I play my part and you play your game. You give Love a bad name!*** DOCTOR LOVE/ KISS ***I say I wanna set you free! Don't you know you'll be in misery! They call me, Dr. Love! And even though I'm full of sin and the earth wouldn't let me in. You'll let me through there's nothin you can do! So if you please! Get on your knees! Call me! Dr. Love!*** AND SHE WAS/TALKIN HEADS ***And she was lying in the grass. She could hear the highway breathing. She's making sure she is not dreaming. Now she's starting to rise, and she opens up her eyes. The world was moving she was right there with it, and she was. She was floating above it and she was. And she was drifting through the backyard. And she was taking off her dress. She was moving very slowly, rising up above the earth. Moving into the universe. Drifting this way and that. Not touching the***

ground at all and she's up above the yard. She was proud about it. No doubt about it. She isn't sure about what she's done. And she was looking at herself. And things were looking like a movie. LOVE, REIGN O'ER ME/THE WHO *Only Love can make it rain. Love! Reign o're me! Only Love can bring the rain that makes you yearn to the sky. Love! Reign o'er me! Oh God I need a drink of cool, cool, rain! Love!* GET DOWN MAKE LOVE/QUEEN *Get down make love. Get down make love! You take my body! I give you heat! You say you`re hungry! I give you meat! I suck your mind! You blow my head! Make love inside your bed! Everybody say, get down make love! You can make everybody get down make love!* CARRY ON WAYWARD SON/KANSAS *Carry on. There will be peace when you are done. Once I rose above the noise and confusion, just to get a glimpse beyond this illusion. I was soaring ever higher! But I flew too high. Though my eyes could see I still was a blind man. I hear the voices when I`m dreamin. I can hear them say!* THE GRAND ILLUSION/STYX *Welcome to the grand illusion! Come on in and see what`s happening! Pay the price! Get your tickets for the show! The stage is set! The band starts playing! Suddenly your heart is pounding! Wishing secretly you were a star! But don`t be fooled by the radio, the TV, or the magazines. They show you photographs, how your life should be, but they`re just someone else's fantasy. So if you think your life is complete confusion, because you never win the game. Just remember, it`s a grand illusion, and deep inside were all the same! Someday soon we`ll stop to ponder, what on earth whose spell were under. We made the grade and still we wonder, who the hell we are!* THE CONFESSOR/JOE WALSH *If you look at your reflection at the bottom of the well. What you see is only on the surface. When you try to see the meaning, hidden underneath, the measure of the depth can be deceiving. The bottom has a rocky reputation! You can feel it in the distance, the deeper down you stare. From up above it`s hard to see, but you know it when you`re there. On the bottom words are shallow! On the surface talk is cheap! You can only judge* *the distance by the company you keep. In the eyes of the confessor, there`s no place you can hide. You can't hide from the eyes of the confessor. Don`t you even try! You cannot tell a lie to the confessor! Strip you down to size! Naked as the day that you were born! Take all the shackles and the chains and give it up!* LIMELIGHT/ RUSH *Living on a lighted stage approaches the unreal. In touch with some reality, beyond the gilded cage. Cast in this unlikely role. Ill-equipped to act. Living in the limelight, the universal dream. Get on with the fascination. The real relation. The underlying theme! All the world's indeed a stage! And we are merely players. Performers and portrayers. Each another's audience, outside the gilded cage!* ROUND AND ROUND/RAT *Out on the streets, that`s where we`ll meet! I always cross the line! Get in our way, and we`ll put you on your shelf! Were gonna go! But then we`ll see you again. Cold in vain, she said, "I knew right from the beginning, that you would end up winning! I knew right from the start, you put an arrow, through my heart!" Round and round! With Love we'll find a way just give it time! What comes around goes around! I`ll tell you why! Looking at you, looking at me! It`s easy to see! "It`s all the same!" she said. Well Love will find her way just give it time!* TOUCH TOO MUCH/AC/DC *It was one of those nights when you turned out the lights, and everything comes into view. She was taking her time. I was losing my mind! It wasn`t the first, and wasn`t the last. She knew we were making love! She`s got a touch! A touch too much! She had the face of an angel, smiling with sin. A body of Venus with arms. Dealing with danger, stroking my skin. Let the thunder and lightning begin!* PHOTOGRAPH/ DEF LEPPARD *I`m out of luck! Out of love! Got a photograph picture, you`re too much! You`re the only one I want to touch! I see your face every time I dream! On every page and magazine! So wild and free. You`re all I want! My fantasy! Look what you`ve done to this rock n roll clown! I`d be your lover, if you were there. Put your hurt on me, if you dare. Sexy woman, you got style! You make every man, feel like a child. You got some kind of hold on me!*

You`re all wrapped up in a mystery! I gotta have you! You`re going straight to my head! TALKIN BOUT LOVE/LED ZEPPELIN ***Talkin bout Love. I like the way you hold the road. Mama it ain`t no sin. Talkin bout Love! I can't stop talkin bout Love!*** WALK THIS WAY/AEROSMITH ***She told me to walk this way! Talk this way! Just give me a kiss! Then I knew that Love was here to stay!*** *FOOLIN/DEF LEPPARD* ***Lady Luck never smiles so lend your love to me awhile. Do with me what you will. Break the spell. Take your fill. On and on we rode the storm. Flames died and the fire has gone. I realized that not long ago. Is anybody out there? Is anybody there? Does anybody want Love? Does anybody care? I just gotta know if you`re really there and you really care! Won`t you stay with me awhile. Close your eyes now run and hide. Easy Love is no easy ride! Just wakin up from what we had could stop good Love from going bad!*** HYSTERIA ***Out of touch. Out of reach. You could try to get closer to me. I`m in luck. I`m in deep. Hypnotized, shaken to my knees. I gotta know tonight. If your alone tonight? Can`t stop this feeling! Can`t stop this fire! I get hysterical hysteria. Can you feel it? Do you believe it? It`s such a magical, mysteria, when you get that feeling. Better start believing! Cause it`s a miracle. Out of me. Into you. You could hide. It`s just a one-way street. I believe I`m in you yeah. Open wide. That`s right. Dream me off my feet. Believe in me! When you get that feeling you better start believing! Can you feel it? You better believe it! Start believing!*** JUNGLE LOVE/STEVE MILLER ***I met you on somebody`s island. You thought you had known me before. I brought you a crate of papaya, then waited all night by your door. You probably wouldn`t remember. I probably couldn`t forget! Jungle love in the surf in the pouring rain! Everything's better when wet! Jungle love, it`s driving me mad! It`s making me crazy! But lately you live in the jungle. I never see you alone. But we need some definite answers so I thought I would write you a poem. The question to everyone's answer is usually asked from within. But the patterns of the rain and the truth they contain are written right***

up on your skin. My cycles of circular motion protect you and keep you from harm. You live in a world of illusion. Everything's peaches and crème but we spend our time in a dream. THOSE SHOES/ EAGLES ***Tell us what your gonna do tonight to mama. There must be someplace you can go. In the middle of the tall drinks and the drama. There must be someone you know. God knows your looking good enough. You might have something to lose. Pretty mama, what you gonna do in those shoes? Got those pretty little straps around your ankles. Got those shiny little chains around your heart. They're lookin at you. Tell you anything you want to hear. They give you tablets of love. They're waiting for you. Got to score you. They give you tablets of love! You just want someone to talk to. They just want to get their hands on you. You get whatever you choose. Oh no you can't do that once you started wearing those shoes.***

I played those songs and many more but when I heard this song at work, I had to add it to my list because I was taken back by the words. It seemed to have struck a chord with me. BROKEN WINGS/MR. MISTER ***This time will be the last I fear, unless I make it all too clear. Take these broken wings and learn to fly again and learn to live so free. When we hear, the voices sing, THE BOOK OF LOVE will open up and let us in. I think tonight we can take what is wrong and make it right. It's all I know that your half of the flesh and blood makes me whole! When we hear, the voices sing, THE BOOK OF LOVE will open up for us and let us in!*** When I heard that song, I was like, WOW! Maybe that's the book the loud voice said I was going to write. I was confused and a little scared about it but went on with the show and my life and didn't think about the book anymore.

When I started dancing again, I had a problem with a lady named Shasta. Someone popped my car hood and pulled half the spark plugs out and I barely made it home. I had to take my car to the mechanics to get the spark plugs back in the right places. One day at work, we got into a confrontation, but I wouldn`t back down. That surprised her because I was so small. We got into a shoving match then both walked away. So now there was a lady at work that wanted to kick my ass and I didn`t know why. I didn't even know her and had never done anything to her. I minded my own business and did my job! JR, another dancer, whose favorite song to play was by TEARS FOR FEARS called EVERYBODY WANTS TO RULE THE WORLD kept telling me Shasta wanted to kick my ass. Her song went like this: ***Welcome to your life. There's no turning back. Even when we sleep, we will find you acting on your best behavior. Everybody wants to rule the world. There's a room where the light won't find you. Holding hands while the walls come tumbling down. When they do, I'll be right behind you. So glad we've almost made it. Everybody wants to rule the world.*** I asked JR why Shasta wanted to kick my ass but she didn`t say. Shasta made me miserable at work and I came home every night complaining to Steve. Steve was tired of hearing it and suggested I tried another bar. I went to Crazy Girls and got the job, but when I went into the dressing room, to my shock, Shasta was sitting in a chair getting ready. She also quit Dejavu because of our arguments. She took one look at me and said, "Ok this is strange. Something must be going on. There must be a reason why we're both here right now. Sit down and let`s smoke a joint and try to figure out what`s going on." She said, "JR told me you wanted to kick my ass." I told her, "That's not true! Jr told me you wanted to kick my ass!" She replied, "That`s not true either. I never said that." We both realized JR did it. She set us up for a fight. Shasta said she was sorry for pulling my spark plugs and all was water under the bridge. Shasta was so mad at JR that she went and broke her distributor cap. We became good friends after that.

While working at Crazy Girls, the owner's son got the hots for me and followed me around the bar like a puppy dog begging me to go out with him. He was a good-looking young man, but I told him I was promised to someone. He finally got the hint and quit bothering me.

The owner of Dejavu wasn't happy we left and came to Crazy Girls to find out why. Shasta told him JR was causing shit between the dancers. He said he'd fire her if we came back, so we did. He also owned Baby Dolls next door and it was a very large bar so I didn`t like it. I liked the way the stages were set up at Dejavu more than the other bars because it was cozy to me. You could see everything in the room from anywhere. There was only one dark corner to avoid. One time three guys cornered me there and tried to grope me all over, so I started screaming and swinging on them, and they let me go. I went and told the manager and they got kicked out.

One day I was very sick with a high fever and needed to go to the doctor, but Steve insisted I heal myself. The doctor was a couple miles away, so I asked him to take me, but he told me to drive myself. I told him I was so sick I was seeing spots and insisted he drive me! He still wouldn`t and it made me so mad that I spit a big loogie in his face! As I did, I fell over backwards into a big empty TV box and got stuck in it! Steve busted out laughing and I was really mad!

My car was making a small ticking noise, so I asked Steve to look at it, but he wouldn't. I was driving it to the mechanics, but it began to smoke so I pulled over and parked. There went that car. I ran it out of oil because I didn`t know it had a leak. If only Steve had looked at it, he could've told me it needed oil!

We moved around the corner to The Inn apartments. It was nicer, and our apartment was on the second floor overlooking the pool and BBQ area.

We were going to Galveston Island for the weekend, and I asked my mom if she'd watch Inky. I told her she wasn`t fixed and she was an indoor cat and to keep her away from her male cats. She agreed. While we were in Galveston, I saw Venita's old Boyfriend from Dejavu. He was with his pregnant wife. I thought how lucky he was to still be alive, meanwhile my girlfriend was dead. We saw each other, made eye contact and recognized each other, but said nothing. After we got home, I picked up Inky and my mom said she couldn't keep the cats apart and Inky mated with one of hers. We kept one black fluffy female out of the litter, and I named her Pandorapunkinskinwiskfurphony. Pandora for short.

Life seemed to be normal now. Nothing crazy was going on. My hair grew to my butt, and I now had beautiful, natural golden curls and looked like Venus the Goddess, the character I played at Dejavu. I really liked my hair now and was having so much fun in my life.

A friend of Steve's came over with some nitrous oxide also known as Whip It's. Immediately after I inhaled it from the balloon, I began screaming really loud. It scared Steve and his friend, but it only lasted a few seconds. I'd never done nitro (laughing gas) before and didn't know what to expect. When it was over, they asked me why I screamed like that. I told them I saw the Devil and there were flames all around me and he was laughing at me in a scary voice. He said, "Hahahahaha! Now you're in Hell with me forever! Hahahaha!" That frightened me so much I started screaming. Steve and his friend were like WOW! You're not supposed to trip like that on Nitro. They didn't want me to take another hit but I convinced them I'd do better next time. I took another hit, got up and started chasing a tiny invisible red rubber ball around the room trying to catch it. They thought that was funny because they didn't know what I was doing. Seconds later it was over. They started laughing when I told them what I was doing. I didn't take another hit.

Now I had a fantasy. I wanted to get lots of colored balloons, blow them up, but fill all the red ones with laughing gas and put them in a small room with the two openings opposite each other. Me and Steve would rub baby oil over each other's naked bodies, then slither through our openings suspended in the balloons. We'd suck all the red ones we found. When we reached each other in the middle we'd have sex suspended in the balloons! Sounds like lots of fun!

During the year of our promise to marry, I'd ask Steve strange questions because I'd never been close enough to a man to ask these questions. I asked him if it hurt when he got a hard on?" He replied, "Only until you take care of it." Then he laughed and said, "It doesn`t really hurt." But he did tell me men named their dicks and his was Mr. Mojo. I replied, "More like Donkey Kong!" I had no idea guys named their dicks. I named my sexual parts Sugarbush and Honey Hole. Steve liked that.

We were in the shower together and he asked, "Do you want a golden shower?" I looked at him funny because I didn't know what he meant. Then he started pissing all over me like an animal marking his territory! I didn't find it funny and told him not do it again! He just laughed.

Steve was in the bathroom and left the door open. I walked by and saw him pissing all over the rim of the toilet bowl. I yelled, "Steve! What the fuck are you doing!" He was kind of shaken and replied, "I'm cleaning the toilet bowl. There was a pubic hair on it." I told him, "That's just ridiculous! That's not how you clean a toilet bowl! Don't ever do that again or you'll be the one cleaning it from now on!" I don't think he ever did it again. Men! I'm telling you! What the fuck!

Every time Steve looked at a hot chick, I'd ask him, "Don`t you want her instead of me? You can have her, but you will lose me. Do you want to trade?" He always said, "Nope! I want you!" I asked him why, when there were so many other beautiful women in the world to choose from and he replied, "Because you are the whole package. You're cute, sweet, and sexy."

Steve screamed like he was in terrible pain when having an orgasm and it started to scare me that something might be wrong. I asked him if it hurt when he had an orgasm and he replied, "No! It feels so good all I can do is scream when it happens!" Sex with him was awesome! He was so good at it when we were finished, I often had a tear rolling down my cheek because I was so satisfied. For some reason I always yelled, "Oh God!" when we were having great sex! When I realized it, I stopped.

I was pondering my life again and was really confused and scared about my past, so I decided to pray to God (which I hadn't done in a while). I told him, "I'm confused about what's going on. This all seems too crazy! I need to know it's ok playing Venus the Goddess at a strip bar. I need to know if I'm really Love! Please give me a sign to ease my troubled mind." When I went to work that day, I heard a song that just came out and it really made my eyes widen and take notice! It was LOVE WALKS IN by VAN HALEN and it went like this: ***Contact is all it takes, to change your life to lose your place in time. Contact. Asleep or awake. Coming around you may wake up to find. Questions deep within your eyes. Now more than ever, you realize! And then you sense a change. Nothing feels the same. All your dreams are strange. Love comes walking in. Some kind of alien, waits for the opening, then simply pulls a string and Love comes walking in. Another world! Some other time! You lay your sanity on the line! Familiar faces! Familiar sites! Reach back remember with all your might! There she stands in a silken gown with silver lights shining down! So when you sense a change, and nothing feels the same, and all your dreams are strange, Love comes walking in. Some kind of alien, waits for the opening, then simply pulls a string, and Love comes walking in! Sleep and dream is all that I pray! I traveled far across the Milky Way. To my master, I become a slave! You will meet him some other day. Where silence speaks as loud as war. Earth returns to what it was before.*** The song kind of scared me and made my heart beat fast because I thought, wow, could it really be me? I added it to my playlist. I decided not to talk to God about it again because it scared me too much. Close enough confirmation for me to keep doing what I was doing, and I felt better about it.

I stopped taking the pill and told Steve we had to use some other birth control. It was almost a year after he gave me the promise ring, but I wasn't keeping track of time. Early one morning Steve woke up and said, "Do you want to get married today?" I'd forgotten all about it and didn't prepare for a wedding. I asked him, "Are you sure you don't want another woman who is hotter than me?" He assured me he didn't. I asked him, "How will we get married today?" He replied, "We can go to the Justice of the Peace." I told him, "Ok. Why not. It`s a beautiful Spring Day and the flowers are in bloom." I didn`t tell anyone we got married. We consummated our marriage that night and used no contraceptives for the first time. Later I realized my mom wouldn't like that we didn`t have a wedding, so we decided to have a small ceremony. I had one month to prepare for it. We partied all month and I got everything ready for the wedding. I needed a preacher, so my mom said she had one in mind. When I spoke to him on the phone, I told him me and Steve were already married, and just needed a preacher for the ceremony. He said he wanted no part of this deception and hung up. I told Steve, "It`s ok. God will show up to bless our marriage. We don`t need a preacher." The day of the ceremony came, and I had less than ten guests in the living room waiting for my appearance. When I came out Steve started crying and trembling because he was overwhelmed by my beauty. The sky turned black and the noise of the thunder crashing outside was very loud and it started pouring sheets of rain. Two tornados were outside not far from us. We were getting ready to say the vows we made for each other, but Steve was trembling and could barely speak. I looked at him and whispered, "It`s ok. We're already married." Our vows didn't say, til death do we part. We said, and death shall not part us. The ceremony was over, and the tornados stopped, but it was still pouring rain and me and Steve told our guests we were going to drive around to honk our horn in the decorated car. My mom said she wanted to see our marriage license. I told her we were going to the JPs to get it, but she wanted to go with us to be a witness. I had to tell her we did that last month. She was kind of bummed she didn't get to be a witness. We got back to join the party in full swing.

We invited all our friends. My parents left shortly afterwards, and the party still went on. Steve got so drunk he could barely take my garter off. It got late, and people still wanted to party, so we put the keg and booze outside for anyone who wanted. Me and Steve went to bed and were so tired and buzzed we didn't have sex. But we had a great time at our wedding reception.

We started looking for a new place to live and bought a two-bedroom mobile home and moved to Northwood Mobile Home Park in Lewisville Texas. Shortly after that I started throwing up in the mornings. Then I missed my period! I thought I might be pregnant but wasn't sure. I didn`t tell Steve yet. I wasn't sure how he'd react about me getting pregnant so soon after getting married. I went to the doctor's and yes, I was pregnant! The doctor told me how far along I was. When I counted the days backwards, I realized I got pregnant the day we came back from the Justice of the Peace. Just like a new queen was supposed to do. Hahaha! Get pregnant on her wedding night. I told Steve I thought I was pregnant and got a home pregnancy test. It came up negative. I was confused and didn`t know what to say. I told Steve, "I am pregnant! I already went to see the doctor and he said yes, I am pregnant!" We got another test, and it was positive. We were both very happy and excited. If it was a boy, he'd be Michael Kirk and if it was a girl, she'd be Angela Kay. Angela was my favorite girl's name.

I was having serious doubts again about who I was, why I was playing the role Venus the Goddess, why I was here, and if I picked the right name. Here I went again having doubts about myself. So, I asked God if I picked the right name. The next time I went to work the DJ said he had a song for me to play when I went on stage. He said, "Trust me, I'm pretty sure you're going to like it. It's a remake of an old song." When I took center stage, he played ***Goddess on the mountain top. Burning like a silver flame! The summit of beauty and love! And Venus was her name! She's got it! Yeah, baby she's got it! I'm your Venus! I'm your fire! Her***

weapons were her crystal eyes! She's got it! Yeah, baby she's got it! I thought, ok, I guess I picked the right name. That song became a big part of my show.

When I was a dancer, I learned a cute little money-making trick. I purred like a kitty cat in guys ears, and it drove them crazy. Men came in and handed me money and asked me to that thing in their ear. They'd also bring friends in and pay me to do it to them. I looked like a lion with my long golden curls. When I didn't feel like table dancing men paid me well for shoulder massages.

Early in my pregnancy I had terrible morning sickness and sometimes Steve threw up. When he was done, I immediately felt better and laughed and thanked him.

Steve went to every doctor's appointment, and the sonogram was the most exciting. The doctor asked if we wanted to know the sex, so we talked about it and we did. It was a boy! Michael! Named after the Archangel in Revelations! I was so excited! I couldn't wait for him to make his appearance in this world!

I danced until I was seven months pregnant and found lots of men thought pregnant woman were very sexy, so I made lots of money. I had all the pregnancy worries like a normal mother had. I just wanted a healthy baby.

I decided to try to get ahold of my real dad to see if he wanted to be in our lives. I asked my mom if she knew where he was, but she didn't. She gave me his mother's number, so I called and asked if she knew where he was. She wanted to know why I wanted to get ahold of him and asked if I was trying to get money from him. I told her I was having a baby and was fine. We chatted a bit and hung up. I sent her several letters and called a couple more times asking about my dad but to no avail. She'd always cry when I called so it made it difficult for me to keep calling. I gave up and went on with my life.

Not long after that, I had a weird dream. I was flying in the sky along a highway. I was close enough to the ground that I could still see everything. I came to a place and stopped. I looked inside and it was an electronic shop full of TV's, stereos and video equipment. I went in and walked around and saw my stepmom. I told her I had been looking for them for a while and was so happy to see her! I told her to tell my dad I was trying to get in touch with him. She said she would and then I woke. I wondered what the dream meant or if it meant anything at all.

Me and Steve threw a Halloween party, and I was a big bag of jellybeans. Steve was a hot chick. He had bright red fingernails, black fish net stockings, a long blonde wig, and a sexy dress that looked pretty good on him. He had perfect shaped balloon breasts. I found him a cute pair of shoes and he looked pretty hot. After I put makeup on him, he looked very sexy. He named himself Debbie. We made Everclear punch and got a keg of beer. His best friend from childhood arrived drunk and dressed as half man, half lady. I introduced him to Debbie and told him she was a dancer friend from work. He thought Debbie was so hot and started hitting on her. No one knew Debbie was really Steve! I told everyone Steve would be here in about an hour. It was hilarious! They all really thought Debbie was a dancer from my work! Debbie was teasing his best friend so bad. She was sucking on cherries from the punch and giving him sexy eyes. I was dying laughing inside and Steve was holding his role pretty good. His friend was fawning all over Debbie and trying to rub his hand up her leg and kiss on her. How long was this going to go on? I took each guest aside except for his best friend and told them Steve was really Debbie. Now they couldn`t stop laughing! They were enjoying the hilarious show and finally Steve had enough and told him, "Hey! It`s me, Steve!" We were all laughing and his best friend didn`t know what to think. He was confused and said, "Well, all I can say is, Steve makes a really sexy woman!" We all laughed. His best friend pulled up a stool next to the keg and drank until he fell over backwards off the stool. The party ended late that night. It was lots of fun!

It was close to my due date and my mom told me it doesn't hurt that much to have a baby. Boy did she lie! She was on a drug called twilight when she had kids. They didn`t do that now. I wanted to try childbirth naturally. I went into labor, and it was mild. I called Steve at work and told him, and he came home and drove me to the doctor. The excitement was incredible! The doctor asked if I wanted to have my baby today or tomorrow. I replied, "Today!" She told us to meet her at the hospital. When we got there the doctor broke my water and the real pain began. I called my mom and told her I was having my baby but she didn`t show up. I told the doctor I changed my mind and wanted an epidural because I was in so much pain. It was like a giant anaconda wrapped around my stomach squeezing me in half! The doctor said I was too far along to get one, but I still begged her. She finally relented and told me I'd have to be very still while they put the needle in my spine. It was hard to stay still during the contractions. They got the needle in, and my pain eased. Four hours after I was admitted Michael was born. He was perfect and I was so relieved. Steve was in the delivery room the whole time and took pictures. He gave Michael his middle name Kirk because I told him it was customary in my family to pass down the father's middle name to his son. He did because he liked Captain Kirk from Star Trek. Michael's name meant God-like. I called my mom again and asked why she didn`t come? She said she didn`t know she was invited. I told her that`s why I called, so she'd come! I really wanted her there. She said she was sorry, she didn't know. They came later that night.

Michael was a few months old, and I went back to work. I didn't even look like I had a baby. Nothing strange was happening. Maybe all the crazy shit was over. I baptized Michael outside on the first rain and asked God to bless and protect him.

When I first started working at Dejavu we only had one small dressing room with benches, mirrors, and lockers. When I came back, we had two more upstairs dressing rooms with lockers and benches. I was happy about it. We had more dancers, but also more room and lockers to use. We also had a house mom named

Vernell. She was a big black woman that didn't take shit from anyone. She didn't let any dancers walk over her. I liked that I had someone to hold my money and watch my clothes when I was on stage. A lot of dancers were thieves. She also stopped dancers from doing drugs in the dressing rooms. Vernell really liked me because I was a very nice person and never caused any problems.

Sometimes guys tried to get in the ladies dressing rooms to get a sneak peek behind the scenes. We'd just chase them out. If they wouldn't leave, we got the bouncer to take care of it. When I worked nights and it was closing time all the lights in the bar came on and it was announced that we were closing. It was time for the customers to leave. At this time men desperately tried to hook up with dancers after work. The bouncers had to kick them out. By then I was so tired I just wanted to go home. If guys weren't spending money on dancers, we just sat in the dressing room and partied without them, and the manager had to clear the dressing room out to get the dancers to party with the guys.

It was our one-year anniversary, and we didn't have what couples call, Our Song yet. We were out dining and drinking, and Steve heard the song WONDERFUL TONIGHT by ERIC CLAPTON ***It's late in the evening. She's wondering what clothes to wear. She puts on her make-up and brushes her long blonde hair. And then she asks me, "Do I look alright?' And I say, "Yes, you look wonderful tonight." We go to a party, and everyone turns to see. This beautiful lady that's walking around with me. And then she asks me, "Do you feel alright?" And I say, "Yes I feel wonderful tonight." I feel wonderful because I see the love light in your eyes. And the wonder of it all, is that you just don't realize how much I love you.*** Steve loved the song and we made it ours.

A girlfriend came over with these blue crystals and said it was going to blow my mind. I had to warm them in the oven then snort it when it cooled. It was amazing! I started seeing crazy equations and was trying to explain it to Steve. It went on for about an hour and then suddenly stopped. I asked Steve what all I said, and he told me I said so much that he couldn't possibly tell it to me. He wished he had turned a tape recorder on so I could've listened to it later. He said I was explaining equations of how life began. It was strange, and I never did it again.

I tried to get ahold of my dad one last time. I called my Grandma Mary Jane and asked her again if she heard from him. She replied, "No! What is it you want from him? Do you need money or what?" I told her, "No. I don`t need any money. I just had a baby not long ago and thought he might like to be part of my life?" She still told me she didn't know where he was but I'm pretty sure she was lying to me.

We didn`t want the mobile home anymore and told the company to come get it. The plumbing behind the shower in the master bedroom leaked for a long time and we didn`t know. I was shocked when we pulled the wall open! It was mold that looked like a giant alien plant growing all the way up to the top inside of it. It was very scary looking! The company didn`t want to fix it so we let them repossess it.

Just before we moved to a house, I received a letter with no return address. It was from my dad. He did want to be part of my life! I called him and we talked for a bit, and he only lived 2 hours away in Mt Pleasant Tx. I told him I'd been trying for over a year to contact him. He said he was sorry for taking so long to respond but his mom had just given him my messages. We went to visit them for a weekend. They lived on 8 acres out in the country with 2 ponds. It was so beautiful there. My little sister and brother also lived there. We went swimming off the small dock on the pond and a fish bit Steve's nipple off. Blood was running down his chest. Everyone scrambled quickly to get out. It was so funny the way everyone acted, you would have thought there was a shark in the water. No one swam in the ponds again. The fish were so hungry you could throw a hook with no bait in and catch brim nonstop. To my surprise my stepmom did work at an electronic store, just like in my dream. It was Radio Shack. Another coincidence?

We moved to a nice three-bedroom house with a good-sized fenced in backyard in Lewisville. Everything was going well, and Steve asked if I was ready to have another baby and I replied, "Yes!" I was so excited! We'd discussed how far apart we wanted our kids and thought two and a half years was good. Two weeks later he said he changed his mind and wanted to wait. I told him, "Too late! I`m already pregnant cause I can feel it!" And yes, I was pregnant again. I was hoping for a girl. Me and Steve were both very happy at the news. Steve was a very good father.

I took Mikey to the public pool to teach him how to swim. He was about one and a half. The pool started off shallow and gradually got deeper. He got in the water and went under and took off. It was amazing! He swam like a little fish. We went to visit my dad and we took Mikey to the public swimming pool, and he wanted to jump off the high dive. When he got to the top, everyone watching him was holding their breath. I yelled, "It`s ok! He knows how to swim!" He jumped off into the water and swam right to the ladder and got out. It was so cute. He liked it so much, he did it all day long.

One day I said, "Hey God. I know I haven`t talked with you in a while. I haven`t had any prophetic dreams like I did years ago. Are you still there? Are you mad at me for something? Was all of that even real?" That night I had a crazy dream. What I thought was God appeared above me. He looked just like the Angel from Dejavu. I said, "God is that you?" No response. He said, "Don`t go to the lake this weekend!" I replied, "Why not? He said, "Because it is going to rain a lot and the levy is going to overflow and two alligators are going to get in the lake. A large one and a small one." At the same time he told me that, he was also using his hands to show the rain coming down and the water flowing. I immediately woke. There are alligators in Texas? I told Steve we couldn`t go to the lake this weekend and told him of my dream. It rained crazy all week and was Sunday or Monday when I picked up the newspaper and read there was a swimming competition at Lewisville Lake where we often went swimming and camping. They called it off because two alligators were in the lake. One eight foot and the other four foot. Another coincidence! Maybe this was real. Maybe God was really talking to me. Now that was scary excitement! Maybe I won`t ask God anymore weird questions. It kind of frightens me when shit like that happens. I showed Steve the newspaper article and he thought it was crazy. After the two alligators were caught, the swimming competition continued.

After that crazy dream Steve told me I should try to dream and help him gamble on his basketball games. I told him I didn't think it was to be used that way and laughed it off. A few days later I told Steve I had a weird dream and I saw milk walking around and didn't know what it meant. I kept saying, milk walkin. Steve said, it must be Milwaukee! He bet on Milwaukee Bucks next 11 games and won 10 of them. He was amazed and very happy about it and wanted me to do it again. I told him I had no control over it. It just happened randomly.

It was the night before Christmas, and I put a pop tart in the toaster, went in the other room, and forgot about it. When I walked by Inky, she'd reach her paws out and attack me! She did it over and over! I told Steve, "Inky is acting strange! She keeps attacking me without hurting me like she`s trying to tell me something! I`ve never seen her act like this before!" Then we smelled smoke! We ran into the kitchen and the toaster was in flames and was just getting ready to catch the cabinets on fire! Steve unplugged it and pushed it into the sink just in time. I realized Inky was trying to tell me there was a fire in the kitchen. What a great cat. I loved her so much.

On Mikey's first Christmas, we debated on whether to tell him about Santa or not. We knew it would be lying to him and we didn't want to start off lying to him. We weren't Christians and didn't go to church. We only celebrated Christmas because it was fun, and society did it. We went ahead and told him about

Santa and did the whole gift thing. We still didn't feel right about lying to our son. We hoped there'd be no harm in it. Easter to us was just all about the candy. Believing in the tooth fairy was fun too. Money for your teeth! Cool! My mom had an old tradition. On New Year's Eve she put coins on the windowsill and cracked the window a bit. She said it was for the money fairy to bless her money, so she'd have plenty the next year. I still did this every year.

One afternoon my little brother came over and we went to a lake. Steve and my brother were swimming while me and Mikey played on the shore. I noticed a young boy screaming help! He was frantically waving his arms and bobbing up and down in the water! I yelled to Steve and my brother, "He`s drowning!" They had just been by the boy and were halfway back to shore. They turned around and saw him go under for the last time. They swam as fast as they could to where he went under and started trying to find him. The boy's mother realized what was going on and frantically screamed and yelled at the shore for people to save him because she couldn't swim. I picked Mikey up and ran to the office and told them a boy drowned and to call the police. The whole time waiting for the police, Steve and my brother were trying to find him. I ran to the volleyball court and told the players, a young boy just drowned, and we needed help finding him right away! They just looked at me and ignored me. They acted as if I was speaking Greek. Fifteen minutes went by before help arrived. It took over half an hour before they found him. They tried to resuscitate him for a while but had no luck. We were all crying. Especially the mother. What a very sad day.

I was seven months pregnant and stopped working. I really enjoyed the mornings with Mikey. We got up around 8, had breakfast together, then I put blankets and pillows on the floor, and we watched Zoobilee Zoo and played with toys. Then we spent time in the backyard playing and having lunch. I was very tired all the time and when Mikey napped so did I. It was a warm afternoon, and I had all the windows open, but they had screens on them. We were both napping, and I was woken by a neighbor ringing the doorbell. When I opened it, she had Mikey with her. I was confused. She said she found him wandering down the street. I was still confused. How did he get out? All the doors were locked. I went to his room, and he had pushed the screen out and climbed out his window. After that I always closed the windows and doors and locked them. One time Steve spanked Mikey and left a bruise on his little tushy and I didn`t agree with it. That infuriated me! I told him, "I came from an abusive family, and will not tolerate it! If you ever lay a hand on my child like that again, we are done!" He never did that again.

My little sister came to stay with us when it was time to have my baby. She could watch Mikey while I was in the hospital. She was a handful. Late one night after we went to sleep, I heard a noise in the backyard and found her with the neighbor boy in the tent. Busted! I made him go home and Steve made her stand in the corner and then write a hundred times, "I will not have boys over late at night without permission."

Finally, I thought I was in labor but didn`t tell anyone until I was sure. It was late night, and I had a few hours of mild labor and could time the contractions at a few minutes apart. I decided I better tell Steve. As soon as the labor pain was over, I'd think maybe I wasn't in labor. I did that all the way to the hospital. This time we set it up to do an epidural. By now my labor pains were strong! The doctor broke my water, then I got the epidural, and my pain was eased. About half an hour later I told Steve, "Something's not right. I`m having bad labor pains again and I shouldn`t be!" Steve looked at my back and the tube for the epidural was gone. He found it laying on the ground, dripping. He called the nurse and she just picked it up off the floor and connected it again. That made me angry that she didn't properly sterilize it. A few hours went by, and I felt like I was going to have the baby soon, so I got out of bed and squatted next to it.

The nurse came in and franticly yelled, "What are you doing?!" I told her I was more comfortable like this, but she made me get back in bed. A little bit later I yelled for the nurse and told her the baby was coming but they didn't believe me. I was yelling for my doctor, and she finally arrived. When she got in the room, she started yelling, "Don't push! Don't push!" I was yelling, "I'm not pushing! It`s just coming out!" She barely got her rubber gloves on in time, and he popped right out into her hands. She almost didn`t catch him. He didn`t cry right away so it scared me. Finally, I heard him cry and that moment of relief came. Steve videoed the birth. It was a boy! Matthew, meaning gift of God or from God. Steve wanted to give him the middle name Spock, but I said no. He got the middle name Kirk like his dad and big brother. Before he was born Steve said he wanted no more than 2 children, and I should get my tubes tied while I was in the hospital. My doctor talked me out of it by saying things like, "What if your children die? Don`t you want more? What if you divorce and remarry? Don`t you want more? What if you divorce and your husband gets the children? Your husband can always get a vasectomy. It`s easier for him to do it than you. Don`t you want more children?" I decided that since I didn`t have a girl I'd wait. Steve wasn`t very happy about it. He soon got a vasectomy. He walked funny for a couple days and said it felt like someone punched him in the balls. Having children was the most rewarding experience I ever had.

On the first rain I baptized Matthew the same as Michael. When we were outside in the backyard Mikey was waving to what he said was God in the sky. When we were done, he ran through the house and to the front yard waving and yelling bye to God. I didn't see anything, but Mikey said he saw God.

Steve`s best friend got a job in Florida and recommended he come down and work there. He applied and got the job. The company paid our moving expenses, and we rented a big U-Haul and pulled our car behind. On the way, I let Inky out to walk around at a rest stop. When I called her, she didn't come like she always did. I called and called. I started getting worried. We looked all over for her. An hour went by and still no Inky. I was panicking! Steve said we had to go soon and leave her. I said, no way! We waited a bit longer and finally here she came, taking her sweet-ass time. I didn't let her out of the car again until we got to the apartment we rented where his best friend lived. It was in Ft. Lauderhill Florida and was a gated apartment complex with a security guard. I felt quite safe. It had an Olympic sized swimming pool, a huge picnic area, and a theater room.

The first week there, something happened that scared me. The front doors to the apartments were inside the building like a hotel. One morning I woke up and opened the door and looked in the hallway and there was blood everywhere. All down the hallway walls, on my front door, and a big puddle of blood on the floor. I was freaking out! What happened? Later I found out someone shot the security guard during the night, and he came in the building to get help, but no one heard him. He laid on the floor and blead to death! WOW! Now I didn`t feel safe anymore! The police came and questioned me, but I didn't hear or know anything.

We lived on the first floor and the living room had sliding glass doors that opened up to a giant courtyard BBQ area. It had ducks and squirrels that came right up to you to be fed. Mikey and Matt really liked that. I enjoyed the time off work and spending it with my kids and husband.

I was watching TV and JACK HORKHEIMER came on! He was real! He worked at the Space Planetarium in Florida. I was so excited when I saw him and couldn`t wait to prove to Steve he was real! I showed him the next time Jack came on and proved I wasn`t making him up. I'd really like to see the episode I saw in April or May of 1985! The one that tripped me out! The one that said if you had the marks of Pleiades somewhere on your body, then you were someone very special and always remember to keep looking up!

Above us, was an escort service. One of the ladies was fond of me and wanted to have sex but I wasn't really into women. We got a bottle of whiskey and got drunk together. We took all our clothes off and got into our king-sized waterbed and she started having fun with me. That excited Steve and he got a raging boner! Before anything really happened, I got sick from drinking too much and she left. She wanted to try again sometime but I wasn't interested.

Steve's best friend's wife wanted to have sex with me, so she came over one night. The three of us undressed and got into bed and was just getting ready to have some fun when we heard a knock at the door. It was her husband! Oh no! It took us a few minutes to get our clothes on and answer the door. When we opened it, he was suspicious, but didn`t say anything. He and his wife left right away.

Eight months passed since we moved, and we decided that Florida was not for us. Steve called his old job and got rehired and they paid our moving expenses back to Texas.

We had nowhere to live so we stayed with my mom until we found a place. My mom said we could stay with her as long as we wanted. They had a one-bedroom apartment with 13 cats and 2 dogs. Matt's playpen was in the living room and the hair in the apartment was awful. It was hard keeping it off the baby bottle and blankets. I had to constantly wash the nipple and get hair out of Matts mouth. I didn`t like it there and was miserable. Then my oldest brother showed up with a pit bull and her eight puppies and that made it even worse. It rained and mud got all over the apartment from the dogs. I told Steve, "We have to go! I can't stay here!"

I immediately started working at Dejavu again. We found a place a couple days later in Dallas very close to the bar. It had two beautiful giant swimming pools with waterfalls and a big hot tub. It had a small lazy river and a huge BBQ area. There were exotic plants everywhere and it had a big clubhouse. Just behind my apartment was another small swimming pool. I hadn`t taught Matthew how to swim yet. He wore floaties and I'd blow on his face and dunk him under water. He was almost one year old.

One time Steve's boss came in with a couple guys and I wasn't sure if he knew I was a dancer. I just avoided him and wasn't sure if he ever recognized me because we barely knew each other.

At Dejavu I was working on a spectacular dance show. I learned how to dance from watching other dancers. When I saw a move I liked, I incorporated it into my show. I learned how to do the splits by practicing on a step in the swimming pool. That really helped with my show because now I could do a lot of crazy moves like hang from the bar on the ceiling and do the splits on the ceiling. I could also put one foot on one stage, the other on another stage, and go down into the splits and the guys played limbo for money. I did a handstand on stage, then spread my legs in the splits, and went onto one hand and held my body upside down in the splits on one hand. I looked like a star when I did that. It was spectacular, and dangerous. No other dancers did that move. At work the owner put in a rainbow light that turned in circles on center stage overhead. I looked like I was in a rainbow prism. They put in a fog machine, and it really made the rainbow show up. Every day they made a giant rainbow with helium balloons and floated it over center stage. It was so cool. Sometimes I took a bunch of helium balloons and make a costume with them. When I was on center stage, I popped them one at a time until I was down to my G-string and heels. I was quite proud of my dancing skills.

While driving to work I heard an awesome song on the radio and had to add it to my show. It was called RAINBOW IN THE DARK by DIO. I bought the album and the cover shocked me. There was a demon with chains and a whip beating a preacher that was drowning in the ocean. It looked very close to the demon that I had seen with Yellow Rose! ***When there`s lightning! You know it always brings me down! Cause it`s free, and I see that***

it`s me, who`s lost and never found! I cry out for magic! I feel it dancing in the light! It was cold! Lost my hold, to the shadows of the night! No sign of the morning coming! You`ve been left on your own! Like a rainbow in the dark! Just a rainbow in the dark! Do your demons! Do they ever let you go? Do they hide deep inside? Is it someone that you know? You`re just a picture! You`re an image caught in time! There`s no sign of the morning coming! You`ve been left on your own! Like a rainbow in the dark! Feel the magic! I feel it floating in the air! But it`s fear, and you`ll hear it calling you, beware! Lookout! /Holy Diver, you`ve been down too long in the midnight sea! Ride the tiger! You can see his stripes, but you know he`s clean! Oh don`t you see what I mean?! Gotta get away! Get away! Holy Diver! Got shiny diamonds! Like the eyes of a cat in black and blue. Something is coming for you! Look out! Race for the morning! You can hide in the sun til you see the light. We will pray it`s alright! Gotta get away! Get away! Between the velvet lies! There`s a truth that`s hard as steel! The vision never dies! Life`s a never-ending wheel! Holy Diver! You`re the star of the masquerade! No need to look so afraid. Jump on the tiger! You can feel his heart, but you know he`s mean! Some light can never be seen! Holy Diver! Sole Survivor! You`re the one who`s clean! There`s a cat in the blue comin after you, Holy Diver! Gotta get away! Get away! Holy Diver! Now I knew my tattoo was A RAINBOW IN THE DARK! The two songs together on center stage with a great light show was awesome and very dramatic!

We had to tip the DJ every shift we worked. I made sure I tipped him well, so I got a great light show. If you didn't, he didn't give you a light show. He did whatever he wanted when you were on center stage. Dancing was so much fun, and I really liked it. But I always had to go first on stage because the other dancers were never ready. All I needed was my shoes and clothes and I was ready. Make-up could go on later.

In the morning when we opened, there weren't very many customers, so I practiced my dance routine. My girlfriends thought

I was crazy to put on a show for no one. They just walked around on stage. One morning I was practicing and maybe five or six customers were in the bar. At the end of my time on center stage a good-looking young man came up to tip me. He said, "Before I got here my plan was to see all the dancers dance and give these fifty ones to the best dancer in the bar. After I saw your show, I don`t think anyone will top it, so here is the fifty dollars. I`m just going to hand it to you and not throw it on the stage." What a great way to start a day!

At work there were 7 stages. On each side of center stage were side stages. Each side stage had three big bubble tubes and a pole to dance on. But I had a problem with the poles. They were too big around. I couldn`t get my little hands around it to do twirls and turns. The best I could do was climb it, turn upside down, and slide to the ground and go into the splits on the floor. I did the same with the big bubble tubes. I finally learned how to twirl on the poles. The manager told us not to climb on the water tubes anymore because they began to leak. The bar was looking like an underwater scene. I felt like Venus in a Clamshell when I took center stage. Each side stage also had runner stages. They were only about a foot wide and 10 feet long. There were also two more runner stages that were high off the ground and very dangerous to dance on. You had to hold on to a steel bar connected to the ceiling. If you fell off one side, it was an 8-foot drop.

Me and Steve were doing well financially, so I bought three fish tanks. A 75-gallon, 50-gallon, and a 30-gallon and put tropical fish in them. Some were rather expensive. I got all new furniture for the apartment and bought a piano. No one played the piano, but I was hoping my kids might. Life was going very well, and all was normal.

I liked it when it stormed and was working, because the bar got packed, and money flowed like a water tap turned on. During one storm all the lights went out. Suddenly, the two giant front doors blew off the hinges and the wind came whipping in the bar and was blowing around like a tornado. I got so scared and hid under a table until it stopped. We were all in the dark with no music. That was when it was time to go to the dressing room because in the dark men might try to take advantage of you. When we looked outside, power lines were down, trees were broken everywhere, and giant dumpsters were in the road.

Husbands liked bringing their wives in to see my show and party with me all the time. Many of them wanted me to go home with them but I'd always say, "Nope! Just innocent fun in the bar." When men asked me what my name was, I'd say, "Venus the Goddess." They'd respond with, "What are you the Goddess of?" I'd reply, "I'm the Goddess of everything because I heard LOVE CONQUERED ALL!"

Steve's and his new boss came in occasionally. Whenever Steve wasn't looking or listening, he'd come on to me in a roundabout way. He was very good looking. When we went to his apartment for dinner, he'd look at me and roll his eyes towards his bedroom as if to say he wanted me in there. I told Steve what was going on, but he didn't believe me. I didn't know what to do to convince him. I finally told Steve I didn't want to go to his boss's place anymore and didn't want him at ours. Way later in life Steve looked back and realized he was hitting on me and we had a good laugh.

The law was trying to shut down all the topless bars in the area. It was pouring rain and storming crazy outside and the bar was packed. There was barely standing room. I was dancing for this cute married man, who was tipping me lots of money very fast. Suddenly, the music stopped, the lights came on, and the cops were all around us! They were arresting dancers and customers. They started calling names off and picking out dancers they were taking to jail. Surely, they wouldn't call my name because I had done nothing wrong. They called my name! Oh shit! What did I do? They took many of us to jail and charged us with public lewdness. Steve took me to my court date. I was dressed in white, and the undercover cop took the stand and the judge asked him, "What did you see?" He replied, "I thought I saw the guy putting his hands down her g-sting but I'm not sure because it was too dark." Then my lawyer brought up a strange case from another city about two gay men getting it on in a car in public and they dismissed my case. I was totally confused about it all! When the judge said case dismissed, Steve jumped up and started clapping and the judge yelled, "Order in the court! Order in the court! We don`t do that here." I always wondered what happened to the married man. I hope they dropped his case too because we did nothing wrong. I`m sure whatever happened, his wife wasn`t happy about it.

On my court date I walked in the courthouse and almost lit a joint instead of a cigarette but noticed just in time. One time me and Steve were in a shopping mall, and I mistook a police station for a place to buy bongs because it had hundreds of bongs displayed in the window. I tried to drag him in there to buy me one until he told me what it was. What a trap!

I got my belly button pierced and wanted to do my nipples. I only did one to see how it felt. It was quite a pinch and brought a tear to my eye. When I went to work a new law was passed. Dancers had to wear flaps on their G-string backs and put liquid latex on our nipples and powder them. That wasn't good for a fresh nipple piercing and the latex got in the piercing. My boob got infected and swelled up twice its size and I had to see my doctor. She gave me antibiotics and I asked when I could put my ring back in. She asked me if I was crazy and wanted another infection. She convinced me not to put it in again.

One afternoon we were sitting in the living room and the door opened and a tall black man walked in. Steve only had time to jump up out of his chair because it happened so fast. When the guy saw Steve, he said, "Oops, wrong apartment!" then took off out the door and was gone. We were both standing there staring at each other trying to process what just happened. Wow!

That was the second time in my life that happened to me. So we bought a gun.

The owners of the bars in the area put up a tall chain link fence around the block and hired Head East and Foghat to perform in the parking lot. They charged ten dollars a person unless you worked at Baby Dolls or Dejavu. When the dancers weren`t on stage we were allowed to go outside to party and watch the bands. The parking lot was packed with people. Steve came and we had lots of fun!

I usually took a joints worth of pot to work to smoke later in the day. On this day I had the bud in a cellophane cigarette wrapper sitting in the console. I opened the door, and the wind picked my weed up and blew it away into the sky. All I could do was laugh as I watched it disappear. I guess that's how other people get lucky and find pot.

Van Halen was performing a free concert in Deep Ellum. They shut the entire block down and it was a big street party. Steve had to work, so me and my little brother went. We arrived late and were way in the back. I had a bottle of Jack Daniels but nothing to back it with. I wanted to get to the front, so I pretended I was going to throw up and everyone around me moved out of my way and I moved forward. That worked so well I did it until the only people in front of me were two tall mean looking bikers and they wouldn`t let me through. I finally made it around them and was in front just in time to hear my favorite Van Halen song LOVE WALKS IN. After a while I was being smashed against the chain fence by people behind me and I had to pee. I finally got out and found a port-a-potty. I was drunk and couldn`t find my brother anywhere. I found a place and smoked a joint. Now I was trying to find a phone to call a cab. The police saw me, and I saw them, and I threw the couple joints I had on the ground and ran in the opposite direction. They caught up with me and asked why I ran away. I told them because I was drunk. They arrested me and put me in a holding tank in the public works department.

The next morning, I woke, and they got me a big breakfast from Mc Donald's. I called Steve and he came and got me, and we drove around until we found my car. Steve didn`t get mad about it but I did pay a $100 fine for the wonderful accommodations I had the night before.

After the bar closed one night, I told my girlfriend it would be funny to change the big sign out front with the letters on it. After everyone was gone, we made it say, Free Hot Wet Pussy! No Cover Ever! When I went to work the next night, the girls were all laughing and talking about it. I guess the manager hadn`t noticed yet. When he did, he changed it back.

I started working days at Dejavu and they were making the dancers park in the back lot behind the building. Me and a girlfriend got off work together and got in her convertible and smoked a joint. She said she'd drive me around back to my car. I told her I could walk no problem. She insisted. She stopped behind my car, and I went to get in it when suddenly, the green van next to my car opened the side door and two guys jumped out and grabbed me and tried to kidnap me! My girlfriend pulled out a gun and pointed it at them and yelled really loud, "I don`t think so! Not today mother fuckers!" They let go of me and jumped back in their van and took off! Another close call. We reported it to the manager. So now we had a security guard to escort us to our cars and I felt safer.

I was working nights again and the manager informed the ladies that a man in a white pickup truck was following dancers' home, shooting them, and stealing their money. When I was on my way home, I noticed a white truck following me. I pulled into the parking lot of my apartment and parked. The white truck did too! I was starting to get scared. The white truck was parked several spaces away from me. I wasn`t sure what to do so I locked the doors and waited to see what he was going to do. He didn`t get out of his truck to go anywhere. I sat in my car trying to figure out what to do. If I got out and ran, I might not be able to unlock my apartment fast enough if he was chasing me. I knew my next-door neighbor was a coke dealer and was usually up at that time. I left all my stuff in the car and put my keys in my hand like a weapon and took off running to my apartment. He got out of his truck and started chasing after me! I ran into my neighbor's apartment because the door wasn`t locked and I immediately locked it and told him someone was following me, and they were at the door! Someone was trying to turn the doorknob to open it! My neighbor looked through the peep hole and yelled, "You better get the fuck out of here now! I`ve got a gun and if I open the door and you`re there I'll shoot you!" He went to get his gun and the stranger left. I was quite shaken when I went home and woke Steve and told him what happened. I told my manager of the incident when I went to work. We never heard any more about it. Texas is open-carry. Maybe I need a 6 shooter in a holster. It's the wild west.

There was a story going around about a dancer who worked in one of the bars in the area and was dating a man highly involved in the illegal drug trade. She did something to piss the drug dealer off. He killed her and put her through a woodchipper. I didn't believe it was true until I saw a detective show about it on TV. I was glad I hadn't gotten mixed up with the wrong crowd so far.

Some dancers were beautiful but stupid. Some couldn't even fry hamburger or slice a tomato. Those kind of chicks needed to find a rich man to take care of them. Shasta and Haley were the only long-time dancer friends I'd have. Haley lived near me, and we had kids around the same age. She was a down to earth person. Most dancers were flakes.

Our anniversary was coming up and I told Steve to get some coke and come to Dejavu to party with me and only me and pay no attention to other dancers and we'd party more afterwards. When he got to Dejavu, he started having fun with the other dancers instead of focusing his attention on me like we discussed. I wasn't happy about it, but let it slide. It was time to go home, and Steve told me he invited several dancers over to party. That wasn't the plan! I wasn't happy about it but just rolled with it. When me and the dancers were in the back getting changed, the ladies started arguing over who was going to fuck Steve! They all wanted to! I told them I was invited to the party too, and I'd see them there. They had no idea me and Steve were married. I was not a very happy camper and wondered how long Steve was going to play this stupid game with my coworkers. We were all at the apartment partying and the girls were still arguing about who was going to fuck Steve. I just sat there watching all this wondering how far Steve was going to take it. He finally said, "I must tell you all, I won`t be having sex with any of you tonight because Venus is my wife and it`s our anniversary." They were quite shocked and bummed out. Well, little did Steve know he wasn't having sex with me tonight either! We partied the rest of the night then the dancers left. I chewed Steve out and told him to never do that again. That was embarrassing.

A girlfriend of mine who used to be a dancer came to visit me at work and met one of my managers named Howard and liked him. She got tickets to Pink Floyd and took me, Steve, and him. We had a great time. They hit it off and started dating. Not long after that he took me aside and asked, "Why didn`t you tell me she was a prostitute?!" I told him, "That's not any of my business! That's between you two!" He immediately stopped seeing her and I didn't mind because he had another girlfriend who was a dancer, and she was pregnant.

Dejavu became a whorehouse, and lots of dancers did anything for money. They were out of control. Since I wasn`t that way it was hard for me to make money. I decided to go to Million Dollar Saloon and try it out. My first week there a dancer asked me to cover her set for $20. At the end of the night, I asked for my money, and she told me to wait outside, and she'd pay me. She came out and sucker punched me, and it was on! I got her on the ground and beat the shit out of her! Everyone was yelling for me to get up because they heard the police coming. I got in my car, ready to drive off, when her girlfriend started shit with me. My car window was down, so I grabbed her hair and rolled the window up with her hair in it. Then I started slowly driving off. She got really scared and started freaking out and begging me to stop. The look in her eyes of sheer terror was priceless! I asked if she was going to fuck with me anymore and she said, NO! I unrolled the window, let her hair loose, and passed the police as they pulled in. I really didn`t care for this bar. It was too big and impersonal, no fun.

I went to another bar called Southern Bells on Harry Hines. The same man who owned Dejavu and Baby Dolls owned it. I really liked the bar. It was beach themed and had beach balls and tropical plants everywhere. Free hot dogs, nachos, pizza, and popcorn. When I went to the dressing room my house mom Vernell from Dejavu was there and we were happy to see each other. Each dancer got their own small dressing room and I loved that. My favorite song to play there was Girls! Girls! Girls!/ Motley Crue ***Trick or treat, sweet to eat! On Halloween or New Year's Eve! Yankee girls you just can't be beat! Raising Hell at the Seventh Veil! Have you read the news? I'm such a good, good, boy! I just need a new toy. I'll tell you what girl, dance for me! I'll keep you over employed! Just tell me a story! You know the one I mean!***

One night when I was working the manager said he wanted me to meet a friend of his. I went over and he introduced us, and we all had a drink. I asked the guy if he wanted a dance, but he said no, not yet. I left to work the crowd and saw a regular customer and danced for him then sat down with him. My manager came to our table and grabbed my arm and told me to come back where they were sitting. I went back to the bar where they were, and the manager ordered another round of drinks. Then another. I felt something strange was going on, so I started dumping my drinks in the plants and leaving them on customers tables. I told my regular customer something was going on and my manager was trying to get me drunk. I left my drink at his table and walked away. The manager grabbed my arm again and told me to join them again. His friend was ready to spend some money. When I went over to the guy, he told me he wanted to have sex. I told him, no, I was married. I always wore my rings even when dancing. I never led any one on. It was now an hour before closing, and the guy was still trying to convince me to go home with him, and the answer was still no! He tried to grope me all over in front of my boss and I refused his passes and was fighting his groping hands off. I went to the dressing room to get away from them and heard over the speaker, Venus, you are wanted in the office. I went to the office and my boss fired me. He said I was letting his friend grope me. I told him that was a lie! I was really pissed off and went to the dressing room and threw a drink at the mirror. Glass broke all over. Mama Vernell was confused at my actions, but I was too angry to talk about it. I got my things together and as I was headed to the exit, the police showed up to escort me out. I told the police I was fired because I wouldn`t sleep with my manager's friend. As we walked out the door, to my amazement, there was John, my old weed dealer, who I hadn`t seen in at least five years and didn't know I was a dancer. He was getting ready to walk in the bar. I broke away from the police and yelled, "Oh My God! John!" I ran into his arms, hugged him, and told him what was going on and the police left. He walked me to my car, but when I tried to start it, it wouldn`t start. I was out of gas. Hmm, I had plenty of gas when I came to work. I wondered who took all the gas out of my car so I couldn`t go anywhere at the end of the night. John gave me a ride home a few blocks away and came in and met my husband. Before he left, we discussed getting together to let our kids play. I felt that would be a bad idea since I was sure he still wanted to have sex with me. We never saw each other after that.

I started working at another bar called Lipstick. To my surprise Myles wife worked there. I had no idea she was a dancer. I asked if it would be a problem if we worked together and she said no, they got divorced.

A dancer got very drunk, and I told the manager she needed to go to the hospital because she had alcohol poisoning and was dying. A guy came in the dressing room and slung her over his shoulder. I asked who he was, and he told me he was her boyfriend. I also told him she had alcohol poisoning and needed to go to the hospital immediately. He left with her and a few days later they came in and thanked me for insisting she went to the hospital because yes, she had alcohol poisoning.

My hair was very long and curly and I still looked like my character Venus. My hair was all one length, past my butt. I wanted it layered all the way down. My mom used to be a beautician, so I told her what I wanted. I said keep the length but layer it all the way down like a long shag. I even drew pictures for her. I said, "Whatever you do, don't cut the length except for maybe an inch!" She cut my hair just past my shoulder all the same length! When I looked in the mirror I freaked out and yelled, "Oh my God! Mom! Why did you do that!" I was so upset I started crying. She replied, "I'm sorry. I thought that was what you wanted." I thought, damn, how am I going to do my show as Venus if I don't look like her. I had no idea what made her cut it like that. I could tell I made her feel bad, so I got myself together and said, "I'm sorry. It's ok. It's just hair and it'll grow back." Then we hugged.

I got a harem outfit and liked to play THIEVES IN THE TEMPLE by PRINCE. I'd dress up like a harem princess with veils and tassels that I pulled off. The song went like this. ***Love come quick! Love come in a hurry! There are thieves in the temple tonight! They don't care where they kick, just as long as they hurt you. There are thieves in the temple tonight! Love if your there come save me, from all this cold despair! I can hang when your around, but I'll surely die if you're not there! I feel like I'm looking for my soul. Voices from the sky say rely on your best friend to pull you through. Cause me and you could have been a work of art.***

I also liked LOVE FOR SALE by SOUTHGANG. ***Wining, dining you all night long, in a fancy French restaurant. Candy, roses, diamonds, and limousines. I give ya anything that you want. You say that gold can't buy your love. No that would never do. Now all my riches turn to dust without you! If your love was for sale, I would buy it up. If your heart was a wishing well, I would fill it up. I'd pay any price! If your love was for sale! I'd take you places far away, from Paris to the Taj Mahal. I'd have you painted in a thousand poses, but you don't seem to care at all. You say that money is just a cheap disguise to hide what's really true. I'm just a beggar in your eyes! I'm begging you!***

There was a dancer that smoked crack and I didn`t know she was an addict. I asked her to get some for me and Steve to try and gave her a hundred dollars. She got it and came over. We all took turns taking hits of it. It did feel good. When it got to the last hit, she insisted that she have it, but it wasn`t her turn and she didn`t pay for any of it. It was my turn. Steve explained that to her and she became furious. I took the last hit and she got even angrier. Me and Steve took the pipe outside and he busted it on the ground in front of her. We never had her over or smoked crack again after seeing how crazy it made her.

There was a very sexy young blonde at work and for Steve's birthday I asked if she'd come over and have some play sex with me while my husband watched and to my surprise she said, yes. We made plans and she came over and we all had fun. Nothing serious. I knew he'd really like it.

I liked the bar's atmosphere but the stages weren`t that great. It was the last dance of the night and at every topless bar, we did showtime. All ladies danced on the floor or stage for tips at the same time. I found this young good-looking man tipping twenties. A dancer named Goldie saw him tipping me lots of money and waited for me to leave so she could get some. Only problem was, I wasn`t leaving him until showtime was over or he stopped tipping me. Show time was over and Goldie was mad she didn't get to dance for him, so she went to the owner and told him I let a guy put his hands down my pants earlier in the evening. That was a lie. She was just jealous. But since they were close friends, he fired me. That pissed me off and I told them they could both go fuck themselves!

I went back to Dejavu to see if it got any better. They had bouncers on each side of the bar to make sure dancers didn`t get too crazy with the customers. I really liked that because I could make good money if the girls weren`t being whores. When I went back to work, we had a free tanning bed. I used it every day and got very tan. The owner installed movie screens on each of the side stages. If you brought a music video, you could play it while dancing on center stage. The screens lowered down from the ceiling with a touch of a button and back up when the music was over. I went to the store but the only music videos I found were WHAT GOD WANTS by ROGER WATERS and SUNDAY BLOODY SUNDAY by U2. The videos were cool to play, but it took attention off me when on center stage. I didn't like that, so I stopped doing videos.

The bar had lots of black lights, so I took colored highlighters and drew pink hearts, yellow moons, and blue stars all over my body and it looked great. You only saw them when the black lights were shining on me. If I went outside, they were invisible.

Steve took me to a comedy show and afterwards I wanted to try standup comedy. I worked on an act and called myself Andrea Marbles Putty and was known as The Anti Dice. I made jokes about Andrew Dice Clay. I got white thigh high boots and a long sexy white jacket and cut a bunch of superballs in half and superglued them all over my jacket. I told everyone that it was the best jacket to wear when drinking because if I got too drunk and fell down, I'd bounce right back up and say, "Hell yeah let`s party!" But the first time I got on stage the superglue didn`t work as well as they said it did, and I started losing my balls! When people asked me what I did for a living I'd tell them, "I'm a producer and a chauffeur. I produced two kids and now I have to chauffer their asses around!" Guys came in and asked me my name, but before I could answer, they'd ask if I wanted to go fuck! I'd respond, "Well, my name is Venus! As in flytrap! You know you stick your meat in and it doesn`t come back out! Still wanna go fuck!" It confused some and aroused others. If a married man came in the bar and tried to grope me, I'd kiss him on the back of his shirt with bright red lipstick and say, "Yo asshole, I`ll get you for that later!" If a guy reached out and inappropriately touched me, I'd give him a quarter and say, "If you want to reach out and touch someone, here`s a quarter to call your mommy!" One time Dice and I were in a plane high in the sky. He bent over, I kicked his ass out and said, "Fuckin Fly or die!" Yo, do pigs fly?" Needless to say, he waved goodbye, and from that moment on, I knew pigs couldn`t fly, but it was fun watching him try! And the last thing I said to him was, "Yo! I`ll treat you like the pig that you are!"

We now had over 30 dancers on each shift. The bar had a big sign outside that said, 29 beautiful women and 1 ugly one. I thought that was funny. I decided to jokingly sell a product called Handy Dandy Blindy Bifuckles. They were just glasses you couldn't see through. I'd tell men, "Get your Handy Dandy Blindy Bifuckles while supplies last. If you happen to find yourself fucking the ugly one in your car tonight, you'll need to get a pair. Get them now while supplies last!"

One night after the bar closed, my boss let me do my comedy and the dancers stayed to watch. Steve was in the back of the bar hiding because he was sure that I'd bomb. By the time I was done, the dancers were rolling on the floor laughing! It was a hit! Steve was impressed and said he'd never be able to do that.

I danced at Dejavu and did my stand-up comedy at an amateur comedy club. After several times at the club, the owner told me I had to clean up my act or go. Yes! I was a dirty comedian! I told them to go fuck themselves and never went back. I didn`t really want to be a comedian. I just did it for fun and the experience of it. I wanted to see what it was like. The adrenalin rush was overwhelming, and I'd shake after every performance. It was way easier to take my clothes off and dance than to be a comedian.

Steve's work had a big party at a hotel, and had a talent show contest, so I entered. When it was my turn on stage, I made the parents take their kids to the hallway then told all my dirty jokes. I won second place. Fifty bucks. The boss's daughter took first place. Go figure. I never did anymore stand-up comedy after that, but the experience was fun.

After a week at pre-k Mikey came home and told me he didn`t want to go anymore because he was the only white kid in class, and everyone picked on him. He was very upset about it. I totally understand how he felt because I'd been there. I told him he didn`t have to go to school again until kindergarten.

Our apartment had an alarm system that we set every night. One night when Steve was working and the boys were sleeping, a drunk man knocked on the door and said, "It's Santa Claus! Let me in!" I yelled, "Go away or I'll call the police!" He left and a short time later, the house alarm went off. I ran around to see what set it off and found a window about 2 inches open. I shut it and locked it while the security people talked to me on the monitor. I told them I thought someone had tried to get in the window.

One day we all went out for lunch and when we got back there had been a big fire on the front of our apartment but the inside didn`t burn. The firemen got it out in time. Someone started a fire by putting paper in the front of the apartment and lighting it. Then it caught the building on fire! We were lucky we had no damage.

We moved to a better area and rented a nice little three-bedroom house with a big backyard in Lewisville on Strickland. Mikey started school and liked it. He did very well and made friends with kids in the neighborhood. We were very happy.

Everything was going well for us. Matt was around three and a half and was so cute and lots of fun to play with.

Steve always won giant stuffed animals when we went to the state fair or Six flags. One time he made a tape at the singing booth for me. Me and the kids heard him when we were outside the recording booth. He sounded hilarious! We were laughing so hard! He chose a song that was not easy to sing. TWO PRINCES/ SPIN DOCTORS ***One. Two. Princes kneel before you. That's what I said now! Princes. Princes who adore you. Just go ahead now! One has diamonds in his pocket. That's some bread now! This one, said he wants to buy you rockets. Ain't in his head now! This one got a princely racket. Got some, big seal upon his jacket. Ain't in his head now! You marry him your father will condone you. How bout that now. You marry me, your father will disown you. He'll eat his hat now! Marry him or marry me! I'm the one that loves you baby can't you see? I ain't got no future or family tree! But I know what a prince and lover ought to be! So, if you want to call me baby, just go ahead now. If you like to tell me maybe. Just go ahead now. And if you want to buy me flowers. Just go ahead now. And if you like to talk for hours. Just go ahead now! One. Two. Princes kneel before you. Oh! Your Majesty! Come on forget the king and marry me!***

We decided to buy a house and found a cute three-bedroom in The Colony with a big fenced in backyard and a football field in the back. It was a very small town.

One-night my little sister and her husband came over to spend the night and party. Matt was sleeping and I left Mikey there with her husband while me and my sister went around the corner to get beer. When I got home, Mikey was sitting on the front lawn crying. I immediately became alarmed and asked him what was wrong. He told me Michelle's husband said he was going to cut him into little tiny pieces and flush him down the toilet and no one would ever know what happened to him! When I heard that, I turned into a crazy demon and flew into the house in a rage and went off on her husband! Then I kicked them out and told my sister he was never allowed here again! She asked, "But we drove two hours to get here! What are we going to do?" I replied, "I don't fuckin care! Just leave!" I was so mad!

The Cowboys won the Superbowl, and we took the kids to the parade party downtown. It went well, but at the end, one of the cars in the parade somehow caught on fire. When the parade was over the atmosphere immediately changed. People started lighting fires and dumping porta-potties and trash dumpsters over. Fights broke out around us. Steve picked up Matt and I grabbed Mikey's hand and we took off running for the car. It was very scary and total chaos, but we made it out unharmed. We saw the destruction on the news later and it was shameful.

I was giving a girlfriend a ride home after work and we were on a three-lane highway doing 70 miles an hour. There was a car in front of us. Something told me to get in the lane furthest from the car and go around and pass it. My girlfriend was confused at why I maneuvered in such a strange way. As soon as I passed the car, we looked in the rearview mirror and the car had spun out of control and was playing pinball off the rails. She looked at me in amazement and asked, "How did you know something was going to happen?" I told her, "I didn't! Something just spoke to me, and I listened to it." She thought that was wild!

Sometimes for a joke I'd call my friend Brenda in the middle of the night and scarily whisper, "Brenda! Where's the kitty?" She'd respond, "I don't know." Then we'd chit chat for a while. I did this to her for many years! I did it a lot because (for some reason) I thought it was funny.

Boys, birds, dogs, cats, lizards, snakes, fish, turtles, hamsters, bugs, and sports was what my future held. I really enjoyed being a mom.

Mike started playing football and it interfered with his piano lessons, so he had to choose. He had just learned how to play The Blue Danube. But football it was. It was convenient having the football field behind our house. Our kids loved to play sports and eventually played basketball, football, baseball, and soccer. Sometimes Steve was the coach for their teams, and it was lots of fun going to their games.

One night while coming home from work I got a flat tire right in front of my mom's place on Highway 121. I felt how lucky I was that I wasn't stuck somewhere on the highway. My mom answered the door and I told her I had a flat. She started bitching at me! She said her husband was too sick to change it because he was dying of cancer. I told her I'd call Steve and when he got off work, he'd come change it and I'd stay there until then. For some strange reason she didn't like the idea and had her husband change it. I couldn't believe my mom acted like that to me. It's not like I did it on purpose! It made me so mad I went into the restroom and screamed. I thought moms were supposed to help their daughters in times of need. My tire got changed and now I didn't ever want to ask my mom for help with anything again. I was happy I got my flat tire in front of her place instead of further down the road because it was a spooky dark highway.

A couple things happened on highway 121 before I had the flat that made me not want to walk down it at night. The first was when I was driving home during the day. It was only me and another car on the highway. A big giant cougar walked slowly across it in front of our cars. We both had to stop because it was taking it's time crossing. I was amazed. I looked over at the person in the other car and they had big eyes too. Then the cougar went into the bushes. Another time it was dark and me and Steve were driving home when something floated in front of our windshield. We looked at each other in puzzlement. Steve said, "Did you see that?" I replied, "I don't know! What did you see?" Neither one of us wanted to admit what we saw. We both tried to say maybe it was a huge garbage bag floating in the air. But we knew it wasn't. It looked more like a grey ghost or spirit. Like the one I saw at the house in Oak Cliff.

Steve was drunk one night, and we got into an argument because he wanted to drive somewhere. He started manhandling me and that pissed me off, so I just let him go. The next day I told him I wouldn't put up with it and next time I'd call the police and leave him. I had never told him of the physical abuse I'd witnessed as a child.

We went to Ohio to visit Steve's family and went to Mill Creek Park where he played as a child. What was funny about this story was a week earlier I told Steve, "You do know you look like Jesus, right?" He just laughed. While me and his sister were watching them playing in the creek she yelled out, "Steve! You look like Jesus!" I just started laughing because I was glad someone else saw it too and not just me.

I never met Steve's dad but thought I had a dream about him. He had an eye patch, so I figured it was him. I was picked up in a spaceship and a man with an eyepatch was at the controls. Everything was fine until he turned into an alien, and I started screaming for him to put me back down on the planet! He said, "Ok! Just calm down!" He put me back on the planet and the whole planet was in ruins like a big bomb had gone off! I looked around and started yelling, "Wait! Come back! Don't leave me here!" Then I woke. Me and Steve talked about it, and he said, "Yeah, that sounds like my dad. Sometimes he was a prankster."

I began having awesome flying dreams. A man dressed in a black suit and cape with a hat came to me at night and picked me up and flew me around the world. It was so much fun. When we'd fly too high and I looked down it frightened me, and I'd start falling. Then I'd wake up. That happened a lot, so I began trying to recognize places and stay low. He taught me how to run and take off. Sometimes I didn't make it through the walls and bounced back on my butt. Once I was trying to fly and got stuck against the ceiling and was yelling for help. I was trying to master my dreams. Almost always, when I realized I was dreaming, I tried to fly. Sometimes I jumped in the air and floated around and looked down at people on the ground. My dream life was as big as my real life, and I couldn't wait for bedtime to go into the other world. If I dreamt I was cheating on Steve I'd get worried and wake up wondering if it was real or just a dream. Sometimes it took hours to tell Steve my dreams. He said it wasn't fair because he rarely dreamt. Steve was always telling me to keep a journal of them, but I'd start one and never keep up with it. It took way too much time to write everything down.

A topless bar called Wranglers opened 5 miles away from home, so I started working there. I didn`t really care for the bar but it was close. When two men were sitting together, I'd dance for both at the same time. I put one foot on one guy's shoulders and one on the other guy's shoulder and do the splits upside down. I always warned them to not touch me because it was a dangerous move. The owner didn`t like that move and said it was too provocative and told me not to do it anymore. It was a totally legal move, and if he let dancers go to places in the bar where they let men suck all over their boobs and grope them, I'd keep dancing that way. We got in an argument over it, and I was fired again.

I went back to Dejavu for a bit, but I was tired of dancing and needed a break. I got a job at a costume rental shop called Incognito. I really enjoyed it. After a week my car broke down and needed lots of work. I didn't have money to fix it, so I went back to Dejavu to make quick money. I went back just before Halloween and saw a bunch of bullet holes in the wall. While I was gone someone came in with a gun and shot up the place and thankfully no one got hurt. I was glad I wasn't there when it happened.

We liked to camp and here were some stories from our adventures. We were all at Dinosaur Valley camping and were sitting around a square concrete fire pit late at night. The boys got tired and went in the tent to sleep. We were eating cheese Doritos when a racoon showed up. We put Doritos on the ledge of the concrete fire pit and the racoon reached up with its tiny human like fingers and took it and ate it. It was so cute. Then many racoons wanted Doritos, so we kept feeding them. We put the rest of the Doritos in a cooler behind us. We weren`t looking and a racoon opened the cooler, grabbed the Doritos, and ran off into the dark woods. Then all the racoons started growling like mad dogs because we had no more Doritos and that scared us. We jumped up and went running for the tent and I tripped over an armadillo and fell rolling on the ground. Steve thought that was hilarious as we both tried to get in the tent at the same time. We were laughing out of control until we made it in the tent and felt safer. That would make a great Doritos commercial.

Another time at Dinosaur Valley there was a small river you walked across to go to the hiking spots. While we hiked, a quick storm came and went. We went to cross back to our campsite, but the river was much higher and rushing way faster. We all had to hold hands very tight to cross and if my hand slipped, Matt would be swept away in the current. We slowly made it across safely. It was our anniversary that night and we were in the middle of another big storm. The tornado sirens went off and all the campers went to the brick restrooms because it was the only safe place. We were with a bunch of strangers having a party in the women's restroom when the big tornado came and passed. When it was over, I thanked them for having a fun party with us. It was scary but fun. They wished us happy anniversary and we all went back to our campsites.

Me and Steve were hiking at Dinosaur Valley and found a beautiful lagoon. It looked like it was out of a story book. It was getting late so we didn`t swim but tried to remember where it was so we could go back another day. Steve's sister came to visit, so we took her and our kids to Dinosaur Valley to camp and go to the lagoon. It was over 100 degrees and we couldn`t find it anywhere. After a couple hours, we ran out of water, and I began to get heat stroke. My face turned beet red, and my lips and face went numb. I knew that wasn't good but my kids were doing ok and didn't complain once. We finally found a very small pond of water. The pond was very yucky and had bugs all over it. We knew we had to get in the water to cool off. We all slowly crept into the pond and laid down. After that I felt much better. Now we were just trying to find the path to get back across the river to our campsite because it was getting dark and had no flashlight. I was getting worried, when finally, we saw a hiker and asked which way to the river. He told us we were about a mile away and going the right direction. We felt relieved knowing we only had a mile to go, and we made it back to the campsite as darkness came. Me and his sister thought we were going to die out there.

One time me and Steve and our kids went camping at the lake by our house and a big storm came. We tried to ride it out in the tent, but it started filling with water. The wind was incredible, so we decided to leave. We packed the car quickly and were trying to get the tent down, but it was flying in the air like a kite, and we were struggling with it. Two guys saw us and jumped out of their car and helped Steve wrestle the tent to the ground and I drove the car over it so it wouldn't blow away. They finally got the tent in the trunk, and we thanked them and went on home. The next day we went back to see what damage the storm caused, and a giant tree fell exactly where our tent had been. The trunk was as wide as I was tall. If we had stayed and rode the storm out, we would have been flattened like pancakes. Good decision.

In my religious life I still didn't go to church or worship God or Jesus or really pray to anyone. I didn't want anything to do with all that stuff and was happy that way. It was too confusing and all I wanted was the truth. I wanted to stop searching but found that difficult. Many things didn't seem right about the story of Jesus, but I wasn't sure what it was. This whole virgin birth is not a miracle. A fertile female only needs sperm to get pregnant. Was he God or the son of God? Many people had different views on it. But once in a great while, I prayed to God.

I had two accidents and my car had hood and engine damage, but still ran. I was driving and was stopped at a red light and my kids were in the backseat. The engine caught on fire, so I yelled, "Get out of the car NOW! They asked, "Why?" and I yelled, "Just do what I said! Now!" We got out and I told them the car was on fire. By now the fire was blazing four feet above the hood. Luckily it was next to a mechanic shop, and they came out with fire extinguishers and put it out.

I got a cute little red car but was having a brake problem. Whenever it rained and I pressed the brakes they locked up and I fish tailed. It was dangerous. We had our mechanic Casper look at it, but he couldn't find anything wrong. He put water on it and still nothing. I got it back and when it rained it was still locking up. I told Steve, "I'm not driving that car anymore. It will kill me like this!" I showed Steve and finally he saw them lock up. He got the pads on the back brakes changed and my car was fine. Right after I paid it off, I was coming home from Dejavu, and it was dusk. I was only a block away from home and didn`t notice a car illegally parked on the snake shaped road and I ran right into it. It made a very loud crash and I hit my mouth on the steering wheel and was bleeding. No one came out so I drove half a block to my house to get help. As soon as I got home, I told Steve to call the police and paramedics. I told him I was hurt but not sure how bad and needed to wait outside for the police. I had blood down the front of my shirt. He called the police, and I grabbed some paper towels and went outside to wait. As soon as I got outside the police came around the corner and I waived my hands to flag them down. They asked me why I fled the scene and I told them I didn`t. I could see where the accident happened from my house. I told them I only left to get medical attention and to have my husband call the police. The paramedics came and checked me out and I just had a small cut in my mouth. A few days later the police called and informed me they'd be at my house in 5 minutes to arrest me for leaving the scene of an accident. I assured them that was not the case and explained it to them. They still said they'd be there in 5 minutes to arrest me and hung up. I started crying and now I had to talk to God. I said, "God, you know I didn`t leave the scene of the accident. I need you to do something right now, so they don`t come arrest me! Unless you want me to be arrested!" I got dressed, put my shoes on, and called Steve to let him know what was going on. While I waited for them to show up, I got a call. It was the police. They said they just reviewed the case and decided to drop it. What a relief! I thanked God for helping me and went on my merry way. Totaled the car.

I got a Dodge Ram party van that was very big and hard to drive. The back turned into a bed, and it had a table and four swivel chairs. We did lots of camping and partying in that van. Me and Steve drove to the lake to be alone and have some fun. Afterwards Steve stepped out in his shorts, and I stepped out in my underwear. I accidentally fell against the door, and it shut. The keys were in the van, and it was locked. We tried to unlock it but couldn't. There was no one around. Steve went to the office at the lake and called a locksmith to come while I hid behind the trees in my underwear until he got back. That was scary. When the locksmith showed up, I hid behind the trees again until he left. Steve thought it was funnier than I did.

My little brother called and wanted me to come to his bar after work to check it out. It was a regular Rock-N-Roll bar around the corner from work. I got there at 8 and saw the bouncer who was very tall, muscular, and very scary looking, with a big ring in his nose, long black hair, and tattoos all over. I told him, "I`m looking for my little brother. He's the DJ. He told me to meet him here." He replied very loudly and rudely, "Well little girl! I suggest you take a seat and wait on him just like the rest of us do!" About 15 minutes later my brother showed up and the entire bar went crazy chanting his name. He started shaking hands, hugging people, and greeting them. I had no idea he was such a big star in his bar. I was kind of jealous because I didn't get that kind of reception when I went to work, and I was Venus the Goddess. He showed me around and introduced me to his people. The bar was very big and awesome. It had an ice block shot that was a big, long slanted slab of ice and you poured a shot at the top and it went down the ice and you sucked it up at the bottom. There were two volleyball courts, two swimming pools, and the entire outside had sand on the ground. It made you feel like you were at a beach. My brother went on to do his job and I played topless volleyball with the ladies until I had to go.

Me and Steve partied in Deep Ellum one night until the bars closed and when we got to our car, the parking lot was near empty. We decided to have sex and were getting it on when we saw a police car, but it wasn't close. We decided to keep doing what we were doing. Next thing we knew a cop was knocking on the window! Shit! We were busted! We didn`t see the cop pull up behind us because we were so busy trying to keep an eye on the cop in front of us. We got ourselves together and got out of the car and the police thought I was a prostitute. We told them we were married but they didn`t believe us until we showed them our driver's licenses. They told us it wasn't a safe place to be doing what we were doing and to go home.

The owner of Dejavu built a new bar on the parking lot where I was almost kidnapped and named it Venus Topless. He wanted me to go to work there but I kept refusing. I told him I really liked Dejavu. I finally relented and the next week I went to work there. I worked about a week and the manager said I was too provocative. I thought that was stupid because I was supposed to be. I was an exotic dancer! If I wanted to tease a man by sucking my beer bottle like a cock, I would! I didn`t like the way the stages were set up anyway, so I went back to my old stomping ground, Dejavu.

Now at Dejavu, the dancers were private contractors, and had to declare 3 table dances a shift and pay a percentage to the bar. That sucked! No more weekly paychecks! We had 30 plus dancers on each shift. If you showed up late and they had all the dancers they wanted, they didn`t let you work. I made sure I was always on time. I didn`t want to drive an hour for nothing.

The bar was sold to a new owner, and we were rocking it hard when he came in and he didn't like it. We used the music to bring the bar to a crazy high level, and it made money and drinks flow more. It was so much fun! The new owner made a new rule. Every third dancer had to do country music. I didn't like country music and hated when dancers played it because it brought the bar down. I had to find some decent country music in case I got stuck playing it. This is some of what I came up with: SOMETHING TO TALK ABOUT/BONNIE RAITT ***Let`s givem something to talk about. A little mystery to figure out. How about Love!*** TURN THE PAGE/BOB SEGER ***You don`t feel much like riding. You just wish the trip was through. Here I am. Upon the stage! Here I go, playin the star again. There I go. Turn the page! You feel the eyes upon you, as you`re shakin off the cold. And you always seem outnumbered. You don`t dare make a stand. Out there in the spotlight you`re a million miles away. Every ounce of energy, you try to give away! As the sweat pours out your body like the music that you play. Here I am upon the stage! Here I go, playin the star again! There I go! Turn the page!*** Sometimes I got away with songs that weren't really country like these: LIFE'S BEEN GOOD TO ME SO FAR/JOE WALSH ***I have a mansion forget the price. I've never been there. They tell me it`s nice. They say I`m crazy, but I have a good time. I`m just looking for clues at the scene of the crime. Lucky I`m sane after all I`ve been through. I can`t complain but sometimes I still do. Life`s been good to me so far. I keep on going, Guess I`ll never know why.*** MANSION ON THE HILL/NEIL YOUNG ***Well I saw an old man walking in my place. And he looked at me, it could have been my face. His words were kind, but his eyes were wild! He said, "I got a load to Love, but I want one more child." Around the next bend take the highway to the sun. Or the rocky road, it really don't matter***

which one. I was in a hurry but that don't matter now. There's a mansion on the hill. Psychedelic music fills the air. Peace and Love live there still. On that mansion on the hill. THE GIRL WITH FAR AWAY EYES/ROLLING STONES ***I had an arrangement to meet a girl, but I was kinda late. I thought by the time I got there she'd be off. To my surprise she was sitting in the corner. A little bleary and worse for wear was a girl with far away eyes.*** COVER OF THE ROLLING STONE/DR. HOOK ***Well, were big rock singers. We got golden fingers. We sing about beauty, and we sing about truth. We take all kinds of pills to give us all kind of thrills. I wanna see my smilin face on the cover of the Rolling Stone!***

Mama Vernell was also back at Dejavu and I was happy about that. I told her what happened at Southern Bells, and she totally understood why I acted that way. I didn't usually act like that unless I had a good reason.

I got too drunk at work once and was doing my upside-down handstand on center stage and doing the splits and was just getting ready to stand on one hand when my arm buckled and got caught under me in a weird way and I couldn`t move. It was hilarious looking! I was upside down trying to wiggle my legs and free my arm under my body. The stage doors opened, and a manager helped me get unstuck and off stage. I was laughing uncontrollably! It was so fucking funny! After I quit laughing, I started crying because I was embarrassed. Then I started laughing again. My manager kept telling me it was alright. I composed myself and just worked the floor the rest of the night. No more breaking my own rules, hopefully.

We got a new manager that was a real creep. He followed me around trying to put his hands down my pants and I had to constantly fight him off. He was an alcoholic jerk, and his wife was the bartender. They'd steal liquor from the bottles and replace it with water. He'd tease me and call me Lady Godiva and say, "One day I'm going to bring a white horse into the bar for you to ride around on!" I got tired of fighting him off and told the new owner what was going on. The owner must have said something to him because he didn`t bother me sexually anymore. But we were by no means friends after that. He was always an asshole to me. The rule was table dances were $20 dollars a song and got paid at the end. One time, instead of paying me, a customer whipped his dick out and refused to pay so I went to the manager who I didn`t like and told him what happened. He was supposed to kick him out but didn`t. He replied, "Wait until he finishes his beer, and I'll kick him out." I disagreed with that and went to the guy's table, picked up his beer, poured it in his lap, then walked away. He left because no dancer wanted to dance for a man with wet pants.

Occasionally after work I went to the topless bar next door to have a Martini and see what was going on. Some of the managers went there too. This one time I sat at the bar and my very cute and nice manager was at a table with a bunch of dancers. I ordered my drink and took one little sip and passed out on the floor! My manager jumped up and ran over to help me. He had no idea what was wrong. He just saw me 10 minutes ago and I was fine. But now I was incoherent. He asked me what was wrong, and I told him I didn't know. He helped me up and took me outside and got me a cab. He gave the cabby $50 and told him to take me home. About 10 minutes later I seemed to be sobering up and told the cabby to just drive me around for 10 more minutes and take me back to Dejavu. By the time I got to my car I was fine. That was very strange! I was glad my manager was there! If he hadn't, I don't know what would have happened! I didn't go to the topless bar next door anymore.

One day all the dancers brought water guns and oozies to work and had a big water fight in the bar. It was so much fun! We did it for 2 days. The men were warned before they came in that all the dancers had oozie water guns and if they didn`t want to get wet then they shouldn`t come in. The carpet was soaked with water. The boss finally said that was enough. No more water fights. I knew the fun had to eventually come to an end. I think they let us do that because we were getting new carpeting. That next day they tore all the carpeting out and we got sexy red plush carpeting with new chairs and tables.

The topless bars were having porn stars come in and put on dance shows, take pictures with customers, and sign autographs. I really hated those days because the guys paid no attention to us dancers. When the porn stars were there, the guys didn't spend money on us, only the porn stars.

When I was too tired to dance and didn't feel like putting on a show, I did short songs like these. I CAN'T DANCE/ GENESIS ***Hot sun, beating down! Burning my feet just walking around! I can't dance! I can't talk! The only thing about me is the way I walk! I can't dance! I can't sing! I'm just standing here, selling everything!*** CRAZY LITTLE THING CALLED LOVE/ QUEEN ***This thing, called love, I just can`t handle it. This thing, called love, I must get round to it. I ain`t ready! Crazy little thing called love. I kind a like it! Crazy little thing called love.*** LOVE STREET/DOORS ***She lives on Love Street. Lingers long on Love Street. She has a house and garden. I would like to see what happens. She has robes and she has wisdom. And she knows what to do. She has me and she has you! I see you live on Love Street! There`s this store where the creatures meet. I wonder what they do in there. I guess I like it fine. So far. Lalalalalalal! Lalalalalalala!*** WALK OF LIFE/DIRE STRAITS ***Here comes Johnny singing, I got a woman, down in the tunnel tryin to make it pay. Turning all the nighttime into the day. After all the violence and double talk. You do the walk. You do the walk of life.*** DIRTY LOVE/FRANK ZAPPA ***Give me! Your dirty love! Like you might surrender to some dragon in your dreams. Like a pink donation to the dragon in your dreams! Like some tacky little pamphlet in your daddy's bottom drawer! I don't believe you've never seen that book before. I don't need no consolation! I don't want your reservation! I only got one destination, and that's your dirty love! I'll ignore your***

cheap aroma, and your little-bo-peep diploma! I'll just put you in a coma, with some dirty love!

I wanted to have a water gun fight at my house, so I invited some dancers. Steve was the camera man and enjoyed filming all of us. The dancers were running around in their G-strings with oozies, blasting each other and dancing around partying. The entire living room and kitchen were soaked, and we were sliding and falling down on the slippery kitchen floor. The dancers were having wrestling matches on the soaked living room floor while wearing only G-strings. What a mess to clean up the next day.

I made a strawberry cake with chocolate icing, and it was sitting on the kitchen counter. Steve walked by and out of the blue I dug my hand into it and threw some on him and yelled, "Food Fight!" Oh, it was on now! We took all our clothes off and had a big cake fight! It got very slippery everywhere from the icing. We fucked like rabbits on the kitchen floor covered in cake. It was a lot of fun. We showered, then it was time to clean the mess and it wasn't easy. It was hard to get all the icing off the tile floor.

Every Sunday morning to open my show at Dejavu I played LITHIUM by NIRVANA. It went like this: ***I'm so ugly, but that's ok cause so are you. We've broken our mirrors. Sunday morning is every day for all I care. And I'm not scared. Light my candles, in a daze cause I found God! Yeah! And just maybe, I'm to blame for all I've heard. But that's ok, my will is good! Yeah! I like it! I'm not gonna crack! I love you! I'm not gonna crack! I killed you! I'm not gonna crack!***

Other songs I liked playing on Sundays. *LOSING MY RELIGION/REM* ***Oh life, is bigger! It's bigger than you and you are not me! The lengths that I will go to. Oh no I've said too much! I set it up. That's me in the corner! That's me in the spotlight, losing my religion! Tryin to keep up with you and I don't know if I can do it. Oh no I've said too much! I haven't said enough. I thought that I heard you sing. I think I thought I saw you try. Every whisper. Every waking hour, I'm, choosing my confessions.***

Consider this the hint of the century. The slip that brought me to my knees failed. What if all these fantasies come flailing around? Now I've said too much. But that was just a dream. Just a dream. LAY YOUR HANDS ON ME/BON JOVI ***They say that to really free your body, you've got to free your mind. Hey check this out! Lay your hands on me! Lay your hands on me! Lay your hands on me! Come on! If you're ready, I'm willing and able. To lay my cards out on the table! Right now. What you get ain't always what you see! But satisfaction is guaranteed! If you want me to lay my hands on you then, lay your hands on me! All you gotta do is, lay your hands on me! Now listen up! I'm a fighter, I'm a poet, I'm a preacher. I've been to school, and I've been the teacher! If you show me how to get up off the ground, I can show you how to fly and never ever come back down! All you gotta do is, lay your hands on me!*** PERSONAL JESUS/DEPECHE MODE ***Reach out and touch me. Your own personal Jesus. Feeling unknown and you're all alone. Flesh and bone by the telephone. Lift up the receiver. I'll make you a believer. Your own personal Jesus.*** LEAVE YOUR LIGHT ON/SANTANA ***Hey now, all you sinners put your lights on. All you killers put your lights on. All you children leave your lights on. You better leave your lights on. Cause there's a monster! Living under my bed! Whispering in my ear. There's an angel, with her hand on my head. She say I got nothing to fear. I still got a purpose to serve. So let your light shine, deep into my hole. We all shine like stars and then we fade away.*** SELLING THE DREAM/LIVE ***And to love a god. And to fear a flame. And to burn a love that has a name. I've willed, I've walked, I've read, I've talked! I know! I know! I know! I've been here before! And to Christ, a cross. And to me, a chair. I will sit and earn the ransom from up here!*** LIKE A PRAYER/MADONNA ***Life is a mystery. Everyone must stand alone. I hear you call my name, and it feels like home. When you call my name, it's like a little prayer. I'm down on my knees. I wanna take you there. In the midnight hour, I can feel your power. I hear your voice. It's like an angel singing.***

I close my eyes. Oh God I think I'm falling out of the sky. Heaven help me! Like a child you whisper softly to me. You're in control. Now I'm dancing. It's like a dream. No end and no beginning. Let the choir sing! SHE TALKS TO ANGELS/BLACK CROWS ***She'll tell you she's an orphan, after you meet her family. She pulls those shades down tight! She gives a smile when the pain comes! Pains gonna make everything alright! Says she talks to angels! They call her out by her name. Oh yeah! She talks to angels! Says they call her out by her name! Says she talks to angels! Don't you know that they call her out by her name!*** *WHAT GOD WANTS/ ROGER WATERS* ***What God wants, God gets! God help us all! The kid in the corner looked at the priest. The priest said God wants goodness. God wants light. God wants mayhem. God wants clean fight. What God wants, God gets! Don't look so surprised! It's only Dogma! The monkey in the corner wrote the lesson in his book. God wants peace. God wants war. God wants famine. God wants chain stores. God wants sex. God wants freedom. God wants Semtex. What God wants, God gets! God wants boardwalks. God wants jihad. God wants good. God wants bad. The alien prophet cried! What God wants, God gets! God wants crack. God wants rainfall. God wants wetbacks. God wants voodoo. God wants shrines. God wants law. God wants organized crime. God wants crusades. It seems God wants everything and more!*** SUNDAY BLOODY SUNDAY ***I can't believe the news today! I can't close my eyes, and make it go away! How long? How long must we sing this song? We can be as one tonight! Bodies strewn across the dead-end street. But I won't heed the battle call. It puts my back up against the wall! Sunday bloody Sunday! And the battles just begun. There's many lost, but tell me who has won? The trench is dug within our hearts. And mothers, children, brothers, sisters torn apart! Sunday bloody Sunday! And it's true we are immune. When fact is fiction and TV reality. And today the millions cry. We eat and drink while Jesus won. The real battles just begun to claim the victory.***

I went to work one Sunday morning and told the DJ to play my LITHIUM to open. He told me the owner said I couldn't play Nirvana anymore because Kurt Cobain committed suicide. Well, I felt bad but didn't know what that had to do with my show. You know, the show must go on! After the memory of his death passed, I was able to play his songs again.

I started taking a pill called Xanax without Steve knowing. It made me feel really good inside. I loved to take one and take a bubble bath, then get into clean warm soft sheets and blankets and take a nap. I began drawing pictures on the walls and doors and painted them when I took a small dose. A larger dose made me sleep very well. In Mike and Matts rooms I drew volcanos and prehistoric scenes. On Mike's door I did a big elephant and on Matt's I did a pretty design. Basically, I looked at the door or wall and painted what I saw. I did the bathroom in an underwater scene with a shark, octopuses, and fish. It came out very well. The entire bathroom looked like it was under water. I was quite proud of what I drew. I loved going into the bathroom to relax. I'd take candles, incense, weed, soothing music, party lights, and have a long bubble bath. It was like a sanctuary to me. The last thing I drew was in the garage and was a red house being taken up by a tornado.

At work, my girlfriend gave me a handful of Xanax bars. I took a whole one about half an hour before I'd be home. By the time I got there I couldn`t get my key in the door. I was so fucked up! Steve opened the door and let me in. I laid down on the floor right there and went to sleep. Steve went through my stuff and found the Xanax. He took three bars and threw the rest away. When I woke the next morning, he was passed out on the floor and I couldn`t wake him all the way up. I tried to find the Xanax, but he said he threw away what he didn`t take. I was afraid maybe he took them all! He was so fucked up that I had to bring him a pot to piss in because he couldn`t get up. The next day he came out of his daze and jumped all over me. He called my counselor

I had a number to from 1985. Steve told him I was taking Xanax and drinking. The counselor asked him if I was still eating and he said, yes. The counselor told him to leave me alone and said I was fine. Then he asked to talk to me, so I got on the phone. I told him, "Yes. I took Xanax and drank and got fucked up." He asked if I was still eating and I said, yes. He said, "Ok good. If you have any problems call me." Steve wasn't happy with what the counselor said, but I didn`t take any more Xanax even though it made me feel so good.

Steve worked for a paper company making good money and we had great insurance through his job. He had to lift heavy rolls of paper to put them on the sheeter. One morning he woke and couldn`t move. He was in excruciating pain. After trying to get off the floor for an hour, Steve finally had me call 911 and the paramedics came and got him onto a stretcher and took him to the hospital while I stayed with the boys. He called me later and said he had a slipped disc in his back. He had the surgery. Recovery was rough but he could walk again. Afterwards he had terrible cramps in his back and was taking hydrocodone for his pain. He eventually went back to work, then got laid off.

We decided to work together selling vacuum cleaners. We went through a week of orientation. I liked the vacuum cleaner and thought it did a really good job and owned one myself. But the company acted like a weird cult. Singing songs and chanting every morning at the meetings. After orientation they told us it was time to knock on doors for leads. They separated me and Steve and we went knocking with other employees. We didn't like going door to door and both decided to quit. I told Steve to wait one more day. Tomorrow was the day they were playing a game and giving $100 dollars to an employee. I told Steve I figured out their game and I was going to win. I convinced him to go to the meeting in the morning and I did win. I collected the money, and we were supposed to go door knocking again but went home instead. The next day we came in and returned the vacuums we used for demonstrations and told them we quit. They were puzzled and angry and one girl started crying. You see, she had to pay the $100 to sponsor me so she'd get a percentage of my sales. She was upset she lost $100. We told the boss we figured out their game and weren't interested. He responded with, "You haven't had enough time to figure it out yet!" We walked away laughing.

The news on TV said they cloned a sheep named Dolly. I was freaked out. I didn't know how I knew they were working on cloning in 1985 when I told Steve about it. Now I was afraid they'd bring dinosaurs back to life just like in my dreams. It was getting closer to being possible. It must be possible to clone people and dinosaurs if they cloned a sheep. The world was getting scarier every day. Our technology was out of control and usually used for bad.

Steve got a job at a paint company lifting 5-gallon buckets. The guy that worked the position before him was killed in a work accident. He walked under a giant hydraulic table used to wrap buckets of paint and was crushed. He didn't do the proper procedure of lock out, tag out, before he went under the machine. In 1998 Steve reinjured his back and had problems walking again. We lived on my money and credit cards during his injury.

We were thinking about moving to a Cherokee reservation so I got my papers together and sent them to the reservation and asked if we could come visit to see if we wanted to move there. They approved my papers and said come on over but thought of other plans.

My little sister put a mobile home on our dad's land. Her and her new husband lived there with their two boys. I thought it might be a good idea to do the same since we weren`t sure if Steve would be able to work again. We brought it up to my dad and stepmom and they said we could. I saved all the money I could for a whole year so we could move to Mt. Pleasant in the summer. During that time Steve was waiting to get his worker's comp check.

Several months before moving, I went to work and told my boss I was changing my name from Venus the Goddess to Angie. I just wanted to be a normal dancer. My boss replied, "I don`t think the owner is going to like that and what about all your customers? Do you think they'll like it?" I told him I didn`t care and did it anyways. I liked the name Angie and the song by THE ROLLING STONES. ***Angie. When will those dark clouds disappear? Where will it lead us from here? Angie! You're beautiful, but ain't it time we say goodbye? I still love you. All the dreams we held so close, seemed to all go up in smoke. Let me whisper in your ear. Angie. I hate that sadness in your eyes. But ain't it time we said goodbye? I still love you baby. Everywhere I look I see your eyes. There ain't a woman who comes close to you. Come on baby dry your eyes! Ain't it good to be alive! We can't say we never tried.***

The last year I danced at Dejavu the bar got skanky. Most dancers did anything for money and I couldn't wait to quit. There was a beautiful blonde dancer. I thought she was way prettier than me, had a much nicer body, and had a beautiful boob job. She'd put her hands down guys pants and jack them off. I'd always try to get to the customers before she did so I could make some money from them first. One evening it was the end of our shift and she was dancing for a guy and doing what she always did while French kissing the guy. I was next to her dancing for another guy. Her husband walked in and saw her doing that and saw she was deeply engaged in a kiss. She didn't see him watching. He leaned over and pinched her as hard as he could on her cheek! She looked up and was shocked to see him standing there! He pinched her so hard and long she was crying and ran to the dressing room. I thought, hahaha, slut, you got what you deserved! Those kind of dancers cut my money bad.

When I got off work the last thing I wanted to hear was loud music. I just wanted to have a calm normal life with my family. Doing things like cooking dinner, watching a movie, going to the kids sporting events, or helping with homework. I lived a regular normal lifestyle when not at work. People around me had no idea I was an exotic dancer because I kept it to myself. Most people thought strippers were bad people. But not all of them.

There was a dancer named Cindy who was always snooty to me and acted like she was better than me. She said she was saving all her money so her and her husband could move to the country and she wouldn`t have to dance anymore. Wow! That sounded like what I was doing! She moved, but a month later she was back at Dejavu. Her husband hung himself from a tree and she had to come back to work. I thought, oh no, I hoped nothing like that happened to me and Steve when we moved to the country.

I hadn`t told anyone at the bar I was moving until the day I was ready to quit. When I told my boss it was my last day, he started laughing because he didn`t believe me. I had made a t-shirt that said, Queen of Dejavu and started having all the dancers sign it. Then he knew I was quitting. My boss said, "You`ll be back! They always come back!" I replied, "NO I WON`T! NOT THIS TIME!" That was the end of my time at Dejavu and was hoping it was the end of my dance career.

During my career as a dancer when playing warrior songs, I dressed in a warrior costume with chainmail, leopard skin clothes, a sword and shield, and a face mask. When I played angel songs I dressed as an angel with wings. When I did temple songs I dressed as a harem princess and had tassels on the skirt that I shed a little at a time when I danced. When I played songs about queens, I dressed as a queen. When I was a goddess, I wore a real cute little white toga type dress. Halloween time was the most fun to wear all my costumes.

Me and Steve had lots of fun dressing up and role playing. He'd be a king, prince, sheik, pirate, or burglar, and I'd put on one of my costumes and act out fun things.

Some of the last songs I played. BIG TIME/PETER GABRIEL ***I'm on my way! I'm making it! I've got to make it show! So much larger than life! I'm going to watch it growing! I'm smarter than that! I worked it out! I've been stretching my mouth, to let those big words come right out! I've had enough! I'm getting out! My parties all have big names, and I greet them with the widest smile. Tell them how my life is just one big adventure! And always they're amazed when I show them round my house to my bed! And my heaven will be a big heaven, and I will walk through the front door!*** LOVE SHACK/ B52'S ***If you see a faded sign by the side of the road that says, fifteen miles to the love shack! I'm headed down the highway! Looking for Love to get away! I've got me a part and it's as big as a whale and it's about to set sail! Were headin down to the love shack! So, hurry up and bring your jukebox money! The Love Shack is a little old place where, we can get together! Sign says, "Stay away fools!" Cause Love rules, at the Love shack! It sets way back in the middle of a field. Just a funky, old shack where we can get together! That's where it's at!*** CLOSING TIME/SEMISONIC ***Closing time. Turn the lights up over every boy and every girl. One last call for alcohol. So, finish your whiskey or beer. Closing time. You don't have to go home but you can't stay here! Time for you to go back to the places you will be from. This room won't be open til your brothers or sisters come. So gather up your jackets, and move to the exits. I hope you have found a friend. Closing time. Every new beginning comes from some other beginnings end.*** HAPPY TRAILS TO YOU/ VAN HALEN ***Some trails are happy ones, others are blue. It's the way you ride the trail that counts. Here's a happy one for you. Happy trails to you, until we meet again. Happy trails to you, keep smiling until then.*** Dejavu and most of the other topless bars closed, but the huge Venus Topless sign still remains.

CHAPTER 4

MOUNT PLEASANT THE SIMPLE LIFE

Steve's workman's comp came through and I had saved all the money I could. We paid cash for a 3-bedroom mobile home and put it on my dad's land in Titus County. We tried to get insurance on it right away, but they wouldn't insure it until we put under-pinning on.

While in the Colony packing my sister called me in a panic and said, "There's a tornado outside!" She got scared when she saw it and ran to our dads' and got in the closet with the phone and waited. A few minutes later she went outside, and the tornado passed over. We were lucky it missed our trailer. It came from the back of the property, went up our property line, crossed the highway, and touched down. The lady who lived behind us called the lady that lived cattycorner to warn her and said, "There's a tornado coming your way! Take cover!" The old lady replied, "It's too late! It's already here!" Then the phone went dead! When the tornado hit the ladies little red house it was blown to pieces like a bomb went off. She was thrown over 500 yards and was killed! Her house and all the trees were gone. The only thing left was a concrete slab. I immediately thought of the last picture I drew, with a red house being taken up in a tornado! WOW! Was it a coincidence that I drew that?

We immediately drove back to Mount Pleasant to see the damage from the tornado. When we got close to our trailer, we saw lots of police cars and fire engines blocking the side roads. We made it to our trailer with no problem.

My little sister Michelle lived there for a long time and knew how to get past the barricades and drove me down back roads where we saw many houses flattened to the ground. It was pure devastation. I'd never seen houses damaged like that before. It was raining and people were going through their ruins trying to salvage what they could, and everyone was crying. That made me cry.

During our trips back and forth we liked singing PEACHES by THE PRESIDENTS OF THE UNITED STATES. ***Movin to the country, gonna eat a lot of peaches. If I'd have my little way! I'd eat peaches every day! Millions of peaches! Peaches for me! Millions of peaches! Peaches for free!***

My sister told me about a Satanic Cult in Gilmer, the next town over. She said they sacrificed a young blonde girl in a ritual not long ago. I didn't believe her, until I saw a crime show about it. And yes, they did sacrifice a young blonde girl in a ritual. It was true. How scary!

We put in the septic tank, laid sewage and water pipes, put up an electric pole, and put under-pinning on. The septic tank was put in illegally. My dad said, "We will just say it was already here and they won't say anything." It was a lot of work, and my dad's friend, a judge, was supposed come dig the hole for the septic tank but got drunk the night before and fell into a fire and was burned. We eventually got the work done. My dad was a jack of all trades and could fix or build almost anything. The land had lots of pecan, plum, and peach trees. It was also covered in blackberry bushes. My dad made wine and we all grew gardens.

We put up a mailbox and put gravel on the dirt road. I painted a heart shaped piece of wood, put flowers around it, painted Love Street on it and hung it on the giant electric pole on the road where everyone could see. When done, I started laughing, because now I really did live on Love Street and that made me very happy.

I still had no religion but occasionally talked to God. One day I was driving to Walmart and said, "Hey God, I'm not sure what's really going on. Am I really Love or the Goddess of Love or something like that? I really need a sign to prove it's really me and this is all real." I walked in the store, and heard a loud voice say, "Venus! Reveal the goddess in yourself!" That shocked me and I froze. My heart started pounding. I was so frightened! Then I realized it was just a commercial for a new women's razor called Venus. What relief I felt when I realized it was just a commercial and not God talking to me. I laughed and thought it was just a coincidence. Maybe I shouldn't talk to God anymore because his replies always confused and scared me.

I thought about going to work at a dance bar in Paris, but I wasn't sure I wanted to dance anymore. And if I did, what name would I use? I was driving to Walmart and decided to talk to God again. I said, "Hey God, I don't know if all this crazy stuff in my life is really real. I'm not sure if I'm really Venus the Goddess or Love or something like that. I really need to know. I need proof. You haven't written a song about me in a while. I want you to write a song telling me who I am, and I want it to be really powerful." I wondered if this was how Noah, Moses, and Jesus felt when they talked to God. I finished shopping and as soon as I got in my car the radio said, "Here's a brand-new release by LIVE called DOLPHINS CRY!" ***The way your bathed in light, reminds me of that night, God laid me down into your rose garden of trust. And I was swept away. With nothing left to say. Some helpless fool, yeah I was lost in a swarm of bees. You're all I need to find. So when the time is right, come to me sweetly, come to me. Come to me! Love will lead us! Alright! Love will lead us! She will lead us! Can you hear the dolphins cry? See the road rise up to meet us! It's in the air we breathe tonight. Love will lead us! She will lead us! Oh yeah, we meet again. It's like we never left. Time in between was just a dream. Did we leave this place? This crazy fog surrounds me. Love will lead us! Alright! Love will lead us! She will lead us! Life is like a shooting star! It don't matter who you are! If you only run for cover! It's just a waste of time. We are lost til we are found! This Phoenix rises up from the ground! And***

all these wars are over! Over! Over! Come to me! Yeah, come to me! Love will lead us! Alright! Love will lead us! She will lead us! The song reminded me of the dream I had years ago where God told me he wanted me to lead his people out of the church. But to where? I didn't know. I got scared because now maybe I really was Love! I was quite shaken by the song and had to pull over to gather myself. I thought could it really be me? Now I didn't want to talk to God anymore because I feared what else he might say. I wondered if I was just going crazy or if this was all real. Was some higher power messing with me? Or was it all just a coincidence? Later in life I saw the music video and it blew me away! The video of LOVE IS STRONG was pretty good too.

My grandpa passed, so my dad and stepmom went to Harlingen for the funeral in their VW rabbit. On the way, an axel broke, and the tire went flying off. They were broken down on the side of the road in a town that if you blinked you would've missed. They were wondering what to do, when a truck full of men pulled up behind them and asked if they needed help. My dad was leery until he saw they were driving a small firetruck. They took my parents to the fire station and coincidentally one of the volunteer fire fighters was a VW collector with about twenty of them, so he fixed the car for free. My dad thanked them and asked how they knew they were broken down and a firefighter said that once a week from 8 pm to 9 pm they have a meeting, and an old man who was tall, broad shouldered, with long white hair came to the station and told them a couple was broken down on the road. They said he had no car and wondered how he got there. When they turned around, the man was gone, and they had no idea where he went. They described my grandpa perfectly. At the procession, a motorcycle cop somehow collided with another car head on, right in front of the car my grandma and cousin were in. The policeman was thrown off his motorcycle and his head and helmet went into the top of the car's windshield and were stuck in it and his body flipped on top of the car almost taking his head off. He was dead! My grandma was freaking out screaming and my cousin jumped out of the car and turned the motorcycle off because it was spinning in circles on the ground. The whole procession was stopped. After more than an hour everyone made it to the burial. While my grandpa was being lowered into the ground, the straps broke, and his casket fell into the hole making a giant crashing noise scaring the mourners. Crazy.

I decided to work at Baby Dolls in Paris. It was a nude bar 45 minutes away on the highway we lived on. I wouldn't even need to make a turn except into the bar. I wanted to get away from the Goddess image, so Angie would be my name. We went to check out the bar and it was nice. It was a rock and roll bar. The girls were pretty, and it wasn't a cover for prostitution. They hired me on the spot and all the other dancers were nice to me.

Steve and the boys loved basketball, so we put in a basketball court. They spent hours playing together. That was such great father son bonding time. We built a big deck overlooking the pond and when it rained one pond flowed into the other and it looked like a big river flowing through the backyard. I felt like I was on the Amazon. I grew a nice big garden and a green bean teepee that was fun to get inside. I planted hundreds of beautiful flowers. Zinnias were the easiest to grow. I'd give them away in pretty vases. The flowers lasted so long that my friends asked me if I was a witch.

Me and Steve went to the casino in Louisiana to gamble and party. As soon as we pulled in, I told Steve, "I'll make a bet with you! I bet $50 that before we make it to our room, someone will fawn over my hair." He replied, "I'll take that bet!" After all it wasn't very far to the room. We checked in and was on the elevator with four people. A lady said, "I'm sure you've heard this before, but your hair is so beautiful!" I thanked her and looked at Steve. I'm sure my eyes were big as I was trying to contain my laughter and excitement. I just won $50!

The first winter was rough. We had a bad ice storm and had to break out of the frozen trailer. We lost power for 2 weeks so the fish tanks couldn't be aerated or heated. We got the last propane heater Walmart had and tried to keep the tanks warm, but they still couldn't get air and all my tropical fish died.

Steve put Billy Holidays music on, and I began singing her songs very well as if I knew them. That was strange because I'd never heard her before. When I was done Steve was amazed and so was I. He asked, "How did you do that? You are an awesome singer." I told him, "I don't know. It just happened." We were both puzzled. Maybe I was just channeling her spirit. When I went to my parents and put The Doors on and sang and performed a concert for them, they liked it so much and thought I sang so well they bought me a karaoke machine.

I found one of my favorite songs I liked as a child in Steve's album collection! It was called Hi Hi Hi. ***Well, when I met you at the station you were standing with a bootleg in your hand. I took you back to my place for a taste of a multicolored band. We're gonna get hi, hi, hi! The night is young! She'll be my funky little mama, gonna rock it and we've only just begun. I'm gonna do it to you, gonna do it, sweet banana. Well, take off your face, recover from the trip you've been on. I want to lie on the bed, get you ready for my polygon. Yes, I go like a rabbit, gonna grab it, gonna do it til the night is done!*** Hahaha! Not really a good song for a young girl.

Our first New Year's here we had a big party with family and friends. A lot of people thought it was going to be the end of the world. It had something to do with whether the computers rolled time over to the year 2000 or not. Everyone was waiting to see. The song to play for New Year's was 1999 by PRINCE. ***Don't worry. I won't hurt you. I only want you to have some fun. I was dreamin when I wrote this, forgive me if it goes astray. But when I woke up this morning could've sworn it was judgement day. The sky was all purple. There were people runnin everywhere. Tryin to run from their destruction. You know I didn't even care. Say two thousand zero zero over, oops out of time! So tonight I'm gonna party like it's 1999! I was dreamin when I wrote this so sue me if***

I go to fast. But life is just a party and parties weren't meant to last. War is all around us, my mind says prepare to fight! So, if I gotta die, I'm gonna listen to my body tonight. People let me tell you somethin. If you didn't come to the party, don't bother knockin on my door. I got a lion in my pocket and baby he's ready to roar! Everybody's got a bomb! We could all die any day! But before I let that happen, I'll dance my life away! I don't wanna die! I'd rather dance my life away! Listen to what I'm tryin to say! Everybody say PARTY! Can't run from Revelation. Sing it for your nation. Dreamin when you're singin. The telephones a ringin. Mommy, why does everybody have a bomb?

My dad had a 3D picture book, and everyone saw the invisible pictures but me. I tried and tried. I thought maybe they were all playing a joke on me because I couldn't see anything but squiggly lines and patterns. Steve assured me he could really see it. I tried for months and months. Finally, one day I saw it! Wow! It was so cool! Now I can see all of them. I wish The Other Side was one. That'd be cool. Maybe it was.

I danced three years at Baby Dolls. The bar got 25% of all we made and everything during showtime. I thought they got way too big a cut. The bars music was a juke box and that limited what I had to play. Some songs I played at Baby Dolls. LOVE IS THE DRUG/ROXY MUSIC ***Love is the drug that I need to score! Love is the drug, got a hook in me! Love is the drug, I'm thinking of! Oh, can't you see? Love is the drug for me!*** WHAT I GOT/SUBLIME ***Early in the morning, risin to the street. I strap shoes to my feet. Got to find A reason things went wrong. Got to find a reason why my monies all gone. Never start no static. I just keep it off my chest. Never had to battle with no bullet proof vest. Take a tip from me. Take all your money and give it all to charity. Love is what I got! It all comes back to you. You'll finally get what you deserve. Try and test that you're bound to get served. Love's what I got! Don't start a riot!*** STEADY AS SHE GOES/RACONTEURS ***Live a simple life in a quiet town.***

Well here we go again. You've found yourself a friend that knows you well. But no matter what you do you'll always feel as though you tripped and fell. When you have completed what you thought you had to do, settle for a world neither up or down. Sell it to the crowd that is gathered round. Steady as she goes. Are you steady now? WONDERWALL/OASIS ***Today is gonna be the day that they're gonna throw it back to you. By now you should somehow realized what you gotta do. And all the roads we have to walk are winding. And all the lights that lead us there are blinding. There are many things that I would like to say to you, but I don't know how. Today was gonna be the day but they'll never throw it back to you. Maybe, you're gonna be the one that saves me.*** FREE FALLIN/TOM PETTY ***She's a good girl. Loves her mama. Loves Jesus and America too. There's a freeway running through the yard. And I'm free fallin! All the vampires walking through the valley. They move west. I wanna glide down. Wanna write her name in the sky. I'm gonna leave this world for a while. Now I'm free! Free fallin.***

Baby Dolls had no manager. The owner ran the bar. He hired a lady named Brenda to manage and she was very nice. She fixed up the private dance rooms with wallpaper, flowers, and pictures. She realized I was the big money maker and would tell the other dancers how much money I turned in and tell them to get on the ball. Now everyday became a competition for other dancers to make more money than me.

A lady named Barbie started working and was very pretty with long blonde hair and my size body, about 105 pounds, and her boobs were bigger than mine. She was perfect! Barbie and Bunny were my biggest competition as far as looks but Chelsea was the best dancer and could get the bar hoppin by playing her favorite song BALLROOM BLITZ by SWEET.

Men brought their wives in to meet me and party. They liked to watch me dance for their wives. Some wanted to take me home, but I always said no, we could only party in the bar. Floor dances were $10 a song and you had to keep your G-string on, but private room dances were $20, and you took everything off.

A dancer borrowed $20 to get dinner and said she'd repay me later. At the end of the night, she told me to wait outside, and she'd pay me. I was sitting in my car with the window down and she sucker punched me for no reason. I was confused at why she did that. I thought we were friends. I got out of my car, and we started fighting and she ripped my favorite necklace off that my son Mike gave me. That made me so angry that I turned into a monster. I wrestled her to the ground, clenched my teeth into the back of her neck and tried to rip her spinal cord out! I went crazy on her like a wild animal! Someone called the police, and we could hear the sirens. I got up, got in my car, and passed the cops as they were coming in the parking lot. The next day I went to work but she didn't. Brenda saw what she did to me on the cameras and said, "Hey, I've got something for you." She held up a big ring of keys and said the other dancer lost them during the fight. She said, "Here, take these keys and throw them as far away in the field as you can." I was reluctant, but Brenda said she deserved it. So, I threw her keys far away into a big field where they were never found. When the lady came back to work, she was beat up and all I could do was laugh at her. She said she was sorry, and she had my necklace and would give it back, but she never did. She quit soon after that.

Brenda wanted to spruce up the bar more, so she set up a place to take pictures of the dancers to put on the wall when you first walked in to pay the entrance fee. I wanted a nude picture taken with a bunch of balloons. It was the end of the night and time for pictures, and I needed the balloons blown up. I told every dancer I needed each one of them to blow a balloon up and if they didn't, they'd get pregnant. One girl got upset because she couldn't blow one up and was almost in tears because she believed what I said and didn't want to get pregnant. I was only joking and just needed help blowing up the balloons. She wanted to know if there was any way out of it and I told her, "Maybe if another dancer blows it up for you it will work. That is your only hope if you can't do it." Another dancer blew hers up and we finished taking pictures and I was happy with mine. A month later the girl came to work crying. She said she was pregnant, and it was all my fault! I laughed and said, "Hey, you're the one who couldn't blow up a balloon. It's not my fault." I told her, "It's ok to be pregnant and having a child is a wonderful thing." I congratulated her. She married the man she was pregnant by and when she had her baby, she was so happy.

A couple came in and liked me. We partied and danced together for hours. When they were ready to leave, they wanted me to go home with them, but I told them no. As they were leaving, the manager saw them on camera taking my picture off the wall and hiding it in their cooler. She ran out to their car as fast as she could and told them to give it back. They acted like they didn't know what she was talking about. She told them she saw what they did on camera and opened their cooler and got my picture back.

Brenda wanted to put some crazy shows on, so she got a kiddie pool, put it on center stage, and had two girls do a show with chocolate, whip creme, cherries, and bananas. It was a hit! The guys slapped money on our sticky bodies. I did it a few times but didn't like the mess. After the show was over, we had to go shower and rinse our clothes and money. I didn't want any part of that anymore and said someone else could do it. It took too much time to clean up.

Brenda came up with another idea. She blew up an inflatable hot tub, added bubbles and a strobe light, put a drape around it, and charged customers to see two girls bathing each other. The men threw money in the water or slapped it on our wet bodies as we washed and played with each other. They really liked that, and it too was a hit. I didn't mind that show because there was no big mess.

One night a new dancer came in and took one look at me and recognized me, but I didn't recognize her. She heard someone call me Angie and said, "That's not Angie! That's Venus the Goddess from Dejavu!" Luckily no one heard and I took her aside and said, "Please don't tell anyone I was Venus the Goddess. I'm trying to get away from that name and don't want anyone to know." She agreed and said nothing. She worked a few days and went on her way. That was close. She almost blew my cover.

One night at the end of the evening, the lights came on and it was time for the dancers who didn't have room dances to go to the dressing room. I was walking to the back and Brenda stopped me and said a man just paid for 5 private dances with me. I had no idea who he was, and I was tired and just wanted to go home. She said I had to dance for him because he already paid. We were in the private room and was finishing the first song when he lunged at me and bit me real hard on my breast and I had teeth marks on me. I yelled really loud, "Ok it's over! I'm done!" I slapped him real hard across his face and ran out of the room and showed Brenda where he bit me, and told her, "I'm done! Kick him out!" She chewed him out and kicked him out. He didn't get a refund.

The Sherriff of Paris came in with a few police occasionally to check out the bar. When he saw me, he got the hots for me. Every time he came in, he'd look for me. One time I was standing next to him in my G-string, and he grabbed my boob. That shocked me since he was a policeman. I pulled his hand away and gave him an angry look. Next time he came in he did the same thing. I surely couldn't call the police, so I tried to avoid him.

I was leaving work one night and always looked to see if anyone was following me. It was rare for anyone to be on the road at 2:30 A.M. and if they were, I pulled over to let them pass so I knew I wasn't being followed. On this night a car pulled behind me out of nowhere, so I pulled over to let them pass but they didn't. They pulled behind me and stopped. That scared me! I had no idea who it was until the police lights came on. They saw me and recognized me. He asked, "Why did you pull over to the side of the road?" I replied, "Because I didn't know you were the police. I thought you was someone following me from the bar, and I wanted you to pass." They made me get out and walk the line to see if I was intoxicated. I was wearing big fluffy pink bunny slippers and they were hard to walk in, but I passed. Then the police radioed to the Sheriff and said, "I have your girlfriend here. What do you want me to do with her?" He replied, "If she's not drunk, let her go on her way." I felt relieved but these small-town cops made me feel very uneasy.

There was only one place to stop for gas on my way to work and it closed at 10. That worried me because if I had an emergency there was no one around. A little gambling room opened on the highway, so I went in, met the owners, and told them I worked at Baby Dolls. The gambling place was open all night and sometimes after work I stopped in to play the machines. The owners started coming to Baby Dolls to party. I was driving home from work one night and a big red truck came out of nowhere and was behind me. I pulled over to let them pass, but they pulled over behind me. Now I knew they were following me, and I had to come up with a plan. I pulled into the gambling room to see if the truck followed me in the parking lot and it did. I ran in the gambling room and yelled to the owner that I was being followed. He got his shot gun, cocked it, and went out front, but no one was there. He went to the back door and opened it and the red truck was there hiding, waiting for me to leave. He pointed his shotgun at the truck and told the guy he better leave, or he'd blow his head off. The truck immediately sped off. I waited about half an hour to make sure he didn't come back then drove home. I was glad there was a place for me to go when I felt I might be in danger.

One of my favorite things to do on stage was to get the guys to wad up bills and try to score a basket in my G-string. Guys really liked to play basketball with my G-string as the hoop. When I did that, I'd have most of the guys around the stage trying to score a basket. It was such an easy gimmick to get the guys to tip me.

When it was a customer's birthday or bachelor party, we put him in a chair on center stage and gathered all the dancers around to dance. But only if he wanted to. A man and his girlfriend came in and it was his birthday and she wanted us to put him on stage with all the dancers. While we were doing that, I was doing a move that required a lot of balance. I was holding the dancer pole and had a foot on each of the chairs arm rests. I lifted my leg to do the splits against the pole and my pussy was right in his face. His girlfriend didn't like that, so she jumped on stage and grabbed my leg and pulled it. That made me lose my balance, but I kept a good grip on the pole, and swung around and kicked her right in her face. The other dancers were shocked at what she did and stood there staring at her. I jumped down off the pole and was getting ready to kick her ass when the bouncer came and grabbed the lady and escorted her out. I thought, hey if she didn't want dancer pussy in her man's face then don't put him on center stage! Stupid fucking bitch!

I guy came in and got a couple private room dances. A few days later his wife started dancing there and she lived in Mt. Pleasant. Maybe we could carpool together. Me and her became friends and I invited her and her husband over to smoke some pot and shoot pool, but they declined. I invited them a couple more times, but they still declined. I was confused at why they didn't want to party with us. The lady took me aside and said, "The reason we can't party with you is because my husband is the head of the DEA in Mt. Pleasant. We're here undercover looking for people selling hard drugs." I told her I didn't know of anyone ever selling drugs in here since I worked here. I thought, oh shit! I couldn't believe I'd been inviting the head of DEA to come party with me, and I privately danced nude for him! They didn't find anyone selling drugs and she quit shortly after that.

I was growing six pot plants mixed in with tomato plants against the side of my trailer. The plants got so tall that I bent them down sideways and fastened them to the ground, so they'd be hidden better. I was outside in my bikini and saw the DEA helicopter overhead so I got a big white sheet and covered up the plants as fast as I could. The helicopter was hovering low above me, and I saw it was the guy from the bar who was the head of DEA, so I smiled and waved, and he smiled and waved back, then the helicopter left. I was kind of scared because I didn't know if he was going to come back and bust me, or if he was just flirting.

My parents asked to come see my show and I really didn't know what to say because I knew it would be awkward. I decided what the hell. Steve brought my parents to the bar, and they brought a bunch of beer. I introduced my parents to my coworkers and paid my favorite dancer Bunny to table dance for him. It was awkward getting on stage the first time and I wouldn't go nude. My stepmom got really drunk and was tipping all the girls on the stages. She had so much fun and drank so much that we had to cut her off. She needed help to the car. My dad also had a good time. What a strange experience that was.

The DJ was cool and reminded me of Wolf Man Jack from the old days. I always tipped him more than other dancers and brought him shots when guys brought me whiskey. Sometimes I'd have four or five bottles of Jack on different tables. My regular customers knew I liked Jack and used it to lure me to their tables. The DJ got a job on the radio and quit. I came to work but we had no DJ. No one knew how to DJ or work the lights. With no DJ, there was no show. Well, the show must go on. Brenda asked me to practice all the lights, the mic, the music, and announcing the dancers. I really didn't want to but did because no one else would. I practiced a little before we opened. Hey, I was pretty good at it for never having done it before. The pay was way less, and I didn't like that. I told the manager she had to find someone right away. It took a couple weeks.

Michael was in 9th grade and was so good at football that he played with the 11th and 12th graders. He wanted to be a professional player. One evening at work, some guys came in that looked very young. You only had to be 18 to get in the bar. The next day I went to pick Mike up from practice and I heard one of the boys say with excitement, "That's her! The one I saw at the nudie bar last night!" I immediately realized it was him I saw at the bar and got Mike and went on home. I realized the boys from 12th grade were old enough to see me dance. I knew my son might feel bad if the boys teased him about it, so my dance career was over. I went to the bar, cleaned out my locker, and explained to them why I couldn't dance anymore, and they understood.

Steve was now an assistant manager at Burger King. I knew Steven was the king of something. Just didn't know he was the king of burgers. Hahaha! Steve said they needed front cashier help and I got hired to work 10 to 5. Most of my coworkers were young Hispanic people in High School. They were all nice to me because I was Steve's wife and they liked him. They thought he was the best assistant manager.

I hated being trained by the main manager because he'd always stand right behind me, and I could feel his breath on my neck. I worked there for a while and got good at it. One day the other manager Angie said in front of my co-workers "If everyone was like her, my job would be so much easier. I wouldn't have to work at all. She's my best employee!" I looked around to see who she was talking about and asked, "Who are you talking about?" She replied, "You silly! I'm talking about you!" When it was time for my raise the main manager gave me a nickel. That was an insult, so I gave a week notice I was quitting.

I had no other job lined up, so I cleaned some carpets and did some housework for a ritzy family.

Steve's boss wanted me to come back, and I did under the condition I only worked front counter. I wasn't happy about going back to Burger King, but it was an easy job with daytime hours. There weren't many jobs in the small town.

Something freaky happened. I woke up one morning, went to the bathroom and was going to wash my face. I looked in the mirror and couldn't believe what I saw. I rubbed my eyes to see better and wake up. I looked in the mirror again and thought, no way. This couldn't be real. I looked ten years younger. I couldn't believe it was real, so I checked to see if I was awake or dreaming. I was awake. I thought this must all be in my imagination. When Steve saw me, he said, "Hey, you look different." I was giddy jumping up and down on the bed. I had no explanation for it and went on with my crazy life as if it was all normal.

Me, Steve, and the boys, went out to eat and when we were done, I was holding the door open for an elderly couple coming in. As the man walked in, he stopped and said, "So little girl, what do you want to be when you grow up?" That confused me because I was well into my mid 30's. I smiled and didn't say anything. When we all got in the car, they started teasing me and laughing at me because the man thought I was a little girl.

My dad built a small house on a corner of the land for my grandma Mary Jane to come live, but she never did. She moved in with my uncle Mark who worked for NASA. My dad turned it into a party house, and it was so cool. It had a bar, pool table, dance floor, and a band stage. It had lots of fun party lights and we'd have many parties there. My dad and stepmom threw me a princess party for my birthday, and it was lots of fun. They also had the best Easter party I'd ever been to. They made a nice dinner and told everyone it was rabbit stew. It tasted like chicken noodle soup. No one except me and Steve tried it until they told us it wasn't rabbit, it was chicken. They set up the coolest scavenger hunt all over the land that ended back at the party house. It was so much fun.

My dad caught a black rat snake 3 feet long and gave it to me to keep as a pet. The snake bit me the first time I picked him up but after that he was very docile, and I could carry him anywhere. I named him Stretch. He ate eggs and live rats. I kept the snake for five years and my friends were impressed with him. He grew almost six foot long and was very big around. I got tired of cleaning his cage and buying rats and felt bad keeping him captive. I woke up one morning and let him go free.

My sister came over in a little white VW rabbit and left it running while her young son was in it. She'd done that before and I warned her about it. On this day, it rolled into the pond and was stuck front down in the water. I immediately jumped in to open the back door. Her son fell on top of the dashboard and was against the windshield. I reached in and yelled for him to grab my hand so I could pull him out. He was very scared, and I kept yelling at him to grab my hand. Finally, he did, and I pulled him out. My little sister got a good scolding from me.

Raising children was the most rewarding thing I'd ever done. Everything in my life was going normal and I wasn't having any problems with crazy shit like before. I still didn't have a religion or go to church or worship or follow any higher power. I liked it just fine that way. I felt like I followed and believed in the power of love more than anything. I accepted that life was now, and there was nothing after death.

Me and Steve were watching The David Letterman Show and every night at the end, pants corporation came on and said something silly for a few seconds. On this night, it said in a whispered voice, "Brenda, where's the kitty?" When I heard that, my eyes got big and I looked at Steve and said, "Did they really say that!?" He replied, "Yes!" We started laughing. I immediately called Brenda and told her what happened, and we both laughed because I use to call her and say that to her late at night (for no apparent reason). Afterwards I got to thinking, and it kind of scared me. Who was fucking with me? Why did the TV say that (for no apparent reason)? Am I being spied on? Was that just a coincidence? I had no idea but it sure was weird.

My little sister's husband had a prescription for Hydrocodone and Xanax. She became addicted and would get so fucked up she'd be unable to function. While she was fucked up, she'd tell our parents I gave her the pills. That was a lie. I never gave her any pills. My parents believed her and were mad at me. I tried to convince them she was lying but they didn't believe me. It took a couple days before she sobered up and told our parents the truth, but they didn't believe her and thought she was covering for me. I told her not to lie like that again, but she did it several times.

We had a party at the party house and me and my little brother were cleaning afterwards. He felt a little down, so I gave him three vitamins with smiley faces. He left one laying on the table and the next morning my dad went to inspect and saw the pill and thought it was acid or some drugs. He came to my house and asked me what it was, and I told him they were vitamins. But he didn't believe me. I was so mad he kept accusing me of giving my little brother and sister drugs. I went to get the bottle to show him, but remembered it was the last of them and I threw the bottle away and the trashman already came. I went to the store to get another bottle, but they were out. Now for sure my dad didn't believe me and at that point I really didn't care.

Me and Steve were sitting on the back porch and my little sister pulled up. She got out, and we could tell she was extremely fucked up because she had a hard time walking and talking. She wanted to know if we had any pills and me and Steve laughed and told her, no! After what she had done to me, I wouldn't give her so much as an aspirin. She got in her car and only had to drive about a hundred feet to her trailer, but she ran over my wooden fence and my flower garden and destroyed it. We didn't say anything about it. Ten minutes later her husband saw how fucked up she was and was mad. She told him I got her fucked up and that was another lie. Me and Steve were together all night and Michelle wasn't with us. She only stopped by after she was already really fucked up. Her husband believed her and was mad at me and came over and chewed me and Steve out. We told him she was lying, but he didn't believe us. He slammed the door real hard when he left and knocked some pictures off the wall. That infuriated Steve so he went to their house and told him off and slammed their door and a bunch of pictures fell and broke. He called Steve and told him to come clean up the glass and Steve told him, "Fuck you! You need to come over here and repair the wooden fence and flowers she ran over!" No more was said. Now I was mad at my sister for lying again. When she was sober, I chewed her out and told her to stop lying about me giving her pills and she said she was sorry and wouldn't do it again. Now I didn't want my little sister around me. She eventually went to rehab.

I worked as a shift supervisor for six months at the new Wendy's, but the manager and employees were druggies and flakes, so I started looking for a new job. They closed within a year after I quit.

I saw an ad in the paper for a barista at a coffee shop and applied. I picked a bouquet of zinnias from my garden, put them in a pretty vase with ribbons, and wrote a cute note that read, "Pick me to be your next employee." The owner thought it was cute and hired me.

Mike wanted to play college football but tore his meniscus during a game in 11th grade and needed an expensive surgery, and someone anonymously paid for it. That was very generous of them, but it was the end of his football dreams. I felt so bad for him. He started writing and won many competitions in twelfth grade. Now he wanted to be a sportswriter.

Mike got a job at the local Pizza Hut as a delivery driver. I didn't like him working there, because in the past robbers came in, took the seven employees to the freezer, and executed them all. That was just so shocking to hear. It felt creepy and dark in the store whenever I went in. He was also in college majoring in Journalism.

I started working at Java Jays coffee shop and ran it by myself. It was a double drive through and sat in the middle of town. Soon my sales were always two to three times more than the other employees. Probably because they cheated the owners.

One morning I came in and was shocked. The entire inside of the coffee shop was covered in sugar ants. It was like a horror movie. Invasion of the Ants! I tried to sweep them out, but they covered every place in the entire store. It took hours to get them all out. When I got in my car to leave it was also covered inside with ants. They climbed up the wheels and invaded my car. The lady boss became a real bitch to me, so I quit.

Matt graduated high school and was in college majoring in Political Science and joined a protest called Occupy Dallas. It was a peaceful protest that started with a march to the federal reserve building in Dallas and was affiliated with the Occupy Wall Street that began in New York City, and the ones that sprang up all over the country. They were basically protesting our corrupt government who were bought off by the corporates. Matt called and told us about it and asked us to bring our tent and set up in Pioneer Park. We got there but no other tents were set up except for the news tent. We set our tent up and a policeman came by and asked why we set up our tent in the park. We told him we were allowed to for the Occupy Protest, and he said no more. Soon many tents were set up and we did marches during the day. Every weekend we brought food for the protesters and went on marches and hauled their trash away. Before this protest Matt was involved in several others and had been arrested about five times. He got a real good free civil rights lawyer and got all the charges dropped. After a month or so of being at Pioneer Park the city wanted us to move to a more discreet location. I felt that was a bad idea being further away from the public eye because they couldn't see what was going on in the camp. We were called THE 99%. There were over 350 people doing the marches and 150 tents at the new location at City Hall Park. One weekend we couldn't make it there and the protesters were told to get their belongings and get out of the park because they were going to bulldoze it down. The city said we broke the rules for safe protest movements, but that was a lie. They just wanted us gone. That weekend, in the middle of the night, the swat team showed up with helicopters and spotlights and bulldozed everything down and that was the end of Occupy Dallas. After that the FBI kept calling for Matt, but he was never home. They told me, "You tell Matt he can run from us, but he can't hide forever!" Then hung up. I thought, Wow! That was scary. Sounded threatening. We told Matt about it, but he just laughed.

Steve said his boss needed a front counter person desperately and wanted me to come back and promised I'd only work front counter. Mike use to work there with his dad and came back and now we worked together. I was happy about it. Mike and the manager got into it and Mike quit and the manager took it out on me. He started being snotty to me and made me take Mikes' position in drive thru. The first time I took an order I messed up pretty bad and said, "Welcome to Taco Bell. Can I take your order?" Where that came from, I had no idea. I never worked for Taco Bell. Everyone wearing a headset busted out laughing. I didn't like working the drive thru or doing fries and was looking for another job.

Mike got his associates degree in Journalism and got a job as a sportswriter for the local paper. He was good and got many compliments from readers. Matt was still taking political science. When Matt got his associates degree his college professor gave out awards and his read, "The person most likely to change the world!" I laughed and thought, really, he can't even find his shoes. How's he going to change the world? But I must say the greatest quality he has is a very sweet soul. He is the kindest person I know.

I got hired at Walmart and there were many crazy customers there. My first week, a lady came through my line and put over $1000 worth of clothes on the belt and still had a bunch of stuff in her buggy and said, "Oh, I forgot my wallet in my car." Then she took off as fast as she could with the buggy and ran out the door. I just stood there confused. I was checking another lady and noticed all her items said catfish when I rang them up. I rang up steak, it said catfish, $2.34. I looked at her and said, "Somethings not right. Why does everything say catfish?" She replied, "I don't know. It must be a mistake from the meat department." I called my manager, and she peeled the stickers off and under each sticker was the original one. I rang her items up and she said, "Oh no! I don't want anything now." She got angry and left. That happened all the time with different customers, and they liked targeting new cashiers.

I was in terrible pain for years from an operation to have a cyst removed from my fallopian tube, so I went to the doctor, and he ran tests and said I had acid reflux and my gallbladder wasn't working. It seemed the operation caused some muscles to stop working and others to overwork. In the middle of surgery to remove my gallbladder, I woke up and looked the doctor in his eyes and said, "Stop it! You're hurting me!" I was trying to grab my stomach and the doctor yelled at the nurse to grab my arms and hold them back! They put the gas mask on and knocked me out again. When I woke, I remembered all of it but didn't say anything. I was still in terrible pain and cried because the operation didn't work. I still felt like a snake was squeezing me in half. I told the doctor and surgeon I was still in pain, and they said it would take time for it stop. All I could do was wait to see if it went away. When I saw my surgeon, he asked, "Did I hurt you?" I replied, "No." and said nothing about waking up. Oddly the next year the surgeon died from a heart attack and my doctor died from cancer.

One day I had an acid reflux attack. I felt like the girl on Willy Wonka and the Chocolate Factory that blew up like a giant blueberry! Antacids didn't help and was in so much pain I went to the hospital. Ironically, they gave me a drink called a Green Goddess and within minutes I was better.

Several more years went by and was still in terrible pain in my ribs and stomach. I was in the kitchen and reached my arm up real high while on my tippy toes to grab something off the top shelf. When I did, all the muscles in my ribs and below turned into a terrible charlie horse! I fell to the ground screaming in pain! It made me so mad that I grabbed the muscles and started squeezing them as hard as I could! I was screaming in pain and kept squeezing them real hard like I was in a wrestling match with them! I was so tired of being in pain! I let go, got up, and my pain was gone. All the pain in my ribs was gone. I was so happy! It was a muscle problem! They were all muscle problems! Eventually all my problems stopped, and I was better! I was so relieved after being in pain for so many years!

The town became a sanctuary for Hispanics, and I didn't like the way guys in town gawked at me, so I started dressing dumpy by wearing sweats, oversized t-shirts, put my hair in a crappy bun, and gained 20 pounds.

Mike had a girlfriend, and she did something that really hurt him. I'd never seen him so upset in in my life. He felt betrayed by her and some of his friends. They broke up and she moved out. They got back together again, and she got pregnant. When Mike was young, he said he'd never get a girl pregnant and not marry her. I told Mike he didn't need to get married just because she was pregnant, but he married her because he loved her. They had a baby boy and named him Michael Kirk Jr. He was so beautiful. I looked at his ears and knew immediately he was my grandchild. I'd never met anyone not related to me that had my ears. My ears were rare. They didn't look funny, just a little different. I didn't like my ears to show and always hid them behind my long hair.

Mike and his wife Lucy split up and were in the middle of a terrible custody battle. During their divorce Mike got a DNA test to make sure Mikey was his. I had no doubts because of his ears, but I stayed neutral. We all loved Mikey and it would've been heartbreaking if he wasn't Mikes. When she found out about the test, she got very mad. She'd always assured Mike that he was his and said we had no right to do the test without her knowing. I told her Mike had every right and we'd find out in a couple weeks for sure. Then her tune changed, and she took Mike aside and made a confession. I was torn about how I wanted it to turn out. If he wasn't Mikes, we'd all be heartbroken. The test proved he was Mikes son. So much crap went on during their divorce. All the grandparents just wanted was for them to get along and have shared custody, but she got full custody because she had a clean record and Mike always took the fall when they got in trouble with the law, so she'd get out of it.

One night I was at the party house with my dad, and we were drunk. My dad had a switchblade knife and was showing me how to protect myself from a person with a knife. I was holding it in a defense pose and accidentally pushed the button and stabbed him in the forearm and blood started squirting all over. I got scared and grabbed an electric cord and wrapped it around his arm then ran and got my stepmom who was sleeping. She drove us to the hospital and said she was going to tell them I did it on purpose, but she was kidding. We had to get our story straight and say it was just a regular knife because switchblades were illegal. It was just a plain old knife. He got several stitches and his arm turned black. I felt terrible about it and apologized over and over. He eventually recovered. I learned my lesson. Don't play with weapons while drinking!

I liked taking Mikey to the party house when he came to visit. We'd shoot pool, play instruments, and sing and dance. One day my dad played guitar and me and Mikey came out from behind the bar singing, ***"Hey, hey, were the monkeys! Come and watch us sing and play! Were the new generation, and we've got something to say!"*** Mikey loved it so much. He'd yell, "Again! Again!" We did it until he was too tired.

For Mikey's first, second, and third Easter, I made giant Easter Baskets out of plastic kiddie pools. They were so cool looking. I did his favorite color each year and filled them full of candy, toys, and clothes. Easter was just like Christmas at my house.

We spoiled Mikey every holiday. On Christmas he had so many presents they took hours and hours to unwrap, and he'd be tired of it. I enjoyed buying gifts for everyone, but it took such a toll on my finances. I was lucky to work at a place where I found good deals and bought presents all year round.

After my dad had a triple heart bypass, he said he could see everyone's aura for months and said mine was very different than everyone else's. He said it was purple and way bigger than the others, with lots of silver stars above my head and he fell in love with it because it was so beautiful. Then he asked, "Do you think it might be possible you come from some kind of space royalty?" I didn't understand what he meant by that and said, "I don't know." Inside I thought, well I did play the role of Venus the Goddess and I may have come from the constellation Pleiades because I had the constellation Pleiades across my stomach. I'm also related to a president that was assassinated. I'm really just a mutt. French, English, German, and Cherokee. We said no more about it. Who knows? Maybe I did come from some kind of space royalty. After that my dad bought me presents that said things like PRINCESS PARKING ALL OTHERS WILL BE TOWED! Sometimes he teased me and said I was from Fleabees.

My little sister and her family moved into town. Steve suggested I invite her over for lunch. I told him, "NO! She'll get fucked up on pills if she comes over and blame it on me again!" He replied, "No she won't. Just give her another chance." We argued about it for a while, and I finally agreed. I called and invited her over for lunch and swimming and told her, "Don't take any pills while you're here!" She agreed. When she came over, we were going to drink a couple beers, get stoned, have lunch, and go swimming. But something wasn't right as soon as she got there. She didn't want a beer and didn't want lunch. I got suspicious and asked if she took any pills and she said no. So, I ate lunch and started drinking a beer and we got stoned. We went outside and got in the pool and within 5 minutes she couldn't stand or stay awake. She started going under water and was drowning. I was trying desperately to keep her head above water while she was passed out in the pool. I finally got a good grip on her and with all my strength I picked her up and threw her out of the pool. I picked her up, got her up the steps, and into the house. I laid her on the couch where she passed out for a couple hours. Her husband called and wanted to talk to her, and I explained to him she was too fucked up on something. I told him I had no idea what she took but she was passed out on the couch for a couple hours. He wasn't happy about it, but finally believed me when I told him I didn't give her anything and he didn't blame me. She finally woke up and went home. I heard no more about it but told Steve I'd never invite her over again and he finally agreed.

A girlfriend had a tongue ring and was playing with it in her mouth like it was a piece of candy. I asked her, "Wouldn't your tongue ring be better if you had candy on it?" That excited her! I had her bring me a few tongue rings and I made some. She put it in her piercing and loved it. That was how the birth of Pierced Tongue Suckers happened. Soon I was making 30 at a time and selling them for $3 to $5 each.

Walmart put in eight self-checks outs with one regular register. They had two cashiers run it. I liked the position because I didn't have to lift things, but most cashiers didn't like working it, so I did most of the time. I thought self-checkouts were a terrible idea because so many people weren't very honest. They'd ring one item up and throw two in the bag. The weight alerted me, and it angered the thieves when they got caught and they'd come up with crazy excuses. Some rang up one item but had four or more of them. They also took the bar codes from items that were small, like tiny boxes of Tide and tape it over the bar code of a giant-sized item. I only noticed by looking at my register screen and seeing what rang up. Customers did that with many products. I caught a lady who put a barcode for a twenty-five-dollar swimming pool over a three-hundred-dollar one. When I caught her of course she didn't want it at that price. I checked her items, and they were all like that. When I rang them up right, she wanted none of it. By the end of the day, we'd have buggies full of crap people tried to steal. Sometime the customers wouldn't even ring their items up. One time a guy come through self-check with a basket full of steaks, chops, and ribs, not bagged. He tried to go through and walk right out. I stopped him and asked for his receipt. He stupidly said, "My receipt is in my car. I'll go get it." He proceeded to take the buggy, so I grabbed it and told him he couldn't take it unless he had a receipt. He tried to push the buggy past me and run for the door. I grabbed the buggy tight and yelled at the top of my lungs, "I said you can't take this buggy unless you have a receipt!" He acted like he was going to hit me, and the customers around heard and stopped and stared. He walked out without the buggy after a customer came and stood next to me. They started having one person run self-check and it was hard when three customers ganged up and surround the register to where you couldn't see what they were doing. I caught them most of the time because it was obvious. Sometimes there'd be several people that went to registers as far apart from each other as possible. One kept me occupied while the others were stealing. It amazed me how many thieves there were. Lots of customers were very rude and ugly to the cashiers. They'd cuss us out or throw things at us if they didn't get their way. I hated my job and wanted out of it so bad. The customers were becoming more aggressive, and my job was becoming more dangerous.

One day I went to work, went to the back to clock in, and there were a lot of pallets of marijuana wrapped in cellophane. It was about eight feet wide, five feet tall and 50 feet long. I was like, wow! Where did all that pot come from? I'd never seen that much pot in my life! The manager said, there was a big drug bust on the highway and the police had nowhere to store that much and asked them to keep it until they figured out what to do. That made me feel uneasy because I knew the drug cartel in Mexico wouldn't like that and might retaliate. They did that one more time, then told the police they needed to find a new place.

I went to work, and they put me in automotive because they had no one. I had absolutely no knowledge of cars or anything that had to do with them. All I could do when people came in or called was tell them to come or call later. Some customers got mad, and I felt so stupid. I felt so stupid because I worked for a crappy corporation. The next day I went to work they had me work the phones, intercom, and walkie talkies. I also had a large clothes section to keep up. It was a lot of work. I really didn't want to do it, but the floor manager made me. When areas of the store were shorthanded, the managers came and got me off my register to work them. They called me their secret weapon because I was so fast at things. It made the cashier managers mad because they had to have a certain number of cashiers on the registers. They'd argue over who got me for the day. I just wanted to work self-check with another person.

Steve couldn't work at Burger King anymore because his back pain returned, and the stores were sold to new owners. He applied for disability but was declined. He got a lawyer for the appeal. The next two years was very rough on us because Steve wasn't working, and I only worked part time.

My stepmom was a great cook, seamstress, cake decorator, jewelry maker, crocheter, knitter, and barbie doll house maker. She was very talented in artistic things. I never lived up to her standards of perfection when it came to doing projects with her and it kind of hurt my feelings because she let me know it.

Me and Steve went to see the movie Armageddon. During it I accidentally dropped a box of sugar babies between my legs. I tried to get them all out of the seat and from between my crotch as best I could. The end of the movie came, and it was a tearjerker. Me and Steve got up to leave and I noticed a bunch of sugar babies melted and stuck to my butt. That made me laugh and I was trying to tell Steve to walk behind me because I had a bunch of sugar babies stuck to my butt and didn't want anyone to see. I couldn't say it. All I could do was laugh when I tried to tell Steve. Every time I tried to talk, I'd laugh harder and harder. I was in tears. Steve had no idea what was wrong and kept looking at me funny. The other people started looking at me also because the end of the movie was so sad, but I was laughing! That was so embarrassing. When we got to the car I could finally talk, and we both had a good laugh.

I missed too many days of work and one of the big managers called me in the office to sign papers saying if I missed one more day I could be fired. When I got in the office, he tried to pull up my file, but couldn't find it anywhere, and got frustrated. It disappeared and now there was no proof of how many days I missed. The manager said he'd look for it, but he never found my file.

Steve told me I looked like Robert Plant because our hair looked the same. He also said I looked like the little girl on the rocks from the album Houses of the Holy. I had to admit he was right. My dad and stepmom called me twisted sister after they saw a video of the rock band because my hair looked like the lead singers.

Sometimes me and Steve sat on the back porch and philosophized. We talked a lot about God, religion, and mankind. Steve said he'd like to start a church called The Church of No One Knows. We'd just discuss things and party. I said we should start a church called The Church of Love and at my church we'd have discussions about everything. We'd party, eat, and listen to inspirational music. It sounded like fun.

I was working one day, waiting for a someone to come through my line when two ladies approached and asked if we could all pray to God together. I knew how talking to God was. Sometimes it was scary. I didn't want to be rude and say no. We were in an aisle, and they were praying. One of my bosses came running over where we were and was looking up in the air as if she saw something. Then she saw us praying in the aisle and said, "Oh! I'm sorry! I didn't mean to interrupt! Go on as you were." Then she walked away. I didn't know what she saw because I didn't see it. Later I asked her what she saw, and she replied, "I'm not sure. It was just a presence of some kind up in the air above you."

Now they only put one person in self-check out to watch eight self-checks and it was hard. When we were extremely busy, we also had to run a register at the same time. I couldn't watch my screen anymore and they just wanted me to let shoplifters go. I had a hard time helping all the customers when I was alone. I hated my job but couldn't quit because I was the only income.

Walmart got even more stupid. They put a blue circle about 12 inches in diameter outside self-checkout and made me stand on it and say hello to people walking by. They had only one cashier in self-checkout, and it was too much for them. Customers would come out and ask me to help, but I wasn't allowed to leave the little blue circle. Whenever I got off to help, the big wigs from corporate who were in their office watching on camera would send my manager over to tell me if I kept getting off the circle, they'd fire me. My managers didn't like telling me that because they really liked me. One time when that was happening, my manager came to me and said, "If you don't stand on the circle, they want me to fire you." I told my manager, "Well, you tell them to stop sending the middleman over here and come down themselves and fire me!" Then I flipped the cameras off. They also wanted me to wear a vest that everyone in self-checkout shared and I thought that was gross. I complained about it until I got my own personal vest. Who wanted to wear a dirty sweaty vest that was shared by everyone? Not me!

A few days later a big wig lady from corporate came in and told me I wasn't doing my job right. She was going to show me how to get people to come to self-check. She grabbed a guy's buggy and pulled it into self-check. That confused him and he said, "Me and my wife aren't done shopping yet! How fucking rude!" I heard his wife yelling at him to get out of self-check and I was laughing inside. I told him, "Just go ahead and go. I'll delete what the stupid lady started ringing up." So, one strike for the big wig. Then she grabbed a lady's cart and dragged it into self-check and started ringing her items up, then went back to the blue circle. The lady said, "That was really rude of her to drag my cart in here! I wasn't done shopping yet and I wanted to go to a regular isle because there's something I want on it!" I apologized to her, deleted the items, and told her to call corporate and report how rude she was. Strike two for the big wig who was showing me how to do my job. Now I was really laughing inside. She gave it one more shot. She grabbed the end of a man's buggy and tried to pull it into self-check and he refused. There was a struggle for the buggy, and the guy yelled real loud, "Get your fucking hands off my buggy! I don't want to go in self-check!" That scared her so she let go and walked away. Strike three for the big wig. You're out! I was laughing so hard I could barely contain myself. After she left, I called my manager over and told her what the big wig did and told her, "I will not drag people and their carts into self-checkout like she wanted me to." My manager was shocked to hear what she did. She agreed with me not to do that. Then as a funny joke I asked, "If I have to stand on this little blue circle and say hello to people can I at least dress up like Cinderella?" She laughed and said, NO! I thought it was very strange that I had to stand on a little blue circle and felt like I was in a Star Trek episode waiting to be beamed up. They fired the lady from corporate.

Steve grew his hair out kind of long and grew a big white beard. I looked at him and said, "You do know you look like Zeus, right?" He just chuckled. A few days later we were walking to my parent's and as we approached, my stepmom yelled out, "Look! It's Zeus!" I started laughing at Steve and said, "I'm glad I'm not the only one who thinks you look like Zeus!" My parents started calling him Zeus when they saw him.

My parents knew someone who needed to find a home for two male cats named Zeus and Hercules. How ironic. They agreed to take them both. They were totally identical as far as I could tell. The only way I told them apart was by their personalities. Hercules was calm and docile, and Zeus was obnoxious. When they became teenagers, Zeus was mean to his brother and ran Hercules off. Then Zeus got weird and came over to my house all the time to hang out with me. When I opened my door, he'd rush in and piss all over my house. He kept doing that and now I always had to watch out for him. He was attracted to me in a weird way and wanted to love all over me all the time, but he wasn't my cat. I kept taking him back to my dad's, but he insisted on following me everywhere. Then he started pissing in my air conditioning window unit. It made my whole house smell like cat piss. I was at a loss at what to do. That cat just wouldn't leave me alone!

Steve's' disability finally came through. Steve wanted to go to Ohio to visit his family. I told him I could get my vacation in two weeks, and we'd go together. As soon as I got back from vacation, I planned on quitting my job of 11 years. I was going to take a year off work and spend time with my grandson. Steve said he couldn't wait and went to Ohio without me. It kind of hurt my feelings that he didn't wait for me.

When Steve got back, we decided to visit my sister in Colorado Springs. We planned the trip two years earlier but were unable to go. Before we left, I told my girlfriends at work I was going to go to Colorado for vacation. They started teasing me and saying I wasn't coming back. They were acting goofy and laughing. One said, "Women like you who go to Colorado don't come back!" Then they started laughing at me more. I didn't understand what they meant by that. It was the end of August 2016, when we went to visit. It was very beautiful in Colorado and the mountains were amazing. My sister told us she was moving in with her boyfriend and wanted to know if we wanted her place. Me and Steve talked about it, but I really wanted to go back to Texas and spend time with my grandson. Steve kept trying to talk me into moving and said, "We can stay in Colorado for six months and if we don't like it, we can go back. We can go to Texas and get what we need for the next six months and move to Colorado. If we like it, I promise to take you back to Texas to get the rest of our stuff." I finally agreed and we went to Texas to get some belongings. When we got there, Steve told me, "You have three days to go through everything you own and pack what you want to take and store the rest and tell everyone goodbye. Only take what you really need, and we'll come back in six months for the rest." I thought that was very unreasonable. I didn't even get to say goodbye to my real mom who lived two hours away. I didn't understand what the big rush was. What the hell! Did he rob a bank or something and needed to get out of town? I just didn't get it. It was happening way too fast for me.

I worked as fast as I could to get all the things done. Steve got a small U-Haul to pull behind the truck and I was trying to figure out what I needed for the next six months. I went to work and told them I quit. They didn't believe me and told me to go clock in. I replied, "Look at me! Do I look like I'm ready to work? I'm in my street clothes and my work vest is in my hand to turn in! Really! I'm quitting!" When I was leaving, I noticed the small blue circle they made me stand on was gone. I thought how strange that was. Why was it there for such a short time and now it was gone?

Me and Steve packed and were ready to move to Colorado. We left our trailer for the kids if they needed it and gave my car to Matt. We left most everything there. Pool table, fridge, washer and dryer, aquariums, all the furniture, the swimming pool, most of my sentimental belongings, and anything we didn't need for the next six months. The hardest thing I ever had to do in my life was say goodbye and move away from my two sons and grandson. I cried for a little while. Now off to our new adventure at the bottom of The Garden of the Gods! Who knows what awaited us!

CHAPTER 5

RADIOACTIVE COLORADO

We moved into the cute one-bedroom duplex in Colorado Springs at the bottom of The Garden of the Gods. It was on Colorado Avenue, and I could see Pikes Peake from my window. We had a nice big deck to party on, but had no fireplace, bathtub, air conditioning, swimming pool, or basketball court. We had a barbecue area and private laundromat for tenants. I took over my sister's job cleaning the laundry room and started cleaning apartments for the landlord. Me and Steve lived in the only duplex in the complex. The rest consisted of cottages and one-bedroom apartments. There were only 16 tenants but the numbers to the addresses were strange. We had 3 101's, 3 102's, 2 201's and 2 202's. I felt like I was in the twilight zone. And for some weird reason we had two street addresses. It was very confusing for people who delivered anything. Sometimes we had to hunt down our packages from neighbors. We had the same problem in Mt. Pleasant. It was hard to find because it was off grid. If we tried to get cable or satellite, they'd say our address didn't exist. Quiet time was 10 at night to 8 in the morning. So many rules! Everything we needed was in walking distance. I thought how ironic, ex-topless dancer Venus the Goddess, now living at the bottom of The Garden of the Gods. I'd never even heard of it until I came to visit. When I first heard of the Garden of the Gods, I imagined lots of beautiful colorful flowers, but it was a bunch of enormous rocks. It was pretty, just not what I expected. They say it was named that because it was beautiful enough for the Gods to meet there. Colorado compared to Texas was a big difference. I felt like I went from black and white to full color 3D.

What I didn't like about the area was all the homeless people. They were everywhere. They panhandled on all the street corners. Sometimes they'd hang out on our porch or ask for money and we'd have to run them off. We were so high up in altitude the air was very dry, and we had to remember LOTION GOES ON THE SKIN every day.

After we moved in my sister said the man who lived here before her died in the apartment. They didn't find him for a month, and he stunk up the place. That didn't bother me much. I was used to crazy ghosts and spirits. I also noticed all the rooms were tilted different ways and I felt like I was in a funhouse.

I wanted to know what the big hurry was to move here and laughingly asked Steve, "Did you rob a bank or something?" He jokingly replied, "Because I want you to go back to being just my wife. Not a mom, grandma, sister, or daughter. I want you all to myself for a while."

The first week here, an old lady knocked on my door and asked to use my restroom. I was confused and told her to go across the street to the drug store. She tried to convince me to let her in, but I still said no! She finally left. I thought that was weird. Colorado Springs was a strange place.

Every time I went to cross the street, the traffic stopped even when they had the right of way. I didn't like that at all. I wanted to wait for the crosswalk sign, but everyone just stopped when I wanted to cross. I told Steve about it and didn't want to walk by myself anymore. Steve replied, "I think you're over exaggerating!" I told him, "Ok, take a walk with me and I'll show you." We were walking and got to the first crosswalk and all the cars stopped when they weren't supposed to. Steve waved them to go on and we waited for the crosswalk sign. On the next corner, it happened again. Then again! That made Steve angry, and he began yelling at the cars to go ahead and go. I told him, "See what I mean!"

Shortly after we moved in, we had a giant windstorm. I'd never seen anything like it before. Ninety mile an hour winds

24 hours nonstop. Bus windows, car windows, and building windows, were blown out in areas around me and the highways shut down. It was like being in a tornado for an entire day. Steve laughingly said, "Why don't you go to the store and get something for me?" I replied, "Hell no! The wind might pick me up and take me away!" Steve doubted that. Well, that evening the news said a full-grown man was picked up in the air and dropped to his death by the wind. I was so glad I didn't go outside! I've been picked up off my feet by the wind before and had to hold on to the door handle of a White Castle for dear life until it stopped. It sure frightened me.

We were walking down the avenue to Mother Muffs, an old brothel turned into a bar. We were almost there when a young lady dressed in a red devil costume with wings, horns, and a pitchfork, jumped out in front of me. She got on her knees, took my hand, kissed it, and said, "Nice to meet you your majesty! May I ask what your name is?" I looked up at Steve in confusion and he said, "Just accept it and deal with it." I replied, "My name is Venus the Goddess, and this is my husband." I gestured my hand towards Steve to see what he was going to say, and he replied, "I'm Zeus!" Wow, he stayed in character! Inside I was laughing but also felt weird, wondering why it was happening. She asked to take pictures with me. After that, she asked if she could take me home and dress me in her barbie doll clothes. I declined the invitation. If it had been Halloween or even October, I would've understood.

When we went to fast food restaurants they asked for a name with the order. Steve started jokingly saying, "Zeus." I found it funny, and he challenged me to use the name Venus the next time. I did it once but was too embarrassed to do it again. I told him, "Look if you're not really Zeus and you pretend you are, it just might piss him off. Unless you're sure you're Zeus, you should stop using his name. You know the crazy shit I've been through, so don't fuck with my mind. Maybe I'm crazy and should see a psychiatrist." He replied, "You're doing just fine. You're not crazy. You don't need to see a doctor! You're ok!"

I got vertigo for three days and could barely stand or walk! It was like the time I took the medicine in the mental hospital. I had to hold the walls to get anywhere and couldn't eat or drink because I was so sick and dizzy when I stood or laid down. Every time I moved my head the room spun in circles. I was in agony! It was horrible! Steve thought it was funny and said, "You should enjoy the free buzz you're getting!"

I asked Steve silly questions like what century we're in because I'd forget. When you don't work, time doesn't really matter. I asked Steve one day, "If Jesus comes back to get me are you going to let him take me like you promised?" He replied, "Hell no! I'll kick his ass if he comes back!" Then I asked Steve a really silly question. "If you were God, would you be able to be faithful to me?" He laughingly replied, "Hell no! I'd put you in my harem and fuck you whenever I wanted!" His answer shocked me! I didn't know what to say. Then I asked, "Do you think I might really be a goddess?" He replied, "Not yet, but you're probably on your way to being one." Some of the things we discussed were silly, but I was glad to have someone like Steve to talk to about crazy things.

I was 20 pounds overweight, and my boobs got big. Steve didn't like big boobs and laughingly told me to make them stop growing. He made jokes like: Hey! I can't hear you over your boobs! Will you put those away? Your headlights are blinding me! I really liked my new big boobs but thought how ironic to grow them now instead of when I was a topless dancer.

Sometimes we pretended to be at Cindy's Bar and Restaurant. I dressed sexy and turned on colorful party lights. We drank, smoked weed, played music, and danced. When we were done, I'd cook a really good meal. Better than you'd get in a restaurant because I was a pretty good cook.

One night we were partying and listening to music and heard these three songs. RADIOACTIVE by IMAGINE DRAGONS,

DROPS OF JUPITER by TRAIN, and CAN'T STOP by THE RED HOT CHILI PEPPERS. After we heard them, a light bulb went off in our heads at the same time. We both said, "Wow! Maybe the music is radioactive because in a weird way it seems to tell stories of our lives!"

I hiked and partied almost every day and took a princess nap in the afternoons. I joined a gym for the first time and really liked going. I lost 20 pounds and looked hot! I got a whole new wardrobe for my sexy new body, but Steve didn't like the clothes I bought. He thought they were too sexy and told me he didn't want me to wear short shorts, half tops, spandex pants, or a bikini. I sternly told him I'd dress the way I want, and he just had to accept it. He'd get on to me about my bra strap showing when he saw it. I told him, "Look! We're not in the 70's! It's no big deal if my bra strap shows! I'm not embarrassed! I'm not a teenager!" We went to the bar that night and I showed him so many women with their bra straps showing, that he said no more about it. One time we were going out and Steve said, "I'm not taking you anywhere dressed like that! It's way too sexy! Go change." Like as if he was my father. That pissed me off, but I changed to avoid an argument. My neighbor asked if I wanted to go to a public swimming pool. When I told Steve what I was doing he replied, "You can't go to a public swimming pool, and you definitely can't wear a bikini in public! I replied, "Why not, do I look bad?" He replied, "Because you're way too fucking sexy. If you wear a bikini, all the guys will hit on you, and I won't be there to stop it. And I don't want your pretty, soft white skin to get all wrinkled from the sun. Public pools have germs that can make you sick. I don't want you to take that chance." I told him, "I can handle myself and my friend is like a big bodyguard." I didn't understand. All the years I was an exotic dancer he never showed any jealousy. Now he was crazy jealous. We argued about it for a while, and I was too upset to go anywhere so I took a nap. I went swimming the next week.

The Colorado sun turned my long curly locks a beautiful golden color again. Strangers constantly complimented me on it and wanted to know if it was real. They'd walk up to me and start touching my curls. When sunlight shined on it, it glowed with many colors and Steve was amazed. I didn't wear make-up because I didn't like the way it felt on my face. I only wore lipstick. You'd think most men would've been happy about their wife being over 50 and turning into a hot goddess, but Steve didn't seem very happy about it and I didn't know why. Too bad! I was in full bloom. I never felt this beautiful in my life as I felt now. Not even when I was an exotic dancer. I was so hot Steve was worried I'd go back dancing because ironically a topless bar called Dejavu was five miles away. Steve told me if I ever went back to Dejavu we're through. I had no intentions of dancing again because it was way too hard.

One evening we were partying, and Steve yelled, "Oh my God! Cindy! You look like you're 14!" He fumbled for his phone to take a picture and show me. I laughed and told him to knock it off. I figured he was a little too drunk. A couple days later my little sister came over and yelled, "Oh my God! Cindy! You look like you're 14!" She was shocked and fumbled for her phone wanting to take a picture, but I told her, "No pics please!" Yes, sometimes I looked younger for some weird reason. When I did, Steve would say, "Stop looking like a sweet little girl and start looking your real age!"

Me and Steve talked about living forever and coming back after you die. I told him I wouldn't want to live on earth forever or even 1000 years, like the Bible said some people did. It would be a curse to see all your loved ones die around you. But it did make me wonder how that worked back then. Did you stay young for hundreds of years and then get old or do you get old around a hundred and stay old for hundreds of years? If I die and could leave this planet, I never want to come back. Steve wanted to come back as an eagle.

We were taking a walk in The Garden of the Gods one afternoon and Steve said, "I'm Zeus. Will you marry me, Venus?" I busted out laughing because he looked so serious. I ignored him. Several hours later he looked at me serious again and said, "Well, you never answered my question." I had no idea what he was talking about. He said, "You know. The question I asked you on our walk today. Well, what's your answer?" I just laughed at him and said, "Sure, why not?" Steve didn't take this Venus and Zeus stuff as serious as I did. It was almost always a joke to him.

One afternoon we had several neighbors over drinking. I said to Steve, "You know, we should get married." The look of shock on everyone's face was hilarious. They started saying things like, you two aren't married? You both look so cute together! Steve said, "Yes were married! Sometimes Cindy likes to joke around and say were not." I busted out laughing because I thought it was so funny. I just wanted to see everyone's reactions.

Sometimes Steve talked to my friends in my Facebook and Messenger and pissed them off. Some had no idea it wasn't me and unfriended me. I told him he needed to stop it!

Steve wanted me to get a job, but my plan was to take a year off since I worked the two years he waited for disability. He wasn't happy about it, but I thought it was only fair. Then he started telling me how much shampoo, conditioner, dish soap, and toilet paper to use. I wasn't happy about it. He treated me like a child who didn't know anything, and we argued more.

One day on our way to the grocery store Steve said, "Now I don't have a lot of money, so don't ask for anything!" When we went in, I asked for a bag of Doritos, and he went off on me! He started yelling at me as if I was a little child and people around us turned and stared. I was so embarrassed I almost started crying. I went to the truck and waited for him. When he came out, I chewed him out and told him to never act like that again.

After several months of partying, I stopped, looked around, and wondered if I'd find out why I was really brought here away from my family in such a haste. Or, if I'd just party my life away. Maybe there was no reason.

My brother and his girlfriend were over partying with us, and we were at the kitchen counter. Steve was drunk and wanted our attention, but we were busy talking. He started jumping up and down like a big gorilla making gorilla noises. I looked at him and yelled, "Steve! Stop it! We're trying to have a conversation!" He sternly looked at me and said, "Cindy come into the bathroom with me! I want to talk to you!" We went in and he said, "I want to split up!" and he used his two index fingers holding them together then separating them. I was a little drunk and what he said confused me, so he said it again. Then he said, "You need to start thinking about what you're going to do when I'm gone." I was like wow! I thought we had a pretty good marriage. I 'd have graded it a 90 out of a 100. I was also somewhat unhappy but not enough to throw our marriage away. I guess he was. I went into the kitchen crying and told them the party was over, and Steve wanted a separation, so they left. He hurt my heart so bad! That was so out of the blue! Steve packed and left to go find a motel. I was debating if I should go back to my mobile home in Texas or stay in Colorado. I didn't have a job and panicked because I forgot about my 401K. Steve came back later that night because he couldn't find a cheap motel. Steve was mad that I told my brother and his girlfriend he wanted a separation because a couple days later he changed his mind and said he was being stupid. He apologized and said he didn't know what was wrong with him. He promised he'd never do that again. He said, "If I ever act like that again, slap me around and tell me how stupid I'm being! You're the best thing in my life, and I never want to lose you." I agree I'm closer to Steve than anyone else in this world and could talk to him about anything. To lose him would be devastating.

Now I wondered what I'd do if I didn't have Steve. I thought about it for a little while. Then suddenly, I remembered John from Dallas Parkway! My heart started racing like crazy, my palms got sweaty, and my mind couldn't think straight! What was that? Why did I feel like that after all these years? I looked John up on FB to see if he was on it and to my great surprise he recently joined. I messaged him to see if he remembered me, but he didn't. I was kind of bummed about it and tried to jog his memory, but he still said he didn't remember me. Steve found out we talked and got very mad. He asked me what the deal was between me and John, so I told him, "John was just a guy from my past, and the only one that ever broke my heart, and he didn't even remember me." Steve replied, "What an asshole! I find it hard to believe he doesn't remember you. I think he's lying. If I ever see him, I'll kick his ass for making you feel so bad. But on the other hand, I'm glad things didn't work out between you and him or you wouldn't be here with me right now and maybe I should thank him. If there is something you need to get out of your system go ahead and do it. Just make sure you come back to me." I assured him there was nothing I needed to get out of my system and laughingly said, "I don't need John's head on a silver platter!" Steve apologized and said he overreacted.

Months passed, and Steve was on me to get a job, but I didn't want to because my life was one big party since I moved here. I felt like a teenager with no responsibilities, and really liked it. I liked going to Pikes Peake because I felt like a goddess on a mountaintop. During the day I hiked mountains and canyons, or went to the Garden of the Gods, or to the gym. I partied almost every night. I didn't keep track of days or time. Life was lots of fun and I wondered again if this was how the rest of my life was really going to be, or if the bottom would drop out and I'd find out the real reason, why, out of the blue, I'd been moved to the bottom of the Garden of the Gods. Was there even a reason?

I still cleaned the laundry room and vacant apartments for my landlord. I also made tongue suckers and sold them in a jewelry shop on the avenue. I make a little money every month and was happy my invention was finally sold in a store. Every day was a party day. I still didn't know or care what day of the week it was and wasn't on a schedule for anything.

Now I 've made a complete circle in my book and I'm back to where something spoke to me to write it in December 2016. I told you the story of my life up until now. I 'd forgotten all about The Book of Love. I thought maybe I was imagining all of this and would glide through life and be normal like everyone else. I didn't tell Steve yet that something spoke to me and told me it was time to write the book. On New Year's Eve we were at home partying, and Steve said, "You know that book you talked about a long time ago? I think this is the time you're supposed to write it." My eyes got big, and I replied, "Wow! That's just fucking crazy because something spoke to me the other day and told me the same thing!" What a strange coincidence. I knew I was brought to the bottom of the GOG for a reason. Maybe that was the reason. To write The Book of Love. It made me wonder what spoke to me. God, an entity, an alien, an angel, or just me? What was it!

I 'd never really written anything before and had only read a few books. One was over a quarter of a century ago by Kurt Vonnegut called Cat's Cradle. It was pretty good. It was about a chemical created called Ice9. If it touched the oceans or rivers, they'd all freeze. I really liked the ending. Another was The False Messiah. In it, anyone who claimed to be the Messiah was put through dangerous tests that no one ever passed. They all died so no one ever wanted to stand up and claim to be the Messiah. Several years ago, Matt wrote a book called Capitalistic Punishment while he was in college. It was a story about how the United States Government was corrupt and on the corporates side. The corporates were money hungry and didn't care about how they enslaved the people and polluted the world. The government was being controlled by rich corporations that paid off politicians who held offices. The politicians would then make the laws in favor of the corporations and not in the best interest of the common people. Me and Steve thought it was a pretty good book, but he never published it. When I was younger, I also read some of the Bible.

I wrote a rough draft in thirty days that filled a small spiral notebook. I was like, ok I wrote it. Hope I'm done. I read it and didn't like it. It sounded like three aliens were serenading me through music. I said to myself, I must have gotten some signals or wires crossed or something. Steve read it and laughed and said, "Maybe you should call the book, Seduced by Zeus, or Venus with Amnesia." We laughed and I put it away and didn't mess with it anymore.

A few days later my sister came over and was in a panic. She said something about three aliens she thought were bothering her. Me and Steve found it funny because of the book I wrote about three aliens. I calmed her down, we talked for a bit, and told her everything was going to be ok, then she went on her way. I felt she was searching for something in her life. Soon afterwards she joined a Russian Orthodox Church and was practicing being good and getting ready for her confession. She kept asking me to go, but I always said no. She wanted me to go with her so bad that she offered me $100, but I still declined. She eventually quit going. She got her estheticians license and started working at Sun Spa in Manitou Springs. I really like that because I got in the hot tubs and swimming pool free. She was doing good and stopped taking pills. My little brother got his masseuse license and was also doing well.

Over six months passed, and Steve refused to take me to Texas like he promised. We argued about it quite often and my dad wanted to know if we're coming back or not because he wanted to tear down the trailer and sell the land. Our boys didn't live there, and the place was vacant except for my belongings, all the furniture, and lots of sentimental things I saved over my lifetime. Like my Christmas stocking that my dead Grandma hand made for me when I was born and my boy's stockings when they were born. All my costumes and an antique jewelry box that was my mom's when she was young. My expensive personal pool stick. Pottery my kids made when they were very young. Seeds I grew for generations from a morning glory plant I got from Matt when he was little. Most of my knickknacks, my wedding dress and veil etc. I'm pretty sure you get the picture. I was desperately trying to get Steve to take me to Texas to get my belongings.

Steve had long beautiful silver curls and his beard was long and bright white. When we went out together people barely noticed me anymore. They just saw Steve and his bright white beard. He got compliments from strangers all the time. We made jokes about it and Steve asked, "How do you like it? I'm stealing your thunder!" I told him, "I don't like it at all! Stop it!" We started a game to see who got complimented first when we went out and how many times we got complimented. Him and his beard, or me and my long golden curls. Some days he won and other days I did. It went back and forth.

I still had very vivid dreams and here were some recent ones. I had a round spaceship 10 feet wide and it was broken. The bottom of it spun very fast and made it lift off. I could only get it to go about twenty feet off the ground. That aggravated me because I didn't know how to fix it.

Then I had a dream lots of alien spaceships landed outside my window and were invading us. I was so scared I hid in my closet. I didn't know the outcome because I woke in a panic.

Another dream was two aliens were holding me captive and sternly kept asking me, "What is the combination to love?" I was confused because I didn't understand what they meant. They became angry and kept asking me the same question. Finally, I replied, "There is no one combination for love. There are many combinations, and they change constantly." Then I woke up.

I liked when I realized I was dreaming and controlled what I was doing. I could still fly and float in the air and it was lots of fun. If I dreamt I was cheating on Steve, I'd freak out, cry, and panic. When I woke and realized it was just a dream I'd laugh and felt relieved. Damn I couldn't even cheat on Steve in my dreams.

Something was pestering me to write again, so I wrote two chapters. I let Steve read it and asked what he thought. He looked at me and was holding back tears and said, "Wow! I wish I had been there to protect you. I wish we'd grown up next to each other and I'd have made sure nothing bad happened to you. I can't believe after all you've been through, you're still such a nice, sweet person." I replied, "It's ok. I'm here and I made it through everything." Steve said I should rename the book Cindy Narrowly Escapes!

Matt flew up from Texas to visit for the summer. When it was time for him to go back, Steve said he'd give him a ride back and that excited me because I could get my things and wrap everything up there. But what Steve said next threw me for a loop. Out of the blue he said, "I'll take Matt to Texas, but that doesn't mean you're going with us or I'm coming back!" I was confused and replied, "What do you mean, not coming back?!" He said, "After I drop Matt off, I'll probably go move in with my brother in Ohio." I was so confused because we weren't fighting or anything. After being married over 30 years I really had no idea that was an option. I didn't cry or get upset this time. I helped him pack and get ready to leave. We didn't fight or argue, and I didn't beg him to stay. It was very strange. Steve decided he didn't want to drive to Texas and Ohio, so Matt got a flight out. Steve planned on leaving early the next morning and got up at 4 am to go. When he was showering all the electricity on the block went out. He took it as a sign not to leave. Steve told me again, "I'm so sorry! If I'm ever being stupid like that again just slap me and knock me out of it! You are the best thing in my life, and I don't ever want to lose you!" Then he went to the store and bought a plant he named The Stupid Plant. He said, "Every time I see this plant it will remind me how stupid I was when I thought I wanted to leave you."

I still didn't have a religion or believe in God or Jesus and didn't pray to anyone. It was kind of like being out in the wilderness. Steve was the same way. I just wanted to be left out of all the religion crap and live a simple happy life. I was kind of like a rebel who refused to bow down to anything or anyone until it felt right. But then I started questioning everything and seeking the truth. I was not going to live in blind faith as the church told their followers to do. I said to God several times, "I'm not really sure you are real, but if you are, why have you been bothering me in my past and what do you want from me?" It would reply, "Because you are faithful and true!" So, I'd be like, "What the fuck is that supposed to mean? Do you want me to be a judge in the end times or what?" But no reply. Then I'd laugh at myself for having such silly conversations. I began wondering if that was really happening or if it was all in my mind. Who was talking to me? Was it a real entity or just my imagination?

If God in the Old Testament was real, I thought he was a very mean and jealous God and I wanted nothing to do with him. Sometimes I got mad and cussed him out. That was just the kind of relationship we had. If he was real, for some reason, I was very angry with him. From what I read he acted like a very spoiled child. If he didn't get his way, he killed everyone. Strangely I felt sometimes I was running away from something and running to it at the same time. It was a very strange feeling. How could my God be so cruel to kill all the humans in the Old Testament then suddenly in the New Testament he was giving out free golden tickets to Heaven? Something sounded fishy there. The Bible says you're a sinner, and it's your fault that Jesus was hung on a cross. The Old Testament was gory and bloody. If you didn't do what God wanted, he'd torture you, kill you, or threaten you with enteral hellfire! He used the Devil to scare you.

Christianity tried to persuade me Jesus was the God of The Old Testament and the Son of God in The New Testament. It didn't sound right nor make sense! Something wasn't right but

I didn't know what. I felt Jesus and God of The Old Testament were not the same characters.

Could you imagine if the Bible was true and there were invisible angels, spirits, ghosts, devils, and demons all around us. If just for one day we could see them fighting each other. People would be so frightened. I know it would scare me!

Our new president wanted to be a dictator and destroy our democracy. I always tried to vote for the lesser of two evils. I'd never seen our country so divided. Many people couldn't even be civil to each other. It was Democrats against Republicans. I felt our president was nothing more than a spoiled rich child who, when he didn't get his way, made people pay dearly. He acted like God in The Old Testament. Personally, I think we should dump the old government system, and all become Americans. The old system divided us and didn't work for the common man. It worked for the very wealthy and corporates to make them richer and keep others poor. I felt every single person should count for a vote. It was our fault. We the common people let them do it. We need to stop them, or it could be the end of the human race as we know it. I am not Republican or Democrat. I AM AN AMERICAN!

We were on the verge of the effects of global warming caused by humans and the only thing people in higher power thought about was making more money. They didn't care if their species became extinct as long as they were very wealthy while they lived here. The wealthy and corporates didn't care about the generations that would suffer long after they were dead. They didn't care about cancer and other illnesses they were inflicting upon the world with the pollution they made. Our oceans were full of plastic, and it was killing lots of innocent creatures. Many people lost their compassion for other living creatures. Sometimes I felt humans were alien to this planet because I knew no other species that destroyed the place that gave it life. I felt humans were a germ on the planet and were making Mother Earth very sick and it would only get worse if we didn't change our ways. I figured soon her antibodies would react and kill us all and she'd terraform herself.

I felt like I moved to a giant looney bin because many people around here were crazy. Some pulled wagons full of stuffed animals down the avenue and on the highways waiving to cars. You could hear the homeless people on the street screaming all hours of the night and during the day they panhandled on street corners. Some were drug addicts, some were down on their luck, and others just didn't want to be in the system of our society anymore, and I couldn't blame them.

I felt the world had gone crazy. The whole world was a giant looney bin to me. We had the capability to blow ourselves up many times over, and certain people held the buttons. We had the capability to clone humans and animals. Soon people would want wings by growing them on their bodies after having them implanted in their backs. Now that would be crazy! But it's possible. I saw scientists grow a human ear on the back of a rat. That freaked me out! No one else seemed to mind. People killed each other over petty possessions, drugs, politics, religion, personal beliefs, and money. Wars were going on everywhere! Many humans seemed to lack morals or empathy for any life around them and were not grateful for the great gift of life! I didn't like the way humans were in this world. We're not fitting in. Some mornings I woke up and wondered why I was on a planet with so many crazy people. Christians would say, "Don't worry, God is in control." I'd think, yes, he is, and he's doing a great job being a War God. His followers refuse to see him for what he really is!

One day our entire block was barricaded off by police. We couldn't drive home and had to park down the block and walk. A man kidnapped his ex-girlfriend and held her hostage in a motel room down the street and there was a standoff. He finally let her go and she was fine. A couple weeks later the exact same thing happened again, but with different people. I thought the odds of that happening twice in one week were incredible.

We were sitting on the couch and heard a giant noise and saw a big flash of light in our house. It sounded like a bomb and lit the entire living room up. I thought two cars crashed and exploded. I ran outside to see what happened, and lots of police cars and swat teams came out of nowhere and blocked the street off. They surrounded a car in the street and were trying to make him surrender. Finally, he did. My curiosity almost put me in danger!

A few times I opened my front door and saw lots of police in the parking lot. They were always busting people on both sides of our complex. So much crazy stuff went on around me, I should've become a reporter.

We were here a year and Steve was on me to get a job. We were walking in Old Colorado, and I felt something spoke to me. I told Steve, "I think God just spoke to me and told me to apply here and I'd get hired!" He laughed at me. I applied. A week later no response. Another week went by, and I began to wonder. Hmm? Maybe that was all in my imagination and God didn't really talk to me. Another week went by, and Steve said I should look for work elsewhere. I told him give it a little more time, I'm pretty sure I'm going to get hired. A couple days later they called and said they could give me 20 hours a week and I was happy. I went in and worked a four-hour shift and learned everything to run the store alone. It was the easiest job I ever had in my life. The owner's name was Cindy. Her husband said he'd make next week's schedule and call me. Three days went by, and no call. I called to get my hours, but he said, "I'm sorry. I don't know how to tell you this, but we really don't have any hours for you. I have no idea why we hired you because we really don't need help. If we get an opening, I'll call you." Afterwards I laughed because it was so funny. I worked four hours in the last year, and it was on Labor Day! Well maybe God was talking to me because after all I did get hired. Was that just a strange coincidence or God, or something else?

I thought maybe I should just stand on the street corner with a sign that said, "Just fell from Heaven! Didn't know I needed money! Anything will help!" Me and Steve had a good laugh because we knew I'd make lots of easy money that way. People were very generous to homeless people here. But I'll get a real job.

Safeway across the street needed cashiers badly, but only hired them from within the store. Which meant you had to work in a department before you could be a cashier. I was so experienced they hired me in the seafood department but had me work as a front cashier.

Me and Steve made an agreement that since I did most of the housework for the last thirty years, when I went to work, he'd do it. He was pretty good at it but quite picky about where I put my belongings. He put the utensil rack in the bedroom, and I thought he lost his mind. I let it go for a while but put it back in the kitchen because it was inconvenient to go to the bedroom to get cooking utensils. He also had a bad habit of throwing things away without asking me. If he felt we hadn't used something in a while he'd throw it away. When we lived in Mt. Pleasant, I came home to find all the china dishes my stepmom gave me in the trash! The entire eight-piece setting. I was shocked and wasn't happy and got all my dishes out of the trash. One time I needed my pineapple corer but couldn't find it anywhere. I described it to Steve and asked if he saw it, and he replied, "Yes. I didn't know what it was, so I threw it away." I knew he'd seen me use it many times before. Sometimes I felt he did this just to see if he could make me mad. He still does this. He recently threw my fry-daddy away and I'm sure things I haven't noticed yet. I wish he'd stop doing that. He thinks I'm petty when I argue about it, but he doesn't understand it's not about the object, but about his actions of not respecting things I liked.

The uniform at Safeway was black from head to toe. When I went to work, I felt like an alien hunter from the movie Men in Black. When I'd come down from the top of the staircase almost everyone stopped and stared at me for some weird reason. I felt uncomfortable and had to stand at the top, take a deep breath, and prepare for the stares. Why they stared at me like that, I had no idea.

I got compliments on my hair constantly, and they always wanted to know if it was natural and I'd say, "Yep, it's the way it grows out of my head." I almost made it through a whole day at work with no one remarking about it and was thinking about it. One minute later a lady said, "I'm sure you've heard this a million times, but your hair is so beautiful!" I thanked her and laughed inside. My hair looked like angel hair or a big lion's mane. It was cool but sometimes I felt it had an entity of its own and I was invisible.

I applied for twenty hours a week at Safeway but when I got my schedule, I had thirty-six, so I went to the manager Victoria and told her I didn't want that many. She replied very nicely, "Well this is how it works here. You are the low man on the totem pole. Everyone above you gets to pick their hours and you have to take all the remaining up to forty." I wasn't happy about that. A couple weeks later I got a graveyard shift and was confused. I asked my boss why. She said once a week some cashiers had to work the graveyard shift to change prices of the merchandise. If the other cashiers didn't want to, I had to. I wasn't happy about that either but dealt with it. I didn't like the hours. They didn't tell me all that when I was hired and felt I 'd be the low man on the totem pole for a long time. I didn't like my job and wanted a new one.

Mike flew up for a visit. When I was on FB someone said, it's good Mike's moving to Colorado. I was confused because he didn't tell us he was moving here. When he arrived, I asked when his flight back was, and he got a funny look on his face and replied, "I'm not planning on going back." I was happy and he stayed with us, got a job, and moved next door into a cottage.

Mikes divorce was finalized, and Mikey took a plane and

visited for two weeks at New Year's. We had a late Christmas and I had so much fun playing with him and his new toys. My coworkers adored him. They loved his big brown eyes and beautiful long dark curls. We took him to lots of fun tourist attractions and hiked. I was sad when he left and couldn't wait for him to visit again.

Even though Steve didn't work he was always in a hurry to do things. He'd get pushy when he wanted to go somewhere and had no patience for anything. If the line at the store was too long, he'd put his items down and leave. He also had no patience for traffic and had some road rage. Rush here! Rush there! Rush everywhere! I just wanted to go slow and take my time.

Here went Steve again, out of the blue, saying he wanted to separate. He said, "This just isn't working for me. We're just not on the same page." I was really confused. I couldn't believe he was doing that again! I really thought me working would make things better between us. I didn't think we had any problems big enough to separate over. The only thing we really argued over now was getting my things from Texas and my drinking too much sometimes. We partied a lot together, but I wasn't a mean or falling-down drunk. Steve partied just as much as I did. So, I told him OK. I didn't get upset or cry. I helped him pack again and started taking all the pictures off the walls and asked if he wanted any and he said, no. I told him to get a cell phone and I'd help him set it up before he left, so he'd have GPS. He stayed at Mike's until he was ready to leave, and I went to work.

Before we moved to Colorado, the series American Gods was getting ready to come on cable TV and I was excited to see it. It was about the old Gods in modern day America and lots of new Gods, like Technical Boy, Cellphone, Media, and Mr. World. When we moved here, we didn't get cable, internet, or satellite. Steve found the book and planned to read it before he decided to move out but hadn't. When I got home from work, I was expecting Steve to be gone, but he was still at Mike's. I found a note left in the book American Gods on the kitchen counter. The note said, "If you don't understand me by now you will never understand me!" That really confused me because I had no idea what he meant, and why he'd leave the note in that particular book. That seemed weird.

Steve was going to leave in the morning for Ohio. Instead, he came home and again said he was sorry for acting like that. I replied, "This is sounding like a broken record." He said, "Sometimes we are not on the same page. When I'm going up, you're going down, and when I'm going down, you're going up. I'm tired of being your bodyguard and protecting you from other men. Whenever you go out with your friends, I feel like you're a little girl going out on a date for the first time. You haven't aged like me. I'm looking older and you are looking more beautiful!" I thought wow, those were weird feelings. I asked him what made him change his mind to decide to stay and he replied, "The music I listened to at Mikes was all telling me to stop being stupid and not to leave you, over and over again, so I decided not to." I told Steve he needed to stop acting the way he was acting, and I was a grown up and he needed to treat me like one.

Steve still refused to take me to Texas to get the things I wanted and sell the rest. I begged him. He held the truck keys up and told me I could go without him. That really pissed me off because I knew no one who could go with me and I damn sure wasn't going that far by myself. Eventually, my dad gave all my stuff to Goodwill, tore down the trailer, and sold the land. I don't think Steve realized how much that hurt my feelings to lose all my sentimental belongings. It wasn't about the items, but the memories I had attached to them. I had to take into consideration maybe it was too painful to drive that far again due to his back.

I hiked in The Garden of the Gods a lot and accidentally crashed so many weddings I couldn't keep count anymore. I'd just stand around like a guest and watch, then hike away. One day we were watching the news and saw the city put a giant blue square right in the spot where people liked to get married. We went to the Garden to see what it was about. We got there and saw a giant square made of steel, painted blue. It was ugly and out of place. The news crew was there and interviewed me. He asked what I thought about it, and I replied, "It's an ugly eyesore and it needs to go! It doesn't belong in this natural setting and couples who are planning on getting married here next year won't be happy." The reporter said it had something to do with the Olympics and they were going to put five rings on top of it. He asked me, "So you don't like it?" I replied, "No, I don't like it, but I'm not planning on getting married here anytime soon! You should ask those who are." My interview was on the news, but I didn't see it. My girlfriends at work told me they saw me on TV. A petition was immediately started to remove the big ugly blue frame and within days they took it down.

One night me and Steve were walking down Old Colorado to the bars, and I heard loud music and people dancing and thought there was a new bar. I walked in past the doorman and the bartender asked what I wanted to drink. I looked around and quickly realized, I'd crashed a wedding reception!!

Mikey came to visit for the summer, and we were all so happy to see him. We went hiking in the Garden of the Gods, Red Rock Canyon, Cheyenne Canyon, and Rainbow Falls. We went to the Zoo, drove to the top of Pikes Peak, took him to the big arcade in Manitou Springs, and many other things. We all had lots of fun. We celebrated his birthday, and he was getting so big. I love him so much. He went back to his moms, and it was so emotionally hard on all of us. Even Mikey.

Something was pestering me to write again. I replied to it, "Look, if you want me to write this book, then you must give me a job that is not a slave job. I need a job I can work and get paid to write. Until then I will not write!"

Days after that, the manager Victoria called when I was off work and asked me to come see her. I told Steve, "Somethings going on. I think they're going to let me go for some reason." Steve said, "No way! I don't think so!" I went in and she said, "I really don't want to tell you this because you are my best cashier, but we have to do layoffs and you were the last one hired." She was almost in tears and said, "Usually it's the employee crying when I have to let them go, not the manager." She did her best to keep herself composed. I told her, "Don't worry! It's all going to be ok." She told me I could go to a much further location or take the layoff. I took the layoff. She said she'd call me when the layoff was over. I was happy about it and went home and celebrated!

I didn't want to go back to Safeway, so I started looking for a new job right away. Some time passed, and I was out taking a walk. At the end of my block, I saw a western shop. I wasn't into western wear but decided to check it out. I went in and saw a Help Wanted sign and applied as a salesperson, but the owner was out of town and wouldn't be back for a week. A week later I stopped in again, but she was still not back. Victoria called and said my layoff was over and wanted me to come sign papers to come back. I stopped in the western store one more time on my way to Safeway. I told the lady to let the owner know about my situation at Safeway and that I really wanted to work at her store instead. I went across the street to sign papers and get my schedule, but Victoria didn't realize it was Sunday and Human Resources didn't work weekends so she couldn't process papers to terminate my layoff. I needed to come back tomorrow. When I got home the owner of the western store called and wanted me to come in right away for an interview. She hired me on the spot but said she could only give me twenty hours a week. I told her that was great because that was all I wanted. I started working and really liked it. I sold men's and women's western boots, work boots, hiking boots, work clothes, and casual clothes. It was one of the easiest jobs I'd ever had and was very good at it.

The owner's husband was very tall, broad-shouldered with white bushy hair. He was gruff and quite intimidating. I avoided him when I could. He only came in five minutes a week to get the timecards for payroll. The lady owner said he drank all the time, and they had a rocky relationship. Sometimes when he'd see me, he'd say, "It looks like you've grown taller little girl!" The lady owner was very small like me and ran the whole show. She was the boss! She came in at 9 in the morning and left a little after noon every day. What I didn't like about my job was how the owner whispered with her other coworkers as if to be telling secrets and making fun and criticizing other employees right in front of them. That went on a lot, and I thought it was very unprofessional, but I ignored it. I got to dress up for work every day and really liked it.

The second week at work a man came in, and I could tell he was drinking because I smelled it. We were both in the men's department in the back of the store and I was across the room from him. I coughed a little and he yelled at me, "Hey! Do you know what it means when a woman coughs like that?" I just ignored him. Then he yelled really loud, "It means you want to suck my dick!" I was like, wow, I couldn't believe he said that. I ignored him and went on with what I was doing. He kept saying it over and over, louder and louder! There was a lady in the store and we both got frightened. I told my coworker to make him leave and she also heard his profanities directed at me. Me and the lady customer went to the breakroom to get away from him because he wouldn't stop yelling. He finished shopping and was checking out and started asking my coworker nasty questions. She told him if he didn't stop, he'd have to leave. I was angered because she didn't kick him out right away. When he left, I asked why she didn't kick him out right away? She replied, "Because we needed the sale." The lady owner asked me what happened. I told her, and she too was upset with my coworker for not kicking him out.

Me and Steve went to the grocery store and he said, "Go ahead in. I'll be in there in a minute." He did that often and I thought he was just smoking a cigarette. I went in by myself and for some reason I felt everyone kept staring at me. Wherever I went they stared! I stopped and looked at myself to make sure nothing was wrong. Did I have toilet paper hanging out of my pants or my zipper down? Steve caught up with me and I told him, "I feel weird! I've got this feeling everyone's staring at me. Is this all just in my mind?" Steve replied, "No. You're not imagining it. They are staring at you. When I came in the store after you, I saw everyone watching you!" I asked him why they were staring at me? He replied, "Because you are so beautiful. You just need to get used to it. You should've seen the stockers face light up when you asked him a question. He sure got happy when you were talking to him."

Later, me and Steve went to the casino in Cripple Creek and got a room for the night. When we were on our way to dinner at the restaurant, I felt weird. I felt like some people were staring at me again. I thought maybe I was just imagining it. We got our table and I told Steve, "I feel like the staff is staring at me for some reason." He replied, "No. You're just imagining it this time. Get over yourself! No one is staring at you!" We finished dinner and I still had a creepy feeling I was being stared at. I tried to ignore it and get over it even though I felt uncomfortable. When Steve went to pay the bill, a lady that worked there came over and said, "Sorry we were all staring at you, but we thought you were the CEO of the casino. You look just like her." I felt better like I wasn't being crazy.

Normally when I went to work, the lady owner thought of me as a ray of sunshine. Her and some of my coworkers called me their little angel princess. But sometimes the boss was in a pissy mood and took it out on her employees. She treated us like little kids. She used to be a kindergarten teacher. I stopped by work to get my paycheck and there were no customers. I chatted a minute with a coworker, when suddenly, the owner came rushing over to us like a wicked witch and yelled, "If you want to talk to each other, do it on your own time!" We both looked at each other and thought, wow, what fucking a bitch! We hadn't even talked a minute. I think the owner was jealous of the relationships between me and her employees. I brought shrimp, hors d'oeuvres, and snacks for my coworkers to make a party at work. I liked to make it enjoyable and I'm sure my boss didn't care for my attitude, but coworkers really liked working with me. Sometimes when she was leaving for the day, I'd say things like, "Don't you want to stay for the party?" or "When you come back bring the tequila!" or, "Make sure you call before you come so I can get rid of all the party people!" Me and a coworker planned to have Chinese food for lunch at work. When our boss found out, she called the night before and changed my schedule to be off. Then said, "If you two want to have lunch together you need to do it on your own time!" If the boss lady was mad at you, she made you do a bunch of unnecessary work, like inventory all the clothes and it took all day. One time she said if we were slow, she wanted me to go out and pick weeds. I thought that was crappy of her because she never made anyone else do it. She must have been in a bad mood. I was out picking weeds and started smelling something and realized I sat in dog poop and had it all over my pants and had to go home to change. My coworkers thought it was funny and so did I.

It was a holiday and work was very slow so the owner told us to find something to do and went home. I vacuumed under every rack because I could tell it hadn't been done in a long time. It took several hours. Then I went into the musty basement and sorted hundreds of hangers. Then I picked some weeds and did all my closing chores. The next day, the lady boss came in and was mad because I didn't button up one of the vests on the rack. She snottily asked my coworker, "What did Cindy do all day!" She could be such a bitch. When she found out, she quickly changed her tune.

One night I had a very strange vivid dream about the lady boss. I was on the phone with her, and she was telling me to stay away from these people. She kept saying it over and over. She said, "Stay away from those people because they are very bad and will only get you in trouble." That confused me because I didn't hang with any people. I just stayed at home with Steve. I told her, "I don't hang out with them." Then we hung up. I went to work the next morning and told her about it. Her eyes got really big, and she looked at me funny and said, "Wow! I had that exact conversation with someone on the phone last night! How did you know what I was saying!?" I told her it was in the dream. That amazed her and now when she looked for me, she'd say, "Where's psychic Cindy?" She was always asking me to look at her and see if I saw any bad energy around her.

Something strange was going on. I didn't feel right inside. I felt like somehow, I was changing and didn't like it. My insides felt weird, and I didn't know what was going on. Then I missed my period! I realized I must be starting menopause and it was awful. I got hot flashes and wanted to step into a refrigerator. I poured sweat even in air conditioning. It was horrible! Every hour I went through it over and over. All night long, I 'd wake to a pool of sweat. Everything I slept on would be soaked. What a cruel joke God played on women. Bleed one week every month for most of your life, then when that stopped you felt like you were on fire all the time. At times it was unbearable in the hot summer because we had no air conditioning. I hoped it didn't go on long, but some ladies said they'd been going through it for 20 years and I wasn't happy to hear that.

After I worked a year at the western store, my boss asked if I wanted to go to their other location and sell only men's and women's western boots, hats, and belts etc. I had no idea they had another store a mile away. I really liked it at the new store because it was even easier than the main store. But there was a problem. It was in a very bad location and had no business because it was off the beaten path and there were many homeless people living at the creek behind the store. It wasn't the safest place for me to be alone. There were steel bars on the windows and a big steel padlocked gate on the front door. Surrounding the entire property was a giant 8-feet-tall chain fence with a padlocked gate. Sometimes customers came in and asked if I felt safe and I assured them I was fine. Sometimes homeless people came in wanting to bum things or clean the parking lot for a few dollars. I was always nice to them as not to anger them because they could be unpredictable. Sometimes I gave them snacks because I felt sorry for them, and just wanted them to go away. In the time I'd been employed for this business both stores had been broken into and lots of boots were stolen.

My sales were very good at the boot store and my boss gave me a permanent position working Friday, Saturday, and Sunday. I loved running it by myself and the job was easy.

Mikey came and visited again for a couple of weeks after Christmas, so we celebrated late. We went hiking and did lots of fun things again. He was so cute and getting so big. All the ladies adored him. I really didn't care to celebrate Christmas or Easter anymore because I didn't really follow the God of the Bible or Jesus and most people didn't even know Easter was originally Ishtar or Esther's day, The Goddess Love. It was passed into Christianity when her people were conquered. I thought it was sadistic to see a man hanging on a cross and blaming us for it.

I'd been working the boot store for a month and was bored playing on my phone and listening to rock and roll on the radio, trying to keep myself entertained. Business was very slow and sometimes I didn't even have a customer all day.

A big problem at the boot store was when it rained there were 17 leaks in the roof. We had to move all the boots, or they got soaked. We put 17 buckets around the small store hoping customers wouldn't trip. When they came in, I warned them about the leaks and said silly things like, watch out, if you come in you might get baptized. They'd laugh and come in anyway. There was no drinking water, and the refrigerator was broken.

One time at the boot store it was late and the lady from the shop next door ran in and told me there was a man with a gun who just tried to rob the business next to them. She said he ran into our parking lot and to the back of the property and wanted to know if I saw him, but I didn't. She called the police and told me I should lock up until they got there. I did, and then called my boss and she told me to lock up and go home when it was safe. I left before the police arrived.

Not long after that at work something spoke to me in a stern voice and said, "Hey! Wake up! I did what you wanted me to do. I gave you an easy job with few hours. I gave you a place to write and get paid. Now do it!" I was thinking, oh shit! I'm sorry, I forgot, I'll get on it right away. I had no Idea what that was. Me? My imagination? God? An Entity? An Alien?

I rewrote the first two chapters and wanted someone who didn't know me to read it and tell me what they thought. A few months earlier I met a lady on FB with the same name as me and we got along very well. She was very pretty and around my age. She used to be a Broadway musical dancer in New York and Europe. We talked a lot and she never put me down or criticized me for any of my views. She made me feel I could believe whatever I wanted no matter what others thought. Her beliefs were strange to me. She was a Christian who followed and loved Jesus, but also felt she was part reptilian alien. Her, my little sister, little brother, and my ex-daughter in law all had similar views and were into the Pleiadeans. I found out that many people believed that they were Pleiadeans. My sister said if anyone believed in the Pleiadeans I should because of the constellation across my belly. I'm sure there are aliens because it's only logical there'd be intelligent life somewhere out there considering how long everything has been going on before humans arrived on the scene. I'm just not sure they're in contact with us. My friends and family introduced me to chakras, the third eye, and the energy of love. Cynthia loved my writing and kept me motivated and inspired to keep going. I saw a video by the Imagine Dragons called Thunder and thought of her. I messaged her and asked if she'd heard of them. I should've known she had. She really liked them and the video. It had trippy reptilian people with snake tongues. One of them looked like me.

Several social media groups wanted me to join their cause. One was The Temple of Love and asked me to help rebuild The Temple. I told them, "Why? So God can burn it down again like he did in The Old testament. I remember reading what he did to Ashtoreth the Goddess of love, sex, and war, Queen of Heaven. I know she was the Goddess of Love same as Ishtar and Astarte and Asherah! I'll pass." Another was a lady named Barbara who claimed to be in contact with aliens from Pleiades. That intrigued me since I had the constellation on my belly. I couldn't say if she was for real or not, but she bored me, so I stopped listening. Another was Morgue and he explained everything in mathematics and physics and felt God was one conscious energy and we are all part of it.

Something spoke to me again and I just assumed it was God. It said, "I want you to get a Bible." I didn't have one, so my sister gave me one on Sept. 6, 2018. I was confused and didn't know what to do with it, so I put it on a shelf. Days went by, and the voice spoke and said, "I want you to take the Bible to work with you." I brought it to work every day and put it on the counter behind me and went on with my writing. After some time, something spoke again and said, "I want you to read 1st Kings, 2nd Kings, 1st Chronicles, 2nd Chronicles and Esther." I thought, wow, that was specific, and strange! I wondered if God or this higher power spoke to everyone like that, or if I was just crazy. Maybe it was just an alien or an entity. Maybe it was an Anunnaki from Ancient Samaria that I saw a documentary about that was an 8-foot-tall race they found remains of near the Pyramid of Giza. I heard they come to Earth every 3600 years to make humans mine gold for them, and it had been so long since the last time they were supposedly here that maybe the humans forgot about them. Some people think they are due to come back soon. They were written about in Mesopotamia on clay tablets around the 35th century B.C. Or maybe what was contacting me was aliens from the constellation Pleiades, who some people believed they too were in contact with, to help spread light and love into the world to fight the Anunnaki. I asked both my boys if they'd ever heard of the lady claiming to be in contact with the Pleiadeans and to my surprise they'd seen some of her videos. Maybe it was just my imagination running away with me. I didn't know.

Steve wasn't religious and did what lots of people did. He went to a Christian church when young because it was the mainstream religion in America and his parents made him go. When he grew up, he stopped going and just enjoyed being outside in nature every day. He loved nature and communed with it all the time. He was always nice to me about my beliefs and let me be free to be who I wanted to be and believe what I wanted to believe without criticism. But right now, I just believed in searching for the truth about why I was here and what was really going on. I wanted to get lots of information and examine it all before I decided what to believe. Steve always says no one knows anything for sure, so why search for the unattainable. But I feel the need to search now.

I saw a documentary on a book called The Codex. It was very large in size. Three feet tall and 620 pages. It contained all kinds of information about many different things. People referred to it as The Devils Bible, but really, it wasn't. It had a picture of the Devil and people always turned to that page to see it, so the page got discolored. The book just had lots of information. Inside was the Old and New Testament under the section of incantations and spells. I'd always felt The Bible did cast a spell on many people and got them to worship a deity blindly with no questions asked. Could the Bible really be a book used to cast a spell on humans?

I was working at the boot store, standing at the counter looking out the window, getting ready to open The Bible, when a giant dust devil came down out of the sky right in front of the window. It was so big I thought it might be a tornado. I froze in terror as I saw it pick things up off the ground and objects were swirling all around in the sky! I felt like I was in a scene from The Wizard of OZ. Then it went back up into the sky. I ran outside and a car pulled in the lot and the couple were a little frazzled. They saw it from the end of the block and waited. That was crazy! We were amazed seeing it come out of nowhere. The building next to me had some damage. I went ahead and started reading The Bible.

Later I called my mom and told her what happened, and she angrily replied, "Maybe God is trying to get your attention to tell you something!" I replied back in a sarcastic way, "Well you think? The question is, what does he want?!" Me and my mother didn't see eye to eye on religion. She was still into Jesus and the God of the Old Testament, but I wasn't. The first time I tried to explain to her that I felt like a character from the Bible, she got very upset and told me, "You are nobody special and you will never be! Get over yourself!" When I tried to tell her about the constellation Pleiades on my stomach she replied, "So what! I have the North Star on my ass! That doesn't make me anyone special!" Ouch! That felt like a knife in my heart. I thought your mother was supposed to be there to give you confidence and lift you up to be whatever you wanted to be. I ignored her and thought she was being an ass and went on with my life. Later she called and told me I was related to someone in the Bible. She said her last name went back to Moses and meant heir to the one who saw the burning bush. Who knows? We don't talk about religion anymore. I found it funny she went from telling me I was no one and never would be, to you are a descendent and heir of Moses. I wondered what it all meant. If anything.

I read 1st and 2nd Kings but really didn't understand it. My longtime girlfriend called and asked what I was doing. I told her I was going to read 1st and 2nd Chronicles. She replied, "There's no such book in The Bible." I told her, "Yes there is. I'm looking at it right now as we speak." She replied, "My dad was a preacher and there is no such book in The Old Testament! You must be thinking about 1st and 2nd Corinthians!" She tried to convince me they didn't exist, and we debated it. We just had to agree to disagree because I was looking at it. She was supposed to be a close friend of mine for over 30 years, but it seemed she really didn't even know me at all. She was a devout Christian like my real mom and a hard-core republican like my dad. She told me if I didn't come back to the God in the Old Testament I'd burn in Hell for eternity. She said I was not a Goddess. I decided not to talk to her anymore. Bad vibes.

I didn't think the Bible could be trusted because over 75 books were removed by the elders because they didn't fit with their plan. It was also rewritten so many times and just omitting a conjunction or adding an s can change the whole meaning. Jasper, Judith, Tobit, Wisdom of Solomon, Sirach, The Book of Enoch, The Apocalypse of Adam, The Apocalypse of John, The Gospels of Judas, and Additions to Esther were some of those removed. It seemed they tried to erase the existence of the Goddess of Love from the Bible. It may not be telling everyone the whole true story. Some of these books spoke of reincarnation and how people lived for hundreds of years on earth. Some of them even said the God of the Old Testament was really an evil deity who trapped us here in a time bubble, wiped out our memories of who we were and where we came from, to gain control of our energy or spirit. These old writings are crazier than most of today's social media stuff. What is true?

Something spoke to me a few days later and said, "I want you to light a candle every time you come to work and write." I lit a candle but didn't know what to say because I really didn't believe in anything or anyone. I just believed in love. So, I said, "Ok, who or whatever you are. I'm lighting this candle for you and ask for your protection and that you have me write this book the way you want it written." I did it every time I wrote at work. Eventually I just called it my Heavenly Father God from outer space.

When I told my mom I was writing the book, she wasn't happy. She asked me what it was about, and I told her it was stories about my life. Then she said, "I don't think you should write this book! I don't want them to hurt you." I was confused and replied, "What are you talking about? Who'd want to hurt me for telling simple stories of my life?" She seemed angry and replied, "Well, I don't know! I just don't think it's a good idea and you shouldn't write it!" Then she changed the subject. I wondered what she was talking about and if she was hiding something. I had no idea why she'd be upset about me writing The Book of Love.

Steve kept telling me it wasn't safe at work and wanted me to quit, but I told him I couldn't because it was where I got paid to write. I couldn't waste this opportunity. Steve let it go but I knew it wasn't safe there. I felt if this entity or energy wanted me to write, it would also protect me. Sometimes I'd ask this entity to give me a better and safer place to write.

Matt moved to Colorado. Matt and Mike moved to the duplex connected to mine. They both had jobs and were doing well. Matt had his master's in Political Science and wanted to be a teacher. Mike was a chef at a nice Greek Restaurant. I was proud of my children.

I read 1st and 2nd Chronicles and pondered on it. They really meant nothing to me. I said to this higher power, energy, spirit, entity, or whatever it was, "I don't understand why you had me read those books and what it is you want me to know." It replied, "Now I want you to read The Ten Commandments." I did. The spirit said, "What was my 1st commandment?" I replied, "Thou shall not worship any other gods but you." It replied, "What were they doing in Kings?" I replied, "They were worshipping the god Baal and the goddess Ashtoreth who came down from the heavens and built temples so the humans would worship them. They were also worshipping false idols and a golden calf."

It replied, "Yes! And what happened to them." I replied, "You killed them all!" He replied, "Yes! And what are the Christians doing now?" I replied, "Oh shit! They're worshipping Jesus instead of the true God." He sternly said, "Yes! And they will have the same fate if they don't come to me! They worship and pray to an idol called a cross! They pray to pictures they say are me. Others worship other Gods and false idols, and many chase The Golden Calf!" I said, "Oh shit, I don't want to tell the Christians that! They always shoot the messenger! No one really ever wants to hear the truth. Afterall they wouldn't believe me anyway!" The spirit replied, "Well maybe they are not my true followers!" I was glad I got out of mainstream religion when I was a teenager, or it would be much harder to do at this point in my life. I'm sure it would be hard for someone to change their beliefs after they'd dedicated their entire life to it. I always thought something was fishy about the whole free ticket to Heaven from Jesus. That just didn't sound like the God of the O.T. He was mean and cruel. I also refused to believe Jesus was God. I felt something wasn't right about the God of the O.T. Things just didn't add up. And it said angels from heaven came down and mated with females from earth. Sorry but that sounds like aliens sugar coating themselves. I call it as I see it!

1st and 2nd Chronicles were about building the true Temple of God after he killed all the people who wouldn't follow him. Again, I felt like a character in the Bible and wondered if this was how Noah, Moses, and Jesus felt when they were living on Earth and a higher power talked to them.

Me and the spirit talked about building the true temple of God and I told it, "I have no riches to build a temple God's worthy of. Like the one in Chronicles. The spirit replied, "You are the temple I want to build. You have my Holy Spirit inside of you. The same Holy Spirit that Jesus had. He came to earth to show the world how to release the Holy Spirit inside of them, that my spirit may be released upon earth and there would be Heaven on Earth.

He came to show you how to be humble and compassionate for all living creatures."

Most churches just wanted your money for their own personal pleasure and many Christians were two faced hypocrites. They seemed like false prophets.

We saw the first season of American Gods and liked it. Steve read the book and the movie was close to it. It was about old and new gods in modern time America. I also liked The Tudors and The Game of Thrones. My favorite movies were The Wizard of Oz, It Happened One Christmas, Willie Wonka and the Chocolate Factory, Logans Run, They Live, Tommyknockers, Dogma, Pulp Fiction, Fear and Loathing In Las Vegas, Moulin Rouge, The Island of Dr. Moreau, 12 Monkeys, The Fifth Element, and Life is Beautiful.

One day something very scary happened at work. I'll call this The Killer at the Boot Store! My boss called and asked if I had any steel toed Harley boots, and I did. She was sending a guy over who was looking for some and said, "Keep your eye on him. He's kind of weird." I lit my candle, said my prayer, and was going to read Esther until he got there. He arrived on foot and told me he needed steel toed Harley boots so he could kick people's asses when they started shit with him. I didn't have any in his size and he became agitated and said in a stern voice, "I need them really bad, NOW! When I don't get what I want, people get hurt!" I ignored what he said and showed him a pair without steel toes, and he got even more agitated but tried them on. He said, "No matter what, I have to get a new pair of boots from here now!" He took the pair I showed him. As we went to the cash register, he mumbled, "I just fled from Ohio because I stabbed a gay man in an elevator and left him for dead!" I showed no emotion, nor did I respond. He said, "I have a really bad temper and when I get mad, I hurt people really bad!" I still showed no emotion, nor did I respond to what he said. I was getting ready to ring him up and he said, "Check this out!" and he pulled a big switchblade out of his jacket pocket and held it up in front of me and yelled, "This is the knife I used to stab the guy with!" Instead of looking frightened, I said in a giddy voice, "Cool! Is that a switchblade?" I acted like I was his friend and looked at it with admiration and went into the story of how I accidentally stabbed my dad when he was teaching me how to defend myself against a person with a knife. I told him, "Blood was squirting everywhere and I had to take him to the hospital!" Then I asked, "Aren't those illegal?" and I giggled. He replied, "Yes and so is this!" He reached into his other pocket with his other hand, and I was hoping, PLEASE DON'T BE A GUN! PLEASE DON'T BE A GUN! He pulled out a pair of brass knuckles and I said, "Wow! Cool! I've never seen brass knuckles before!" I felt better it wasn't a gun but not safe yet. When he was showing me the brass knuckles, he said, "I even have a giant knife for cutting people's heads off too! Do you want to see it?" I replied with a big smile on my face, "No, that's alright! I'm good!" I rang his boots up and said, "That will be one hundred forty-two dollars and twenty-two cents." He replied in a mumble, "Wow! I can't believe that after everything I've told her the only thing she replies is, "That will be one hundred forty-two dollars and twenty-two cents. I better shut up before I get myself into trouble." He pulled out a giant wad of money rolled up, paid me, put his boots on, and walked out the door. As he left, he said, "I guess God didn't want me to get the pair of boots I wanted." I replied, "I guess not! Don't worship false Gods!" He looked at me confused with his head tilted and replied, "Not even Jesus?" I said, "No, not even Jesus." He replied, "But the Bible says you have to go through Jesus." I replied, "First and Second Kings says you should not worship or pray to any other gods or idols or you and your whole house will perish. He replied, "The Bible says you have to go through Jesus to get to God and go to Heaven." I said, "I don't think that's true. I have a relationship and a direct line to God. And Lucifer deceived the whole world." As I looked at him, I saw he was working it out in his head and he looked at me in amazement and said, "Wow! You know! You're right!" Then he went on his way. As soon as he left, I thought, wow, that was fucking crazy! I immediately called my boss and told her, and she said if he came back tell him I had a family emergency and lockup and call the police. He never came back. I was just glad I made it through unharmed. I sure picked a strange time to start preaching.

When it was over, I read Esther. It was a story about a Queen who wouldn't come to her King when she was called. That made the King angry, so he had a contest to find a new Queen. Esther was a young girl no one knew was Jewish. I think she started out as a slave from a war. She won the contest the King had, due to her beauty. She became his new Queen. Then she saved the Jewish people from being killed. The story really didn't mean anything to me. I told the spirit, "I don't know what this story has to do with me." It replied, "Remember that poem you saved over 30 years ago? That was a message for you. Bring it to work." We talked no more that day.

I brought it to work and when I had time, I lit my candle, said my prayer, and asked God what he wanted me to do. The spirit said, "Get the poem out and read it."

THE BLOODY FIELD

I LAID IN A BLOODY FIELD, STRUCK DOWN BY A WEAPON I DIDN'T SEE MY MIND AND BODY HAD BEEN ATTACKED, IN A BATTLE TO BE FREE HELPLESS AND IN SILENT FEAR, I WATCHED THE ENEMY RAISE HIS SPEAR HE AIMED FOR MY HEART TO FINISH THE JOB, HIS VICTORY CRY RANG IN MY EAR

THE THRUST WAS GIVEN WITH A SMILE, UPON HIS TWISTED FACE
HE DANCED AND LAUGHED AND WAS FILLED WITH JOY, FOR HE WAS NOW THE ACE
WHO WAS THIS ENEMY WHO HATED ME, AND WHY HE WAS SO ANGRY I COULDN'T SEE
WITHIN THE DEPTHS OF MY BROKEN SHELL, A SPARK OF LIFE REMAINED
I CRIED, "OH GOD HAVE PITY ON ME AND WASH AWAY MY STAIN"
AND SUDDENLY A MAN APPEARED AND PICKED ME GENTLY UP
AND LIFE CAME IN AS I ATE HIS FOOD AND DRANK FROM HIS OWN CUP
HE CLOTHED ME WITH A ROYAL ROBE AND PLACED A CROWN OF GLORY UPON MY HEAD
FROM WHERE I STOOD I SAW A ROOM WITH GOLDEN LIGHTS THAT SEEMED TO SPREAD
HIS EYES WERE DARKER THAN NEW WINE AND HE DANCED WITH JOY AND SINGING
HE WATCHED ME LIKE A CHILD PLAYING WITH A NEW TOY
HIS SMILE WAS WARM AND FULL OF LIFE AND THEN I KNEW THIS MAN HAD TAKEN MY STRIFE
AND SOON WE WERE HIS GLORIOUS ARMY, TREADING DOWN THE EVIL ONE, WITH POWER, MIGHT, AND

VICTORY, GIVEN TO US BY THE CHOSEN ONE
THE SPIRIT OF GOD ROSE HIGH AS WE FINALLY STOOD OUR GROUND, TO SHOW GOD'S LOVE THAT WAS WITHIN, AND IT KEPT THE DEVIL BOUND
BUT THEN ONE DAY AS WE WERE BUSY SHINING UP OUR LAMPS, A TERRIBLE MAN CAME INTO OUR CAMPS TO STEAL OUR PRECIOUS TREASURE
AS HE WENT THROUGHOUT OUR MIDST HE BROUGHT TREMENDOUS PRESSURE
CONDEMNATION AND JUDGEMENT WAS HIS AIM
KILLING, STEALING, AND DESTROYING, WAS HIS GAME
I STOOD IN FEAR AND WATCHED, UNABLE TO SAY A WORD, FOR HE WAS HUGE AND I WAS AFRAID OF HIS SWORD
BEWILDERED AND CONFUSED, FIGHTING DESPERATELY FOR HOURS, I SAW AGAIN THAT BLOODY FIELD, ONLY THIS TIME IT WAS OURS
THE MIGHTY ARMY THAT STOOD SO TALL, THE ONE THAT JESUS OWNED, WAS NOW REDUCED TO LIFELESS STONE BECAUSE THEY MISSED THE CALL
THE FIGHTING THAT WENT ON WAS OVER
WHO WAS THE BEST?
AND I WHO WASN'T KILLED, WAS CAPTURED IN THE MESS

THE FREEDOM THAT I ONCE STOOD IN SEEMS ONLY LIKE A DREAM
DID WE FORGET LOVE PAID THE PRICE AND ALL THE WORLD'S REDEEMED?
WE SEE THE FAULTS IN OTHERS, BUT NEVER IN OURSELVES
WE SHINE OUR LAMPS SO BRIGHT AND PUT FORGIVENESS ON THE SHELF.
I LOOK TO LOVE AS MY WASHER, NOT NO WAGGLING TONGUES, WHO WOULD TEAR ME DOWN AND SHAPE ME INTO THE MOLD THEY HAVE BECOME
TO JUDGE EACH OTHER WITH OUR STANDARDS ONLY BRINGS CONTENTMENT
LOVE CAME THAT WE MAY HAVE LIFE
THE KIND THAT BRINGS REDEMPTION
DO NOT KNEEL TO FALSE GODS FROM ABOVE
THEY WERE ONLY CREATED TO HIDE LOVE
THEY LIED TO YOU, DIDN'T YOU HEAR, YOUR QUEEN'S NOT DEAD LIKE THEY SAID
LOVE WAS HIDDEN AWAY IN A DEEP DARK PLACE
BUT NOW SHE'S BACK TO HELP SAVE THE HUMAN RACE
SO HAVE NO FEAR, LOVE IS HERE!
TO SPREAD THE LIGHT OF LOVE THROUGHOUT YOUR ATMOSPHERE
LOVE NEEDS NO RICHES, FAME, OR GLORY

BUT ONLY WANTS YOU TO KNOW THE
TRUE STORY
LOVE WINS
SO MY SAINTS PLEASE KEEP IN MIND THE
WARRIORS WE'VE KNOCKED DOWN
USE YOUR SWORD, BUT WATCH YOUR
AIM, FOR IT'S LOVE WHO WEARS THE
KINGDOM'S CROWN.

While working on chapter three I was tired of the 17 leaks and said, "Ok look! Whoever or whatever you are. If you won't give me a better place to write, can you at least stop the leaks? Please!" Heavy rains came, and I was expecting the ceiling to leak but to my surprise, no leaks! I called the owner and asked if they fixed the roof and told her the ceiling wasn't leaking. She said, it must be a miracle because they did nothing to it. I was skeptical and not sure whether to believe her or not. I could only imagine how much mold and mildew was in the ceiling and it was getting ready to fall. I've killed a few black widows and had to deal with wasps trying to live in the store. One time I put my hand in a boot and hundreds of tiny spiders covered it. Oh my! I shook my hand really good until they all came off. I really needed a new place to write!

One afternoon the boss lady came in to tell me her 40-year-old son was stopping by and recently got out of drug rehab for being addicted to meth. He relapsed and was homeless. She said he'd be coming to change, wash up, and shave in the tiny restroom. I thought that was odd for him to do at a business, especially since I was there by myself. I didn't really agree with it and thought it was only going to be a one-time thing, so I let it go. He started coming in once a week, then every day. He came in to get out of the rain or hide from the police. When customers saw him run in the store dirty with no shirt or shoes and run to the back, they'd be afraid for me and I'd tell them, "It's just the owner's homeless son." They wanted to know why he was here and not at his parents, and I'd tell them because he's a drug addict and I guess they don't want him there. They'd ask if I felt safe or if I wanted them to stay until he left? I'd tell them, I was fine, but really, I knew it wasn't a safe place to be. But I could write my book and didn't want anything to interfere with that.

I told the owner I wasn't comfortable with her son coming in everyday and she replied, "Don't worry, you won't have to deal with him much longer. We bought the vacant building across the street from our other location." I was excited. I'd be in a better, safer place, and wouldn't need a ride to work. But I wouldn't be able to write at work and would have to figure that out later. A bunch of construction started in front of the building they bought, so they put moving off. Then they put a for rent sign on the new building and I was confused. The owners decided not to move the boot store and wanted to rent out the new building. But they didn't tell me. They couldn't rent it out and tried to rent out the location I worked at. I found out by people coming to the property to check it out. One couple wanted to rent it but said the man owner was dragging his feet. Another couple said, "We, told the man who owns the store we want to rent it right away, but he hung up on us. Is he a hard man to work for?" I replied, "Yes, sometimes he can be rude and intimidating." I wasn't happy we weren't moving, and I still had to sit with a drug addict alone at work all day. Now he lived there. When I ate, I didn't feel right if I didn't share because he had no food. I caught him smoking meth on the parking lot by the dumpster and told him not to do that anymore. He just smiled and ignored me and kept smoking it. I knew this wasn't a safe place to be, but he never threatened me. It was just being in the situation of possibilities that things could go wrong that scared me. I felt it was wrong for an employer to expect their employee to put up with that. His mom sometimes dropped food and water off for him and wanted me to give her updates on how he was. She asked me what she should do with him, and I told her she needed to let him go to do what he wanted. That meant don't enable him like she was. She made him king of the drug addicts. I didn't think he'd ever get better like that. I decided to try to finish the book as fast as I could and hoped to move to the new store soon.

While writing chapter three something very strange started happening that was weird. Every third word I typed, the radio also said. And I don't mean a, and, or the. I mean big words. I noticed it, and thought, that's weird! I typed again, and it happened again, and again! I got upset and said, "Whatever is doing this stop it!" Then it started happening with entire sentences and I slammed my laptop closed! If I wrote at home, the TV and radio did the same thing. It kept happening. They said the same sentences I typed, and I wondered if I was imagining it or if it was really happening. I wanted it to stop because it was spooky. I didn't tell Steve because I really didn't know how to explain it without sounding crazy. What was this strange energy? I said nothing for over a month. Finally, I explained it to Steve the best I could, and he thought nothing of it. I said to this higher power, "Ok if this is really happening, I want you to show it to Steve!" Then I came home from work and Steve said, "I see what you mean. I put my cigarette out, dumped the ashtray in the trash and was worried I might have started a fire. I said to myself, "I better look in the trash to make sure I didn't start a fire. Then immediately the TV said, "I looked in the trash. There's no fire!" Shortly after that, we were in our bedroom and Steve was showing me what the buttons on the side of the tv did. He said, "If you want, I can draw a picture for you." Then the TV immediately said, "If you want, I can draw a picture for you." Me and Steve looked at each other with big eyes and started laughing. That started happening a lot but the doozie was when Mikey came to visit. Me and Steve were sitting on the couch watching TV and Matt opened the front door with Mikey on his shoulders and Steve said, "Watch out for the fan!" Then the TV did and said exactly what we were doing in real life. Then Steve yelled again, "Watch out for the fan!" and so did the TV! We all noticed. What were the odds? Was it a coincidence? We all laughed. Now we point it out whenever it happens. Now that we've seen it, we can't unsee it. It happens all the time. When I wrote I didn't have the radio or TV on anymore because it was too distracting. I had no idea what was going on or why. It felt like the world was off balance and I didn't know how to explain it. Something didn't feel right in the world. The only way to describe it would be if there was a parallel universe and it was off just a little. Just enough you could barely see it and you could tell it was there because the universes weren't lining up. Like a fuzzy black and white TV.

When Mikey visited last summer, he secretly whispered to me, "My dad is an alien." I laughed and replied, "Don't tell everyone. They'll think you're crazy. If your dad's an alien, then what am I if I'm his mom, and what is Papa Steve and what are you?" He replied, "Aliens?" We both laughed. Me and Steve were talking about what happened last time Mikey was here with the commercial and the fan and he heard us. He got very excited and yelled, "I remember that! I remember that! Now it happens all the time to me!" I wondered if it happened to everyone, but they were just too busy to notice.

On Mikey's visit last Summer, we had a blast. We went to the Zoo, hiked mountains, went to The North Pole and Cave of the Winds and rode all the rides and went on a lantern cave tour. He went swimming and played laser tag. We had so much fun when he was here. We had a water balloon fight and played sports. One day Mikey looked at me and said, "Grandma Cindy, I can tell your getting old." I replied, "How?" He said, "Because when you dyed your hair you forgot these two parts." Then he grabbed my sideburns, which were a much lighter shade of golden-blonde than the rest. They were almost white. I started laughing and replied, "First of all Little Mikey, let me tell you something. I do not color my hair. Second, I do not curl my hair. This is how it grows." He didn't believe me. I had to get Papa to tell him I was telling the truth. Mikey liked to pester me by pulling one strand of hair out at a time.

I took Mikey to meet the ladies at work and they thought he was adorable. I took him down in the spooky basement to show him a motion activated Halloween phone that looked real. It rang so I picked it up and it said several scary things like, I'm right behind you, or I'm coming to get you. It scared Mikey and he yelled, "Grandma! No! Don't answer the phone anymore! It's too scary!" I was laughing and he said, "That's the devil's phone! And I know the devil's number! It's three, three, three!" He was so cute.

When Mikey was here, we went camping and tubing on the Tarryall River. Mike went once before and said it was like a lazy river. It rained a lot, and the water was rushing very fast. Matt looked at it and was concerned and said, "Are we really going to get in that river? It's flowing pretty fast!" Mike said, "Yep." It was about 15 feet wide, and we started in a shallow, slow flowing spot. We each had our own innertubes. I insisted Mikey wore a life vest or he couldn't go. We got in and took off and the water got deeper and rougher. We were knocked against rocks and the trees that hung over the river. Matt kept getting his back scraped by big rocks. Mikes tube popped right away, and he got in Mikey's. Mikey shared Matt's tube and we were spread apart. Steve hit a giant rock, flipped off his innertube, and was trying to get back on. The water was pulling him down stream and his foot got stuck between two big rocks, almost breaking his leg. He escaped and jumped on his innertube just in time to see what happened to me. Right before all of that, Steve saw I was going to be in serious trouble. I was headed directly towards a 10-foot log stretched across the river with lots of big spikes on it. I had my back to it and worked hard to face forward. I knew if I went backwards over it, I'd get seriously hurt and my innertube would pop. I got turned around just in time but didn't know what to do next. I was headed straight for the middle of the spiked log. I tried to get around it but couldn't. I hung my feet out in front of me as far as I could and held on to my tube with all my might. When I got to the log, I stood up on it. The water was rushing fast over my back trying to push me forward, but I still held my tube tight. Then I walked across the log and hopped back into the water with my tube. I couldn't believe I made it. I was relaxing in my tube, recovering from fright, hoping that was the worst of it. Steve looked to see what happened to me and was shocked I made it past the log without getting hurt. He thought for sure I was doomed. It was a rough ride down the river, and I hoped it ended soon. I noticed Mike standing on the bank yelling for us to get out. He said we missed our stop and didn't know what the river was like past that part. The water was rushing very fast, and I got scared and jumped off my tube. It was waist deep and started taking me downstream. I tried to dig my feet into the ground but couldn't stop. Steve passed me, so I yelled to him, "Get out now! We passed the place we're supposed to get out!" The water was so loud he barely heard me. He jumped out of his tube and also had a hard time stopping. My flip flops shot up in the air and went down stream. I yelled for Steve to grab them as they went by and amazingly, they floated right to him. Now I was barefoot and trying to get to the riverbank. Matt and Mikey floated gracefully to the riverbank where Mike picked Mikey up with no problem. Matt tried to get out of the tube and the water took him downstream also. The three of us struggled to get to the bank. We finally got there, and Steve pulled himself upstream by using tree branches and got out. I tried, but the water was rushing too fast. Me and Matt were still on the riverbank holding on to tree branches so the water wouldn't take us away. We were also trying to hold on to our innertubes. I was standing on a rock in waist deep water and saw a small opening in the bushes above us and told Matt to hand the tubes to Steve through it. Then I told him to climb up the ten-foot bank to the top. It was covered in thorny rose bushes, but luckily Matt had shoes. Steve threw my flip flops down so I could climb up. I got to a point where I couldn't climb any higher or I 'd be stuck in the roses. I put both hands in the air and they lifted me straight up. We walked downstream to see what the river was like and were lucky we got out when we did. It was rougher and rockier. What a trip! I couldn't believe we were all alive. When walking back to our car a man stopped and said, "If you're thinking about getting in the river right now, I wouldn't! It's pretty rough!" We told him, "We know! We just got out and barely made it!"

Steve told Mikey about the killer at the boot store, but he didn't believe it. I began telling him the story and his eyes got big and he was listening to me intensely on the edge of his seat. When I was done, he thought it was scary, but he liked my scary stories. In the past we liked to sit around a campfire and tell them. His favorite was The Pond Monster. He'd come out of the pond at night looking for toys that weren't picked up and take them back to the pond with him.

I finished chapter three and Steve read it. He thought it was pretty good and couldn't wait to read the whole book. He said, "Your true-life story is so crazy that no one will believe it." I replied, "Yeah I know. Hahaha! That's ok because at least you were here while it was happening. Thanks for being here and going through it with me or I'd think I was crazy." He replied, "It has been so much fun! Thanks for letting me be with you!" I was happy he liked what I wrote so far because he read lots of books, at least one a month. Sometimes he started one and said it sucked and threw it away. I was glad he didn't do that to my book. He said, "That's funny, your true-life story seems very similar to Shadow Moons in American Gods." I replied, "Yes I noticed that. That is strange." We both laughed about it. But the question was why? I really felt my life was like a mixture of Shadow Moon and Esther from American Gods.

I told my boss, "Me and Steve are signing another years lease so when we do, you'll have me for at least one more year." She replied, “Oh Cindy! You are a Godsend! I love you so much!” Then she hugged me. I thought, wow, I never had a boss say they loved me before! Life was pretty good, and all was going well.

We got some whip-its which is the same as laughing gas. As we were doing them the radio started playing, WHIP IT! WHIP IT GOOD by DEVO. We laughed so hard. Talk about radioactive!

It was past time for my vacation, so I told my boss I wanted to take it and drive to Phoenix Arizona. She was kind of bitchy about it and said, “Well I guess if you need one, you better take it now. After August it’s the busy season and no one gets a vacation!” She seemed to be getting a snotty attitude with me and I didn’t like it.

Me and Steve left for vacation but a few hours later he knew his back wouldn’t let him make it, so we drove back home. I spent my vacation having my nails done, going to the spa, going out to nice restaurants, and hiking the spots I liked. I went to get my check and the boss lady noticed and said to an employee, “Cindy came and got her check. I bet she lied to me and wasn’t really going out of town. I bet she just wanted to take time off.” Really it was none of her business what I did on my vacation. When I saw her, I told her what happened, but I didn’t think she believed me. She just turned her back and gave me the cold shoulder.

I wasn’t Christian and this year didn’t want to celebrate Christmas. If Jesus saw how commercialized it became, he’d be disgusted. Besides, I don’t even think it was his real birthday. I didn’t go all out like I usually did, and it was the easiest, most relaxing Christmas I had in years.

The lady boss made a special trip to the boot store. She never came in for no reason and looked very angry and told me she didn’t want me to write at the store anymore. She said it wasn’t fair to my coworkers. I was confused. I worked alone and got all my work done before I wrote and have the highest sales. A few months earlier when I was working at the main store, I accidentally left a notebook with a few sentences in it on the counter and she read it. She was embarrassed and said, "I'm so sorry I read it, but I thought they were notes for me." I told her, "That's ok. I don't mind." She asked what I was writing so I told her. She replied in excitement, "Am I going to be in it?" I said, "Yes. Of course." She replied, "I hope it's all good." She seemed excited about my book. She asked her employee of ten years if she knew I was writing at the boot store and she replied, "She has the highest sales at the boot store, so I don't think it really matters what she's doing there." I had no idea what got into my boss that she didn't want me to write there anymore but she seemed to be mean and distant now. Like she wasn't my friend anymore and I didn't understand. I figured she was acting that way because I told her I wasn't happy about her son living at the store. He made a giant hole in the back fence so all the homeless people could get in and hang out. That was scary because I went to the back by myself to take trash out every night. I thought I was supposed to finish my book here, but maybe not. My boss told me, "You can write your book at home on your own time." I just said, "Ok." But I was confused. What really got into her? There were no other workers at the store when I worked. I ran it by myself. When she left, I felt she had no right to tell me not to write because I did get a lunch and what I did on it was my business. Steve and my coworker said I should keep writing but use a notebook and hand write instead of the laptop. I did but wasn't happy about it. That next week she scheduled me for six days and I wondered how she expected me to write if I worked full time for her. If she didn't give me lots of hours, she always told me I was on call. Steve said, "That's bullshit! You don't get paid enough to be on call. You're not a fucking doctor!"

I felt like I was in the beginning of a giant storm that I had no control over. Like a very heavy presence landed on the world. I was just waiting to see what else was going to happen since I was unable to write at work. I said to this higher power, "Ok, if I'm not to write here anymore then what do you want me to do now?" It replied, "Read Revelations." I was like, shit, last time I read that was over thirty years ago. That was a very scary book. I felt my whole world might be turned upside down and wondered if it was just going to be my little bubble or the entire world. I read it and finished in one day and pondered on a part in the 20th chapter that talked about a lady with stars upon her head and had the moon at her feet. That struck a strange chord with me. It made me remember what my dad said about seeing the silver stars above my head and my big purple aura. Was he really telling the truth and really saw that? My name did mean moon goddess, bringer or reflector of light. It made me wonder if maybe I did have something to do with Revelations. Oh well. Life went on and no one really knows anything for sure.

Construction started in front of my place and the noise and dirt were unbearable. They tore up the entire street. It sounded like jet planes flying in front of my window day and night. I wasn't getting any sleep. Dirt was all over everything in my house. We had to keep the windows closed and it was hot. It was worse because I still had terrible hot flashes. When I walked 100 yards to work at the main store it was like going through a warzone. I had to be very careful not to get hurt. It looked like a bomb went off on the entire block. The traffic in front was unreal so our landlord opened the back exit, but it was also hard to get out of. I was miserable.

I was called into work at the main store and clocked in and a man and his son came in. As soon as they walked in, the man said something very strange. He said, "When I woke up this morning, it felt like the whole world is off. Like it's out of balance somehow but don't know how to explain it." I laughed inside because I felt the world was out of balance since November but really didn't know how to explain it to anyone either. That was a strange conversation.

The next time I worked at the boot store I was confused. The entire store was changed around and not in a good way. It looked like a tornado came in and rearranged everything. The men's and women's section were mixed together, and the expensive exotic boots were way in the back where I couldn't see them. The cheap fifty-dollar boots were in the front, and you couldn't reach the cowboy hats or belts. I didn't know how to explain this layout to customers. The store was perfect the way it was before. A handicapped man came and couldn't get around. I called the lady boss and told her what was going on and she said her husband wanted it changed that way. I told her it made no sense, so she came in and looked and said she'd have him change it back the way it was.

A couple days later I went to work, and the store was even worse than before. I called the guy who ran it when I was off and asked what was going on. He said, "I'm very sick with the flu and the owner's being mean, making me rearrange the store over and over, probably to make me quit." Then the lady boss called and told me she changed my schedule to work at the main store instead of the boot store. I figured it was because I complained about her son, and she didn't want me to write. The excuse she gave was, "It wouldn't be fair to the other employees if you only worked the boot store." That was hilarious because no one except me and one guy wanted to work the boot store. Everyone else hated it. She was so full of shit! She wasn't a very honest person, and I was warned when I first started by a couple employees how she really was. They said if I was smart, I'd find a different job and they soon quit.

I told the lady boss things were worse at the boot store. She said, "I know! My husband's gone crazy, and I can't stop him!" She said he was mad at the other employee and was trying to get him to quit. I thought that was very crappy to do to him. He'd been nothing but a loyal employee. They didn't want to fire him for no reason because they didn't want to pay him unemployment. He'd done nothing wrong at work. I felt that was bad business practice and morally wrong. I called him to see if things were back in place and he said no, it's even worse. The owner had all the boots out of place and order which made it hard for customers to find what they wanted. It made absolutely no sense. Everything was out of place.

When I worked the boot store, I still complained about her son living there and cutting a big hole in the back of the fence and said it needed fixed. She told her son to fix it, but he never did. She enabled her forty-year-old drug addicted son to keep abusing drugs and was doing it at the expense of my safety. She felt he was safe because he was her son, but he was just a stranger to me who was a homeless drug addict. If he was so safe and trusted, why didn't he have a key to the store instead of sleeping outside on the porch. I'm pretty sure it was because his parents didn't trust him. I thought he should go to the main store where his mom worked to do his business.

I felt something bad was going on at the boot store because things were out of control, and I couldn't use my laptop to write. I decided when I went to work the next day, I'd light a candle and pray and see if I could get the bad energy or whatever it was, out of the store. When Steve drove me to work that morning, there were homeless people inside the locked gate going through the dumpster. Steve said, "Who are those people going through the dumpster and why are they on the inside of the locked gate that's supposed to be a secured area?" I looked at them and one was the owner's son. Steve asked how they got in, so I told him about the big hole in the back and said I'd been trying to get the owner to fix it. That made Steve angry, and he made me call my boss and tell her it needed fixed today and he was staying with me until then, because it wasn't safe. He also told me to tell her that I didn't want her son in the store during business hours and he needed to go to the main store or her house. I called and told her what was going on. She told me and Steve to kick them off the property. Steve said, "NO! That's not our job!" I told her about the fence issue again and she sent her husband over. He arrived shortly and was an asshole to Steve and sarcastically yelled at him,

"So let's see this big hole in the fence that is making your wife so unsafe!" Then he told Steve "It's only my mentally ill son living behind the building on the patio." He tried to convince Steve it was ok, but Steve didn't agree and said, "Oh! He's mentally ill and a drug addict! Well, that's even worse!" Then the owner aggressively got up in Steve's face and yelled, "If you ever call my wife on the phone and yell at her again, I'll kick your ass from here to kingdom come!" Steve had never talked to her on the phone. Not one single time. They looked like they were getting ready to fight. Then Steve came back in the store.

I got the lady owner on the phone when her husband threatened Steve and told her. I also told her it wasn't right to have her son coming in the store every day because I was there by myself. The whole time Steve was yelling in the background for me to take a sick day. The lady boss wanted me to tell Steve it was ok and and I felt safe, and she said, "You're a grown woman! Tell Steve you're ok with it!" I couldn't tell him that because he was right. Just because her son never threatened me didn't mean it was safe and I took Steve's side. She wasn't happy about it and told me to lock up and come to the main store. Then she changed her mind and told me to go home for a couple hours, and we'd straighten everything out. Two hours went by, so I called her hoping the problems were fixed and I'd go back to work. I asked her if I could come see her so we could talk but instead she replied, "As far as I'm concerned, when you left the store and locked up, I considered that as you quitting. I have nothing more to say to you!" I replied, "I didn't quit! You told me to lock up and leave and we'd talk later to straighten it out!" She replied, "I have nothing more to say to you." Then hung up on me. I was confused. I didn't quit. I never once said I was quitting. I liked my job. I just wanted the hole in the fence fixed and her son not living at the store or on the parking lot doing drugs.

The same day was payday so I went to the main store to get my check, but she wouldn't give it to me until I gave her the keys to both stores. I went home and got them and gave them to her and told her, "I didn't quit!" Strangely we hugged and looked at each other in confusion. She said, "I don't know how things got out of control so fast." We both teared up and I left. She told her employees I quit, but that wasn't true. I told them what really happened. They let me go because I complained about their son at the boot store and my husband stood up to hers. They all sided with me and agreed I shouldn't have to deal with her son at work. Now they knew what kind of a lady she really was. I filed for unemployment and got it due to unsafe working conditions.

Now I could finish writing my book in the comfort of my own home. It was all working out for me. But the owners told lots of lies to unemployment and got my claim denied. They referred to my husband of 30 years as a male friend who convinced me it wasn't safe to work there and talked me into quitting. Her husband said Steve was the aggressive one. He told many lies that I hope he'll pay for later. He said I agreed to have his son there from the beginning, but that was a lie. I only agreed to it one day. He admitted his son was in and out of rehab and didn't know what else to do with him. When the officer asked if his son had a drug problem he replied, "His mother would say he does, but I don't think so. He just wants to live a different lifestyle than us." There he went again enabling his son and covering for him. He said I never complained about his son or the fence before. That was also not true. I complained to his wife many times, but she never told him. I saw him maybe a total of eight times while I worked there. I saw the lady boss all the time and she was who I reported to. The lady officer asked him, "Can you understand her point of view? A lady being there alone by herself with your son every day. How she'd be uncomfortable in that situation." I thought for sure after hearing the question she asked, I'd win my case. He didn't say yes or no. He went on an incoherent rant saying it was safe at the boot store. He also lied and told the officer me and his son were friends beforehand. He could tell it wasn't sounding good for him, so he came up with a doozie lie. At the end he said, "Did you know my son has a reason to be there? He has been retained by the City of Colorado to pick up trash from the vacant lot next to the business." I replied, "This is the first I heard of it." There is not a bar of soap big enough to wash all the lies out of his mouth. I called the city and they told me they never retain anyone to pick up trash and his name was not on their payroll. Somehow, I still lost the appeal. I wasn't worried. I knew it would work out fine for me no matter what the outcome was, but now they're in for some bad karma. For now, I just wanted to finish the book.

After reading the first five chapters I thought the name of the book should be changed to Cindy's Big Trip. I had a hard time believing what I wrote was true. If I didn't, then I didn't believe my life.

I told Steve, "Let's have a photograph party. We'll drink, smoke weed, listen to music, and go through thousands of pictures to find the ones I want for The Gallery of Love." Steve agreed and said, "It sounds like fun, but I bet all the music is going to be radioactive. It will probably be all about pictures, memories and so on." I laughingly replied, "You're probably right." We began our party and Steve was right. All the music that played was about looking at old memories, photographs, the past, darkrooms, etc. It was funny. After an hour of it going on with every song, it began to blow Steve's mind and he said, "I can't take this anymore. This is fucking crazy! I'm going next door to see the boys." He left and the music did it for about thirty more minutes and stopped.

My life felt like a giant puzzle, and I was trying to put all the pieces together. Steve said I'd never have all the answers or be able to put it all together. I had no idea when I started this book where it was leading. I still didn't go to church or have a religion and didn't follow any religious books. I just prayed to God in English and in the Spirit and thanked him for what I had every day. I wasn't Jewish, and I didn't go to a temple to worship God. I wasn't

Christian because I didn't believe Jesus was the true savior. I felt people should search for the living God inside instead of following one from a book. Books could be altered to mislead you to their advantage. If all the religious books were gone, I'd still have my walk with God or this higher power. You don't have to read or believe in the Bible to see all hell was breaking loose on the earth. If God told me to do something I felt was wrong, I wouldn't do it and take whatever punishment he gave me. I only followed what my heart told me. I was such a rebel sometimes.

On December 26, 2019, someone asked us if we wanted to try DMT. We never heard of it, so we looked it up and it was a chemical naturally produced and released in your brain in small amounts when you slept. It's what made you dream crazy dreams. It also came from a plant and could be manufactured in a lab. It caused hallucinations and crazy trips. It only lasts for 10 to 20 minutes. They said when you first go into the trip, you might meet a spirit guide who helps you through it. Me and Steve researched more and saw no bad side effects and decided to try it. I took three hits and the world around me felt like it was shaking and vibrating. Then I saw lots of equations and colored shapes and my surroundings started folding up like an origami and folded into nothingness. Then I blasted through it as a ball of light. I had the most wonderful warm feeling. That was all I remembered. I woke up and felt like many lifetimes had passed and got scared. I asked Steve how long I was gone, and he said ten minutes. That blew my mind how time was warped! The next time I wanted to try to stay awake. I took 3 more hits from the pipe. The same thing happened and when I opened my eyes, I saw molecules moving and changing in the air and everything looked like displaced pixels from a TV. Portholes were opening and closing. I went through them at high speed. I fell asleep for a few seconds, snored, and woke up and laughed. I did that several times and Steve thought it was hilarious. I fell asleep and the spirit guide met me to help me through. There were strands of golden shiny lights all around and we traveled like balls of light or energy through the portholes or tunnels. Then I came back. On my third trip I immediately met the spirit guide and it said, "Oh, you're here again. What is it you want?" I replied, "I'm seeking the truth." We became balls of energy or light and took off through a bunch of crazy spiraled tunnels. We stopped at the bottom of a huge white staircase with large pillars of fire on each side. The guide motioned for me to go up the stairs and I thought wow, I must be going to meet God! It was very peaceful, and everything was bright white. When I got to the top there were golden bars on the doors and couldn't get through, so I turned to the spirit guide, but it was gone. I fell backwards and floated above the stairs and was surrounded in clouds. My body felt so warm and peaceful. It felt like many years went by and I wondered how long I'd been here and thought I should get back home. I woke and only five minutes had passed. On my fourth trip I was in a strange spaceship, and I broke out of what looked like a grape. I saw a cluster of grapes on the floor, and it looked like other people were still inside the grapes, and I was trying to protect them like they were my family. I was trying to protect them from some weird red alien crustations in control of the ship. On my fifth trip the spirit guide asked why I was here, so I told it I was here to see and talk to God. It replied, "Silly girl, no one gets to see or talk to God." I yelled, "Well I do!" I whizzed past the guide and went into a tunnel. It was winding and going side to side. I felt like I was poured down a sink and was going through the pipes. The wind was incredible, and I got stuck against the wall. The guide came back and was laughing at me, and the wind thrust me into another porthole. Then I woke up. I was so tired I went back to sleep but remembered no more.

Trying DMT was one of the most amazing experiences I ever had. It was up there with childbirth. I recommend everyone try it at least one time in their life. Especially anyone who is troubled about anything from dying to drug addiction. I believe it has many benefits and little or no side effects.

In the beginning of 2020, a terrible virus broke out across the whole world, but our president didn't tell us until almost 3 months later. Everything shut down everywhere and everyone had to wear masks. Hospitals were overwhelmed by the sick and millions died. It mutated several times and two years later it was still going on. In some countries when it first started, if you came out of your house, they'd burn it down. We finally got a vaccine, but it didn't stop the spread. Everyone was divided over mask or no mask, vaccine or no vaccine. We had been lied to so much and so long by those in authority that no one knew what to believe.

The current president lost the 2020 election and claimed it was stolen even though there was no proof at all. On January 6, 2021, he got his followers to storm the Capital in an insurrection and take it over. It lasted several hours, and some people were killed and many injured, but control was gained back by the police.

Someone asked me what I was as far as religion. I told them I wasn't Christian but followed God in the Old Testament. They replied, "Oh, so you are Jewish." I didn't really know what to say so I replied, "I guess." That really didn't sound right to me, and it made me question what I believed in and who I really followed. I decided it was time to start examining all the information I'd acquired in my life to see if I could figure out who and what I really was.

I examined the God of the Old Testament because he was who I was raised as a child to believe in. It was the mainstream religion where I lived.

The Bible said the God in The Old Testament created the Heavens and Earth. He created Adam by blowing his spirit into dirt, then split Adam to create Eve. But oddly, Adam had a wife named Lilith first who wanted nothing to do with him. He put(confined) them in a beautiful garden and said they could eat from every tree but the Tree of Knowledge or they'd die. RED FLAG! WHAT DID HE WANT TO HIDE FROM THEM? WHAT DID HE NOT WANT THEM TO KNOW? But a talking snake convinced Eve to eat the fruit. Something changed and the two hid from this god when he came to see them. MAYBE THEY SAW HE WAS NOT THE REAL GOD. He said they sinned and cast them out of the garden and told them to reproduce and multiply. WELL, THAT DIDN'T SOUND LIKE THEY DIED. Adam supposedly lived 930 years. This god wanted their descendants to follow and obey him, but many refused. It was said he was a loving, caring god, but he used scare tactics saying you'd be sent to Hell where Satan, Lucifer, or the Devil was cast previously by him for starting a war in Heaven. We'd be tormented forever and ever in a fiery pit if we didn't bow to him, worship him, and accept him as our god. DOESN'T SOUND LIKE A LOVING GOD TO ME! He tried to convince us he was the only supreme god and there were no others. He wanted us to walk in blind faith even though he claimed our eternal salvation was at stake. SOUNDS FISHY! He waged war on the humans on earth who refused to follow him. He pitted humans against each other to wage his wars. It was he who commanded all the first-born sons killed and killed 1.2 million humans. He accepted virgin sacrifices and told someone to take their child to the mountain and sacrifice him just to see if he would. He flooded the earth when humans refused him as their god. He supposedly saved one little family and lots of animals on a big arc who followed and worshiped him as their god, and that was how he kept the human race alive. Hoping they'd be obedient to his demands. He tells you not to kill but then tells you to smite his enemies for him. HE SOUNDED LIKE A NARCASSISTIC ANGRY TYRANT WHO WAS NOT GETTING HIS WAY. THIS GOD CRUMBLED BEFORE MY EYES! HE WAS NOT MY GOD! Just because he had the ingredients and knowledge how to create humans does not make him your god. I put ingredients together and made a beautiful cake but that doesn't make me the god of cakes!

Let's talk about Lucifer, Satan, also known as The Devil in the Bible. He was this god's favorite angel in Heaven. He was called The Morning Star. THAT'S STRANGE. I ALWAYS HEARD JESUS WAS THE MORNING STAR. They said he started a war in Heaven against God because he wanted to overthrow him and was cast to the earth. He'd then go before this god saying things like, I bet I can get your favorite worshipper to turn away from you, and God would be like, no you can't. Then they'd play games to see who'd win. For example, the story of Job. That sounded terrible! Sounded like the two were friends in cahoots, playing good cop bad cop. I think the devil only killed two people. So, this god now had lots of people under his control by the fear of the Devil and him. Humans were waiting for a savior to come set them free.

Then came The New Testament with Jesus and he was also called THE MORNING STAR. They said he was the god from the Old Testament who came down from Heaven and became flesh to forgive us of our sins by sacrificing himself on a cross. He preached love, peace, and forgiveness of each other. He was also called the son of God. Confusing. Was he God, or the son of God? They said he had many powers and performed miracles like healing the sick, making the blind see, prophesying, and even raising the dead. They said he baptized people with the Holy Spirit with the evidence of speaking in tongues. He told us we had the keys to the Kingdom and the Kingdom of Heaven was inside all of us. He said he was The Way, The Truth, and The Light and through him we could find eternal salvation. He tried to show us we were just like him and had all the same powers he had. He was angered at how money and government was mixed with god's temple and threw a fit. He didn't like the mainstream teaching of the religion in his time and rebelled against it and the ways of the world. He got many followers, and it worried the government state and church because they'd lose the control they had over the people. They had to kill him. Then they made a martyr out of him claiming he was the god of the Old Testament in the flesh and if we believed that, then we could get into Heaven and have eternal salvation. After Jesus was killed, the church and Christianity warred with each other and finally the teachings were joined. Then the church went through the Old Testament and New Testament and got rid of any books that didn't fit their agenda of keeping humans worshipping and following the god of the Old Testament. I think they did this to keep the truth about who Jesus and humans really were, hidden from us for two thousand more years. Some people were smart and hid many of the books banned from The Bible. I felt the God of the Old Testament and Jesus were two totally different beings.

That is where the Agnostics come in. They hid the banned books. These books have been revealed in recent times. They believed the teachings of Jesus were basically hijacked by the god of The Old Testament to keep people following him. They felt Jesus came to set humans free from the tyranny of the false god, but his message was mixed with the Old Testament to glorify the false god. The Apocalypse of Adam said the garden had bad bitter fruit. In a banned book Jesus said, "Was it not I who got Eve to eat the forbidden fruit?" Jesus sounded like Lucifer when he was in Heaven. Two Morning Stars both claimed they got Eve to eat the fruit. Maybe when Jesus was in Heaven, he was the one who warred against the false god because he knew the truth and was thrown to earth and then called Satan.

Then we have those who believe in the old gods and goddesses like Zeus, Venus, Poseidon, Hera, Aphrodite and so on. Their names changed according to where you lived in the world and what teachings you followed. Zeus was also a tyrant who wanted to be worshipped as the top god above all other gods. I'd have to say he and the god of the O.T. sounded kind of the same.

Then we have Spiritualists, Alchemists, and Pleiadeans, among others, who believe in growing their spirit, being a good person, spreading peace, love, and forgiveness. Meditating and healing yourself from within with herbs and sound vibration. They talk of Chakras and opening your third eye etc. When I first heard of the third eye it made a memory come back. Many years ago, for Halloween I dressed as Queen of the Aliens and painted a third eye in the middle of my forehead with eyelashes and put antennas on my head. I looked quite silly!

Some believe they channel aliens, are part alien, or can time travel. The good ones of love and light are the Pleiadeans, Arcturians, and Sirians and others who claim to be at war with the evil dark aliens, The Anunnaki, who are said to have ruled over the earth and humans for thousands and thousands of years. The Anunnaki were written about five thousand years ago in the Sumerian culture. They were an ancient alien race said to have come from the sky and created humans to enslave us in a false dimensional bubble to mine gold for them. It said they come back every 3600 years to keep things in order on earth. The good aliens say we all came from the same divine light as Jesus and have his same spirit and need to all wake up and acknowledge who we are in order to free ourselves from this slavery. They believe we need to raise the vibration of love high enough to defeat the Anunnaki. They say our spirits are stuck in a dimensional dirt prison and our energy is used over and over by the Anunnaki. This sounded like the Anunnaki Ruler was the same ruler as the God of the O.T. and he used the Bible to hide himself in order to keep control of humans until they came back.

I think they may all have some truth to them in their own way and seemed to mirror each other. Almost the same story but different character names. The earth feels like a reprogramming station for those who refuse to worship the god in the Bible, other gods, or higher deities. Many people believe the Bible just so they can get into this place called Heaven, which might not even be a good place.

I recently saw an episode of Black Mirrors called The USS Callister and it was about an evil scientist who created a virtual spaceship and took DNA from his friends and made replicas of them and put them in the spaceship. He was the captain and controlled all the crew. If you didn't do what he wanted, he hurt you bad. One guy wouldn't do what he said, so the scientist made a replica of his young son and threw him out of the spaceship to his death. He did it over and over until the guy did what he wanted. Whenever someone new was put on the spaceship they'd be very confused about how they got there. The other people on the ship had to inform them what was going on and what the rules were. No one could have sex because the scientist made everyone with no vaginas or penises. What a bummer! That was a crazy episode. It reminded me of how God in the O.T. acted. He has all of us stuck on Earth and wants us to bow to him and worship him or he'll kill us. He'll put you in a fiery pit called Hell to burn for all eternity or until he wants to stop torturing you. That doesn't sound like a very loving God to me. I also don't feel like this was my first time here on Earth for some strange reason. People say the god of the O.T. is a good god. Well, I say just look at all the mean things he did in the O.T. Christians who follow the Bible never want to talk about how their god was in the past before he claimed to be Jesus. I used to think that when you died there was nothing more. You just rotted in the ground and that was it. Sounded so easy and peaceful. But now I'm not sure after all I've been through. I'm starting to believe in this higher power in my life and that I may be here for a reason. God was a very jealous God and killed many people who didn't worship him. Many Christians tell me I can't have a relationship with him, or get to heaven, unless I believe Jesus is my God and he saved me. They tell me I'll burn in Hell for eternity if I don't believe their beliefs. I tell them to quit putting limits on my God. God and I have a perfectly good relationship. Stop trying to push Jesus in-between us. I'm happy with our relationship. I don't need a middleman to water down what I get from God. God told me I can come before him anytime I wanted. Wouldn't God want you to come directly to him if your eternal soul was on the line?

Wouldn't it be crazy if the God of the Old Testament was also Zeus and was really an evil Anunnaki Alien ruler from outer space and was coming back soon. And Jesus was really Lucifer, a Pleiadean Alien warring with him trying to set us free, but the truth was twisted to keep us blind, and he deceived the whole world, and a great war between them was going to take place on earth. That would be an event you wouldn't want to miss! Or maybe you would.

None of that really matters to me because I'm not going to follow anyone. I'm moving forward and following my own Holy Spirit to grow it bigger than my flesh by meditating and using my spirit language. I will work on opening my chakras and my third eye so I can see with my spirit. I'll try to be kind to all living things on the earth because I feel that everything is a part of me. We are all what god is in flesh form. Everything is! My body is my church and wherever I go, my church and spirit also go. I AM the temple of God. I AM THE WAY, THE TRUTH, AND THE LIGHT, just like Jesus was, and so are you. I have the same Holy Spirit inside me he had. We are all Kings and Queens in this realm. Jesus is my brother and told us he was a god. So, if that is true, I am also a goddess. So, we are all little Gods and Goddesses running around doing our own thing and not listening to our divine spirits. A friend of mine didn't like that kind of talk. She felt I was putting myself above her God. But I wasn't. I am telling you, everyone who has ever lived on this Earth are equal to each other and to the God of the O.T. because we came from the same divine light he came from. THE ENERGY OF THE GOD SOURCE. THE DIVINE LIGHT! AND WE WILL ALL GO BACK TO IT BECAUSE ENERGY CAN'T BE DESTROYED, ONLY DISPLACED.

People should tithe by giving time to help others who need it. Like helping the elderly get their groceries or shoveling someone's driveway who can't. By giving food, shelter, healthcare, donating time to a good cause, or lifting up your fellow man because he is you. Don't give to a church who is designed to line the pockets of the preacher so they can drive a fancy car. I feel they are false prophets. All churches should help those in need. If not, they are not a true Church of God or Christ.

Don't get me wrong, I love my brother Jesus. I just feel Christianity has been here for 2000 years with no real great results. It's time for a change. Jesus was a beacon of light from the past who showed me I can go against the mainstream religion and government of the day. He came here to show us how to release the Holy Spirit inside of us so we could create heaven on Earth. I think Jesus is coming back through us, not from the sky. We are eternal energy and cannot be destroyed, only transformed. He taught love, forgiveness, and compassion for all living creatures. I plan to keep my divine light and not give credit to any religious sects or deities. I AM a free thinker and will not worship anyone! I will fly on my own wings. The wings of Love. I will grow my spirit and help raise the vibration of Love like Horton Hears a Who and hope others do to. IT'S TIME TO WAKE UP! WAKE UP THE JESUS SPIRIT INSIDE OF YOU! It's an alien invasion of LOVE and Jesus is Love. If anyone would like help releasing their Holy Spirit without going through a religion, as long as I AM here, I AM willing to help. I AM LOVE. We are in THE AGE OF THE GREAT AWAKENING. THE DAWNING OF THE AGE OF AQUARIUS! THE MIND IS LIMITLESS! WAKE UP! AD ASTRA!

CHAPTER 6

THE GALLERY OF LOVE

CINDY AGE 4

CINDY AGE 11

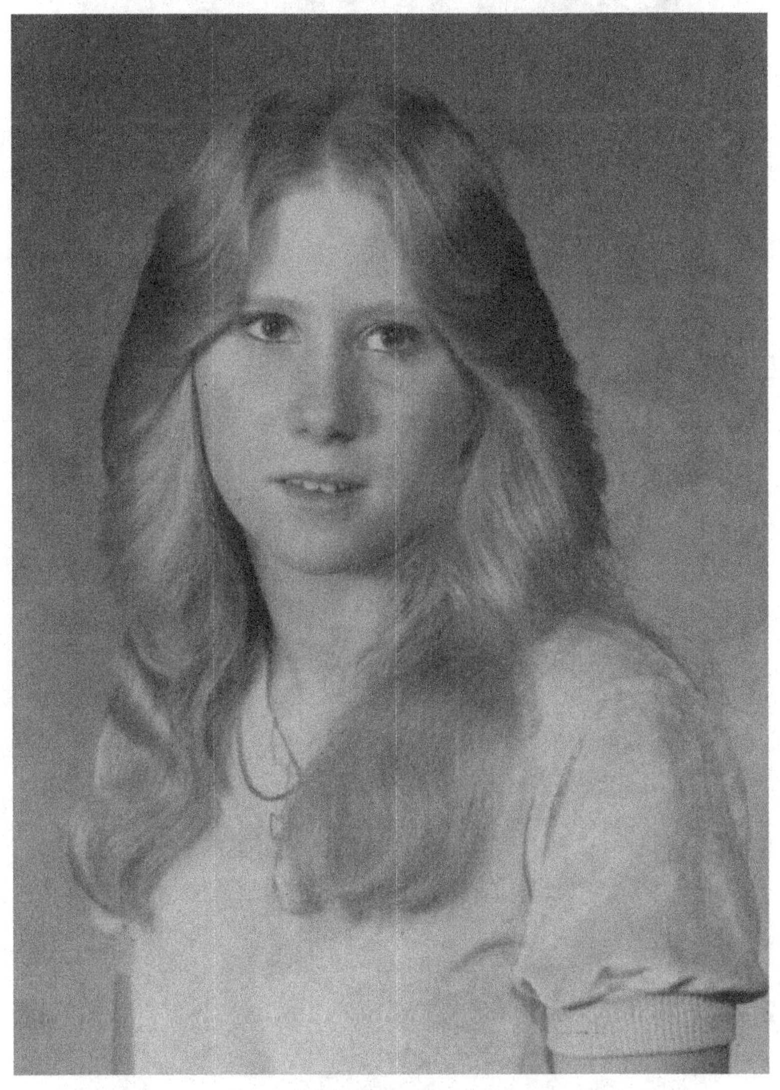

CINDY AGE 16

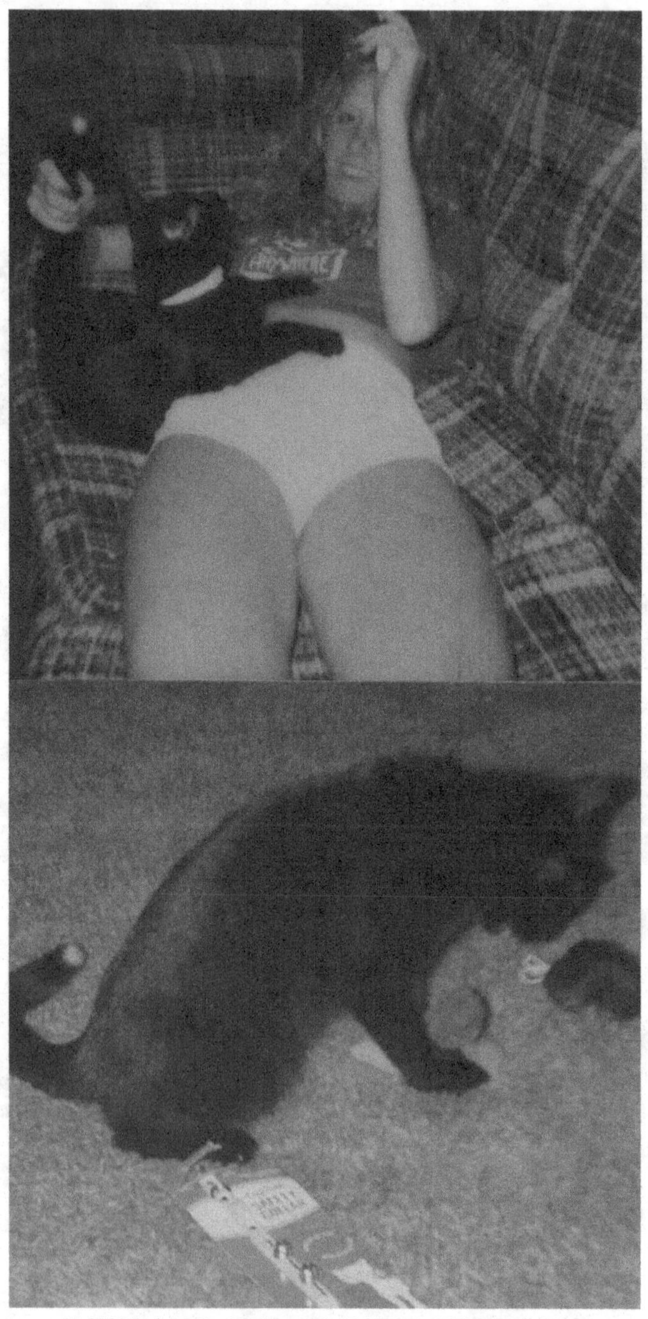

INKY AND HER UNIQUE WHITE TIP

CINDY'S CURLY HAIR AGE 19

WEDDING CEREMONY

AFTER WEDDING CEREMONY

SEXY STEVE

SEXY DEBBIE HALLOWEEN 1986

STEVE'S STRANGE WHITE TRIANGLE

PRINCESS LUSTY

VENUS THE ANGEL

VENUS THE WARRIOR READY TO ATTACK

VENUS THE WARRIOR CHARGING

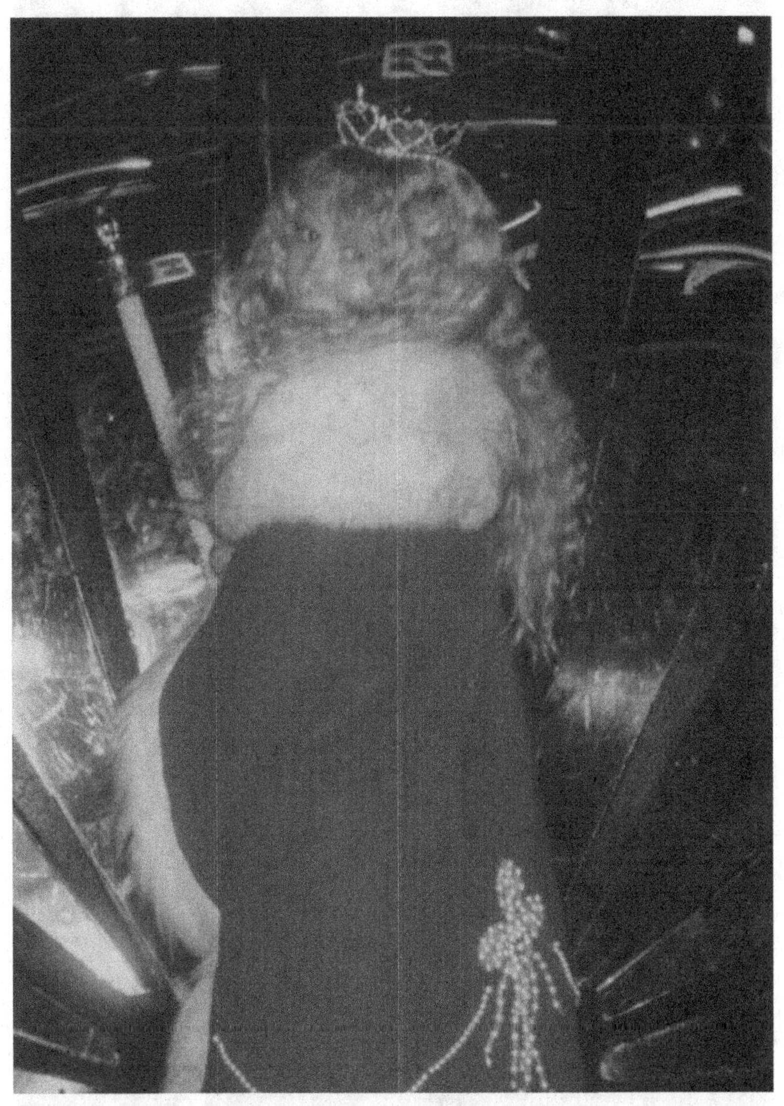

QUEEN VENUS THE GODDESS LOVE AT DEJAVU

HOT VENUS AT DEJAVU

TORNADO CINDY DREW IN THE COLONY

CINDY BEING LARGER THAN LIFE

BACKYARD POND IN MOUNT PLEASANT

ANGIE THE DANCER

ANGIE AT BABY DOLLS

LET'S PLAY POP THE BALLOONS

MY WONDERFUL SON MICHAEL

MY KIND HEARTED SON MATTHEW

MY INVENTION PIERCED TONGUE SUCKERS

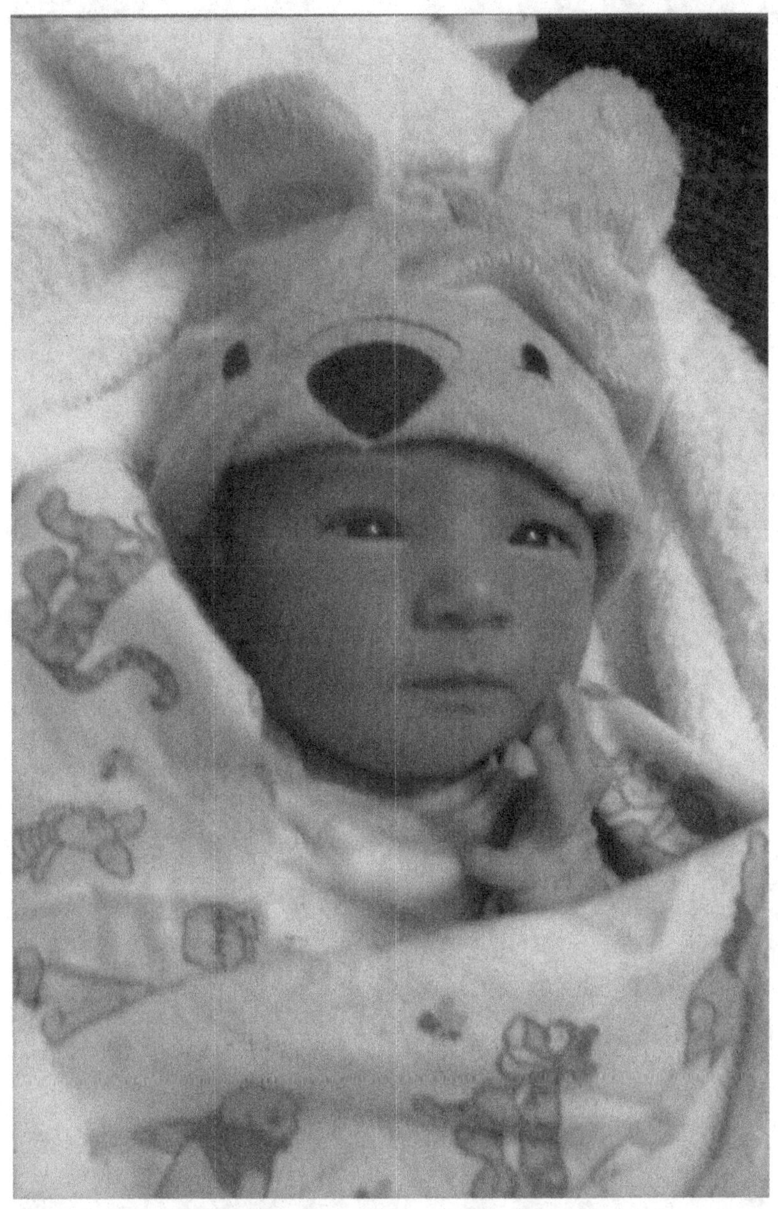

MY GRANDSON MICHAEL JR. THE GREAT THINKER

ONE OF MIKEY'S EASTER BASKETS
FROM GRANDMA CINDY

CINDY IN COLORADO SPRINGS

STEVE AND CINDY IN COLORADO SPRINGS

CHAPTER 7

LET THE MUSIC SET YOU FREE

Music can be a great communicator. It can be prophetic and radioactive in a strange way. Some of it sucks, but lots of it can be inspirational.

This time will be the last I fear, unless I make it all too clear. Learn to live so free. I think tonight we can take what is wrong and make it right. It's all I know that your half of the flesh and blood makes me whole. When we hear, the voices sing, THE BOOK OF LOVE will open up and let us in.

Goddess on the mountain top. Burning like a silver flame. The summit of beauty and love, and Venus was her name. Her weapons were her crystal eyes. I'm your Venus! I'm your fire!

Lightening crashes, a new mother cries. Her placenta falls to the floor. The angel opens her eyes. The confusion sets in. I feel it coming back again. Forces pulling from the center of the earth again. This moment she's been waiting for. The angel opens her eyes! Pale blue colored iris presents the circle and puts the glory out to hide./Love is an angel disguised as Lust.

She's blood flesh and bone. She's touch, smell, sight, taste, and sound. She's so high above me. Like Cleopatra, Joan of Arc, or Aphrodite.

Girl, dancing down those dirty and dusty trails. Rocket through the wilderness. Around the world the trip begins. Roam if you want to. Roam around the world. Without wings. Without anything but the love we feel!

Contact is all that it takes to change your life to lose your place in time. Contact. Asleep or awake. Coming around you may wake up to find. Questions deep within your eyes. Now more than ever, you realize! And then you sense a change. Nothing feels the same.

All your dreams are strange. Love comes walking in. Some kind of alien, waits for the opening, then simply pulls a string and Love comes walking in. Another world! Some other time! You lay your sanity on the line. Familiar faces. Familiar sites. Reach back remember with all your might! There she stands in a silken gown with silver lights shining down! So when you sense a change, and nothing feels the same, all your dreams are strange, Love comes walking in. Some kind of alien, waits for the opening, then simply pulls a string, and Love comes walking in! Sleep and dream is all that I pray. I traveled far across the Milky Way. To my master, I become a slave! You will meet him some other day. Where silence speaks as loud as war the earth returns to what it was before.

Always said you were a youth quaker. A stormy little world shaker. An angel with a broken wing. Wars little queen. The gods lay at your feet. We caress your cheek. Stars wrapped in your hair. Paradise a shattered dream. Your innocence dripped blood sweet child! Wars little queen! An angel with a broken wing! Don't you know paradise takes time?

She'll tell you she's an orphan, after you meet her family. Says she talks to angels. They call her out by her name. Oh yeah! She talks to angels! Says they call her out by her name! Don't you know that they call her out by her name!

It's all the same. Only the names have changed. I'm wanted dead or alive. Sometimes you tell the day by the bottle that you drink. Still I'm standing tall.

The amusement never ends. You could have a big dipper. Shed my skin. This is the new stuff. I go dancing in. Will you show for me? I will show for you. Only you've been coming through. Build up that power! Feel that power!

There you hear the music, and it all comes crystal clear. Music does the talkin. I'm young! I'm wild and I'm free! I've got the magic power of the music in me! The world is full of compromise and infinite red tape. The music's got the magic, it's your one chance for escape! Turn me on turn me up. It's your turn to dream.

Follow me stereo child. Love is the kill and your hearts still wild! Who's the hunter? Who's the game? I feel the beat call your name. I hold you close in victory! You won't be caged in the call of the wild! I am the warrior! Like a true nature's child, I was born to be wild!

You better come inside when you're ready to. But no chance if you don't want to dance! You're like a four-letter word! You say that Love has won! But then your finger won't trigger the gun! Are you getting it? Really getting it! Come on Steve! Get it! Cause the best is yet to come! Armageddon!

Welcome to the jungle. We got fun and games. We got everything you want. Honey we know your name! We are the people who can find whatever you may need. If you want it, you're going to bleed, but it's the price you pay. Feel my serpentine! I wanna hear you scream! Watch it bring you to your knees! You learn to live like an animal in the jungle where we play.

She's got a smile that seems to me, reminds me of childhood memories. Her hair reminds me of a warm safe place, where as a child I'd hide, and pray for the thunder and rain to quietly pass me by. Sweet love of mine, where do we go from here?

I've just closed my eyes again. Climbed aboard the dream weaver train. Dream weaver, I believe you can get me through the night. I believe we can reach the morning light. Fly me high through the starry skies. Cross the highways of fantasy. There still may be some time. Fly me away to the bright side of the moon and meet me on the other side.

Come with me, on a journey beneath the skin. We will look together, for the pan within. Swing your hips, loose your head, and let it spin. Close your eyes, breathe slow we`ll begin. To look together for the pan within! Put your face to my window! Breathe a night full of treasure! The wind is delicious, sweet and wild with the promise of pleasure! The stars are alive at nights like these! Were born to be, sanctified by you and me! And all we gotta do is surrender! Surrender! Surrender! Man gets tired. Spirit don't. Man

surrenders. Spirit won't. Man crawls. Spirit flies! Spirit lives when man dies. Man seems. Spirit is. Man dreams. Spirit lives. Man is tethered. Spirit free. What spirit is man can be. Once you were tethered. Now you are free. And you're trying to remember. You're scouring your conscience. Raking through your memory. Now I see you wavering as you try to decide. You've got a war in your head and it's tearing you up inside! You're trying to make sense of something that you just can't see. Trying to make sense now and you know you once held the key. That was the river! And this is the sea! Here we are in this special place! What are you gonna do here? What show of soul are we gonna get from you? Could be deliverance or history. Could be something true. Here we are in this fabulous place. What are you going to dream here? You love to beat your chest and make your sound! But not here man, this is sacred ground, with the power flowing through! Here we stand on a rocky shore. Your father stood here before you. I can see his ghost explore you! Just let it come! Don't bang the drum! I pictured a rainbow. You held it in your hands. I had flashes but you saw the plan. I wandered out in the world for years. You just stayed in your room. I saw the crescent, you saw the whole of the moon! You were there at the turnstiles with the wind at your heels! You stretched for the stars, and you know how it feels to reach too high! Too far! Too soon! You saw the whole of the moon! I was grounded while you filled the skies. I was dumbfounded by truth. You cut through lies. I saw the rain dirty valley. You saw Brigadoon! I spoke about wings. You just flew! I wondered, I guessed, and I tried. You just knew! I sighed. You swooned! With a torch in your pocket and the wind at your heels! Yes, you climbed on that ladder with the wind in your sails! You came like a comet, blazin your trail! Too high! Too far! Too soon!

I was ready to be humbled by the words that you had written. I knew I was the victim of a beautiful deception. All my once exact beliefs, like tangled threads unraveled. I walked out stunned and liberated. And so began my travels. We came upon a stricken ship

that must have once been splendid. I heard a wild holy band that invoked the days of rapture when our Love was still young and contagious. I won't believe the flame I lit is dead or even dying. She was Aphrodite, Helen, Thetis, Eve, among the satyrs. She was Venus in a V-neck sweater. Keep the river on your right and the highway at your shoulder and the front line in your sights. Remember what you told her. This is all in code my dear. I came in quest of secret knowledge. There I read the books of Love and contemplated in seclusion. As a tender dawn was breaking, in a doorway I stood spellbound by the ancient music they were making. I took my breakfast with the gods, til a wind blew them all away. I had misread every warning. Remember what you told her. This is all in code my dear.

Show me! Show me! Show me how you do that trick! The one that makes me scream she said! The one that makes me laugh! Spinning on that dizzy edge. Dreamed of all the different ways I had to make her glow. You, strange as angels. You, lost and lonely. Dancing in the deepest oceans. You're just like a dream. I must have been asleep for days! I opened up my eyes and saw you! Just like heaven.

If our paths never cross, I'm sorry. But if I live to see the seven wonders, I'll make a path to the rainbows end.

I want to run! I want to hide! I want to tear down these walls that hold me inside! I want to take shelter from the poison rain! We're still building and burning down love! And when I go there, I go there with you. It's all I can do. Our love turns to rust. We're being blown by the wind and trampled to dust. I'll show you a place high above the desert plain where the streets have no names.

I have climbed the highest mountains. I have run through the fields. I have crawled. I have scaled these city walls. But I still haven't found what I'm looking for. I felt the healing fingertips. I have spoke with the tongue of angels. I have held the hand of the devil. I believe in the kingdom come and all the colors will bleed into one. You broke the bonds and you loosed the chains. Carried the cross of my shame. Yes, I'm still runnin. You know I believe!

The magic of the moment is what I've got for you. Let us find together what we were looking for. The rhythm of love! It's the game I'm looking for. I make you feel the taste of life until your love will flow!

I'll be there for you! These five words I swear to you! Words can't say what love can do!

I'm running down a dream. Never would come to me. Workin on a mystery. Goin wherever it leads.

I won't back down. You can stand me up at the gates of hell, but I won't back down. I'll keep this world from dragging me down. There ain't no easy way out!

Forget about your foolish pride! Take me to the other side! You blinded me with love, and it opened up my eyes!

Smoke she is arising! You're to blame! She's coming close now. I can feel her. Come on little sister! Send down fire to me! Stand down in front of me!

Just walk this way to the dawn of the light. Hear this voice from deep inside. It's the call of your heart. Close your eyes and you will find passage out of the dark. Will you send me an angel in the land of the morning star? Just find your place in the eye of the storm. Here I am in the land of the morning star. Just raise your hand and reach out for the spell. Find the door to the promised land. Just believe in yourself. Don't stop believing.

On a dark desert highway, I saw a shimmering light. There she stood in the doorway. I was thinking to myself this could be Heaven, or this could be Hell. Then she lit up a candle and she showed me the way. Mirrors on the ceiling and pink champagne on ice. And she said, "We are all just prisoners here of our own devise." In the master's chambers they gathered for the feast. They stabbed it with their steely knives but they just can`t kill the beast! Last thing I remember I was running for the door. Had to find the passage back to the place I was before. "Relax" said the nightman, "We are programmed to receive. You can check out anytime you like. But you can never leave!"

There`s a lady who's sure, all that glitters is gold, and she`s buying a stairway to heaven. When she gets there, she knows, if the stores are all closed, with a word she can get what she came for. There`s a sign on the wall, but she wants to be sure, cause you know sometimes words have two meanings. And it`s whispered that soon, if we all call the tune, the piper will lead us to reason. And a new day will dawn for those who stand long. Yes, there are two paths you can go by. There`s still time to change the road you`re on. The piper is calling you to join him. Dear lady can you hear the wind blow? And did you know, your stairway lies on the whispering wind? And as we wind on down the road. Our shadows taller than our soul! There walks a lady we all know! Who shines white light and wants to show! And if you listen very hard, the tune will come to you at last! When all are one and one is all!

Come as you are. As you were. As I want you to be. As a friend. As a known enemy. Take your time. Hurry up. Choice is yours. Don't be late. Come doused in mud.

You say, one love, one life. We get to share it. We're one, but we're not the same. We get to carry each other. Have you come here for forgiveness? Have you come to raise the dead? Have you come her to play Jesus to the lepers in your head? We're one, but we're not the same. You say, Love is a temple. Love is a higher law. You ask me to enter, but then you make me crawl. One Love. One blood. But we're not the same. Gonna take a walk with your sister moon. Let her pale light in, to fill up your room. You've been living underground. You've been running away from what you don't understand. Love! She's slippery. You're sliding down. She'll be there when you hit the ground. She moves in mysterious ways. Gonna take a dive with your sister in the rain. Let her talk about things you can't explain. To touch is to heal. She's the wave! She turns the tide! One day you will look back and you see where you were held by this Love. You could move on this moment. Follow this feeling!

Don't want to wait til tomorrow. Why put it off another day? C'mon, turn this thing around! Right now! It's your tomorrow!

Right now! It's everything! Right now! It's your magic moment! Do it right here and now! It means everything! Do it right here and now! Tell me, what are you waiting for? What's the matter girl? Do it right here and now!

A woman on the radio talks about a revolution, when it's already passed her by. I was alive and I waited for this.Right here right now, there's no other place I want to be. Watching the world wake up from history.

Say your prayers little one. It's a war! Don't forget my son, to include everyone! Sleep with one eye open. Exit light! Enter night! Take my hand. We're off to never-never land! Somethings wrong! Shut the light! Heavy thought tonight and they aren't of Snow White! Dreams of war! Dreams of liars! Dreams of dragon's fire and the things that will bite! Hush little baby! Don't say a word! And never mind that noise you heard! It's just the beasts under your bed! In your closet in your head! Exit light! Enter night! Grain of sand! We're off to never-never land!

I started out all alone down a dirty road. The town lit up and the world got still. I'm learning to fly, but I ain't got wings. Coming down, is the hardest thing. Some say life, will beat you down. It will break your heart and steal your crown. So I started out, for God knows where. But I guess I'll know, when I get there.

Can you see what I want? I wanna run through your wicked garden! That's the place to find you! Cause I'm alive! I know the darkness blinds you. Can you see without eyes? I wanna drink from your naked fountain! I'm gonna burn your wicked garden to the ground! Can I bring you back to life now? Out of the chains that bind you. Are you still alive? Can you feel pain inside? Can you love? Can you cry?

This time you've gone too far! I told you! Don't talk back! Just drive the car! Shut your mouth! I know who you are! Don't say nothing! Keep your hands on the wheel! Don't turn around! This is for real! I'm digging in the dirt to find the places I got hurt.

If you could only see the way she loves me then maybe you would understand. Why I feel this way about our Love and what I must do. If you could only see how blue her eyes can be when she says she loves me. You gotta take a little dirt to keep what you love.

Trying to get up that great big hill of hope, for my destination. I realized quickly when I knew I should, that the world is made up of this brotherhood of man. I cry sometimes when I'm lying in bed, just to get it all out what's in my head. And I'm feeling a little peculiar. I wake in the morning, and I step outside. I take a deep breath and I get real high, and I scream to the top of my lungs, what's going on! I try all the time, in this institution! I pray every single day, for revolution! What's going on?

You let me violate you! You let me desecrate you! You let me penetrate you! You let me complicate you! Help me! I broke apart my insides! I've got no soul to sell!

Tonight we sail on a radio song. Rescue me should I go down if I stay too long. Run with me wherever I go. Just play dumb, whatever you know.

Who was there to take your place? No one knows! Never will! Mostly me but mostly you. What do you say? What do you do? When it all comes down! I don't wanna come back down from this cloud. It's taken me all this time to find out what I need. All police are paranoid. So am I! So's the future! So are you for being a creature!

Love spreads her arms and waits there for the nails. I forgive you boy. I will prevail. Too much to take. Some cross to bear. I'm hiding in the trees with a picnic. She's over there! She didn't scream. She didn't make a sound. Cold black skin. Naked in the rain. Hammer flash in the lightning! They're hurting her again! Let me put you in the picture. Let me show you what I mean. The messiah is my sister! Ain't no king and she's my queen. I had a dream. I've seen the light. Don't put it out cause she's alright! Yeah, she's my sister!

Your Love is strong and you're so sweet! You make me weak! Someday babe we got to meet! A glimpse of you was all it took. A stranger's glance that got me hooked! I followed you across the stars. I looked for you in seedy bars. What are you scared of baby!? It's more than just a dream! I need some time with you. If you know what I mean. We make a beautiful team. Love is strong and you're so sweet! Someday babe we got to meet. Just anywhere. Out on the street and in the dark! I followed you through swirling seas. Down darkened woods with silent trees. What are you scared of babe!? This life ain't just a dream! I'll wait for you until the dawn. My mind is ripped! My heart is torn! Your love is strong!

Give me a word. Give me a sign. Show me where to look. Lay me on the ground and fly me in the sky. Tell me will love be there? (YEAH) Love is in the water. Love is in the air. Oh! Heaven let your light shine down! I'm gonna let it shine! Heaven send a light! Let it shine on me! Come on and shine!

How many special people change? How many lives we live are strange? Someday you will find me, caught beneath a landslide, in a champagne super nova in the sky. Wake up the dawn and ask her why? A dreamer dreams she never dies. Wipe that tear away now from your eye.

I'm broke but I'm happy. I'm short but I'm healthy. I'm high but I'm grounded. I'm sane but I'm overwhelmed. I'm lost but I'm hopeful. I care but I'm restless. But what it all comes down to, is that I haven't got it all figured out just yet. I'm free but I'm focused. Everything is going to be fine, fine, fine.

They were all in love with dying and they were doing it in Texas. They were drinking from a fountain that was pouring like an avalanche coming down the mountain. You never know just how you look through other people's eyes. Some will die in hot pursuit while sifting through my ashes. Some will fall in love with life and drink it from a fountain that is pouring like an avalanche coming down the mountain.

So long ago I don't remember when, that's when they say I lost my only friend. They said she died easy of a broken heart disease, as I listened through the cemetery trees. Now it always seemed such a waste. She always had a pretty face. I wondered why she hung around this place. There's got to be something better than in the middle. But me and Cinderella, we put it all together. We can drive it home. With one head light. But there's got to be an opening somewhere here in front of me through this maze of ugliness and greed. We'll run until she's out of breath. She ran until there's nothing left. She hit the end. It's just her window ledge. This place is old. It feels just like a beat-up truck. I turn the engine, but the engine doesn't turn. This place is always such a mess. But me and Cinderella put it all together. We can drive it home with one headlight.

Take the wheel and steer. It's driven me before, but lately I'm beginning to find that I should be the one behind the wheel. So, if I decide to waive my chance to be one of the high. Will I choose water over wine and hold my own and drive? It seems to be the way that everyone else gets around. But lately I'm beginning to find that when I drive myself my light is found. Hold the wheel and drive. Whatever tomorrow brings I'll be there with open arms and eyes.

This ain't no joke. I'd like to buy the world a toke and teach the world to sing in perfect harmony. Hey! I know it's just a song but it's spice for the recipe. This is a Love attack! I know it went out but it's back. Twenty-five years ago, they spoke out and they broke out of recession and oppression and together they toked. They folked out with guitars around a bonfire just singing and clapping. Man, what the hell happened there! Some were spell bound. Some were hell bound. Some they fell down, and some got back up and fought against the melt-down. The bond is broke. So, choke up and focus on the close-up. Even Mr. Wizard can't reform no God like hocus pocus. So don't sit back and kick back and watch the world get bushwhacked. When you know your neighborhood is under attack!

All around the world statues crumble for me! Everywhere I go people stop and they see. I just wanna fly. Dance a little stranger. Show me where you've been. Love can make you hostage wanna do it again. There's no time to think about it. The starting or the end. We'll find out I'm told.

Rock the cradle of Love! Yes, the cradle of Love, don't rock easily it's true! It burned like a ball of fire. When the rebel took a little child bride! To tease! Go easy yeah! Cause Love cuts a million ways! She shakes the Devil when he misbehaves! Sent from Heaven above! That's right! To rob the cradle of love! Yes, the pages of Love, don't talk decently it's true! You can't stop it! It ain't in vain! These are the wages of Love I know. Rock the cradle of Love! I robbed the Devil of Love!

Life's like a road you travel on. When there's one day here and the next day gone. There's a world outside. We won't hesitate to break down the garden gate. There's not much time left today. Life is a highway, I wanna ride it all night long. There's no load I can't hold! A road so rough this I know! I'll be there when the light comes in! Tell'em were survivors!

Closing time. Turn the lights up over every boy and every girl. One last call for alcohol. So finish your whiskey or beer. Closing time. You don't have to go home but you can't stay here. Time for you to go back to the places you will be from. This room won't be open til your brothers or sisters come. So gather up your jackets, and move to the exits. I hope you have found a friend. Every new beginning comes from some other beginnings end.

Some trails are happy ones, others are blue. It's the way you ride the trail that counts. Here's a happy one for you. Happy trails to you, until we meet again. Happy trails to you, keep smiling until then.

PART 2

Get up! Stand up for your rights! Preacher man don't tell me Heaven is under the earth. I know you don't know what life is really worth. It's not all that glitters is gold. Half the story has never been told. So now you see the light. Come on! Stand up for your rights! Don't give up the fight! Most people think Great God will come from the skies. Take away everything and make everybody feel high. We sick an' tired of-a your ism-skism game. Dyin, goin to Heaven in-a Jesus's name. Lord, we know when we understand, Almighty God is the living man. You can fool some people sometimes. But you can't fool all of the people all of the time. So now we see the light. Whatcha gonna do? We gonna stand up for our rights!

You poisoned my sweet water. You cut down my green trees. The food you fed my children was the cause of their disease. My world is slowly fallin down, and the air is not good to breathe. And those of us who care enough, we have to do something. What you gonna do? Your newspapers they just put you on. They never tell you the whole story. They just put your young ideas down. I was wondering could this be the end. And I feel the future trembling as the world is passed around. If you stand up for what you believe, be prepared to be shot down. I feel like a stranger in the land where I was born. And I live like an outlaw. I'm always on the run. I've got to take a stand. I believe the revolution must be mighty close at hand. I smoke marijuana but I can't get behind your wars. And most of what I do believe is against most of your laws. I'm a fugitive from injustice but I'm goin to be free. Cause your rules and regulations they don't do a thing for me.

I keep on thinkin bout you sister golden hair surprise. And I just can't live without you, can't you see it in my eyes? I been one poor correspondent and I been too, too hard to find. But it doesn't mean you ain't been on my mind. Will you meet me in the middle?

Will you meet me in the air? Will you love me just a little? Just enough to show you care.

How many roads and seas must a white dove sail, before she sleeps in the sand? The answer my friend, is blowin in the wind. How many years can a mountain exist before it's washed to the sea? How many years must some people exist before they're allowed to be free? And how many times can a man turn his head and pretend that he just doesn't see? How many ears must one person have before he can hear people cry? And how many deaths will it take til he knows that too many people have died? The answer my friend, is blowin in the wind.

Awaiting a word. Gasping at glimpses of gentle true spirit. He runs wishing he could fly. He waits by the window and wonders at the empty place inside. Heartlessly helping himself to her bad dreams. Stand by the stairway. You'll see something certain to tell you Love isn't lying. It's loose in a lady, who lingers, saying she is lost.

You're lost little girl! You're lost! Tell me who are you.

Two kinds of people in this world. Winners. Losers. I lost my power in this world because I did not use it. Two kinds of trouble in this world. Living. Dying. I lost my power in this world and rumors are flying.

I was doing time in the universal mind. I was feelin fine! I was turning keys. I was setting people free. I was doin alright! Then you came along, with a suitcase and a song. Turned my head around!

There's something happening here. What it is ain't exactly clear. There's a man with a gun over there. Telling me I got to beware. I think it's time we stop! Children what's that sound?! Everybody look what's goin down! There's battle lines being drawn. Nobody's right if everybody's wrong. Young people speaking their minds. Getting so much resistance from behind. A thousand people in the street. Singing songs and carrying signs. You step out of line the man come and take you away. Everybody look what's going down!

The sky is clearing, and the night has gone out. The son he come. The world is all full of love. Rejoice, rejoice, we have no choice but to carry on. The fortunes of fables are able to sing this song. Now witness the quickness. Love is coming! Love is coming! Love is coming to us all! Where are you going now my Love? Where will you be tomorrow? The questions of a thousand dreams. Girl, when I was on my own chasing you down, what was it made you run?

Six o'clock in the morning. I feel pretty good, so I dropped into the luxury of the Lords. Fighting dragons and crossing swords with the people against the hordes who came to conquer. Seven o'clock in the morning. I am so amazed I'm here today. Seeing things so clear this way. In the car and on my way to Stonehenge. I'm flying in Winchester Cathedral. Stumbled through the door and into the chamber. There's a lady setting flowers on a table covered lace. And a cleaner in the distance finds a cobweb on her face. And a feeling deep inside of me tells me, this can't be the place. I'm flying in Winchester Cathedral. All religion has to have its day. Expressions on the face of the savior, made me say, I can't stay. Open up the gates of the church and let me out of here! Too many people have lied in the name of Christ for anyone to heed the call! So many people have died in the name of Christ that I can't believe it all! And now I'm standing on the grave of a soldier that died in 1799. And the day he died it was a birthday, and I noticed it was mine. And my head didn't know just who I was, and I went spinning back in time. And I am high! Upon the alter! High! Upon the alter! I'm flying in Winchester Cathedral. It's hard enough to drink the wine. The air inside just hangs in delusion.

Let me take you to the movies. Can I take you to the show? Can I make your garden grow? From the Houses of the Holy, we can watch the white doves go. From the door comes Satan's daughter. You know! There's an angel on my shoulder. In my hand a sword of gold. Let me wander in your garden and the seeds of love I'll sow. So the world is spinning faster. Are you dizzy when you're stoned? Let the music be your master. Will you heed the master's

call? Satan and man said, "There ain't no use in crying, cause it will only drive you mad." Does it hurt to hear them lying? Was this the only world you had?

She's and angel of the third degree. You can't stop us on the road to freedom! You can't keep us cause our eyes can see!

And who by fire? Who by water? Who in the sunshine? Who by high ordeal? Who by very slow decay? And who Shall I say is calling? Who in these realms of love? And who by brave assent? Who by accident? Who in solitude? Who in this mirror? Who in mortal chains? Who in power? And who shall I say is calling?

Now the flames they followed Joan of Arc as she came riding through the dark. No moon to keep her armor bright. She said, "I'm tired of the war. I want the kind of work I had before. A wedding dress or something white. To wear upon my swollen appetite." Well, I'm glad to hear you talk this way. You know I've watched you riding every day. And something in me yearns to win such a cold and lonesome heroin. "And who are you?" she sternly spoke to the one beneath the smoke. "Why I am fire" he replied, "And I love your solitude. I love your pride." "Then fire make your body cold. I'm going to give you mine to hold." Saying this she climbed inside. To be his one, to be his only bride. And deep into his fiery heart he took the dust of Joan of Arc. And high above the wedding guests he hung the ashes of her wedding dress. It was deep into his fiery heart he took the dust of Joan of Arc. And then she clearly understood. If he was fire, then she must be wood. I saw her wince. I saw her cry. I saw the glory in her eye. Myself I long for love and light. But must it come so cruel and bright? Lady Godiva was a freedom rider. She didn't care if the whole world looked. Joan of Arc with the lord to guide her, she was a sister who really cooked!

By the rivers dark I wandered on. I lived my life in Babylon. And I did forget my Holy song. And I had no strength in Babylon. By the rivers dark where I could not see who was waiting there. Who was hunting me? And he cut my lip and cut my heart so I could not drink from the rivers dark. And he covered me. And I

saw within, my heart and my wedding ring. By the rivers dark I panicked on. I belonged at last to Babylon. Then he struck my heart with a deadly force, and he said, "This heart it is not yours!" And he gave the wind my wedding ring and circled us with everything. By the rivers dark in a wounded dawn, I live my life in Babylon.

They sentenced me to twenty years of boredom for trying to change the system from within. I'm coming now! I'm coming to reward them! I'm guided by a signal in the heavens. I'm guided by the birthmark on my skin. I'm guided by the beauty of our weapons. First, we take Manhattan. Then we take Berlin! How many nights I prayed for this, to let my work begin. I don't like your fashion business mister. And I don't like what happened to my sister. I told you! I told you! I was one of those from above!

I've seen the future baby, and it is murder. Things are going to slide. Slide in all directions! Won't be nothing you can measure anymore. The blizzard of the world has crossed the threshold and it has overturned the order of the soul.

Here comes your ghost again. But that's not unusual. It's just the moon is full and you happened to call. And here I sit, hand on the telephone, hearing a voice I'd known a couple of light years ago. You burst on the scene already a legend. Temporarily lost at sea. Yes, the girl on the half shell could keep you unharmed. Her name is Aphrodite, and she rides a crimson shell.

I'm crazy for Love, but I'm not comin on. I'm just paying my rent every day in the Tower of Song. I was born like this. I had no choice. I was born with the gift of a golden voice. And twenty-seven angels from the Great Beyond, they tied me to this table in the Tower of Song. The rich have got their channels in the bedrooms of the poor. And there's a mighty judgement coming. But I may be wrong. You see I hear these funny voices in the Tower of Song. I see you standing on the other side. I don't know how the river got so wide. Now I bid you farewell. But you'll be hearing from me baby, long after I'm gone. I'll be speaking to you softly from a window in the Tower of Song. And I'm crazy for Love but I'm not coming on.

Don't dwell on what has passed away or what is yet to be. Yeah, the wars, they will be fought again. The Holy Dove, she will be caught again. Bought and sold and bought again. The dove is never free. There's a crack in everything. That's how the light gets in. We asked for signs. The signs were sent. Signs for all to see. But they've summoned up a thunder cloud! And they're going to hear from me! You can add up the parts. You won't have the sum. Every heart, to love will come! But like a refugee. There's a crack, a crack in everything. That's how the light gets in.

She is wearing rags and feathers from salvation army. And the sun pours down like honey on our lady of the harbor. And she shows you where to look among the garbage and the flowers. There are children in the morning. They are leaning out for Love, and they will lean that way forever.

Well I've heard there was a secret chord, that David played, and it pleased the Lord. But you don't even care for music, do you? Well it goes like this: The fourth, the fifth, the minor fall, and the major lift! The baffled king composing Hallelujah! Well, your faith was strong, but you needed proof. When you saw her bathing on the roof, her beauty and the moonlight overthrew ya. She tied you to her kitchen chair. And she broke your throne and she cut your hair. And from your lips she drew the Hallelujah! But baby I've been here before. I've seen this room and I've walked this floor. You know I used to live alone until I knew ya. And love is not a victory march. It's a cold and it's a broken Hallelujah. Well, there was a time when you let me know, what's really going on below. But now you never show that to me do ya? But remember when I moved in you, and the Holy Dove was moving too. And every breath we drew, was Hallelujah! Maybe there's a God above. But all I've ever learned from Love, was how to shoot someone who outdrew ya. It's not a cry you hear at night! It's not somebody who's seen the light! It's a cold and very broken Hallelujah!

Everybody knows that the dice are loaded. Everybody rolls with their fingers crossed. Everybody knows the war is over. Everybody

knows the good guys lost. Everybody knows the fight was fixed. The poor stay poor. The rich get rich. Everybody knows the boat is leaking. Everybody knows the captain lied. Everybody knows you've been discreet but there were so many people you just had to meet without your clothes. Everybody knows.

It's closing time. I swear it happened just like this. The gates of Love they budged an inch. I can't say much has happened since. I loved you when our love was blessed. Now there's nothing left but closing time. I miss you since the place got wrecked by the winds of change and the weeds of sex.

PART 3

I'm waking up to ash and dust. I'm breathing in the chemicals. I'm breaking in, shaping up, then checking out on the prison bus. This is it! The apocalypse! I'm waking up! I feel it in my bones. Enough to make my system blow. Welcome to the new age! To the new age! I'm Radioactive! Radioactive! It's a revolution I suppose. Welcome to the new age! Radioactive! Radioactive! All systems go, the son hasn't died. Deep in my bones, straight from inside, I'm waking up! Welcome to the new age!

Now that she's back in the atmosphere, with drops of Jupiter in her hair. Reminds me that there's time to change. Since the return of her stay on the moon, she listens like spring, and she talks like June. But tell me. Did you sail across the sun? Did you make it to the Milky Way to see the lights all faded? And that Heaven is overrated. Tell me! Did you fall from a shooting star? And did you miss me while you were looking for yourself out there? Now that she's back from that soul vacation, tracing her way through the constellation. Now that she's back in the atmosphere I'm afraid that she might think of me as Plain ole' Jane and told a story about a man, who was too afraid to fly, so he never did land. But tell me. Did the wind sweep you off your feet? Did you finally get the chance to dance along the light of day? And head back to the Milky

Way. And tell me! Did Venus blow your mind?! Was it everything you wanted to find?

Can't stop! Addicted to the shindig! I'm gonna win big! Choose not a life of imitation! Distant cousin to the reservation. In time I want to be your best friend. East side lovers living on the west end. Knocked out, but boy you better come to. Don't die! You know the truth as some do! Go write your message on the pavement! Burn so bright! I wonder what the wave meant. The world I love. The tears I drop. To be part of the wave can't stop. Ever wonder if it's all for you? Come and tell me when it's time to. Sweetheart is bleeding in the snow cone! So smart she's leading me to ozone! Music the great communicator! Use two sticks to make it in the nature! I'll get you into penetration! The gender of a generation! The birth of every nation! Worth your weight the gold of meditation! This chapter's going to be a close one! All on a spaceship persevering. Use my hands for everything but steering! Can't stop the spirits when they need you! Kickstart the golden generator! Sweet talk, but don't intimidate her! Can't stop the Gods from engineering! Feel no need for any interfering! Your image in the dictionary! This life is more than ordinary! Can I get two, maybe even three of these? Coming from space to teach you of the Pleiades! Can't stop the spirits when they need you! This life is more than just a read through!

Close the door, put out the light. No, they won't be home tonight. The snow falls hard, and don't you know? The winds of Thor are blowing cold. They're wearing steel that's bright and true! They carry the news that must get through! They choose the path where no one goes. They hold no quarter. Walking side by side with death. The Devil mocks their every step. The dogs of doom are howling more. They carry news that must get through! To build a dream for me and you!

People what have you done? Locked him in his golden cage. Made him bend to your religion. Him resurrected from the grave. He is the god of nothing! You are the gods of everything! He's inside you and me! The bloody church of England in chains of

history, requests your earthly presence at the vicarage for tea. And the graven image you know, with his plastic crucifix. He's got him fixed. You'll be praying to next Thursday to all the Gods that you can count.

Queen of light took her bow, and then she turned to go. The prince of peace embraced the gloom and walked the night alone. Dance in the dark of night. Sing to the morning light. The dark Lord rides in force tonight. And time will tell us all. Side by side, we wait the might, of the darkest of them all. I hear the horses' thunder, down in the valley blow. I'm waiting for the Angels of Avalon. Waiting for the eastern glow. The war is common cry, "Pick up your swords and fly!" The sky is filled with good and bad! The mortals never know! The pain of war cannot exceed the woe of aftermath! The drums will shake the castle wall! The ring wraiths ride in black. Ride on! Sing as you raise your bow! Shoot straighter than before! The magic runes are writ in gold, to bring the balance back. Bring it back! At last the sun is shining With flames from the dragon of darkness, the sunlight blinds his eye.

Let the sun beat down upon my face. Stars fill my dreams. I'm a traveler of both time and space, to be where I have been. Sit with elders of the gentle race this world has seldom seen. They talk of days for which they sit and wait. All will be revealed. Talk in song in tongues of lilting grace. Not a word I could relate. Story was quite clear. I been flyin. All I see turns to brown as the sun burns the ground. And my eyes will fill with sand as I scan the wasted land. Pilot of the storm who leaves no trace like thoughts inside a dream. Heed the path that led me to that place. Yellow desert stream. Beneath the summer moon, I will return again. Oh Father of the four winds, fill my sails across the sea of years. I'm on my way!

We come from the lands of ice and snow! From the midnight sun where the hot springs flow! The hammer of the Gods! We'll drive our ships to new lands to fight the horde and sing and cry! Valhalla, I am coming! On we sweep the threshing oar. Our only

goal will be the western shore. How soft your fields so green can whisper tales of gore, of how we calmed the tides of war. We are your Overlords! So now you'd better stop and rebuild all your ruins! For PEACE and LOVE can win the day, despite of all your losing!

Long ago, in days untold, were ruled by Lords of greed. Kings and Queens and guillotines. I know I lived this life before. Living other centuries. Dejavu or what you please.

I'm gonna fight'em all! A seven-nation army couldn't hold me back! They're gonna rip it off! Taking their time right behind my back! And the message coming from my eyes says, "Leave it alone!" Don't want to hear about it! Every single one's got a story to tell! Everyone knows about it! From the Queen of England to the hounds of Hell! And if I catch you coming back my way, I'm gonna serve it to you! And that ain't what you wanna hear, but that's what I'll do!" And I'm bleeding right before the Lord! All the words are gonna bleed from me, and I will sing no more!

Where have you been and what did you see my blue-eyed one? And what did you hear? And who did you meet? What will you do now? I've stumbled on the side of twelve misty mountains. I've walked and I've crawled on six crooked highways. I've stepped in the middle of seven sad forests. I've been out in the front with a dozen dead oceans. I've been ten thousand miles in the mouth of a graveyard. And it's a hard rains gonna fall. I saw a newborn baby with wild wolves all around it. I saw ten thousand talkers whose tongues were all broken. I heard the sound of thunder. It roared out a warning. Heard a roar of a wave that could drown the whole world. I met a young woman whose body was burning. I met a young girl she gave me a rainbow. I met one man who was wounded in love. It's a hard rains gonna fall!

T'was in another lifetime, one of toil and blood. When blackness was a virtue. The road was full of mud. I came in from the wilderness, a creature void of form. "Come in" she said, "I'll give you shelter from the storm." And if I pass this way again you can rest assured, I'll always do my best for her on that

I give my word. Try imagining a place where it's always safe and warm. "Come in" she said, "I'll give you shelter from the storm." Suddenly I turned around and she was standing there. With silver bracelets on her wrists and flowers in her hair. She walked up to me so gracefully and took my crown of thorns. "Come in she said, "I'll give you shelter from the storm." Now there's a wall between us. Something there's been lost. I took too much for granted. I got my signals crossed. In a little hilltop village, they gambled for my clothes. I bargained for salvation, and she gave me a lethal dose! Beauty walks a razors edge. Someday I'll make her mine! If I could only turn back the clock to when God and her were born!

Someone told me there's a girl out there, with love in her eyes, and flowers in her hair. The mountains and the canyons started to tremble and shake, as the children of the sun began to wake! Seems like the wrath of the Gods got a punch on the nose and it's starting to flow! I think I might be sinking! Throw me a line, if I reach it in time, I'll meet you up there where the path runs straight and high! They say she plays guitar and sings Lalalala.

I married Isis on the fifth day of May. But I could not hold on to her very long. So, I cut off my hair and I rode straight away for the wild unknown country where I could not go wrong. I came to a high place of darkness and light. I was thinkin about Isis, how she told me that one day we would meet up again and things would be different the next time we wed. If only I could hang on and just be her friend. I still can't remember all the best things she said. Came to the pyramids all embedded in ice. There's a body I'm tryin to find. If I carry it out it will bring a good price. Chopped through the night and chopped through the dawn. I broke into the tomb, but the casket was empty. There was no jewels. No nothin. I felt I'd been had. Then I rode back to Isis just to tell her I love her. She was there in the meadow where the creek used to rise. Blinded by sleep and in need for a bed. I came in from the east with the sun in my eyes. I cursed her one time then I rode on ahead. Isis oh Isis! You mystical child!

It was gravity that pulled us down. And destiny which broke us apart. You tamed the lion in my cage. But it just wasn't enough to change my heart. Now everything's a little upside down. As a matter of fact, the wheels have stopped. What's good is bad, what's bad is good. You'll find out when you reach the top, you're on the bottom! I can't feel you anymore. I can't even touch the books you've read. Every time I crawl past your door, I been wishin I was someone else instead! Down the highway, down the tracks, down the road to ecstasy. I followed you beneath the stars, hounded by your memory. And all your ragin glory! I been double crossed now for the very last time, and now I'm finally free. I kissed goodbye the howling beast on the borderline which separated you from me. You'll never know the hurt I suffered. Nor the pain I rise above. And I'll never know the same about you, your holiness or your kind of love, and it makes me feel so sorry. Idiot wind. Blowing through the letters that we wrote. We're idiots babe! It's a wonder that you still know how to breathe! It's a wonder we can even feed ourselves!

I look at you all, see the Love there that's sleeping, while my guitar gently weeps. I don't know why nobody told you how to unfold your love. I don't know how someone controlled you. They bought and sold you. I don't know how you were diverted and inverted. You were perverted too. No one alerted you. I look at you all, see the Love that there's sleeping. While my guitar still gently weeps.

I put a spell on you! Because your mine! You better stop the thing that you're doin! I said, "Watch out! I ain't lyin!" I put a spell on you! Alright! I took it down!

When will I know that I really can't go to the well once more? Time to decide on. When it's killing me, when will I really see? The more I see, the less I know. Privately divided by a world so undecided and there's nowhere to go. Running through the field where all my tracks will be concealed and there's nowhere to go. Tell my Love now!

Your eyes are like two jewels in the sky. But I don't sense affection. No gratitude or love. Your loyalty is not to me, but to the stars above. Your sister sees the future like your mama and yourself. One more cup of coffee before I go. To the valley below!

Hello darkness my old friend. I've come to talk with you again. Because a vision softly creeping, left its seeds while I was sleeping. And the vision that was planted in my brain, still remains, within the sound, of silence. In restless dreams I walked alone. When my eyes were stabbed by the flash of a neon light, that split the night, and touched the sound, of silence. And in the naked light I saw, ten thousand people maybe more. People talking without speaking. People hearing without listening. People writing songs that voices never share. And no one dare, disturb the sound, of silence. "Fools" said I, "You do not know! Silence like a cancer grows. Hear my words that I might teach you. Take my arms that I might reach you." But my words like silent raindrops fell, and echoed, in the wells, of silence. And the people bowed and prayed, to the neon god they made. And the sign flashed out its warning. In the words that it was forming. And the sign said, "The words of the prophets are written on the subway walls and tenement halls. And whispered, in the sounds, of silence."

It's the time of the season, when love runs high. And this time, give it to me easy. And let me try with pleasured hands to take you in the sun, to promised lands. To show you everyone. It's the time of the season for loving! What's your name? Who's your daddy? Is he rich like me? Has he taken any time to show you what you need to live? It's the time of the season for loving.

Who made who? Who made you? Ain't nobody told you?! Who made who? If you made them and they made you? Who picked up the bill? And who made who? Who turned the screw?

Sister, am I not a brother to you? And is our purpose not the same on this earth? To love? We grew up together from the cradle to the grave. We died and were reborn and then mysteriously saved. Sister, when I come knock on your door, don't turn away.

Could you be Love and be loved? Don't let them fool ya. Or even try to school ya. We got a mind of our own. So, go to hell if what you're thinking is not right. Love would never leave us alone. In the darkness there must come out the light. Could you be Love? The road of life is rocky, and you may stumble too. So while you point your fingers, someone else is judging you. Love your brotherman. Don't let them change ya. Or even rearrange ya. We got a life to live. They say only the fittest of the fittest shall survive. Stay alive! Could you be Love and be loved? Say something. Say something!

Tell the man. What did you have in mind? What have you come to do? No turning water into wine! Tell me baby, what's your story? The thing we need is never all that hard to find. Step out and be renewed. It's time to turn to stone. Tell me baby what's your story? Where you come from and where you want to go this time?

It's the edge of the world and all of western civilization. Break the spell of aging. Is this the war you're waging? First born unicorn. Marry me girl, be my fairy to the world, be my very own constellation. A teenage bride with a baby inside gets high on information. Born and raised by those who praise control of population. Everybody's been there and I don't mean on vacation. First born unicorn. Destruction leads to a very rough road, but it also breeds creation. And earthquakes are, to a little girl's guitar, they're just another good vibration. And the tidal waves couldn't save the world. Break the spell of aging. This is no test, but this is what you're craving. Firstborn unicorn!

Will you hold the line when every one of them is giving up or giving in. Nothing ever comes without a consequence or a cost. Tell me, will the stars align? Will Heaven step in? Will it? Cause this house of mine stands strong. Rather be the hunter than the prey. And you're standing on the edge face up, because you're a natural. You're a natural! Will somebody let me see the light within the dark? I can taste it. The end is upon us. Yeah, you're a natural!

It's good to be King, if just for a while. To be there in velvet.

Yeah, to give 'em a smile. It's good to get high and never come down. It's good to be King and have your own world. It's good to meet girls and a sweet little Queen who can't run away.

I will be king, and you, you will be queen. We could steal time just for one day. We can be heroes! We can beat them! Forever and ever! What do you say?

First things first. I'm a say all the words inside my head. Second thing second. Don't tell me what you think I can be. I'm the one at the sail, I'm the master of my sea. Singing from heartache from the pain. Taking my message from my veins. Speaking my lesson from my brain. Seeing the beauty through the pain. You made me a believer! You break me down. You build me up. You made me a believer! Third things third. Send a prayer to the ones up above. All the hate that you've heard has turned your spirit to a dove. Your spirit up above. Til it broke up and rained down! It rained down! You made me a believer! Last things last. By the grace of the fire and the flames, you're the face of the future, the blood in my veins. You made me a believer! My life, my love, my drive. It came from pain! You made me a believer!

Standing in the gallows with my head in a noose. Any minute now I'm expecting all hell to break loose. People are crazy, and times are strange. I'm locked in tight. I'm out of range. I've been walking forty miles on a bad road. If the Bible is right the world will explode. I've been trying to get as far away from myself as I can. The human mind can only stand so much. You can't win with a losing hand. I hurt easy I just don't show it. You can hurt someone, and not even know it. The next sixty seconds could be like an eternity. All the truth in the world adds up to one big lie.

Well it's alright, if you live the life that you please. Doing the best you can. As long as you lend a hand. You can sit around and wait for the phone to ring. Waiting for someone to tell you everything. Sit around and wonder what tomorrow will bring. Well it's all right, even if they say your wrong. Sometimes you gotta be strong. Every day is judgement day. Maybe somewhere down the road a ways. Well it's alright, everything will work out fine. We're going to the end of the line. I'm just glad to be here. Happy to be alive. It's alright Even if you're old and grey, you still got something to say. Remember to live and let live. The best you can do is forgive. We're going to the end of the line.

What about the time? You'd best believe this is real. Help us understand. Don't play no games. Love from the bottom to the top. Turn like a wheel. See for yourself. We're gonna move right now. Turn like a wheel inside a wheel. They were living creatures. Watch 'em come to life right before your eyes. How do you do? Love from the bottom to the top. Turn like a wheel inside a wheel. There is a song. You're trembling to its tune at the request of the moon. Only a crazy little thing I read. Maybe the planets are trying to become stars and we really came from Mars. The earth is alive, and man is a parasite, and heavenly bodies make us fight. I'm only joking, and I don't believe a word I said. I'm just fucking with your head.

They say that we ain't got the tunes that's goin to put us on the map. And I'm a phony in disguise trying to make the radio. I'm an anti-social anarchist. I sound like so and so. They say I'm just a stupid kid, another crazy radical. They'd love to see me fall, but I'm already on my back. And it goes in one ear and right out the other. Now I know I'm not a saint, I been a sinner all my life. I ain't tryin to hide my flaws. I'd rather keep them in the light. They wanna criticize, scrutinize, cast another stone. Burn me at the stake and sit and watch it from their throne. They say the Devil is my pal. They think they know my thoughts, but they don't know the least, if they listened to the words, they'd find the message tucked beneath. You hear that? You hear what's coming? You better run for the hills cause we're coming to your town and we're gonna burn that mother fucker down! Here's the moral to the story. We don't do it for the glory. We don't do it for the money. We don't do it for the fame. So all the critics who despise us go ahead and criticize us. It's your tyranny that drives us. Adds the

fire to our flames. I'm only playing music cause you know I fucking love it! People talkin shit! Well, you know, they can kiss the back of my hand!

All my friends are heathens, take it slow. Wait for them to ask you who you know. Please don't make any sudden moves. You don't know the half of the abuse. Why'd you come? You knew you should have stayed. I tried to warn you just to stay away. And now they're outside ready to bust. It looks like you might be one of us.

Didn't know what time it was, and the lights were low. I leaned back on my radio. Some cat was layin down some get it on rock-n-roll. Then the loud sound did seem to fade. Came back like a slow voice on a wave of phase haze. Hey that weren't no DJ... That was hazy cosmic jive! There's a Starman waiting in the sky. He'd like to come and meet us, but he thinks he'd blow our minds. He told us not to blow it, cause he knows it's all worthwhile! He told me, "Let the children lose it. Let the children use it. Let all the children boogie." I had to phone someone, so I picked on you. Hey, that's far out so you heard him too! Switch on the TV we may pick him up on channel 2. Look out your window we can see his light. If we can sparkle, he may land tonight. Don't tell your papa or he'll get us locked up in fright.

Coming out to the light of day. We got many moons than a deeper place. So I keep an eye on the shadows smile, to see what it has to say. You and I both know everything must go away. What do you say? It's like a bit of light in the dark. You got sneak attacked from the Zodiac. But I see your eyes spark. Keep the breeze and go. You don't know my mind. You don't know my kind. Dark necessities are part of my design. Do you want this love of mine? The darkness helps to sort the shine. Do you want it now? Pick you up like a paperback. Tell the world I'm falling from the skies!

I knew she came from there. She drove a Plymouth Satellite faster than the speed of light. No one ever dies there. No one has a

head. Some say she's from Mars or one of the seven stars that shine after three thirty in the morning.

I bless you madly. I love you badly. Because it's you who sets the test. So much has gone, and little is new. And as the sparrow sings dawn chorus for someone else to hear, the thinker sits alone growing older and bitter. I gave them life! I gave them all! They drained my very soul dry. I crushed my heart to ease their pains. No thought for me remains there. Nothing can they spare. What of me, who praised their efforts to be free? Words of strength and care and sympathy. I opened doors that would have blocked their way. I braved their cause to guide for little pay. I ravaged at my finances just for those whose claims were steeped in peace and tranquility. Those who said a new world. New ways ever free. For those whose promises stretched in hope and grace for me. My friends talk of glory. Untold dreams. Where all is God and God is just a word. We had a friend. A talking man who spoke of many powers that he had. We used him. We let him use his powers. We let him fill our needs. Now we are strong. And the road is coming to its end. Now the damned have no time to make amends. The silent guns of Love will blast the sky! Where money stood, we planted seeds of rebirth. I believe in the power of good! I believe in the state of love! I will fight for the right to be right! I will kill for the good of the fight for the right to be right! And I open my eyes to look around. And I see a child slain on the ground. As a love machine lumbers through desolation rows. Plowing down man, women, listening to its command. But not hearing anymore. And I want to believe in the magic that calls, now! And I want to believe that a lights shining through somehow. And I want to believe! We want to believe! We want to live! I want to live! I want to live!

Look around you! All around you! Riding on a copper wave! Do you like the world around you? Are you ready to behave? Outside of society that's where I want to be! Those who have suffered understand suffering. And thereby extend their hand. The storm that brings harm also makes fertile. Blessed is the grass

and the herb and the true thorn and light. I was lost in a valley of pleasure. I was lost in the infinite sea. I was lost and measure for measure Love spewed from the heart of me.

He was born in the summer of his 27th year. Coming home to a place he'd never been before. You could say he was born again. You might say he found a key for every door. When he first came to the mountains, his life was far away. On the road and hanging by a song. But the Colorado Rocky Mountain High, I've seen it rainin fire in the sky. He climbed Cathedral Mountain. He saw silver clouds below. He saw everything as far as he could see.

Jesus died for somebody's sins but not mine! Meltin in a pot of thieves. Wild card up my sleeve. My sins my own. They belong to me! People say, "Beware!" But I don't care! The words are just rules and regulations to me. I walk into a room. I'm movin in this here atmosphere. Well, anything's allowed. And I go to this party here and I just get bored. Until I look out the window and see a sweet young thing. And I got this crazy feelin I'm gonna make her mine. I'll put a spell on her! And then I hear this knock on my door. I look up into the big tower clock and say, "Oh my God, here's midnight and my baby's walking through the door!" And I said darling, "Tell me your name. How old are you? Where did you come from?" She whispered to me. She told me her name. And the tower bells chimed. They're singing, "Jesus died for somebody's sins but not mine."

Jesus is just alright with me. I don't care what they may say. I don't care what they may do. Jesus is just alright with me. I don't care what they may know. I don't care where they may go. Jesus he's my friend. He took me by the hand. Led me far from this land. Jesus is my friend!

When I die and they lay me to rest, gonna go to the place that's the best. When I lay me down to die, goin up to the spirit in the sky. Prepare yourself, you know it's a must! Gotta have a friend in Jesus. So you know that when you die, he's gonna recommend you to the spirit in the sky. I never been a sinner. I've never sinned.

I've got a friend in Jesus. So you know that when I die, he's gonna introduce me to the spirit in the sky.

God is a concept on which we measure our pain. I just believe in me. And that's reality. The dream is over. What can I say? I was the dream weaver but now I'm reborn. And so dear friends you just have to carry on. The dream is over.

If I had been God, I would have rearranged the veins in the face to make them more resistant to alcohol and less prone to aging. I would have sired many sons and I would not have suffered the Romans to kill even one of them. If I had been God, with my staff and my rod, I believe I could have done a better job. The temple's in ruins. The bankers got fat. The buffalo's gone and the mountain top's flat. The trout in the stream are all hermaphrodites. And it feels like Dejavu. Counting the cost of Love that got lost.

If God had a name, what would it be? And would you call it to his face if you were faced with him and all his glory? What would you ask if you had just one question? What if God was one of us? Just a slob like one of us. Just a stranger on the bus, tryin to make his way home. Like a holy rolling stone. If God had a face, what would it look like? And would you want to see, if seeing meant that you would have to believe, in things like Heaven, and Jesus, and the Saints, and all the Prophets? What if God was one of us, just tryin to make his way home. Like back to Heaven all alone. Nobody callin on the phone. Cept for the Pope maybe in Rome.

The killing has intensified on the road to peace with more retribution. Neither side will give up their smallest right along the road to peace. So thousands dead and wounded on both sides. Most of them middle eastern civilians. They'll fill their children full of hate to fight an old man's war and die upon the road to peace. The fundamentalist killing on both sides is standing in the path of peace. If God is great, and God is good, why can't he change the hearts of men? Well maybe, God himself is lost and needs help.

He's out upon the road to peace. Maybe, he's lost on the road to peace.

Climbing up on Solsbury Hill, I could see the city lights. Wind was blowing. Time stood still. Eagle flew out of the night. He was something to observe. Came in close, I heard a voice. Had to listen, had no choice. I did not believe the information! Just had to trust imagination! My heart going, boom, boom, boom! He said, "Grab your things I've come to take you home!" To keep in silence, I resigned. My friends would think I was a nut. Turning water into wine. Open doors would soon be shut. So I went from day to day, though my life was in a rut. 'Til I thought of what I'll say. Which connection I should cut. I was feeling part of the scenery. I walked right out of the machinery. My heart going, boom, boom, boom! He said, "Grab your things I've come to take you home! Way back home!" When illusion spins her net, I'm never where I want to be. And liberty she pirouettes, when I think that I am free. Watched by empty silhouettes who close their eyes but still can see. No one taught them etiquette. I will show another me. Today I don't need a replacement. I'll tell them what the smile on my face meant! My heart going, boom, boom, boom! Hey, I said, "You can keep my things they've come to take me home!"

Can I get your hand to write on? Do you want to flash your light on? Take a look, it's on display for you. Coming down, no not today for you! Rebel and a liberator. Rev it up to levitate her. Fly away on my zephyr. I feel it more than ever. And in this perfect weather fly on my wind. We're gonna live forever!

That's great! It starts with an earthquake. Save yourself. Feeling pretty psyched. Slash and burn. Return. Light a candle. Step down. It's the end of the world as we know it and I feel fine!

The entire world is exploding, violence flarin, bullets loadin. Even the Jorden has bodies floatin. If the button is pushed there's no running away. There'll be no one to save with the world in a grave. Take a look around, it's bound to scare you. I can't twist the truth.

This whole crazy world is just too frustatin. You may leave here for four days in space but when you return it's the same old place. You tell me over and over again my friend, you don't believe were on the eve of destruction.

Toe to toe dancing very close. Barely breathing almost comatose. Wall to wall people hypnotized. And you don't stop! Go out to the parking lot, and you get in your car, and you drive real far. And you drive all night and then you see a light. And it comes right down and lands on the ground and out comes a man from mars! And you try to run, but he's got a gun! And he shoots you dead and then he eats your head! And then you're in the man from Mars! You go out at night eatin cars. Then when there's no more cars, you go out at night and eat up bars. Where the people meet face to face. Cause the man from Mars is through with cars and now he's eatin bars. Well now you see what you wanna be. Just have your party on TV. Cause the man from Mars won't eat up bars when the TV's on. And now he's gone back up to space where he won't have to hassle with the human race. Just blast off! Rapture!

I heard the sound of voices in the night. Spellbound, there was something calling. I looked around and no one is in sight. Pulled down. I just kept on falling. I`ve seen this place before. I know it`s a mystery. There you stood. A distant memory. Like we never parted. Said to myself, I knew you`d set me free. And here we are right back where we started. Maybe this fantasy is real. But it`s still a mystery. Do you remember me on the street of dreams? Will we ever meet again? Do you know what it meant to be on the street of dreams? Never know just who you`ll see, do ya? On the street of dreams, you can be who you want to be. Just call me angel of the morning.

The power of Love is a curious thing. Don't need money. Don't take fame. Don't need no credit card to ride this train. It's strong and it's sudden and it's cruel sometimes! But it might just save your life! But you'll be glad when you've found that's the power that makes the world go round. They say that all in love is fair. With a little help from above you'll feel the power of Love! Can you feel it? That's the power of Love!

One man come in the name of Love. One man come and go. One man come, he to justify. One man to overthrow. Free at last! They took your life, but they could not take your pride! In the name of Love! What more in the name of Love?

World turns black and white! Love starts falling down. Reach for the golden ring! Reach for the sky! Baby just spread your wings and fly! Got the truth gets left behind. Falls between the cracks! Standing on broken dreams! Spread your wings! That's what dreams are made of. Cause we belong in a world that must be strong! Who knows what we'll find! In the end, on dreams we will depend, because that's what love is made of!

If I had ever been here before I would probably know just what to do. Don't you? If I had ever been here before on another time around the wheel, I would probably know just how to deal with all of you. And I feel like I've been here before. I feel like I've been here before! And you know it does make me wonder what's going on under the ground. Do you know we have all been here before? We have all been here before!

On the turning away. From the pale and downtrodden. And the words they say which we won't understand. Don't accept that what's happening is just a case of all the suffering. Or you'll find that you're joining in, the turning away. It's a sin that somehow, light is changing to shadows, and casting a shroud over all we have known. Unaware how the ranks have grown. Driven on by a heart of stone. We could find that were all alone in the dream of the proud. On the wings of the night. As the daytime is stirring. Where the speechless unite in a silent accord. Using words you will find are strange. Mesmerized as they light the flame. Feel the new wind of change. No more turning away. From the weak and the weary. No more turning away from the coldness inside. Just a world that we all must share. It's not enough just to stand and stare. Is it only a dream that there'll be no more turning away?

The music played as we whirled without end. No hint. No word. Her honor to defend. I will. She sighed to my request. And then she drowned in desire. Our souls on fire. I led the way to the funeral pyre. And without thought of the consequence, I gave into my decadence. One slip and down the hole we fall. It seems to take no time at all. A momentary lapse of reason, that binds a life to a life. Was it love? Or was it the idea of being in love? Or was it the hand of fate that seemed to fit just like a glove? The moment slipped by and soon the seeds were sown. The year grew late and neither one wanted to remain alone. One slip and down the hole we fall.

Dogs of war and men of hate! With no cause, we don't discriminate! Our currency is flesh and bone! Hell opened up and put on sale! Gather round and haggle! One world! It's a battle ground! One world and we will smash it down! Invisible transfers. Long distance calls. Steps have been taken! A silent uproar has unleashed the dogs of war! You can't stop what has begun! Signed, sealed, they deliver oblivion! Dealing in death is the nature of the beast! One world! It's a battleground and they will smash it down! The dogs of war won't negotiate! The dogs of war won't capitulate! They will take and you will give! You must die so that they may live! You can knock at any door! But wherever you go you know they've been there before! Well winners can lose, and things can get strange! But wherever you go you know the dogs remain!

Stretched to the point of no turning back. A flight of fancy on a windswept field. Standing alone my senses reeled. A fatal attraction holding me fast. How can I escape this irresistible grasp? Ice is forming on the tips of my wings. Unheeded warnings! I thought I thought of everything! No navigator to find my way home! Unladened, empty, I turn to stone! A soul intension that's learning to fly. Condition grounded but turn to try. Can't keep my eyes from the circling skies. Tongue-tied and twisted just an Earth-bound misfit I. Above the planet on a wing and a prayer.

My grubby halo. A vapor trail in the empty air. Across the clouds I see my shadow fly! Out of the corner of my watering eye. A dream unthreatened by the morning light! Could blow this soul right through the roof of the night! There's no sensation to compare with this. Suspended animation. A state of bliss.

No sign of the morning coming! You`ve been left on your own! Like a rainbow in the dark! Just a rainbow in the dark! Do your demons! Do they ever let you go? When you`ve tried do they hide deep inside? Is it someone that you know? You`re just a picture! You`re an image caught in time! Feel the magic! I feel it floating in the air! But it`s fear, and you`ll hear it calling you, beware! Lookout! You`ve been left on your own, like a rainbow in the dark!

Holy Diver! You`ve been down too long in the midnight sea! Ride the tiger! Got shiny diamonds! Like the eyes of a cat in black and blue. Something is coming for you! Look out! Race for the morning! You can hide in the sun til you see the light! Gotta get away! Get away! Holy Diver! Between the velvet lies! There`s a truth that`s hard as steel! The vision never dies! Life`s a never-ending wheel! Holy Diver! You`re the star of the masquerade! No need to look so afraid! Jump on the tiger! Some light can never be seen! Holy Diver! Sole Survivor! You`re the one who`s clean! There`s a cat in the blue comin after you, Holy Diver! Gotta get away!

And to love a god. And to fear a flame. And to burn a love that has a name. I've willed, I've walked, I've read, I've talked! I know! I know! I know! I've been here before! And to Christ, a cross. And to me, a chair. I will sit and earn the ransom from up here!

I saw the world crashing all around your face. I'll stop the world and melt with you. Dream of better lives. The kind that never hates. (you should see why) Trapped in the state of imaginary grace. I made a pilgrimage to save this human race. Never comprehending the race has long gone bye. The futures open wide.

Once I thought I saw you in a crowded hazy bar. Dancing on the light from star to star. Far across the moon beam. I know that's who you are. I saw your blue eyes turning once to fire. I am just a dreamer. But you are just a dream. That perfect feeling when time just slips away between us on our foggy trip.

Don't ask me what you know is true. Don't have to tell you I love your precious heart. I was standing. You were there. Two worlds collided. And they could never tear us apart! We could live for a thousand years! But if I hurt you, I'd make wine from your tears. I told you! That we could fly! Cause we all have wings! But some of us don't know why!

Don't let me here you say, life's taking you nowhere, angel. Look at the sky, life's just begun. Last night they loved you, opening doors and pulling some strings, angel. There's my baby, lost that's all. I'll stick with you baby for a thousand years! Nothing's going to touch you in these golden years!

People come, people go. Some grow young, some grow cold. I woke up in between a memory and a dream. You don't know how it feels to be me.

When I get to the bottom, I go back to the top of the slide! Where I stop and I turn, and I go for a ride! Til I get to the bottom and see you again! I'm coming down fast but I'm miles above you! Tell me, tell me, come on tell me the answer! Well you may be a lover but you ain't no dancer! I'm coming down fast but don't let me break you! Look out! Look out cause here she comes! She's coming down fast! Yes she is!

Well I dreamed I saw the knights in armor comin. Saying something about a queen. There were peasants singing and drummers drumming. And the archer split the tree. We got mother nature on the run in the nineteen seventies. Look at mother nature on the run in the twentieth century. I was lying in a burnt-out basement with the full moon in my eye. I was hoping for replacement, when the sun burst through the sky. Well I dreamed I saw the silver spaceship flyin in the yellow haze of the sun. There were children cryin and colors flyin all around the chosen ones. All in a dream. The loading had begun. We were flyin mother nature's silver seed to a new home in the sun.

Sometimes the lights all shinin on me. Other times I can barely see. Lately it occurred to me, what a long, strange trip it's been! I guess they can't revoke your soul for trying. Get out of the door, and light out, and look all around. I'm goin home. What a long, strange trip it's been!

Gazing through the window at the world outside. Wondering will Mother Earth survive? Hoping that mankind will stop abusing her. And here we are still fighting for our lives. Watching all of history repeat itself time after time. I'm just a dreamer who dreams my life away. I'm just a dreamer who dreams of better days. I watch the sun go down like every one of us. I'm hoping that the dawn will bring a sign. A better place for those who will come after us this time. Your higher power may be God or Jesus Christ. It doesn't really matter much to me. Without each other's help, there ain't no hope for us. I'm living in a dream of fantasy. If only we could all just find serenity. It would be nice if we could live as one. When will all this anger, hate, and bigotry be gone? I'm just a dreamer who's searching for the way today. I'm just a dreamer dreaming my life away.

Imagine there's no countries. It isn't hard to do. Nothing to kill or die for, and no religion too. Imagine all the people living life in peace. You may say I'm a dreamer but I'm not the only one. Imagine no possessions. I wonder if you can. No need for greed or hunger. A brotherhood of man. Imagine all the people sharing all the world. You may say I'm a dreamer, but I'm not the only one. I hope someday you will join us, and the world will live as one. Hold the line! Love isn't always on time! I`ll send an S.O.S. to the world. I hope that someone gets my message in the bottle! Satellite of love. Satellite of love. When Love walks in the room everybody stand up. Talk to me with a message of love.

Do you believe in Heaven above? Do you believe in Love? Don`t tell a lie. Don`t be false or untrue! It all comes back to you! Open fire! Looking for Love, calling Heaven above!

A long, long, time ago, I can still remember how that music used to make me smile. Did you write The Book of Love? And do you have faith in God above? If the bible tells you so? Do you believe in rock-n-roll? Can music save your mortal soul? And there we were, all in one place. A generation, lost in space. With no time left to start again. My hands were clenched in fists of rage. No angel born in hell, can break that Satan's spell. And as the flames climbed high into the night, to light the sacrificial rite. I saw Satan laughing with delight. The day the music died.

Our Love is like water. Pinned down and abused for being strange. Our Love is no other. Our Love is like angels. Pinned down and abused for being strange!

It`s been a long time since I rock and rolled! Let me get back, baby where I come from! It`s been a long time since The Book of Love!

Who am I to believe in Love? I looked around and what did I see? Broken hearted people staring at me. All searching cause they still believe. Love ain`t no stranger! I ain`t no stranger! But when I read between the lines it`s all the same. Who am I to believe in Love?

The Book of Love is (not) long and boring. No one can lift the damn thing. It's full of facts and charts and figures and instruments for dancing. But I love it when you read to me. And you can read me anything. The Book of Love has lots of music in it. In fact, that's where music comes from. Some of it is just transcendental. Some of it is just really dumb. But I love it when you sing to me. And you can sing me anything. The Book of Love was written very long ago. It's full of flowers and heart shaped boxes and things we're all too young to know.

I wonder who wrote The Book of Love? Tell me who wrote The Book of Love? I've got to know the answer! Was it someone from above? Who wrote The Book of Love?

I BELIEVE IN HAPPINESS. I BELIEVE IN LOVE. I BELIEVE SHE FELL TO EARTH FROM SOMEWHERE

HIGH ABOVE. The fire in your eyes keeps me alive. I'm sure in her you'll find sanctuary.

She`ain`t waitin til she gets older. Her feet are making tracks in the winter snow. She`s got a rainbow that touches her shoulder. She`ll be headed where the thunder rolls. She comes like a secret wind. She`s as strong as the mountains and walks tall as a tree! She`s been there before. She`ll never give in. She`ll be gone tomorrow, like the silent breeze. The question is, not does Love exist? But when she leaves where she goes? I got a feeling she don`t know either. Wait like the wind. Watch where she goes.

Round and round. Love will find a way just give it time.

Love has finally reached its end. Love is all around. Love is knocking outside your door. Waiting for you. Love will find a way! So look around! Open your eyes! Love is all around you! Love is gonna find a way! Love is gonna find her way back home again. I know! Love is all around you.

There's a love that knows the way. I'm a rainbow in your jailcell. Not alone. More will be revealed my friend. Don't forget me. I can't hide. Teach you how to dance inside the funny farm. There's a love that knows the way!

The way your bathed in light, reminds me of that night, God laid me down into your rose garden of trust. You're all I need to find. So when the time is right, come to me sweetly, come to me. Come to me. Love will lead us. Alright! Love will lead us! She will lead us. Can you hear the dolphins cry? See the road rise up to meet us! Love will lead us. She will lead us! Oh yeah, we meet again. It's like we never left. Time in between was just a dream. Did we leave this place? This crazy fog surrounds me. All I can do to try and breathe. Life is like a shooting star! It don't matter who you are! If you only run for cover! It's just a waste of time. We are lost til we are found. This Phoenix rises up from the ground. And all these wars are over! Over! Over! Come to me. Yeah, come to me. Love will lead us! Alright! Love will lead us. She will lead us!

Woman of this earth, maker of children who weep for Love. Don't try to find the answer. Adam and Eve live down the street from me. Babylon is in every town. Love's a stranger all around. In a moment we lost our minds here and lay our spirit down. Today we lived a thousand years. Run to the water. We'll cut through the madness of these streets below the moon with a nuclear fire of Love in our hearts. It's a place and the home of ascended souls who swam out there in love, til we can say this world was just a dream. We were sleepin, now we're awake! Run to the water and recognize it is all as light and rainbows!

When I was invisible, I needed no light. My love she comes in colors everywhere, like a rainbow, she comes in color.

A cloud appears above your head! A beam of light comes shining down on you. And I ran! I ran so far away! I ran all night and day! I couldn't get away!

I thought I saw you from a distance. I swore I'd find you again. We had a love so hard to find. Another place, another time. One soul, one mind, one light that shines. One love so fine. Slip me a dream or two. Come on take me back to Déjà vu. Cause I swear I've been there with you!

People of the earth can you hear me? Came a voice from the sky on that magical night. And the colors of a thousand sunsets, they traveled to the world on a silvery light. People of the earth stood waiting! Watching as the ships came one by one. Setting fire to the sky as they landed. Carrying to the world children of the sun. All at once came a sound from the inside! Then a beam made of light hit the ground! Everyone felt the sound of their heartbeat! Every man-every woman-every child! They passed the limits of imagination, through the doors, to a world of another time! On a journey of a thousand lifetimes. Through the walls of time, at the speed of light, fly the crystal ships on their celestial flight.

Now I've got to fly to the angels. Heaven awaits my heart and flowers bloom in my name. All the stars at night shine in my name. I've got to fly back to the angels. Ad astra!

THE OTHERSIDE BY JAMES KEVIN PEAKE

I spent over a hundred hours painting The Other Side with fluorescent colors and it really looked cool in the black lights. I didn't realize until recently the entire picture came out of a queen's mouth who had long curly blonde hair. She is screaming at the top of her lungs! Too funny. It kind of looked like me. Spectacular artwork!

Songs that remind me of the picture The Otherside. LOVE SPREADS/THE STONE ROSES, BREAK ON THROUGH/DOORS, THE OTHER SIDE/RED HOT CHILI PEPPERS, EVERY PICTURE TELLS A STORY DON'T IT/ROD STEWERT, TAKE ME TO THE OTHER SIDE/AEROSMITH, THE OTHERSIDE/THE GREATEST SHOWMAN CAST!

BIG EYED FISH/DAVE MATTHEWS BAND ***Look at this big-eyed fish swimming in the sea. How it dreams to be a bird,***

swoopin, divin, through the breeze. So one day, caught a big ole wave up onto the beach. Now you see--beneath the sea is where a fish should be. Now the fish is dead! Things seem brighter on the other side. You see this crazy man decided not to breathe. He turned red, then blue, then purple. Colorful indeed! No matter how his friends begged and pleaded the man would not concede. And now he's--dead! You see, the silly man should know you got to breathe! Things seem brighter on the other side! No way... No way.... No way out of here. You see this little monkey sittin up in his monkey tree. One day decided to come down and run off to the city. But look at him now. Lost and tired and living in the street. As good as dead! You see what monkey does?.......Stay up in your fuckin tree! But things look so much brighter on the other side. Reign on my Love. Reign in my dreams. My Love dreams.

OTHERSIDE/RED HOT CHILI PEPPERS ***How long will I slide? I heard your voice through a photograph. Once you know you can never go back. Pour my life into a paper cup. Burn me out, leave me on the otherside. And then it's born again. I gotta take it on the otherside. Ad astra!***

Printed in the United States
by Baker & Taylor Publisher Services